Principles of Variational Methods in Mathematical Physics

Principles of Variational Methods in Mathematical Physics

Guest Editor

Irina Meghea

MDPI

Basel • Beijing • Wuhan • Barcelona • Belgrade • Novi Sad • Cluj • Manchester

Guest Editor
Irina Meghea
Department of Mathematical
Methods and Models
National University of
Science and Technology
POLITEHNICA Bucharest
Bucharest
Romania

Editorial Office
MDPI AG
Grosspeteranlage 5
4052 Basel, Switzerland

This is a reprint of the Special Issue, published open access by the journal *Axioms* (ISSN 2075-1680), freely accessible at: https://www.mdpi.com/journal/axioms/special_issues/625DU04S41.

For citation purposes, cite each article independently as indicated on the article page online and as indicated below:

Lastname, A.A.; Lastname, B.B. Article Title. *Journal Name* **Year**, *Volume Number*, Page Range.

ISBN 978-3-7258-7042-4 (Hbk)
ISBN 978-3-7258-7043-1 (PDF)
https://doi.org/10.3390/books978-3-7258-7043-1

Contents

About the Editor

Irina Meghea

Irina Meghea graduated from the University of Bucharest, Faculty of Mathematics, Department of Fluid Mechanics, in 1990, and obtained her PhD in Variational Methods in Mechanics in 1999. She has been teaching at POLITEHNICA Bucharest since 1990. The experience gained through her teaching activity was successfully applied in a treatise comprising a total of 3,500 pages, entitled *Treatise on Differential Calculus and Integral Calculus for Mathematicians, Physicists, Chemists, and Engineers in ten volumes*, published by OCP (Philadelphia) and EAC (Paris) in 2015. Her research activity focuses on variational methods applied to the modeling of real phenomena, as well as on statistical methods used in engineering. The results of her scientific work have been reflected in a 540-page monograph published in 2009, entitled *Ekeland Variational Principle with Generalizations and Variants*, together with nine additional books, 36 articles published in ISI-indexed journals, 39 papers included in ISI conference proceedings, one patent, and participation in 26 research projects, of which seven were international. She has also served as project director for three of these projects. Regarding scientific recognition, she has been an invited professor at several universities, is a member of five international professional organizations, has served as president of the national organizing committee for 12 international scientific events, and has acted as a reviewer for 30 ISI-indexed journals, as well as a guest editor for an ISI journal. Her intention for future work is to conduct advanced research aimed at developing new models for various processes that can be addressed using variational methods, to advance statistical applications in engineering, and to promote international collaborations.

Preface

This Reprint brings together several valuable papers published in the Special Issue *Principles of Variational Methods in Mathematical Physics* of the prestigious journal *Axioms*. It represents a collection of articles and reviews centered on the major themes of the fundamental principles of variational methods, the theoretical aspects related to the main theorems and their numerous variants, and various problems in mathematical physics addressed using these approaches.

This series of papers falls within the scope of applying variational methods to fundamental problems in mathematical physics and to the modeling of real phenomena. Within this Reprint, it is once again demonstrated that the foundation of the calculus of variations lies in Ekeland's variational principle, together with its generalizations and variants, as well as the theorems derived from or equivalent to it. These ensure the theoretical framework upon which solutions to problems in mathematical physics are constructed. Based on such constructions, the analysis is further developed through appropriate numerical methods suggested by the variational approaches used to obtain the solutions.

Both theoretical developments and applications are included in order to characterize important real and concrete phenomena. The present studies include methods for solving and/or characterizing solutions to certain problems in mathematical physics involving the p-Laplacian and the p-pseudo-Laplacian. These methods rely on surjectivity and variational results to characterize weak solutions of Dirichlet or Neumann problems for the aforementioned operators, thereby contributing to the completion of solutions for a sequence of models arising from real phenomena.

In addition, a version of Ekeland's variational principle on a weighted graph is established, together with its equivalence to Caristi's fixed point theorem and to Takahashi's minimization principle. The usual notions of completeness and topology are replaced by weaker versions expressed in terms of the considered graph, and converse results, namely, the completeness of weighted graphs for which one of these principles holds, are also investigated.

Furthermore, the inverse problem of the calculus of variations, which seeks the variational antecedent of a given partial differential system, is addressed. Since statements regarding the underlying Lagrangian structure of a dynamical system are typically affirmative rather than constructive, each successful construction is ad hoc and relies on intuitive steps that must be independently inferred for each problem. By exploiting a formal structural affinity between two different physico-mathematical entities, one of which, being second-order in time, possesses a natural Lagrangian structure, the Lagrangian of the other is constructed through an appropriate modification, thereby yielding a well-structured solution.

A systematic approach to the thermodynamically consistent modeling of isothermal dissipative continuum problems, based on the concept of standard dissipative continua, is also proposed and applied to two example problems. The formulation explicitly allows for different spatial regions associated with different physical behaviors, as well as for the description of interfacial processes. The variational approach proves advantageous for both temporal and spatial discretization of the space-time continuous problem; in particular, for certain classes of problems, generic temporal discretization schemes with known convergence properties are employed.

A rigorous mathematical analysis is also provided for the problem of an elastic body with a thin rigid inclusion crossing the external boundary at zero angle. The existence of solutions is established, and an asymptotic analysis with respect to the damage parameter is carried out, considering the limits as this parameter tends to infinity and to zero. The well-posedness of the boundary value problem is demonstrated, and the corresponding limit models are analyzed.

The existence of a solution to an associated optimal control problem is also proved, enabling the determination of the optimal shape of the rigid inclusion. In addition, a study of the data completion problem for the Cauchy-Stokes equation in a cylindrical domain is presented, in which Neumann and Dirichlet boundary conditions are prescribed on part of an overdetermined boundary, with the aim of reconstructing the missing data on the remaining portion. This approach is based on the factorization of elliptic boundary value problems, allowing a direct expression of approximations of the missing data, formulated as an optimal control problem.

In one of these works, a fractal modification of the nonlinear Schrödinger equation is presented for the first time based on the fractal derivative. The semi-inverse method is employed to establish the corresponding fractal variational principle. This principle is expected to deepen the understanding of the nature of physical phenomena in fractal space and to provide new perspectives for the application and further development of variational approaches.

I believe that this collection of eight scientific papers, connected by the common theme of applying variational methods to solving problems in mathematical physics, with a view toward their application in modeling real phenomena, represents a significant contribution to scientific literature.

Irina Meghea
Guest Editor

axioms

MDPI

Review

Solutions for Some Mathematical Physics Problems Issued from Modeling Real Phenomena: Part 1

Irina Meghea

Department of Mathematical Methods and Models, Faculty of Applied Sciences, University POLITEHNICA of Bucharest, 060042 Bucharest, Romania; irina.meghea@upb.ro or i_meghea@yahoo.com; Tel.: +40-756575418

Abstract: This paper brings together methods to solve and/or characterize solutions of some problems of mathematical physics equations involving p-Laplacian and p-pseudo-Laplacian. Using surjectivity or variational approaches, one may obtain or characterize weak solutions for Dirichlet or Newmann problems for these important operators. This article details three ways to use surjectivity results for a special type of operator involving the duality mapping and a Nemytskii operator, three methods starting from Ekeland's variational principle and, lastly, one with a generalized variational principle to solve or describe the above-mentioned solutions. The relevance of these operators and the possibility of their involvement in the modeling of an important class of real phenomena determined the author to group these seven procedures together, presented in detail, followed by many applications, accompanied by a general overview of specialty domains. The use of certain variational methods facilitates the complete solution of the problem via appropriate numerical methods and computational algorithms. The exposure of the sequence of theoretical results, together with their demonstration in as much detail as possible has been fulfilled as an opportunity for the complete development of these topics.

Keywords: modeling real phenomena; mathematical physics problems; p-Laplacian; p-pseudo-Laplacian; surjectivity methods; variational methods; Dirichlet problem; Neumann problem

MSC: 35A01; 35A15; 35J35; 35J40; 47J30

1. Introduction

Problems for partial differential equations involving the p-Laplacian and p-pseudo-Laplacian are mathematical models that often occur in studies on the p-Laplace or p-pseudo-Laplace equation, generalized reaction–diffusion theory, non-Newtonian fluid theory, non-Newtonian filtration, the turbulent flow of a gas in a porous medium, glaciology, non-Newtonian rheology, etc. These fractional order operators are very important mathematical models describing a multitude of anomalous dynamic behaviors in applied sciences. In the non-Newtonian fluid theory, the quantity p is a medium characteristic. Media with $p > 2$ are called dilatant fluids and those with $p < 2$ are pseudoplastics. If $p = 2$, they are Newtonian fluids. The p-Laplacian appears in the study of flow through porous media in turbulent regime at Diaz et al. [1,2] or glacier ice when treated as a non-Newtonian fluid with a nonlinear relationship between the rate deformation tensor and the deviatoric stress tensor, as described by Glowinski et al. [3]. It is also used in the Helle-Shaw approximation for a moving boundary problem by King et al. [4] and also for "power-law fluids" at Aronson et al. [5]. The p-Laplacian also appears in the study of flow in porous media ($p = 3/2$, at Schowalter et al. [6]) or glacial sliding ($p \in (1, 4/3]$, at Péllissier [7]). Quasilinear problems with a variable coefficient appear in the mathematical model of the torsional creep (elastic for $p = 2$, plastic for $p \to \infty$; see in Bhattacharya et al. [8] and at Kawohl [9]). A nonlinear field equation in Quantum Mechanics involving the p-Laplacian for $p = 6$ was proposed by Benci et al. [10].

Surjectivity methods to solve and/or characterize the solutions for Dirichlet problems involving the p-Laplacian and the p-pseudo-Laplacian have been previously used by the author in [11], together with other variational results, in [12] where two solving methods are displayed, in [13] which discusses some Fredholm alternative types, in [14] with solutions for the p-pseudo-Laplacian treated following two approaches, and in [15] involving surjectivity methods. Solving such problems via results obtained with Ekeland variational principle and other generalized variational principles has been the goal of other works of the author where some Dirichlet or Newmann problems have been studied as in [12,14,16] with the use of a perturbed variational principle, in [17] with variational procedures, as also in [18]. Mountain pass theorem variants and applications involved in modeling real phenomena are performed by the author in [19], while other applied variational methods are capitalized on by the author in [20,21], and several variational principles, together with generalizations and variants, have been compared and analyzed in the monograph [22].

The fractional differential equations are frequently used as modeling tools for processes implied in anomalous diffusion or spatial heterogeneity [23]. Also, in water resources, fractional models have been used to design chemical or contaminant transport in heterogeneous aquifers. In the field of magnetic resonance, fractional models of the Bloch–Torrey equation for drawing anomalous diffusion have been considered. Concerning the domain of cell biology, anomalous diffusion has been measured in fluorescence photo-bleaching recovery and fractional-in-time models have been created for simple types of chemical reaction–diffusion equations and for the simulation of microscale diffusion in the cell wall lining of plants. Similar problems appear in models of chemical reactions, heat transfer, population dynamics and so on [24]. Power law diffusion equations with p-Laplacian having constant and/or variable p are significantly related to researches on non-Newtonian fluids, turbulence modeling phase transitions, data clustering, machine learning and image processing. Many studies devoted to power-law diffusions call for the development of efficient numerical methods for solving elliptic partial differential equations with nonlinearities of p-type gradient [25].

The interest in these kinds of operators is topical both for mathematical approaches and results, as at Mukherjee et al. [26], Zhang et al. [27], Benedikt et al. [28], Lafleche et al. [29], Cellina [30], Khan [31], Xu [32], Akagi et al. [33], Gulsen et al. [34] and Lee et al. [35], and also for applications in many models in various fields, as in Rasouli [36], Yang et al. [37], Elmoataz et al. [38], Gupta et al. [39], Liero et al. [40] and Silva [41].

In this paper, several sequences of results are proposed, starting from the most general and abstract theory, passing step by step through many concrete stages until their applications in models issued from design of real phenomena. The focus falls on a very extended justification, containing all the necessary details and displaying all the theoretical arguments. Some of the results presented in this paper are introduced with an integer justification background and they are used to obtain and/or characterize the solutions of equations of mathematical physics proposed by other authors for similar problems for which they gave solutions via different methods. For such problems resulting from mathematical modeling, we came up with original solving methods following the involved abstract frame. From these original approaches stems the novelty of this work. Our interest is now focused on such kinds of problems and their solutions, and this is one of the initial studies for future developments to find a mathematical model (there is none available) that can be applied for describing diffusion phenomena involved in the micro-emulsification of disperse systems in tight connection with surface properties at the interface in self-organized systems.

This article is the first part of review type of the work under this title containing whole theoretical support detailed in a complete exposition of the arguments, while many applications of the results presented here represent the aim of another original paper under the same title, Part two.

2. Surjectivity for the Operators $\lambda J_\varphi - S$: Applications to Partial Differential Equations

2.1. Surjectivity of the Operators of the Form $\lambda T - S$

In this section, a generalization of a theorem from [42] (Theorem 1.1) is presented and in this result the author used: normed space instead of Banach space, bijection with continuous inverse instead of homeomorphism. Two corollaries of this statement, obtained in [12,14], have also been presented.

Firstly, to have a short expression, we introduce the following.

Definition 2.1. *T: $X \to Y$, where X and Y are normed spaces, is (K, L, a), where $K > 0$, $L > 0$, $a > 0$, if*

$$K\,\|x\|^a \le \|Tx\| \le L\,\|x\|^a \;\forall x \text{ from } X.$$

Proposition 2.1. *Let X and Y be real normed spaces, T: $X \to Y$ (K, L, a) odd bijection with continuous inverse and S: $X \to Y$ odd compact operator. For any $\lambda \neq 0$, if*

$$\lim_{\|x\| \to +\infty} \|\lambda Tx - Sx\| = +\infty,$$

then $\lambda T - S$ is surjective.

Proof. Let z_0 be from Y; we state that:

$$\exists\, x_0 \text{ in } X \text{ e.g., } \lambda Tx_0 - Sx_0 = z_0. \tag{2.1}$$

Take $R > 0$ with the property (see the hypothesis)

$$\|x\| \ge R \Rightarrow \|\lambda Tx - Sx\| > \|z_0\| \tag{2.2}$$

and the open ball from Y $\sigma := B(0, r)$, $r := |\lambda|\, LR^a$. If $y \in \partial\sigma$ and $y = \lambda Tx$, then $\|x\| \ge R$, and hence,

$$\|\lambda Tx - Sx\| \overset{(2.2)}{>} \|z_0\| \tag{2.3}$$

Let be the operator A: $Y \to Y$,

$$Ay = ST^{-1}\left(\frac{y}{\lambda}\right)$$

A is compact, odd and $Ay \neq y$ when $y \in \partial\sigma$ (ad absurdum, put y in the form λTx and take into account (2.3), i.e., $0 \notin (I - A)(\partial\sigma)$). Applying Borsuk theorem, the Leray-Schauder degree $d(I - A, \sigma, 0)$ is odd. However,

$$H:\ [0, 1] \times \overline{\sigma} \to Y,\ H(t, y) = Ay + tz_0$$

being a homotopy of compact transformations on $\overline{\sigma}$, we have

$$d(I - H(0, \cdot), \sigma, 0) = d(I - H(1, \cdot), \sigma, 0), \text{ i.e.,}$$
$$d(I - A, \sigma, 0) = d(I - A - z_0, \sigma, 0),$$

consequently, $d(I - A, \sigma, 0)$ is an odd number, particularly different from zero, therefore $\exists y_0$ in σ, e.g., $(I - A - z_0)(y_0) = 0$ and it remains only to take x_0 in X with $y_0 = \lambda Tx_0$ to obtain (2.1). □

Corollary 2.1. *Let X, Y be real normed spaces, T: $X \to Y$ odd (K, L, a) bijection with continuous inverse, S: $X \to Y$ odd compact operator and* $\alpha := \overline{\lim}_{||x|| \to +\infty} \frac{\|Sx\|}{\|x\|^a} < +\infty$. *If*

$$|\lambda| > \frac{\alpha}{K}, \lambda \in \mathbf{R},$$

then $\lambda T - S$ *is surjective.*

Explanations [43], Volume 5, V, §5, 11.9_1, p. 372: $f: X \to Y$, X and Y normed spaces,

$$\overline{\lim_{||x|| \to +\infty}} \| f(x) \| \overset{def}{=} \inf_{\rho > 0} \sup_{\substack{x \in X \\ ||x|| \geq \rho}} \| f(x) \| = \lim_{\rho \to +\infty} \sup_{\substack{x \in X \\ ||x|| \geq \rho}} \| f(x) \| .$$

If $\alpha = \overline{\lim}_{||x|| \to +\infty} \| f(x) \|$, then $x_n \in X\ \forall n$ from $\mathbf{N}$, and $||x_n|| \to +\infty$ implies $\overline{\lim}_{n \to \infty} \| f(x_n) \| \leq \alpha$.

If $\alpha = \overline{\lim}_{n \to \infty} \| f(x_n) \|$, for any (x_n) with x_n from X and $||x_n|| \to +\infty$, then $\alpha = \overline{\lim}_{||x|| \to +\infty} \|f(x)\|$.

Proof. It remains to prove:

$$\overline{\lim_{||x|| \to +\infty}} ||\lambda Tx - Sx|| = +\infty, \tag{2.4}$$

Assuming, ad absurdum, the contrary, obtain $\rho > 0$ and a sequence $(x_n)_{n \geq 1}$, $x_n \in X$, $||x_n|| \to +\infty$, e.g.,

$$||\lambda Tx_n - Sx_n|| \leq \rho\ \forall n \geq 1. \tag{2.5}$$

From (2.5),

$$\lim_{n \to \infty} \left\| \frac{\lambda Tx_n}{||x_n||^a} - \frac{Sx_n}{||x_n||^a} \right\| = 0,$$

hence, $\lim_{n \to \infty} \left[\frac{|\lambda| \|Tx_n\|}{\|x_n\|^a} - \frac{\|S(x_n)\|}{\|x_n\|^a} \right] = 0$, and as $\overline{\lim}_{n \to \infty} \frac{\|S(x_n)\|}{\|x_n\|^a} \leq \alpha$, it results

$$\overline{\lim_{n \to \infty}} \frac{|\lambda| \|Tx_n\|}{\|x_n\|^a} \leq \alpha. \tag{2.6}$$

But the condition (K, L, a) imposes:

$$K \leq \overline{\lim_{n \to \infty}} \frac{\|Tx_n\|}{\|x_n\|^a}. \tag{2.7}$$

From (2.6) and (2.7), we obtain $K \leq \frac{\alpha}{|\lambda|}$. If $\alpha \neq 0$, then $|\lambda| \leq \frac{\alpha}{K}$, which contradicts the hypothesis, and if $\alpha = 0$, then $K = 0$, also in contradiction with the hypothesis, and consequently, (2.4). □

Corollary 2.2. *Under the conditions of Corollary 2.1, if* $\alpha = 0$, *then* $\lambda T - S$ *is surjective for* λ *any in* $\mathbf{R} \backslash \{0\}$.

2.2. Surjectivity for Operators of the Form $\lambda J_\varphi - S$, J_φ Duality Map

2.2.1. Preliminaries—Duality Map

Let X be a real Banach space, X^* its dual (), x^* an element any in X^*, 2^M the set of subsets of M.

Definition 2.2. $\varphi: \mathbf{R}_+ \to \mathbf{R}_+$ *continuous and strictly increasing with* $\varphi(0) = 0$ *and* $\lim_{r \to +\infty}$

φ (see, for instance [43], Volume 2, p. 27r) = +∞ is, by definition, weight or normalization function.

The multiple-valued map $J_\varphi : X \to 2^{X^*}$, φ weight,

$$\begin{cases} J_\varphi 0_X = \{0_{X^*}\}, \\ x \neq 0 \Rightarrow J_\varphi x = \varphi(||x||)\{x^* \in X^* : \ ||x^*|| = 1, x^*(x) = \ ||x||\}, \end{cases}$$

equivalently,

$$x \in X \Rightarrow J_\varphi\, x = \{x^* \in X^*\colon ||x^*|| = \varphi(||x||), x^*(x) = \varphi(||x||)||x||\},$$

is, by definition, *the duality map* (on X) *relative to* φ. (Beurling-Livingstone).

Its name becomes *normalized duality map* when $\varphi(t) = t$ (in this case, $x^* \in J_\varphi\, x \Longleftrightarrow x^*(x) = ||x||^2 = ||x^*||^2$).

Definition 2.3. *Let X be a real normed space. A nonempty set β of bounded subsets of X, having the properties:*

$$1^\circ \bigcup_{A\in\beta} A = X,\ 2^\circ\ A \in \beta \Rightarrow -A \in \beta, \lambda A \in \beta(\lambda > 0) \text{ and}$$

3° β is filtered to the right related to the inclusion "⊂", i.e.,

for any A, B in β ∃ C in β, e.g., $A \subset C$ and $B \subset C$,

is called bornology on X.

Let β be a bornology on X. The function $f : X \to \overline{\mathbf{R}}$, which is locally finite in the point *a* (i.e., there exists a neighborhood of *a* on which *f* is finite), is, by definition, *β-differentiable in a* if there exists φ in the topological dual X* such that for every *S* in β, we have:

$$\operatorname*{limu}_{\substack{t\to 0\\ h\in S}} \frac{f(a+th) - f(a)}{t} = \varphi(h) \text{ (uniform limit on } S \text{ for } t \to 0).$$

φ is the β-*derivative of* f *in* a, and it is denoted by

$$\nabla_\beta f\,(a).$$

If β is the set β_G of the finite symmetrical parts of X or the set β_F of the bounded symmetrical parts of X, the β-derivative coincides with the Gâteaux derivative and Fréchet derivative, respectively.

Proposition 2.2. 1° $J_\varphi\, x \neq \varnothing$ *∀x in X;*

2° *For any x in X, $J_\varphi\, x$ is a convex, closed, bounded part of X** (*it is contained in the sphere of the equation* $||y||_{X^*} = \varphi(||x||)$);

3° $J_\varphi\, x = \partial\psi\,(x)$, *the subdifferential in x, where*

$$\psi(u) = \int_0^{||u||} \varphi(t)dt$$

(apply Asplund theorem; since ψ is continuous and convex, ψ is Gâteaux differentiable in x iff ∂ψ(x) has a single element, and then ψ′(x) = ∂ψ(x); consequently, J_φ is *uni-valued iff* ψ *is Gâteaux differentiable, and in this case,* $J_\varphi\, x = \psi'(x)$);

4° J_φ *is odd* ($J_\varphi\,(-x) = -J_\varphi\, x$ *∀x in X);*

5° $J_\varphi(\lambda x) = \frac{\varphi(\lambda||x||)}{\varphi(||x||)} Jx,\ \forall x \text{ in } X\backslash\{0\},\ \forall\lambda \geq 0;$

6° J_φ *is monotonous; more precisely*: $\forall x, y$ *in X and* $\forall x^*, y^*$ *from* $J_\varphi\, x, J_\varphi\, y$,

$$(x^* - y^*)(x - y) \geq [\varphi(\|x\|) - \varphi(\|y\|)](\|x\| - \|y\|) \geq 0;$$

7° *The normalized duality map is linear iff X is a Hilbert space;*
8° *If* $x^* \in J_\varphi\, x$, *then* $x \in J_{\varphi^{-1}}(x^*)$ *(duality map on* X^**);*
9° J_φ, J_{φ_1} *being duality maps on X, there exists* μ: $[0, +\infty] \to [0, +\infty)$ *such that*

$$J\varphi\, x = \mu(\| x \|) J_{\varphi_1} \; \forall x \text{ in } X;$$

10° *Let x, y be in X. Then,* $\|x\| \leq \|x + \lambda y\| \; \forall \lambda \geq 0$ *iff there exists* x^* *in Jx, J the normalized duality map on X, with the property* $x^*(y) \geq 0$ *(Kato).*

Furthermore, retain that if J_φ is uni-valued, then it is coercive since:

$$\lim_{\|x\| \to +\infty} \frac{\langle J_\varphi x, x \rangle}{\| x \|} = \lim_{\|x\| \to +\infty} \varphi(\| x \|) = +\infty.$$

The Banach space X is, by definition, *smooth* (*Krein*) if

$$\forall x \neq 0 \text{ there exists } x_0^* \text{ unique in } X*, \text{ e.g., } \| x_0^* \| = 1,\; x_0^*(x) \; = \| x \| .$$

Thus, any duality map on a smooth space is uni-valued and reciprocal.

Since x_0^* from X^* is sub-gradient in $x_0 \neq 0$ for $x \to \|x\|$, iff $\|x_0^*\| = 1$ and $x_0^*(x) = \|x\|$ and $x \to \|x\|$ is convex and continuous.

Proposition 2.3. *X is smooth space iff the norm of X is Gâteaux differentiable on* $X \backslash \{0\}$.

From this, combined with Proposition 2.2, 3°, we obtain:

$$X \text{ smooth} \Rightarrow J_\varphi\, x = \varphi(\|x\|)\|x\|',\; x \neq 0.\; (*)$$

To validate this formula, we prove the following:

Proposition 2.4. *Let X and Y be real normed spaces and* $f: X \to Y$ *be Gâteaux differentiable, F:* $Y \to \mathbf{R}$ *of Gâteaux* C^1 *class. Then,* $g := F \, o \, f$ *is Gâteaux differentiable, and* $g'(x) = F'(f(x)) \, o \, f'(x)$ *[43].*

Proof. We use the formula of finite increases [43], Volume 9, p. 93:

Let β be a bornology on X and $f: X \to \mathbf{R}$ β-differentiable on the segment $[a, b]$ from X. There exists θ in (0,1) such that:

$$f(b) - f(a) = \nabla_\beta f(a + \theta(b - a))(b - a).$$

Standard justification. Take F: $[0,1] \to \mathbf{R}$, $F(t) = f(a + t(b - a))$. With δ being small,

$$\frac{F(t+\delta) - F(t)}{\delta} = \frac{1}{\delta}[f(a + t(b-a) + \delta(b-a)) - f(a + t(b-a))],$$

let A be in β with $b - a \in A$ (property 1° from the definition of the bornology), and take the limit for $\delta \to 0$, $F'(t) = \nabla_\beta f(a + t(b - a))(b - a)$, $F(1) - F(0) = F'(\theta)$, with θ in (0,1), etc. □

We continue the proof of this proposition. Let x_0 and h be in X.

$$\frac{1}{t}[g(x_0+th)-g(x_0)] = \frac{1}{t}[F(f(x_0+th))-F(f(x_0))] =$$
$$F'(f(x_0)+\theta(t)[f(x_0+th)-f(x_0)])\left(\frac{f(x_0+th)-f(x_0)}{t}\right),$$
$$\lim_{t\to 0}\frac{f(x_0+th)-f(x_0)}{t} = f'(x_0)(h), \lim_{t\to 0}[f(x_0+th)-f(x_0)] = 0,$$
$$\lim_{t\to 0}\theta(t)[f(x_0+th)-f(x_0)] = 0$$

and hence the conclusion, since:

$$x_n \to a \text{ and } y_n \to b \Rightarrow F'(y_n)(x_n) \to F'(b)(a):$$
$$F'(y_n)(x_n)-F'(b)(a) = [F'(y_n)(x_n)-F'(y_n)(a)]+[F'(y_n)(a)-F'(b)(a)],$$
$$\| F'(y_n)(x_n)-F'(y_n)(a) \| = \| F'(y_n)(x_n-a) \| \le \| F'(y_n) \| \| x_n-a \| \le \| x_n-a \|$$

(the sequence $(\| F'(y_n) \|)$ is bounded, being convergent),

$$\| F'(y_n)(a)-F'(b)(a)\| = \| \langle F'(y_n)-F'(b),\, a\rangle \| \le \| a \| \| F'(y_n)-F'(b)\|. \square$$

Finally, we introduce the following:

Definition 2.4. *F: X $\to 2^{X^*}$ is upper semicontinuous in x_0 if, for any neighborhood V of F(x_0) in the $*$-weak topology on X*, there exists U neighborhood of x_0, e.g., F(U) $\subset$ V.*

Proposition 2.5. *Any duality map J_φ on X is upper semicontinuous on X (Browder).*

Definition 2.5. *A Banach space X is called strictly convex (Clarkson) if one of the following equivalent properties is fulfilled:*

1° $x \neq y$, $\|x\| = \|y\| = 1 \Rightarrow \|\lambda x + (1-\lambda)y\| < 1\ \forall\lambda$ *in (0, 1);*
2° $x \neq y$, $\|x\| = \|y\| = 1 \Rightarrow \|x+y\| < 2$;
3° $\|x+y\| = \|x\| + \|y\|$, $y \neq 0 \Rightarrow \exists\, \lambda \ge 0$ *with* $x = \lambda y$;
4° $\|x\| = \|y\| = 1$ *and* $\|x+y\| = \|x\| + \|y\| \Rightarrow x = y$;
5° *The sphere* $\{x \in X: \|x\| = 1\}$ *does not contain any segment;*
6° *Any x* from X* attains its inferior upper bound on the unity ball of X in at least one point;*
7° *The function* $x \to \|x\|^2$ *is strictly convex.*

Proposition 2.6. *If X* is smooth (respectively strictly convex), then X is strictly convex (respectively smooth). The reciprocal assertions are true when X is reflexive.*

Proposition 2.7. *If the Banach space X is reflexive, there exists a norm on X equivalent strictly convex such that the dual norm is also strictly convex. (Lindenstrauss, Asplund).*

Definition 2.6. *A Banach space is uniformly convex (Clarkson) if*

$$\forall\varepsilon > 0\ \exists\delta > 0 \text{ such that } \|x\| = \|y\| = 1 \text{ and } \|x-y\| \ge \varepsilon \Rightarrow \|x+y\| \le 2(1-\delta),$$

equivalently

$$\| x_n \| = \| y_n \| = 1\ \forall n \text{in } \mathbf{N} \text{ and } \| x_n + y_n \| \to 2 \Rightarrow \lim_{n\to\infty}(x_n - y_n) = 0.$$

A Banach space is local uniformly convex (Lovaglia) if

$$\forall \varepsilon > 0 \text{ and } \forall x \text{ with } \|x\| = 1\ \exists \delta > 0 \text{ e.g., } \|y\| = 1 \text{ and } \|x - y\| \geq \varepsilon \Rightarrow \|x + y\| \leq 2(1 - \delta),$$

equivalently,

$$\| x \| = \| x_n \| = 1\ \forall n \text{in } \mathbf{N} \text{ and } \| x_n + x \| \to 2 \Rightarrow \lim_{n \to \infty} x_n = x.$$

Proposition 2.8. *X uniformly convex ⇒ locally uniformly convex ⇒ X is strictly convex.*

Proposition 2.9. *X uniformly convex ⇒ x is reflexive. (Milman).*

Proposition 2.10. *If X is local uniformly convex, then, for any sequence $(x_n)_{n \geq 1}$, $x_n \in X$,*

$$x_n \overset{w}{\to} x \text{ and } \| x_n \| \to \| x \| \Rightarrow x_n \to x.$$

Here is a characterization of the uniform convexity.

Proposition 2.11. *X and X^* are uniformly convex iff the norm on X^* and X, respectively, is uniformly Fréchet differentiable.*

Clarification. f is *uniformly Fréchet differentiable* $\overset{def}{\Leftrightarrow}$ $\forall \varepsilon > 0\ \exists \delta > 0$ with the property

$$\|h\| \leq \delta \Rightarrow \|f(x + h) - f(x) - f'(x)(h)\| \leq \varepsilon \|h\|\ \forall x \text{ with } \|x\| < 1;$$

$x \to \|x\|$ is uniformly Fréchet differentiable iff it is Fréchet differentiable and the Fréchet derivative is uniformly continuous on the unity ball.

Proposition 2.12. *If X is local uniformly convex and reflexive, then the norm on X^* is Fréchet differentiable.*

Proposition 2.13. *For any reflexive Banach space, there exists on this an equivalent norm for which it becomes local uniformly convex. (Troianski).*

Proposition 2.14. *For any reflexive Banach space X, there exists an equivalent norm on X for which X and X^* are locally uniformly convex. (Asplund).*

Thus, the equivalent norm and its dual norm are Fréchet differentiable (Proposition 2.12).

Proposition 2.15. *If X is smooth, for any weight φ, J_φ is uni-valued and continuous from X, with the strong topology on X^* endowed with the $*$-weak topology.*

Proof. Take Proposition 2.5 into account. □

Corollary 2.3. *If X is smooth and reflexive, any duality map J on X is semicontinuous.*

Proof. Let $x_n \to x$. Setting $x_n^* := x_n$, $x^* := Jx$, we have $x_n^*(u) \to x^*(u)\ \forall u$ from X, i.e., denoting $u^{**} := \Phi u$, Φ is the canonical embedding in bidual, $u^{**}(x_n^*) \to u^{**}(x^*)$, hence $Jx_n \overset{W}{\to} Jx$. □

The strict convexity can be characterized by the duality map.

Proposition 2.16. *X is strictly convex iff any duality map on X is strictly monotonous. (Petryshin).*

Consequently,

Proposition 2.17. *If X is strictly convex and smooth, then any duality map on X is uni-valued and injective.*

Proposition 2.18. *Let X be smooth and local uniformly convex, J duality map on X and* $(x_n)_{n\geq 1}$, $x_n \in X$. *If* $(Jx_n - Jx)(x_n - x) \to 0$, *then* $x_n \to x$.

Proposition 2.19. *Let X be Banach space. A duality map on X is uni-valued and continuous in the topologies of the norms iff the norm on X is Fréchet differentiable.*

Proof. *Necessary.* X is smooth, and the norm is Gâteaux differentiable (Proposition 2.3), even of the C^1 Gâteaux class in accordance with (∗). *Sufficient.* This results from a Cudia theorem. □

Proposition 2.20. *Let X be a Banach space and* J_φ *a duality map on X.* X^* *is uniformly convex iff* J_φ *is uni-valued and uniformly continuous on the bounded sets of X.*

Proof. *Necessary.* X^* is uniformly convex $\overset{\text{Proposition 2.11}}{\Rightarrow}$ $x \to \|x\|$ is Fréchet differentiable ⇒ $Jx = \varphi(\|x\|)\|x\|'$, $x \to \|x\|'$ is uniformly continuous on the closed unity ball. *Sufficient.* J uni-valued $\overset{\text{Proposition 2.3}}{\Rightarrow}$ $x \to \|x\|$ is Gâteaux differentiable $\overset{\text{Proposition 2.11}}{\Rightarrow}$ $x \to \|x\|$ is uniformly Fréchet differentiable $\overset{\text{Proposition 2.11}}{\Rightarrow}$ X^* is uniformly convex. □

Place here the characterization of the reflexivity of a Banach space.

Proposition 2.21. *The Banach space X is reflexive iff any* x^* *in* X^* *attains* $\sup\limits_{\|x\|\leq 1} x^*(x)$.

In the following, there is a characterization of the reflexivity of the duality map.

Proposition 2.22. *Let X be a Banach space and* J_φ *duality map on X. X is reflexive iff*

$$X^* = \bigcup_{x\in X} J_\varphi x.$$

Proof. *Necessary.* Let x_0^* be in X^*. There exists x_0 in X with $\|x_0\| = 1$ and $x_0^*(x_0) = \|x_0^*\|$; take $t_0 > 0$, e.g., $\varphi(t_0) = \|x_0^*\|$, then $x_0^* \in J_\varphi\ (t_0\ x_0)$. *Sufficient.* Use Proposition 2.21. Let x_0^* be any in X^*, $\exists\, x_0$ in X, e.g., $x_0^* \in J_\varphi\ x_0$, i.e., $\|x_0^*\| = \varphi(\|x_0\|)$, $x_0^*(x_0) = \varphi(\|x_0\|)\|x_0\|$. For $y_0 := \frac{x_0}{\|x_0\|}$, we have $\|y_0\| = 1$, $x_0^*(y_0) = \|x_0^*\| = \sup\limits_{\|x\|\leq 1} x_0^*(x)$. □

Corollary 2.4. *Let X be a smooth space and J a duality map on X.*
1° *X is reflexive* $\Longleftrightarrow$ *J is surjective;*
2° *X is reflexive and strictly convex* $\Longleftrightarrow$ *J is bijective.*

Proof. Take Proposition 2.22 and Proposition 2.16 into account. □

Proposition 2.23. *Let X be a reflexive and smooth space and* J_φ *a duality map on X. Then* $J^{-1} : X^* \to 2^X$, $J^{-1}\,x^* = \{x \in X: J_\varphi\ x = x^*\}$ *coincides with* $J^*_{\varphi^{-1}}$, *the duality map on* X^* *coincides with the weight* φ^{-1} *(identification via canonical embedding* Φ *in the bidual). If X is also strictly convex, then* J^{-1} *is uni-valued, and the formula holds true:*

$$J_\varphi^{-1} = \Phi^{-1}\ J^*_{\varphi^{-1}}$$

Proof. The statement is, in accordance with Corollary 2.4, correct. *First assertion.* Let x^* be any in X^*. $x \in J^{-1} x^* \Longleftrightarrow x^* = J_\varphi x \Longleftrightarrow \|x^*\| = \varphi(\|x\|)$ and $x^*(x) = \varphi(\|x\|)\|x\| \Longleftrightarrow \|x\| = \varphi^{-1}(\|x^*\|)$ and $x(x^*) = \varphi^{-1}(\|x^*\|)\|x^*\| \Longleftrightarrow x \in J^*_{\varphi^{-1}} x^*$. *Second assertion.* X^* is smooth (Proposition 2.6). □

Pass to continuity properties of the duality map. A previous result is represented by Corollary 2.3.

Definition 2.7. *A Banach space has the property (h) if*

$$x_n \overset{w}{\to} x \text{ and } \| x_n \| \to \| x \| \Rightarrow x_n \to x.$$

A Banach space has the *property (H)* if it is strictly convex, and it has the property (*h*).

For instance, any local uniformly convex space has the property (*H*) (Propositions 2.8 and 2.9).

Proposition 2.24. *If X is reflexive and X^* has the property (H), then any duality map J on X is uni-valued, surjective and continuous relative to the strong topologies on X and X^*.*

Proof. J is indeed uni-valued (Proposition 2.6) and surjective (Corollary 2.4). Let $x_n \to x$. Then, $Jx_n \overset{w}{\to} Jx$ (Corollary 2.3); moreover, $\|Jx_n\| \to \|Jx\|$ since $\|Jx_n\| = \varphi(\|x_n\|)$ and $\|Jx\| = \varphi(\|x\|)$. Therefore, $Jx_n \to Jx$. □

Combining Proposition 2.24 with Corollary 2.4, one obtains the following.

Proposition 2.25. *If X is reflexive and strictly convex and X^* has the property (H), then any duality map on X is uni-valued, bijective and continuous relative to the strong topologies on X and X^*.*

We next proceed to the continuity of the inverse of the duality map.

Proposition 2.26. *If X is reflexive, smooth and has the (H) property, then any duality map J_φ on X is bijective with J_φ^{-1} continuous relative to the strong topologies on X and X^*.*

Proof. J_φ is bijective (Corollary 2.4), and X^* is reflexive, smooth and strictly convex (Proposition 2.6). Let $x_n^* \to x_0$. Then, $J^*_{\varphi^{-1}} x_n^* \overset{w}{\to} J^*_{\varphi^{-1}} x^*$ (Corollary 2.3), and the formula from Proposition 2.23 imposes $J^*_{\varphi^{-1}} x_n^* \to J^*_{\varphi^{-1}} x^*$ (see (*H*)). □

Combining Propositions 2.25 and 2.26, one obtains the following.

Proposition 2.27. *If X is reflexive and X and X^* have the property (H), then any duality map on X is a homeomorphism of X in X^* relative to the strong topologies.*

We finish this subsection with the following result:

Proposition 2.28. *Any uni-valued duality map J_φ on a local uniformly convex space X has the property S_+:*

$$x_n \overset{w}{\to} x \text{ and } \overline{\lim_{n\to\infty}} \langle J_\varphi x_n - J_\varphi x_0, x_n - x_0 \rangle \leq 0 \Rightarrow x_n \to x.$$

Proof. The hypothesis implies

$$\overline{\lim_{n\to\infty}} \langle J_\varphi x_n - J_\varphi x_0, x_n - x_0 \rangle \leq 0,$$

but

$$0 \leq [\varphi(\| x_n \|) - \varphi(\| x_0 \|)](\| x_n \| - \| x_0 \| \leq \langle J_\varphi x_n - J_\varphi x_0, x_n - x_0 \rangle,$$

consequently,

$$\lim_{n\to\infty} [\varphi(\| x_n \|) - \varphi(\| x_0 \|)](\| x_n \| - \| x_0 \|) = 0. \tag{2.8}$$

We denote t_n: = $\| x_n \|$, t_0 : = $\| x_0 \|$. Somehow,

$$\lim_{n\to\infty} t_n = t_0, \tag{2.9}$$

we apply Proposition 2.11 and obtain $x_n \to x$. Assume, ad absurdum, that $t_n \nrightarrow t_0$. Then there exists (t_{kn}) subsequence of (t_n) e.g., for instance, $t_{kn} \geq \rho > t_0$ $\forall n$. (t_{kn}) is bounded, otherwise it has a subsequence (t_{ik_n}), $t_{ik_n} \to +\infty$, which implies $\varphi(t_{ik_n}) \to +\infty$, $[\varphi(t_{ik_n}) - \varphi(t_0)](t_{ik_n} - t_0) \to +\infty$, in contradiction with (2.8). Thus, (t_{kn}) has a convergent subsequence (t_{lk_n}), $t_{lk_n} \to t_0' \neq t_0$. Consequently, since $\varphi(t_{lk_n}) \to \varphi(t_0') \neq \varphi(t_0)$, from a rank on, we have, with $\delta > 0$,

$$|t_{lk_n} - t_0| \geq \delta, \ |\varphi(t_{lk_n}) - \varphi(t_0)| \geq \delta$$

and one obtains a final contradiction with (2.8). Here is another justification for (2.9). (t_n) is bounded (see above); let t^* be an adherence value any for this sequence (a fortiori $t^* \in$ **R**) and (t_{j_n}) subsequence with $\lim_{n\to\infty} t_{j_n} = t^*$. Then, from (2.8), $[\varphi(t^*) - \varphi(t_0)](t^* - t_0)$, which implies $t^* = t_0$ (ad absurdum !) and, consequently, (2.9). □

2.2.2. Main Results

Proposition 2.29. *Let X be a real reflexive Banach space, smooth and having the property (H), J_φ duality map on X with φ being (K, L, a) function, S: $X \to X^*$ odd compact operator and*

$$\alpha := \overline{\lim_{\|x\|\to+\infty}} \frac{\|Sx\|}{\|x\|^a} < +\infty.$$

Then

1° $\alpha > 0 \Rightarrow \lambda J_\varphi - S$ *is surjective* $\forall\lambda$ *with* $|\lambda| > \frac{\alpha}{K}$;
2° $\alpha = 0 \Rightarrow \lambda J_\varphi - S$ *is surjective* $\forall\lambda \neq 0$.

Proof. J_φ is odd and bijective with a continuous inverse (Proposition 2.26). Moreover, since

$$Kt^a \leq \varphi(t) \leq Lt^a \ \forall t \geq 0,$$

we have

$$K\|x\|^a \leq \varphi(\|x\|) = \|J_\varphi\, x\| \leq L\|x\|^a \ \forall x \text{ from } X,$$

i.e., J_φ is (K, L, a). We apply Corollaries 2.1 and 2.2 from Section 2.1. □

Proposition 2.30. *Let X be a real reflexive Banach space, smooth with the property (H), and J_φ the duality map on X with $\varphi(t) = t^{p-1}$, $p \in (1, +\infty)$. Suppose that X is compactly embedded by the linear injection i in a Banach space Z,*

$$\|i(u)\| \leq c_0 \, \|u\| \ \forall u \text{ from } X \tag{2.10}$$

and N: $Z \to Z^*$ is an odd semicontinuous operator with the property

$$\|Nx\| \leq c_1\|x\|^{q-1} + c_2 \ \forall x \text{ from } Z, c_1, c_2 \geq 0, q \in (1, p). \tag{2.11}$$

Then $\lambda J_\varphi - N$ is surjective for any $\lambda \neq 0$.

Explanation. N is the short notation for the operator, which acts from X to X^*, i' o N o i, *i' being the adjoint of i.*

Proof. It follows to state that

$$\forall h \text{ from } X^* \ \exists u \text{ in } X, \text{ e.g., } \lambda J_\varphi\, u - (i' \circ N \circ i)\, u = h. \tag{2.12}$$

Apply Proposition 2.1 with $T = J_\varphi$ (correctly, as φ is (K, L, a) with $K = L = 1$, $a = p - 1$), $S = i' \circ N \circ i$. S is obviously odd and also compact: let $(x_n)_{n\in\mathbb{N}}$, $x_n \in X$, be a bounded sequence $(i(x_n))_{n\geq 1}$ has a convergent subsequence $(x_{k_n})_{n\geq 1}$; let $i(x_{k_n}) \to \gamma$, $\gamma \in Z$, then $N(i(x_{k_n})) \overset{w}{\to} N(\gamma)$ and, consequently, $i'(N(i(x_{k_n}))) \to i'(N(\gamma))$ since i' is also compact (Schauder theorem). So, to obtain the conclusion, it remains to prove

$$\overline{\lim_{\|u\|\to+\infty}} \frac{\|(i' \circ N \circ i)u\|}{\|u\|^{p-1}} = 0. \tag{2.13}$$

$\|i'(N(i(u)))\| \leq \|i'\|\ \|N(i(u))\| \overset{(2.10),(2.11)}{\leq} c_0\,(c_1\,\|i(u)\|^{q-1} + c_2) \leq c_0\,(c_0^{q-1}\, c_1\,\|u\|^{q-1} + c_2)$, from which it results (2.13) ($\|i'\| \leq \|i\| \leq c_0$ has been used) [11,12,15]. □

In the following, we search for the surjectivity of the operator $\lambda J_\varphi - N$, when N verifies the growth condition (2.11), where $q = p$, i.e.,

$$\|Nx\| \leq c_1\,\|x\|^{p-1} + c_2 \ \forall x \text{ from } Z,\ c_1, c_2 \geq 0. \tag{2.14}$$

For this reason, we present the statement:

Proposition 2.31. *Let X be a real reflexive Banach space compactly embedded by the linear injection i in the Banach space Z,*

$$\|\ i(u)\ \| \leq c_0\ \|\ u\ \|\ \ \forall u \ from\ X. \tag{2.15}$$

If

$$\lambda_1 := \inf\left\{\frac{\|u\|^p}{\|i(u)\|^p} : u \in X\backslash\{0\}\right\},\ p \in (1, +\infty),$$

then

1° λ_1 *is attained and nonzero;*

2° $\lambda_1^{-\frac{1}{p}}$ *is optimal for (2.15) (i.e.,* $\lambda_1^{-\frac{1}{p}} \leq c_0$ *for any* c_0*);*

3° *If X and Z are smooth and* $J_{XX^*} : X \to X^*$, $J_{ZZ^*} : Z \to Z^*$ *are duality maps relative to the same weight* φ: $\varphi(t) = t^{p-1}$, *then* λ_1 *is the smallest eigenvalue of the couple* (J_{XX^*}, J_{ZZ^*}) *[44].*

Clarification. λ is, by definition, *eigenvalue* for the couple (J_{XX^*}, J_{ZZ^*}) if there exists $u_0 \neq 0$ in Z, e.g., $\lambda\,(i' \circ J_{XX^*} \circ i)\, u_0 = J_{ZZ^*}\, u_0$. In this case, u_0 is, by definition, an *eigenvector*.

Proof. The set from the statement is correctly defined: $u \neq 0 \Rightarrow i(u) \neq 0$.

1° We have

$$\lambda_1 = \inf\{\|v\|^p : v \in X,\ \|i(v)\| = 1\}$$

(the two sets coincide, as $\left\| i\left(\frac{u}{i(u)}\right)\right\| = 1$). Let $(v_n)_{n\geq 1}$, $v_n \in X$, be with $\|i(v_n)\| = 1$ and $\|v_n\| \to \lambda_1^{\frac{1}{p}}$.

X being reflexive, $(v_n)_{n\geq 1}$ has a subsequence (we use the same notation for it) that is weakly convergent in X, $v_n \overset{w}{\to} v$ (Kakutani theorem [43], Volume 3, p. 155). Then,

$$\|\ v\ \| \leq \lim_{n\to\infty} \|\ v_n\ \|,$$

$$\|v\|^p \leq \lambda_1. \tag{2.16}$$

On the other hand, since i is compact, we have $i(v_n) \to i(v)$, which implies $\|i(v_n)\| \to \|i(v)\|$, $\|i(v)\| = 1$ and hence $\|v\|^p \geq \lambda_1$, $\|v\|^p \overset{(2.16)}{=} \lambda_1$, and λ_1 is attained and, a fortiori, nonzero.

2° We take the definitions of λ_1 and 1^0 into account.

3° Firstly, we show that λ_1 is an eigenvalue for the couple (J_{ZZ^*}, J_{XX^*}), i.e., $\exists u_0 \neq 0$ in X e.g.,

$$\lambda_1 \,(i' \circ J_{ZZ^*} \circ i)u_0 = J_{XX^*}\, u_0. \tag{2.17}$$

Taking the functional Φ: $X \to \mathbf{R}$,

$$\Phi(u) = \frac{1}{p}\| \, u \, \|^p - \frac{\lambda_1}{p}\| \, i(u) \, \|^p \, .$$

$\Phi(u) \geq 0\ \forall u$ in X (see the definition of λ_1) and, for $u_0 \neq 0$ e.g., $\lambda_1 \overset{1^0}{=} \left(\frac{\|u_0\|}{\|i(u_0)\|}\right)^p$, $\Phi(u_0) = 0$, which imposes (taking into account Proposition 2.3)

$$\Phi'(u_0) = 0 \text{ (Gâteaux derivative)}. \tag{2.18}$$

Then (the formulae: (*) and that from Proposition 2.4), $\forall u$ in X,

$$0 \overset{(2.18)}{=} \Phi'(u_0)(u) = \left\langle \|u_0\|^{p-1} \| \cdot \|'(u_0), u \right\rangle - \lambda_1 \left\langle \|i(u_0)\|^{p-1} \| \cdot \|'(i(u_0)), i(u) \right\rangle = (J_{XX^*} u_0)(u) - \lambda_1 (J_{ZZ^*}(i(u_0))(i(u))) =$$

$$\left\langle J_{XX^*} u_0 - \lambda_1 (i' \circ J_{ZZ^*} \circ i)(u_0), u \right\rangle, \text{ i.e. (2.17)}.$$

Let λ now be an eigenvalue for the couple (J_{ZZ^*}, J_{XX^*}) and u be a corresponding eigenvector. Then

$$\| \, u \, \|^p = (J_{XX^*}\, u)(u) = \lambda \langle J_{ZZ^*}(i(u)), i(u) \rangle = \lambda \, \| \, i(u) \, \|^p,$$

hence

$$\lambda = \frac{\|u\|^p}{\|i(u)\|^p} \geq \lambda_1. \square$$

We can now state the following.

Proposition 2.32. *Let X be a real reflexive Banach space, smooth and have the property (H), J_φ duality map on X with $\varphi(t) = t^{p-1}$, $p \in (1, +\infty)$. Suppose that X is compactly embedded with the linear injection i in the Banach space Z and let N: $Z \to Z^*$ be an odd semicontinuous operator with:*

$$\|Nx\| \leq c_1 \, \|x\|^{p-1} + c_2 \ \forall x \text{ from } Z,\ c_1, c_2 \geq 0.$$

Then, for any λ, if

$$|\lambda| > \overline{\lim_{\|u\| \to +\infty}} \frac{\|(i' \circ N \circ i)u\|}{\|u\|^{p-1}}, \text{ a fortiori if } |\lambda| > c_1 \lambda_1^{-1},$$

where

$$\lambda_1 := \inf\left\{ \frac{\|u\|^p}{\|i(u)\|^p} : u \in X \backslash \{0\} \right\},$$

then $\lambda J_\varphi - N$ is surjective (N means $i' \circ N \circ i$).

Proof. The statement is correct, $\lambda_1 \neq 0$ (Proposition 2.31, 1^0). We apply, as for Proposition 2.30, Proposition 2.29 with $T = J_\varphi$, $S = i' \circ N \circ i$. We prove

$$\overline{\lim_{\|u\| \to +\infty}} \frac{\|(i' \circ N \circ i)u\|}{\|u\|^{p-1}} \leq c_1 \lambda_1^{-1} \tag{2.19}$$

using 2° from Proposition 2.31, which will be sufficient to impose the conclusion. $\|(i' \circ N \circ i)u\| \leq \|i'\| \, \|N(i(u))\| \leq \lambda_1^{-\frac{1}{p}} (c_1 \lambda_1^{\frac{1-p}{p}} \|u\|^{p-1} + c_2)$ ($\|i\prime\| \leq \|i\| \leq \lambda_1^{-\frac{1}{p}}$), and (2.19) becomes obvious. □

Remark 2.1. *Propositions 29, 30 and 32 have been briefly presented by the author in [11,12,15].*

2.3. Existence of the Solutions of the Problems

Consider the problems

$$(*) \begin{cases} -\lambda \operatorname{div}(|\nabla u|^{p-2} \nabla u) = f(\cdot, u(\cdot)) + h, \ x \in \Omega \\ u|\partial\Omega = 0 \end{cases}, \ p \in (1, +\infty)$$

and

$$(**) \begin{cases} -\lambda \sum\limits_{i=1}^{n} \frac{\partial}{\partial x_i} \left(\left| \frac{\partial u}{\partial x_i} \right|^{p-2} \frac{\partial u}{\partial x_i} \right) = f(\cdot, u(\cdot)) + h, \ x \in \Omega \\ u|\partial\Omega = 0 \end{cases}, \ p \in [2, +\infty)$$

In this subsection, we apply (the idea originates in [45]) the results from Section 2.2 to partial differential equations (weak solutions).

2.3.1. Preliminaries for Sobolev Spaces

To prepare the framework for this subsection and to be coherent and understandable, we start with a theoretical recapitulation for Sobolev spaces.

The spaces $L^p(\Omega)$ (Lebesgue integral in $\mathbf{R}^N$).

Let Ω be a nonempty open set in $\mathbf{R}^N$.

$$p \in [1, +\infty) \Rightarrow L^p(\Omega) := \{u : \Omega \to \mathbf{R} : u \text{measurable}, \ |u|_p \text{ Lebesgue integrable}\},$$

$$\| u \|_{L^p(\Omega)} := \left(\int\limits_{\Omega} |u|^p dx \right)^{\frac{1}{p}}.$$

This norm is Gâteaux differentiable on $L^p(\Omega) \backslash \{0\}$ for $p > 1$. It is even of Fréchet C^1 class ([43,46]).

$$p = +\infty \Rightarrow L^\infty(\Omega) := \{u : \Omega \to \mathbf{R} : u \text{ measurable}, \ \exists \, c > 0 \text{ e.g. } |u(x)| \leq c \text{ on } \Omega \text{ a.e.}\},$$

$$\|u\|_{L^\infty(\Omega)} := \inf c.$$

If $\mu(\Omega) < +\infty$, then $\| u \|_{L^p(\Omega)} \leq [\mu(\Omega)]^{\frac{1}{p} - \frac{1}{q}} \| u \|_{L^q(\Omega)}, 1 \leq p \leq q \leq +\infty$.

$$p \in [1, +\infty] \Rightarrow \| u \|_{0,p} := \| u \|_{L^p(\Omega)}.$$

$L^p(\Omega)$, modulo the known factorization, is a Banach space for $p \in [1, +\infty]$, $L^p(\Omega)$ is uniformly convex and hence reflexive (Proposition 2.9) for $p \in (1, +\infty)$, $L^1(\Omega)$ and $L^\infty(\Omega)$ are not reflexive, $L^p(\Omega)$ is separable for $p \in [1, +\infty)$, and $L^\infty(\Omega)$ is not separable.

For p in $[1, +\infty]$, p' is defined by:

$$\frac{1}{p} + \frac{1}{p'} = 1.$$

Then,

$$p \in (1, +\infty) \Rightarrow (L^p(\Omega))* = L^{p'}(\Omega), \ (L^1(\Omega))* = L^\infty(\Omega), \ (L^\infty(\Omega))* \underset{\neq}{\supset} L^1(\Omega).$$

$L^1_{loc}(\Omega) : = \{u : \Omega \to \mathbf{R} : u$ integrable on any compact part of $\Omega\}$.

At the end of this part of the exposure, we prove ([43], Ω is a Lebesgue measurable set):

Proposition 2.33. *When $p \in (1, +\infty)$, $u \to \| u \|_{L^p(\Omega)}$ is of Fréchet C^1 class on $L^p(\Omega)\setminus\{0\}$.*

Proof. For the following calculus, we use the inequalities [47]:

$$\xi, \zeta \in \mathbf{R}^N, p \in (1, +\infty) \Rightarrow \| \|\xi\|^{p-2}\xi - \|\zeta\|^{p-2}\zeta\| \le \begin{cases} c\|\xi-\zeta\|(\|\xi\|+\|\zeta\|)^{p-2}, p>2 \\ c\|\xi-\zeta\|^{p-1}, p\in(1,2] \end{cases},$$

$$c \text{ independent by } \xi, \zeta. \tag{2.20}$$

Let

$$\Phi(u) : = \| u \|_{0,p}, \ \Psi(u) : = \frac{1}{p}||u||^p_{0,p},$$

hence,

$$\Phi(u) = p^{\frac{1}{p}}[\Psi(u)]^{\frac{1}{p}}. \tag{2.21}$$

Ψ is Gâteaux differentiable on $L^p(\Omega)$ and [48]

$$\Psi\prime(u)(h) = \int_\Omega |u|^{p-1}(\text{sgn}u)h\, dx, \ \forall h \text{ in } L^p(\Omega)$$

We prove that $u \to \Psi'(u)$ is continuous on $L^p(\Omega)$ and then (2.21) will impose the conclusion, taking into account Proposition 2.4.

Let

$$u_n \to u_0 \text{ in } L^p(\Omega). \tag{2.22}$$

It follows to prove

$$\lim_{n\to\infty} \Psi'(u_n) = \Psi'(u_0) \text{ in } (L^p(\Omega))^*, \text{ i.e.}$$

$$\lim_{n\to\infty} \sup_{\|h\|_{0,p}=1} |\langle\Psi'(u_n) - \Psi'(u_0), h\rangle| = 0. \tag{2.23}$$

$\|h\|_{0,p} = 1 \Rightarrow |\langle\Psi'(u_n) - \Psi'(u_0), h\rangle| = |\int_\Omega (|u_n|^{p-1}\text{sgn}u_n - |u_0|^{p-1}\text{sgn}u_0)h\, dx| \le \int_\Omega |(|u_n|^{p-1}\text{sgn}u_n - |u_0|^{p-1}\text{sgn}u_0)h|\, dx \overset{\text{Hölder}}{\le} A_n$, $A_n : = \| |u_n|^{p-1} \text{sgn } u_n - |u_0|^{p-1} \text{sgn } u_0||_{L^{p'}(\Omega)}$, since $||h||_{L^p(\Omega)} = 1$, where $\frac{1}{p} + \frac{1}{p'} = 1$.

However, $| |u_n|^{p-1} \text{sgn } u_n - |u_0|^{p-1} \text{sgn } u_0 |^{p'} = | |u_n|^{p-2} u_n - |u_0|^{p-2} u_0 |^{p'} \overset{(2.20)}{\le}$

$$\begin{cases} c_0|u_n - u_0|^{p'}(|u_n| + |u_0|)^{p'(p-2)}, p > 2 \\ c_0|u_n - u_0|^p, p \in (1,2] \end{cases},$$

hence $A_n^{p'} = \int_\Omega ||u_n|^{p-1}\text{sgn}u_n - |u_0|^{p-1}\text{sgn}u_0|^{p'}\, dx \le$

$$\begin{cases} c_0\int_\Omega |u_n - u_0|^{p'}(|u_n| + |u_0|)^{p'(p-2)}dx, p > 2 \\ c_0\int_\Omega |u_n - u_0|^p dx = c_0||u_n - u_0||^p_{0,p}, p \in (1,2] \end{cases},$$

therefore, when $p \in (1, 2]$, $\lim_{n\to\infty} A_n^{p'} = 0$ (see (2.22)), i.e., $\lim_{n\to\infty} A_n = 0$ and hence (2.23), and when $p > 2$,

$$\lim_{n\to\infty} A_n^{p'} = 0, \tag{2.24}$$

i.e., $\lim\limits_{n\to\infty} A_n = 0$ and hence (2.23). (2.24) is proved as follows:

$$\int\limits_{\Omega} |u_n - u_0|^{p'}(|u_n| + |u_0|)^{p'(p-2)}dx \overset{\text{Hölder}}{\leq} \||u_n - u_0|^{p'}\|_{0,\frac{p}{p'}} \|(|u_n| + |u_0|)^{p'(p-2)}\|_{0,\frac{p}{p'(p-2)}}$$

$= (\|u_n - u_0\|_{0,p})^{p'} \| \, |u_n| + |u_0| \, \|_{0,p}^{p'(p-2)}$, $\lim\limits_{n\to\infty} \|u_n - u_0\|_{0,p}^{p'} \overset{(2.22)}{=} 0$, and the second factor is bounded, since $\| \, |u_n| + |u_0| \, \|_{0,p} \leq \|u_n\|_{0,p} + \|u_0\|_{0,p}$ and $\|u_n\|_{0,p} \overset{(2.22)}{\to} \|u_0\|_{0,p}$. □

Corollary 2.5. *When $p \in (1, +\infty)$, any duality map on $L^p(\Omega)$ is a homeomorphism of $L^p(\Omega)$ on $L^{p'}(\Omega)$.*

Proof. $L^p(\Omega)$ is smooth (Proposition 2.3) and uniformly convex, hence local uniformly convex (Proposition 2.8) and, in particular, has the (H) property, even $L^{p'}(\Omega)$ has the same properties (by applying Proposition 2.27). □

Let Ω be a nonempty open set from $\mathbf{R}^N$ and p in $[1, +\infty]$.

$W^{1,p}(\Omega)$ designates the real vector space of the functions u from $L^p(\Omega)$ for which there exists $g_1, \ldots, g_N$ in $L^p(\Omega)$ e.g.,

$$\forall \varphi \text{ in } C_c^\infty(\Omega) \int_\Omega u \frac{\partial \varphi}{\partial x_i} dx = -\int_\Omega g_i \varphi dx, \; i = \overline{1, N}.$$

In the definition, $C_c^\infty(\Omega)$ can be replaced by $C_c^1(\Omega)$. We denote, for each i, $1 \leq i \leq N$,

$$\frac{\partial u}{\partial x_i} := g_i, \text{ the weak derivative.}$$

These are uniquely determined.

Remark 2.2. *By weak differentiation, one remains in $L^p(\Omega)$.*

Additionally, for u from $W^{1,p}(\Omega)$,

$$\nabla u = \operatorname{grad} u := \left(\frac{\partial u}{\partial x_1}, \ldots, \frac{\partial u}{\partial x_N}\right), \text{the weak gradient}$$

$$|\nabla u| := \left[\sum_{i=1}^{N} \left(\frac{\partial u}{\partial x_i}\right)^2\right]^{\frac{1}{2}},$$

$$\operatorname{div} u := \sum_{i=1}^{N} \frac{\partial u}{\partial x_i}, \text{the weak divergence.}$$

$$|\nabla u| \in L^p(\Omega) \colon |\nabla u| \leq g := \sum_{i=1}^{N} \left|\frac{\partial u}{\partial x_i}\right| \in L^p(\Omega), |\nabla u|^p \leq g^p.$$

Moreover, for $p \in (1, +\infty)$ and p' the conjugated coefficient,

$$|\nabla u|^{p-2} \frac{\partial u}{\partial x_i} \in L^{p'}(\Omega), i = \overline{1, N},$$

$$\frac{\partial}{\partial x_i}\left(\left|\frac{\partial u}{\partial x_i}\right|^{p-2} \frac{\partial u}{\partial x_i}\right) \in L^{p'}(\Omega), i = \overline{1, N}.$$

To justify the above two relations, for

$$p \neq 2, \left(|\nabla u|^{p-2}\left|\frac{\partial u}{\partial x_i}\right|\right)^{p'} = |\nabla u|^{p'(p-2)}\left|\frac{\partial u}{\partial x_i}\right|^{p'}, |\nabla u|^{p'(p-2)} \in L^{\frac{p}{p'(p-2)}}(\Omega),$$

$$\left|\frac{\partial u}{\partial x_i}\right|^{p'} \in L^{\frac{p}{p'}}(\Omega), \frac{p'(p-2)}{p} + \frac{p'}{p} = 1,$$

and for $p = 2$—obviously since $p' = 2$.

We define:

$$\| u \|_{W^{1,p}(\Omega)} := \| u \|_{L^p(\Omega)} + \sum_{i=1}^{N}\left\| \frac{\partial u}{\partial x_i} \right\|_{L^p(\Omega)},$$

a norm on $W^{1,p}(\Omega)$.

Sometimes, when $p \in [1, +\infty)$, one takes the equivalent norm:

$$\left(\| u \|^p_{L^p(\Omega)} + \sum_{i=1}^{N}\left\| \frac{\partial u}{\partial x_i} \right\|^p_{L^p(\Omega)}\right)^{\frac{1}{p}}.$$

$W^{1,p}(\Omega)$ is a Banach space for $p \in [1, +\infty]$, it is uniformly convex and reflexive for $p \in (1, +\infty)$ and separable for $p \in [1, +\infty)$. When $p > N$, any function from $W^{1,p}(\Omega)$ is Fréchet differentiable on Ω a.e. ([49], Chapter VIII).

We now provide some clarifications related to the weak derivative, $p \in [1, +\infty]$. If $u \in C^1(\Omega) \cap L^p(\Omega)$ and $\frac{\partial u}{\partial x_i} \in L^p(\Omega)$, $i = \overline{1, N}$ (derivatives in the usual meaning), then $u \in W^{1,p}(\Omega)$ and the weak derivatives coincide with them in the usual sense. In particular, if Ω is bounded, then $C^1(\overline{\Omega}) \subset W^{1,p}(\Omega)$. Reciprocally, if $u \in W^{1,p}(\Omega) \cap C(\Omega)$ and $\frac{\partial u}{\partial x_i} \in C(\Omega)$, $i = \overline{1, N}$ (weak derivatives), then $u \in C^1(\Omega)$.

Let p be in $[1, +\infty)$.

$$W^{1,p}_0(\Omega) := \overline{C^1_c(\Omega)}^{W^{1,p}(\Omega)} = \overline{C_c(\Omega)}^{W^{1,p}(\Omega)}.$$

$W^{1,p}_0(\Omega)$ with the norm induced is a separable Banach space. It is reflexive if $p \in (1, +\infty)$.

Since $C^1_c(\mathbf{R}^N)$ is dense in $W^{1,p}(\mathbf{R}^N)$, $W^{1,p}_0(\mathbf{R}^N) = W^{1,p}(\mathbf{R}^N)$. However, when $\Omega \neq \mathbf{R}^N$, in general, $W^{1,p}_0(\Omega) \neq W^{1,p}(\Omega)$.

Proposition 2.34. *For any p in $[1, +\infty)$,*

$$W^{1,p}(\Omega) \cap C_c(\Omega) \subset W^{1,p}_0(\Omega).$$

The following considerations strongly imply $W^{1,p}_0(\Omega)$ in the theory of partial differential equations.

Definition 2.8. *We define, by local charts, $W^{1,p}(\Gamma)$ with $p \in [1, +\infty)$, Γ regular manifold, for instance $\Gamma = \partial\Omega$, Ω open set of C^1 class with $\partial\Omega$ bounded. In this situation there exists a unique continuous linear operator γ: $W^{1,p}(\Omega) \to W^{1-\frac{1}{p},p}(\partial\Omega)$, the trace, such that γ is surjective and*

$$u \in W^{1,p}(\Omega) \cap C(\overline{\Omega}) \Rightarrow \gamma(u) = u \mid \partial\Omega.$$

By the way,

Proposition 2.35. *Let Ω be of C^1 class and u in $W^{1,p}(\Omega) \cap C(\overline{\Omega})$, $p \in [1, +\infty)$. Then*

$$u \in W^{1,p}_0(\Omega) \iff u \mid \partial\Omega = 0.$$

Here is another characterization of the spaces $W_0^{1,p}(\Omega)$.

Proposition 2.36. *Let* Ω *be of* C^1 *class and u in* $L^p(\Omega)$, $p \in (1, +\infty)$. *Then*

$$u \in W_0^{1,p}(\Omega) \Longleftrightarrow \exists c > 0 \text{ such that } \left| \int_\Omega u \frac{\partial \varphi}{\partial x_i} dx \right| \leq c \| \varphi \|_{L^{p'}(\Omega)}, i = \overline{1,N}, \forall \varphi \text{ in } C_c^1(\Omega).$$

Suppose $\mu(\Omega) < +\infty$. Then $u \to \| |\nabla u| \|_{L^p(\Omega)}$ is a norm on $W_0^{1,p}(\Omega)$ *equivalent* (and hence also *complete*) to $u \to u_{W^{1,p}(\Omega)}$.

We denote:

$u \in W_0^{1,p}(\Omega) \Rightarrow \|u\|_{1,p:} = \| |\nabla u| \|_{L^p(\Omega)}$ $(= \| |\nabla u| \|_{0,p}$, when confusion cannot appear).

This norm, when $p \in (1, +\infty)$, is Gâteaux differentiable on $W_0^{1,p}(\Omega) \setminus \{0\}$ (combine Proposition 2.15 and Proposition 2.4), which assures uni-valued duality maps (Proposition 2.3).

Proposition 2.37. $(W_0^{1,p}(\Omega), \| \cdot \|_{1,p})$, $p \in (1, +\infty)$, *is uniformly convex and hence particularly reflexive.*

Proof ([50]). *The case* $p \in [2, +\infty)$. We use the following inequality: ([51], Euclidean norm)

$$\xi, \zeta \in \mathbf{R}^n, n \geq 1 \Rightarrow \left\| \frac{\xi + \eta}{2} \right\|^p + \left\| \frac{\xi - \eta}{2} \right\|^p \leq \frac{1}{2} (\| \xi \|^p + \| \eta \|^p) \tag{2.25}$$

Let ε be from $(0, 2]$ and u, v from $W_0^{1,p}(\Omega)$ with

$$\|u\|_{1,p} = \|v\|_{1,p} = 1, \|u - v\|_{1,p} \geq \varepsilon. \tag{2.26}$$

Then

$$\left\| \frac{u+v}{2} \right\|_{1,p}^p + \left\| \frac{u-v}{2} \right\|_{1,p}^p = \int_\Omega \left(\left| \frac{\nabla u + \nabla v}{2} \right|^p + \left| \frac{\nabla u - \nabla v}{2} \right|^p \right) dx \overset{(2.25)}{\leq}$$

$$\frac{1}{2} \int_\Omega (|\nabla u|^p + |\nabla v|^p) dx = \frac{1}{2} (\|u\|_{1,p}^p + \|v\|_{1,p}^p) \overset{(2.26)}{=} 1, \left\| \frac{u+v}{2} \right\|_{1,p}^p \overset{(2.26)}{\leq} 1 - \left(\frac{\varepsilon}{2}\right)^p.$$

We take $\delta > 0$ defined by

$$\left[1 - \left(\frac{\varepsilon}{2} \right)^p \right]^{\frac{1}{p}} = 1 - \delta.$$

The case $p \in (1, 2)$. We use

$$\xi, \zeta \in \mathbf{R}^n, n \geq 1 \Rightarrow \left\| \frac{\xi + \eta}{2} \right\|^{p'} + \left\| \frac{\xi - \eta}{2} \right\|^{p'} \leq \left[\frac{1}{2} (\| \xi \|^p + \| \eta \|^p) \right]^{\frac{1}{p-1}}, \tag{2.27}$$

p' the coefficient conjugated with p ([51]).

We remark that, for u in $W_0^{1,p}(\Omega)$,

$$|\nabla u|^{p'} \in L^{p-1}(\Omega), \|u\|_{1,p}^{p'} = \| |\nabla u|^{p'} \|_{0,p-1}. \tag{2.28}$$

Let ε be in $(0, 2]$ and u, v in $W_0^{1,p}(\Omega)$. Then $|\nabla u|^{p'}, |\nabla v|^{p'} \overset{(2.27)}{\in} L^{p-1}(\Omega)$ and as

$$\| |\nabla u|^{p'} \|_{0,p-1} + \| |\nabla v|^{p'} \|_{0,p-1} \leq \| |\nabla u|^{p'} + |\nabla v|^{p'} \|_{0,p-1} \cdot \tag{2.29}$$

Since $0 < p - 1 < 1$, it results:

$$\left\|\frac{u+v}{2}\right\|_{1,p}^{p'} + \left\|\frac{u-v}{2}\right\|_{1,p}^{p'} \overset{(2.28),(2.29),(2.27)}{\leq} \left[\frac{1}{2}(\|u\|_{1,p}^{p} + \|v\|_{1,p}^{p})\right]^{\frac{1}{p-1}},$$

consequently, if $\|u\|_{1,p} = \|v\|_{1,p} = 1$ and $\|u - v\|_{1,p} \geq \varepsilon$, one obtains

$$\left\|\frac{u+v}{2}\right\|_{1,p}^{p'} \leq 1 - \left(\frac{\varepsilon}{2}\right)^{p'}$$

and hence the conclusion. □

The dual of $W_0^{1,p}(\Omega)$, p in $[1, +\infty)$, is denoted

$$W^{-1,p'}(\Omega),$$

p' the coefficient conjugated to p.

If Ω is bounded,

$$\frac{2N}{N+2} \leq p < +\infty \Rightarrow W_0^{1,p}(\Omega) \subset L^2(\Omega) \subset W^{-1,p'}(\Omega)$$

with continuous injections and dense and, if Ω is not bounded,

$$\frac{2N}{N+2} \leq p \leq 2 \Rightarrow W_0^{1,p}(\Omega) \subset L^2(\Omega) \subset W^{-1,p'}(\Omega).$$

The elements of $W^{-1,p'}(\Omega)$ can be characterized by the following.

Proposition 2.38. *Let F be from $W^{-1,p'}(\Omega)$. There exists $f_0, \ldots, f_N$ in $L^{p'}(\Omega)$ such that*

$$F(u) = \int_{\Omega} f_0 u dx + \sum_{i=1}^{N} \int_{\Omega} f_i \frac{\partial u}{\partial x_i} dx \ \forall u \text{ in } W_0^{1,p}(\Omega)$$

and

$$\| F \| = \max_{1 \leq i \leq N} \| f_i \|_{L^{p'}(\Omega)}.$$

When Ω is bounded, one can take $f_0 = 0$.

2.3.2. The Operators $-\Delta_p$, $-\Delta_p^s$ and N_f

$-\boldsymbol{\Delta}_p$, $p \in (1, +\infty)$, the p-Laplacian

Let Ω be an open set, with the *finite Lebesgue measure*, from $\mathbf{R}^N$, $N \geq 2$. The norm on $W_0^{1,p}(\Omega)$ will be $u \to \|u\|_{1,p}$.

Consider the operator $-\Delta_p : W_0^{1,p}(\Omega) \to W^{-1,p'}(\Omega)$,

$$\Delta_p u = \operatorname{div}(|\nabla u|^{p-2} \nabla u). \tag{2.30}$$

This acts according to [45]:

$$\langle -\Delta_p u, v \rangle = \int_{\Omega} |\nabla u|^{p-2} \nabla u \cdot \nabla v dx \forall u, v \text{ in } W_0^{1,p}(\Omega). \tag{2.31}$$

Taking into account the following, the next property of the p-Laplacian—the identification with a particular duality map—is the most important.

Proposition 2.39. *Let* Ψ: $W_0^{1,p}(\Omega) \to \mathbf{R}$,

$$\Psi(u) = \frac{1}{p}||u||_{1,p}^{p}.$$

Then Ψ *is Gâteaux differentiable on* $W_0^{1,p}(\Omega)\backslash\{0\}$, *and*

$$\Psi\prime(u) = -\Delta_p\, u = J_\varphi\, u \forall_u from\ W_0^{1,p}(\Omega),$$

where $\varphi(t) = t^{p-1}$ ([50]).

Proof. Since $\Psi(u) = \int_0^{||u||_{1,p}} \varphi(t)dt$, we have

$$J_\varphi\, u = \partial\, \Psi(u)\ \forall u \text{in}\ W_0^{1,p}(\Omega)\ \text{(Proposition 2.2)},$$

thus, it remains to prove that Ψ is Gâteaux differentiable and

$$\Psi\prime(u) = -\Delta_p\, u\ \forall u \text{in}\ W_0^{1,p}(\Omega). \tag{2.32}$$

$\Psi = g \circ f$, where g: $L^p(\Omega) \to \mathbf{R}$, $g(u) = \frac{1}{p}\ ||u||_{0,p}^{p}$, $f: W_0^{1,p}(\Omega) \to L^p(\Omega)$, $f\ (u) = |\nabla u|$.

From now on, the proof is continued as in [11] and has been proposed by the author.

g is of Fréchet C^1 class on $L^p(\Omega)$ (Proposition 2.33). f is Gâteaux differentiable on $W_0^{1,p}(\Omega)\backslash\{0\}$ and $f\,'(u)(h) = \frac{\nabla u \cdot \nabla h}{|\nabla u|}$ $\forall h$ in $W_0^{1,p}(\Omega)$ [50]. Applying Proposition 2.4, $u \neq 0$ and $h \in W_0^{1,p}(\Omega) \Rightarrow \Psi'(u)(h) = \int_\Omega |\nabla u|^{p-1} \frac{\nabla u \cdot \nabla h}{|\nabla u|}\, dx = \int_\Omega |\nabla u|^{p-2} \nabla u \cdot \nabla h\, dx \overset{(2.31)}{=} \langle -\Delta_p\, u, h\rangle$ and the case $u = 0$ remains to finish with (2.32).

However, $\Psi'(0)(h) = \lim_{t\to 0} \frac{1}{t}\Psi(th) = \lim_{t\to 0} \frac{t^{p-1}}{p}\, ||h||_{1,p}^{p} = 0 = \langle -\Delta_p\, 0, h\rangle$. □

Remark 2.3. Ψ *has even the Fréchet* C^1 *class on* $W_0^{1,p}(\Omega)$ [44,52].

Corollary 2.6. $u \to \|u\|_{1,p}$ *is Gâteaux differentiable on* $W_0^{1,p}(\Omega)\backslash\{0\}$ *and* $W_0^{1,p}(\Omega)$ *is smooth.*

Proof. For the first assertion, apply Proposition 2.4 considering $\varphi(u) = \|u\|_{1,p} = p^{\frac{1}{p}}[\Psi(u)]^{\frac{1}{p}}$; for the second assertion, we use Proposition 2.3. □

Proposition 2.40. *The operator* $-\Delta_p$: $W_0^{1,p}(\Omega) \to W^{-1,p\prime}(\Omega)$ *is bijective with monotonous inverse, bounded and continuous.*

Proof. $-\Delta_p = J_\varphi$ (Proposition 2.39), and $W_0^{1,p}(\Omega)$ is uniformly convex; apply Proposition 2.26 and take into account the formula $J_\varphi^{-1} = \Phi^{-1}\, J_{\varphi-1}$, Φ is the canonical embedding in bidual (Proposition 2.23). □

$-\mathbf{\Delta_p^s}$, $p \in (1, +\infty)$, the p-Pseudo-Laplacian

Let Ω be an open set of finite Lebesgue measure from $\mathbf{R}^N$, $N \geq 2$, and p in $(1, +\infty)$.

$$\|u\|_{1,p} := \left(\sum_{i=1}^{N}\left\|\frac{\partial u}{\partial x_i}\right\|_{L^p(\Omega)}^{p}\right)^{\frac{1}{p}}$$

is a norm on $W_0^{1,p}(\Omega)$ since

$$\left(\sum_{i=1}^{N}\left\|\frac{\partial u}{\partial x_i}+\frac{\partial v}{\partial x_i}\right\|_{0,p}^{p}\right)^{\frac{1}{p}} \leq \left[\sum_{i=1}^{N}\left(\left\|\frac{\partial u}{\partial x_i}\right\|_{0,p}^{p}+\left\|\frac{\partial v}{\partial x_i}\right\|_{0,p}^{p}\right)^{p}\right]^{\frac{1}{p}},$$

applying Minkovski inequality.

The dual of $(W_0^{1,p}(\Omega), \| \cdot \|_{1,p})$ is also designated by $W^{-1,p'}(\Omega)$, where p' is the exponent conjugated with p.

$\| \cdot \|_{1,p}$ is equivalent to the norm $|u|_{1,p} := \sum_{i=1}^{N}\left\|\frac{\partial u}{\partial x_i}\right\|_{L^p(\Omega)}$:

$$\sum_{i=1}^{N}\left\|\frac{\partial u}{\partial x_i}\right\|_{L^p(\Omega)} \leq N\|u\|_{1,p} \leq N\sum_{i=1}^{N}\left\|\frac{\partial u}{\partial x_i}\right\|_{L^p(\Omega)}.$$

However, $|\cdot|_{1,p}$ is equivalent to $\|\cdot\|_{1,p}$ since $\|u\|_{1,p} \leq |u|_{1,p} \leq N\|u\|_{1,p}$. Consequently,

Proposition 2.41. *$(W_0^{1,p}(\Omega), \| \cdot \|_{1,p})$, $p \in (1, +\infty)$, is Banach space.*

Furthermore,

Proposition 2.42. *$(W_0^{1,p}(\Omega), \| \cdot \|_{1,p})$, $p \in [2, +\infty)$, is uniformly convex.*

Proof. The following proof was proposed by the author in [11]. Use the inequality (2.25): $\xi, \eta \in \mathbf{R}^n, n \geq 1 \Rightarrow \left\|\frac{\xi+\eta}{2}\right\|^p + \left\|\frac{\xi-\eta}{2}\right\|^p \leq \frac{1}{2}(\|\xi\|^p + \|\eta\|^p)$ with the Euclidean norm [51].

Let ε be in (0, 2] and define u, v with $\|u\|_{1,p} = \|v\|_{1,p} = 1, \|u - v\|_{1,p} \geq \varepsilon$. Suppose $p \in [2, +\infty)$. $\left\|\frac{u+v}{2}\right\|^p + \left\|\frac{u-v}{2}\right\|^p = \sum_{i=1}^{N}\int_{\Omega}\left(\left|\frac{\frac{\partial u}{\partial x_i}+\frac{\partial v}{\partial x_i}}{2}\right|^p + \left|\frac{\frac{\partial u}{\partial x_i}-\frac{\partial v}{\partial x_i}}{2}\right|^p\right)dx \leq \sum_{i=1}^{N}\int_{\Omega}\frac{1}{2}\left(\left|\frac{\partial u}{\partial x_i}\right|^p + \left|\frac{\partial v}{\partial x_i}\right|^p\right)dx = 1,$

and hence, $\left\|\frac{u+v}{2}\right\|_{1,p}^{p} \leq 1 - \left(\frac{\varepsilon}{2}\right)^p$, take δ defined by $1 - \delta = \left[1 - \left(\frac{\varepsilon}{2}\right)^p\right]^{\frac{1}{p}}$. □

Let Ω be an open set in $\mathbf{R}^N$, $N \geq 2$, of the finite Lebesgue measure and p in $(1, +\infty)$. Considering the operator $-\Delta_p^s$: $W_0^{1,p}(\Omega) \to W^{-1,p'}(\Omega)$,

$$-\Delta_p^s u = -\sum_{i=1}^{n}\frac{\partial}{\partial x_i}\left(\left|\frac{\partial u}{\partial x_i}\right|^{p-2}\frac{\partial u}{\partial x_i}\right).$$

This acts according to [45]:

$$\langle -\Delta_p^s u, h\rangle = \sum_{i=1}^{N}\int_{\Omega}\left|\frac{\partial u}{\partial x_i}\right|^{p-2}\frac{\partial u}{\partial x_i}\frac{\partial h}{\partial x_i}dx, \ \forall u, h \text{ in } W_0^{1,p} \tag{2.33}$$

Proposition 2.43. *The function Ψ: $\Psi(u) = \frac{1}{p}\|u\|_{1,p}^{p}$, $p \in (1, +\infty)$, is Gâteaux differentiable on $W_0^{1,p}(\Omega)\backslash\{0\}$, and*

$$\Psi\prime(u) = -\Delta_p^s u = J\varphi\ u,\ \varphi(t) := t^{p-1}.$$

Proof ([11]). Fix the index i, $1 \le i \le N$, and let g: $W_0^{1,p}(\Omega) \to \mathbf{R}$, $g(u) = \left\| \frac{\partial u}{\partial x_i} \right\|_{0,p}^{p}$. We have $g = F \circ f$, $f : W_0^{1,p}(\Omega) \to L^p(\Omega)$, $f(u) = \frac{\partial u}{\partial x_i}$, F: $L^p(\Omega) \to \mathbf{R}$, $F(v) = \|v\|_{0,p}^{p}$. As $f'(u)(h) = \frac{\partial h}{\partial x_i}$ and $F'(v)(h) = p\int_\Omega |v|^{p-2} vh dx$ ([48]), $g'(u) = F'(f(u)) \circ f'(u)$ (formula from Proposition 2.4),

$$g'(u)(h) = p\int_\Omega \left| \frac{\partial u}{\partial x_i} \right|^{p-2} \frac{\partial u}{\partial x_i} \frac{\partial h}{\partial x_i} dx \tag{2.34}$$

and hence

$$\Psi'(u)(h) = \sum_{i=1}^{N} \left(\left\| \frac{\partial u}{\partial x_i} \right\|_{0,p}^{p} \right)'(h) \overset{(2.34),(2.33)}{=} \left\langle -\Delta_p^s u,\, h \right\rangle.$$

The rest of the proof is the same as for Proposition 2.39. □

Corollary 2.7. $u \to \|u\|_{1,p}$, $p \in (1, +\infty)$, *is Gâteaux differentiable on* $W_0^{1,p}(\Omega)\backslash\{0\}$. *Consequently,* $(W_0^{1,p}(\Omega), \|\cdot\|_{1,p})$ *is a smooth space.*

Proof ([11]). Taking $\Phi(u) = \|u\|_{1,p}$, we have

$$\Phi(u) = p^{\frac{1}{p}} (\Psi(u))^{\frac{1}{p}}.$$

We apply the formula from Proposition 2.4. For the second assertion, we take Proposition 2.3 into account. □

Nemytskii Operator N_f

In the following, some statements from [53] are necessary to develop some results.

Definition 2.9. *Let* Ω *be a nonempty open Lebesgue measurable (L.m.) set from* $\mathbf{R}^N$, $N \ge 1$, μ *the Lebesgue measure in* $\mathbf{R}^N$ *and* $M(\Omega) := \{u: \Omega \to \mathbf{R}: u \text{ L.m.}\}$. *By definition,* $f : \Omega \times \mathbf{R} \to \mathbf{R}$ *is a Carathéodory function if:*

$1°$ $f(\cdot, s)$ *is* L.m. $\forall s$ *in* $\mathbf{R}$;

$2°$ $f(x, \cdot)$ *is continuous* $\forall x$ *in* $\Omega\backslash A$, $\mu(A) = 0$.

Proposition 2.44. *If* $f : \Omega \times \mathbf{R} \to \mathbf{R}$ *is a Carathéodory function, then, for any* u *in* $M(\Omega)$, $x \to f(x, u(x))$ *is L.m.*

Proof. Let $(\varphi_n)_{n \ge 1}$ be a sequence of real functions, simple, L.m., with

$$\varphi_n(x) \underset{x \in \Omega}{\to} u(x).$$

$F_n : F_n(x) := f(x, \varphi_n(x))$ is L.m. on $A_1, \ldots, A_p$, where $\varphi_n \mid A_k$ = constant, $k = \overline{1,p}$ (1^0 from Definition 2.9), hence F_n is L.m. on Ω. $\forall x$ in $\Omega\backslash A$, and since $\varphi_n(x) \to u(x)$, we have $F_n(x) \to f(x, u(x))$ (2^0 from Definition 2.9), which implies, since the Lebesgue measure is complete, $x \to f(x, u(x))$ L.m. □

Definition 2.10. *Thus, one may consider the Nemytskii operator:*

$$N_f : M(\Omega) \to M(\Omega),\ (N_f u)x = f(x, u(x)).$$

Proposition 2.45. *Suppose* $\mu(\Omega) < +\infty$. *Then*

$$u_n(x) \underset{x \in \Omega}{\overset{\mu}{\to}} u_0(x) \Rightarrow N_f u(x) \underset{x \in \Omega}{\overset{\mu}{\to}} N_f u_0(x).$$

Proof ([54]). It is sufficient to show the proof in the case $f(x, 0) = 0\ \forall x$ in Ω and $u_n(x) \underset{x\in\Omega}{\overset{\mu}{\to}} 0$; thus, it remains to prove that:

$$\forall \varepsilon, \eta > 0\ \exists N \text{ in } \mathbf{N}, \text{e.g., } n \geq N \Rightarrow \mu(\{x \in \Omega : |f(x, u_n(x))| \geq \varepsilon\}) \leq \eta. \tag{2.35}$$

Set $\Omega_0 := \Omega \backslash A$. For $k \in \mathbf{N}$, $\Omega_k := \{x \in \Omega_0 : |s| < \frac{1}{k} \Rightarrow |f(x, s)| < \varepsilon\}$ (nonempty set for sufficiently big k; $f(x, \cdot)$ is continuous in 0), we have $\Omega_k \subset \Omega_{k+1}\ \forall k$ and $\Omega_0 = \bigcup_{k=1}^{\infty} \Omega_k$, hence $\mu(\Omega_0) = \lim_{k\to\infty} \mu(\Omega_k)$ and hence $\exists\, k_0$ in $\mathbf{N}$, e.g., $\mu(\Omega_0 \backslash \Omega_{k_0}) \leq \frac{\eta}{2}$. Let $A_n := \{x \in \Omega_0 : |u_n(x)| < \frac{1}{k_0}\}$, $\exists N$ in $\mathbf{N}$, e.g., $n \geq N \Rightarrow \mu(\Omega_0 \backslash A_n) \leq \frac{\eta}{2}$. Setting $B_n := \{x \in \Omega_0 : |f(x, u_n(x))| < \varepsilon\}$, we have, since $A_n \cap \Omega_{k_0} \subset B_n$, $n \geq N \Rightarrow \mu(\Omega_0 \backslash B_n) \leq \mu(\Omega_0 \backslash A_n) + \mu(\Omega_0 \backslash \Omega_{k_0}) \leq \eta$, which implies (2.35). □

Proposition 2.46. *If the Carathéodory function f verifies the growth condition:*

$$|f(x, s)| \leq c|s|^r + \beta(x), \forall x \in \Omega \backslash A \text{ with } \mu(A) = 0\ \forall s \in \mathbf{R},$$
$$\text{where } c \geq 0, r > 0, \beta \in L^p(\Omega), 1 \leq p \geq +\infty,$$

then

1° $N_f(L^{pr}(\Omega)) \subset L^p(\Omega)$;
2° N_f *is continuous* ($p < +\infty$) *and bounded on* $L^{pr}(\Omega)$.

Clarification. A map between metric spaces is *bounded* if the image of any bounded set is bounded.

Proof. 1° Let u be in $L^{pr}(\Omega)$.

$$|f(x, u(x))| \leq c\,|u(x)|^r + \beta(x), x \in \Omega \backslash A, s \in \mathbf{R}, \tag{2.36}$$

but $|u|^r \in L^p(\Omega)$, $\beta \in L^p(\Omega)$, hence $N_f\, u \in L^p(\Omega)$ (when $p < +\infty$, taking the power p, the first member is integrable and measurable (Proposition 2.44); when $p = +\infty$, the justification is obvious).

2° From (2.36),

$$||N_f\, u||_{L^p(\Omega)} \leq ||c\,|u|^r + \beta||_{L^p(\Omega)} \leq c\,||\,|u|^r\,||_{L^p(\Omega)} + ||\beta||_{L^p(\Omega)} = c||u||^r_{L^p(\Omega)} + ||\beta||_{L^p(\Omega)},$$

and hence N_f is bounded on $L^{pr}(\Omega)$.

We proceed to the continuity. Suppose $f(x, 0) = 0\ \forall x$ in Ω, and let

$$u_n \to 0 \text{ in } L^{pr}(\Omega). \tag{2.37}$$

We will prove:

$$N_f\, u_n \to 0 \text{ in } L^p(\Omega). \tag{2.38}$$

For (2.38), it is sufficient to prove that any subsequence $(N_f\, u_{k_n})$ has a subsequence $(N_f\, u_{l_{k_n}})$ convergent to 0 in $L^p(\Omega)$ (if (x_n), the sequence in the metric space X has the property that any subsequence (x_{k_n}) has a subsequence $(x_{l_{k_n}})$ with $x_{l_{k_n}} \to x_0$, and then $x_n \to x_0$ – ad absurdum justification).

Since $u_{k_n} \to 0$ in $L^{pr}(\Omega)$, $\exists\, (u_{l_{k_n}})$ a subsequence with

$$u_{l_{k_n}}(x) \to 0, x \in \Omega \backslash B, \mu(B) = 0$$

and

$$|u_{l_{k_n}}(x)| \leq g(x), g \in L^{pr}(\Omega).$$

From (2.36),

$$|f(x, u_{l_{k_n}}(x))| \leq c(g(x))^r + \beta(x),\ x \in \Omega \backslash (A \cup B). \tag{2.39}$$

Taking the power p in (2.39), the second member is integrable, and as $x \in \Omega \backslash (A \cup B) \Rightarrow f(x, u_{l_{k_n}}(x)) \to 0$, it results in (Lebesgue theorem of dominated convergence)

$$\int_\Omega |N_f u_n(x)|^p dx \to 0,$$

i.e., (2.38).

Pass to the general case and let $u_n \to u_0$ in $L^{pr}(\Omega)$. $g: \Omega \times \mathbf{R} \to \mathbf{R}$,

$$g(x, s) = f(x, s + u_0(x)) - f(x, u_0(x)),$$

is a Carathéodory function. Since $g(x, 0) = 0\ \forall x$ in Ω and $u_n - u_0 \to 0$ in $L^{pr}(\Omega)$, we obtain $N_g(u_n - u_0) \to 0$ in $L^p(\Omega)$ and, hence $N_f u_n \to N_f u_0$ in $L^p(\Omega)$. □

Remark 2.4. *Retain the inequality:*

$$||N_f u||_{L^p(\Omega)} \leq c||u||^r_{L^{pr}(\Omega)} + ||\beta||_{L^p(\Omega)}.$$

2.3.3. The Problem

Consider the problem

$$(*)\begin{cases} -\lambda \Delta_p u = f(\cdot, u(\cdot)) + h,\ x \in \Omega,\ \lambda \in \mathbf{R} \\ u|\partial\Omega = 0 \end{cases}$$

The next two propositions were obtained by the author and are given in [11,12,15].

Proposition 2.47. *Let Ω be an open bounded set of the C^1 class from $\mathbf{R}^N$, $N \geq 2$, $p \in (1, +\infty)$, h be from $W^{-1,p'}(\Omega)$ and $f: \Omega \times \mathbf{R} \to \mathbf{R}$ a Carathéodory function with the properties*

1° $f(x, -s) = -f(x, s)\ \forall s$ from $\mathbf{R}$, $\forall x$ from Ω,

2° $|f(x, s)| \leq c_1 |s|^{q-1} + \beta(x)\ \forall s$ from $\mathbf{R}$, $\forall x$ from $\Omega \backslash A$, $\mu(A) = 0$,

where $c_1 \geq 0$, $q \in (1, p)$, $\beta \in L^{q'}(\Omega)$, $\frac{1}{q} + \frac{1}{q'} = 1$.

Then, for any $\lambda \neq 0$, the problem $(*)$ has a solution in $W_0^{1,p}(\Omega)$ in the sense of $W^{-1,p'}(\Omega)$.

Explanations. The relationship $u \mid \partial\Omega$ from $(*)$ is in the sense of the trace (Definition 2.8). Moreover, $\gamma^{-1}(0) = W_0^{1,p}(\Omega)$. $f(\cdot, u) = N_f u$, where N_f is the Nemytskii operator (see Section 2.3.2 above), and so the equation from $(*)$ can be written as

$$-\lambda \Delta_p u = N_f u + h. \tag{2.40}$$

From 2° of the last assertion, it is determined (via Proposition 2.46) that N_f maps $L^q(\Omega)$ on $L^{q'}(\Omega)$, and it is continuous and bounded. Moreover (Proposition 2.46),

$$\| N_f u \|_{0,q'} \leq c_1 ||u||^{q-1}_{0,q} + c_2,\ c_2 := ||\beta||_{0,q'},\ \forall u \text{ in } L^q(\Omega). \tag{2.41}$$

Since $q \in (1, p)$ and $q < p^*$ (the Sobolev conjugated exponent), $(W_0^{1,p}(\Omega), \|\cdot\|_{1,p})$ is compactly embedded in $L^q(\Omega)$. Let i (linear injection) be such an embedding,

$$\| i(u) \|_{0,q} \leq c_{0,q} \| u \|_{1,q}\ \forall u \text{ in } W_0^{1,p}$$

(using the Rellich-Kondrashev theorem and taking into account that the norms $\|\cdot\|_{1,p}$ and $\|\cdot\|_{W^{1,p}(\Omega)}$ are equivalent).

Let i': $L^{q'}(\Omega) \to W^{-1,p'}(\Omega)$ be the adjoint of i (as $(L^q(\Omega))^* = L^{q'}(\Omega)$!).

u_0 from $W_0^{1,p}(\Omega)$ is a solution for (*) in the sense of $W^{-1,p'}(\Omega)$ if

$$-\lambda\,\Delta_p\, u_0 = (i' \circ N_f \circ i)u_0 + h. \tag{2.42}$$

We proceed to the proof of Proposition 2.47.

Proof. $-\Delta_p \overset{\text{Proposition2.39}}{=} J_\varphi$, where J_φ is the duality map with $\varphi(t) = t^{p-1}$; the Banach space $(W_0^{1,p}(\Omega), \|\cdot\|_{1,p})$ is uniformly convex (Proposition 2.37) and, consequently, has the (H) property, and it is reflexive (uniformly convex ⇒ reflexive). It is also smooth (its norm being Gâteaux differentiable on $W_0^{1,p}(\Omega)\backslash\{0\}$ (Proposition 2.3)). Thus, one can apply Proposition 2.30 with $X = W_0^{1,p}(\Omega)$, $Z = L^q(\Omega)$, $N = N_f$ — odd continuous operator (Proposition 2.46) and $Z^* = L^{q'}(\Omega)$ and take (2.41) into account; the operator $\lambda(-\Delta_p) - S$: $W_0^{1,p}(\Omega) \to W^{-1,p'}(\Omega)$, where $S = i' \circ N_f \circ i$ is surjective, a fortiori the operator $-\lambda\Delta_p - S - h$ is surjective (commutative group) and hence $\exists u_0$ in $W_0^{1,p}(\Omega)$ which verifies (2.42). □

By replacing q with p in Proposition 2.47, 2^0, and by applying Proposition 2.32, we obtain the following:

Proposition 2.48. *Let Ω be an open bounded set of the C^1 class from $\mathbf{R}^N$, $N \geq 2$, $p \in (1, +\infty)$, h from $W^{-1,p'}(\Omega)$ and $f : \Omega \times \mathbf{R} \to \mathbf{R}$ Carathéodory function having the properties*

$1°$ $f(x, -s) = -f(x, s)$ $\forall x$ from Ω, $\forall s$ from $\mathbf{R}$,

$2°$ $|f(x, s)| \leq c_1 |s|^{p-1} + \beta(x)$ $\forall s$ from $\mathbf{R}$, $\forall x$ from $\Omega\backslash A$, $\mu(A) = 0$, where $c_1 \geq 0$, $\beta \in L^{p'}(\Omega)$, $\frac{1}{p} + \frac{1}{p'} = 1$.

Finally, let $i : W_0^{1,p}(\Omega) \to L^p(\Omega)$ be linear compact embedding. Then, for any λ, if

$$|\lambda| > c_1\lambda_1^{-1},\ \lambda_1 := \inf\left\{\frac{\|u\|_{1,p}^p}{\|i(u)\|_{0,p}^p} : u \in W_0^{1,p}(\Omega)\backslash\{0\}\right\}$$

then the problem (*) has solution in $W_0^{1,p}(\Omega)$ in the sense of $W^{-1,p'}(\Omega)$.

Proof. The statement is correct since $(W_0^{1,p}(\Omega), \|\cdot\|_{1,p})$ is compactly embedded in $L^p(\Omega)$ (Rellich-Kondrashev theorem). Apply Proposition 2.32. □

Remark 2.5. *The condition from Proposition 2.48 can be replaced (Proposition 2.32 allows this) by:*

$$|\lambda| > \overline{\lim_{\|u\|\to+\infty}} \frac{\|(i\prime \circ N_f \circ i)u\|}{\|u\|^{p-1}}.$$

Attention to λ_1: $\lambda_1^{-\frac{1}{p}}$ is optimal for the inequality from the statement; it is attained and nonzero, and it is the smallest eigenvalue of the couple $(J_{L^qL^{q'}}, J_{W_0^{1,p}W^{-1,p'}})$ (see Proposition 2.31).

2.3.4. The Problem

Consider the problem

$$(**)\begin{cases} -\lambda\,\Delta_p^s u = f(\cdot, u(\cdot)) + h,\ x \in \Omega,\ \lambda \in \mathbf{R} \\ u|\partial\Omega = 0 \end{cases}$$

The following two statements are obtained by the author and given in [11,12,15].

Proposition 2.49. *Let Ω be an open bounded set of C^1 class from $\mathbf{R}^N$, $N \geq 2$, $p \in [2, +\infty)$, h from $W^{-1,p'}(\Omega)$ and $f : \Omega \times \mathbf{R} \to \mathbf{R}$ Carathéodory function with the properties*

$1°$ $f(x, -s) = -f(x, s)$ $\forall x$ from Ω, $\forall s$ from $\mathbf{R}$,

$2°$ $|f(x, s)| \leq c_1 |s|^{q-1} + \beta(x)$ $\forall s$ from $\mathbf{R}$, $\forall x$ from $\Omega \backslash A$, $\mu(A) = 0$,

where $c_1 \geq 0$, $q \in (1, p)$, $\beta \in L^{q'}(\Omega)$, $\frac{1}{q} + \frac{1}{q'} = 1$.

Then, for any $\lambda \neq 0$, the problem $(**)$ has solution in $W_0^{1,p}(\Omega)$ in the sense of $W^{-1,p'}(\Omega)$.

Explanations (similar to those for Proposition 2.47): The relationship $u \mid \partial\Omega$ from $(**)$ is in the sense of the trace. $f(\cdot, u) = N_f u$, N_f Nemytskii operator, and so the equation from $(**)$ can be written as

$$-\lambda\Delta_p^s u = N_f\, u + h. \tag{2.43}$$

Now, the norm that endows $W_0^{1,p}(\Omega)$ is $\| \cdot \|_{1,p}$, and $(W_0^{1,p}(\Omega), \| \cdot \|_{1,p})$ is a Banach space that is compactly embedded in $L^q(\Omega)$ since $\| \cdot \|_{1,p}$ *and* $|| \cdot ||_{1,p}$, and hence also $|| \cdot ||_{W^{1,p}(\Omega)}$, are equivalent (see above). Let i be the embedding.

Let i': $L^{q'}(\Omega) \to W^{-1,p'}(\Omega)$ be the adjoint of i (as $(L^q)^* = L^{q'}$). u_0 from $W_0^{1,p}(\Omega)$ is a solution for $(**)$ in the sense of $W^{-1,p'}(\Omega)$ if

$$-\lambda\Delta_p^s\, u_0 = (i' \circ N_f \circ i)u_0 + h. \tag{2.44}$$

Proof. $-\Delta_p^s \overset{\text{Prop.2.43}}{=} J_\varphi$, J_φ duality map with $\varphi(t) = t^{p-1}$, the Banach space $(W_0^{1,p}(\Omega), \| \cdot \|_{1,p})$ being uniformly convex (see above, proposition 2.42). It is also smooth (its norm being Gâteaux differentiable on $W_0^{1,p}(\Omega)\backslash\{0\}$). So, we apply Proposition 2.30 with $X = W_0^{1,p}(\Omega)$, $Z = L^q(\Omega)$, $N = N_f$ – odd continuous operator, $Z^* = L^{q'}(\Omega)$, take into account $||N_f u||_{0,q'} \leq c_1||u||_{0,q}^{q-1} + c_2$, $c_2 := ||\beta||_{0,q'}$, $\forall u$ from $L^q(\Omega)$ the operator $\lambda(-\Delta_p^s) - S$: $W_0^{1,p}(\Omega) \to W^{-1,p'}(\Omega)$, where $S = i' \circ N_f \circ i$ is surjective, a fortiori the operator $-\lambda\Delta_p^s - S - h$ is surjective (commutative group) and hence $\exists u_0$ in $W_0^{1,p}(\Omega)$ which verifies (2.44). □

Replacing q with p in $2°$ from Proposition 2.49 and applying Proposition 2.32, obtain:

Proposition 2.50. *Let Ω be an open bounded set of C^1 class from $\mathbf{R}^N$, $N \geq 2$, $p \in [2, +\infty)$, h from $W^{-1,p'}(\Omega)$ and $f : \Omega \times \mathbf{R} \to \mathbf{R}$ Carathéodory function having the properties*

$1°$ $f(x, -s) = -f(x, s)$ $\forall x$ from Ω, $\forall s$ from $\mathbf{R}$,

$2°$ $|f(x, s)| \leq c_1 |s|^{p-1} + \beta(x)$ $\forall s$ from $\mathbf{R}$, $\forall x$ from $\Omega \backslash A$, $\mu(A) = 0$,

where $c_1 \geq 0$, $\beta \in L^{p'}(\Omega)$, $\frac{1}{p} + \frac{1}{p'} = 1$.

Finally, let i: $W_0^{1,p}(\Omega) \to L^p(\Omega)$ be a linear compact embedding. Then, for any λ, if

$$|\lambda| > c_1\lambda_1^{-1},\ \lambda_1 := \inf\left\{ \frac{\|u\|_{1,p}^p}{||i(u)||_{0,p}^p} : u \in W_0^{1,p}(\Omega)\backslash\{0\} \right\},$$

the problem $(**)$ has solution in $W_0^{1,p}(\Omega)$ in the sense of $W^{-1,p'}(\Omega)$.

Proof. The proof is the same as for Proposition 2.48. □

Remark 2.6. *The condition from Proposition 2.49 can be replaced (see Proposition 2.48) by:*

$$|\lambda| > \overline{\lim_{||u|| \to +\infty}} \frac{||(i' \circ N_f \circ i)u||}{\|u\|^{p-1}}.$$

Attention to $\lambda_1 : \lambda_1^{-\frac{1}{p}}$ *is optimal for the inequality from the statement; it is attained and nonzero, and it is the smallest eigenvalue of the couple* $(J_{L^qL^{q'}}, J_{W_0^{1,p}W^{-1,p'}})$ *(see Proposition 2.31).*

Remark 2.7. *The above results will be used to provide solutions, together with their characterizations, for particular problems from glaciology [55–57], for nonlinear elastic membrane [41,58], for the pseudo-torsion problem [9,59] for nonlinear elastic membrane with the p-pseudo-Laplacian as in [60]. They are presented in the second part of this paper.*

3. Results of the Fredholm Alternative Type for Operators $\lambda J_\varphi - S$

3.1. Important Results

In this section, we continue with results that complete the previous theory provided in Section 2. The statements from this section originate from the generalization due to the author in [11,13] of a theorem of Nečas [42,61] in which normed space is used instead of Banach space and the goal function is a bijection with continuous inverse instead of homeomorphism. The results mentioned above have been obtained based on this theorem and also on propositions of the author and presented in the previous section.

Definition 3.1. *Let X, Y be real normed spaces and F: X → Y,* $F_0 : X \to Y$*. F is strongly closed and strongly continuous, respectively, if*

$$x_n \overset{w}{\to} a \text{ and } F(x_n) \to \alpha \Rightarrow \alpha = F(a),$$

and, respectively,

$$x_n \overset{w}{\to} a \text{ and } F(x_n) \to F(a).$$

For instance, any linear compact operator between Banach spaces is strongly continuous [62].

Definition 3.2. *Let a be a real, strictly positive number. F is, by definition, a-homogeneous if F(tu)* = t^a *F(u),* $\forall u$ *in X,* $\forall t \geq 0$.

F *is a-quasi-homogeneous relative to* F_0, and F_0 is a-homogeneous if

$$t_n \downarrow 0,\ u_n \overset{w}{\to} u_0 \text{ and } t_n^a\ F\left(\frac{u_n}{t_n}\right) \to \gamma \Rightarrow \gamma = F_0\ (u_0).$$

F is a-strongly quasi-homogeneous relative to F_0, F_0 *a-homogeneous* if

$$t_n \downarrow 0,\ u_n \overset{w}{\to} u_0 \text{ and } t_n^a\ F\left(\frac{u_n}{t_n}\right) \to F_0\ (u_0).$$

Proposition 3.1. *Let F be an a-homogeneous and strongly closed (respectively, strongly continuous), then F is a-quasi-homogeneous (respectively a-strongly quasi-homogeneous) relative to F.*

Proof. Observe, in both cases, that $t_n^a\ F\left(\frac{u_n}{t_n}\right) \to F_0\ (u_0)$. □

Proposition 3.2. *If F is a-strongly quasi-homogeneous relative to* F_0*, then* F_0 *is a-homogeneous and strongly continuous.*

Proof. *First assertion.* $t > 0$. Let u_0 be arbitrarily fixed from X and $t_n \downarrow 0$, $u_n \overset{w}{\to} u_0$. Then $t_n^a F\left(\frac{u_n}{t_n}\right) \to F_0\ (u_0)$, hence $(tt_n)^a\ F\left(\frac{u_n}{t_n}\right) \to t^a\ F_0\ (u_0)$, but $(tt_n)^a\ F\left(\frac{tu_n}{tt_n}\right) \to F_0\ (tu_0)$ since $tu_n \overset{w}{\to} tu_0$, $t^a\ F_0\ (u_0) = F_0\ (tu_0)$. $t = 0$. It should be shown that $F_0\ (0) = 0$. Take $t_n \downarrow 0$ and $(u_n)_{n\geq 1}$ with $u_n = 0\ \forall n$. Then, $t_n^a\ F\left(\frac{u_n}{t_n}\right) \to F_0\ (0)$, but $F\left(\frac{u_n}{t_n}\right) = 0$, etc.

Second assertion. From the hypothesis,

$$\lim_{t \to 0+} t^{a} F\left(\frac{u}{t}\right) = F_0(u) \forall u \text{ in } X. \tag{3.1}$$

Suppose, ad absurdum, that F_0 is not strongly continuous. Then there exists u_n, $u_n \overset{w}{\to} u_0$, and

$$F_0(u_n) \to F_0(u_0). \tag{3.2}$$

$\varepsilon > 0$ being arbitrarily fixed, from (3.2), there exists a subsequence of (u_n), it is denoted in the same manner, e.g.,

$$\|F_0 (u_n) - F_0 (u_0)\| \geq \varepsilon \; \forall n \geq 1. \tag{3.3}$$

Furthermore, from (3.1), for any n from $\mathbf{N}$ $\exists\, t_n$, $0 < t_n \leq \frac{1}{n}$, for which

$$\| F_0 (u_n) - t_n^{a} F\left(\frac{u_n}{t_n}\right) \| \leq \frac{\varepsilon}{2}. \tag{3.4}$$

Then

$$\varepsilon \overset{(3.3)}{\leq} \| F_0 (u_0) - F_0 (u_n) \| \leq \| F_0 (u_0) - t_n^{a} F\left(\frac{u_n}{t_n}\right) \| + \| t_n^{a} F\left(\frac{u_n}{t_n}\right) - F_0 (u_n) \| \overset{(3.4)}{\leq} \frac{\varepsilon}{2} + \| F_0 (u_0) - t_n^{a} F\left(\frac{u_n}{t_n}\right) \|,$$

and taking the limit for $n \to \infty$, we obtain $\varepsilon \leq \frac{\varepsilon}{2}$, which is a contradiction. □

Proposition 3.3. *The uni-valued duality map J_φ is a-homogeneous iff φ is a-homogeneous.*

Proof. *Necessary*. $\forall u \neq 0$, $\forall t \geq 0$, $J_\varphi (tu) = \frac{\varphi(t\|u\|)}{\varphi(\|u\|)} J_\varphi u$ (Proposition 2.2, 5°), $J_\varphi (tu) = t^{a} J_\varphi u$, and by taking the norm, $\varphi(t\|u\|) = t^{a} \varphi(\|u\|)$, taking into account that $u \to \|u\|$ takes all the values from $\mathbf{R}_+$. *Sufficient*. Use the same formula. □

Thus, for $p \in (1, +\infty)$, $-\Delta_p$ and $-\Delta_p^{s}$ are $(p - 1)$-homogeneous maps on $W_0^{1,p}(\Omega)$ (Propositions 2.39 and 2.43).

Proposition 3.4. *If the Banach space is reflexive, smooth and has the property (H), then any duality map J_φ on X is strongly closed.*

Proof. Let $u_n \overset{w}{\to} u_0$ and $J_\varphi u_n \to \gamma$. We have

$$\langle J_\varphi u_n - J_\varphi u_0, u_n - u_0 \rangle \to 0,$$

but

$$\langle J_\varphi u_n - J_\varphi u_0, u_n - u_0 \rangle \geq [\varphi(\|u_n\|) - \varphi(\|u_0\|)](\|u_n\| - \|u_0\|) \geq 0 \text{ (Proposition 2.2)},$$

hence $\lim\limits_{n \to \infty} [\varphi(\| u_n \|) - \varphi(\|u_0\|)](\|u_n\| - \|u_0\|) = 0$, which implies $\|u_n\| \to \|u_0\|$ (see the proof for Proposition 2.28). With X having the property (H), we obtain $u_n \to u_0$, which implies (X is smooth reflexive $\Rightarrow J_\varphi$ is semicontinuous, Corollary 2.3) that $J_\varphi u_n \overset{w}{\to} J_\varphi u_0$ and hence $J_\varphi u_0 = \gamma$. □

Corollary 3.1. *If the Banach space X is reflexive, smooth and has the property (H), any duality map on X J_φ that is a-homogeneous is a-quasi-homogeneous related to J_φ.*

Proof. Combine Propositions 3.1 and 3.4. □

We proceed to the basis proposition of this section. The conditions are slightly weakened. Previously:

Definition 3.3. *The map $f: X \to Y$, where X and Y are normed spaces, is regularly surjective if it is surjective and* $\forall R > 0\ \exists r > 0$ *e.g.,*

$$\| f(x) \| \leq R \Rightarrow \|x\| \leq r.$$

Proposition 3.5. *Fredholm alternative. Let X and Y be real normed spaces, T: $X \to Y$ a(K, L, a) and a-homogeneous bijection, odd with a continuous inversei and S: $X \to Y$ an odd compact a-homogeneous operator. Theni for any $\lambda \neq 0$, $\lambda T - S$ is regularly surjective iff λ is not an eigenvalue for the couple (T, S).*

Proof. *Necessary.* Let, ad absurdum, $x_0 \neq 0$ be from X such that

$$\lambda T(x_0) - S(x_0) = 0. \tag{3.5}$$

Multiplying (3.5) by t^a, we obtain

$$\lambda T(tx_0) - S(tx_0) = 0 \tag{3.6}$$

and as $\lim_{t \to +\infty} \|tx_0\| = +\infty$, (3.6) imposes (ad absurdum!) the conclusion that $\lambda T - S$ is not regularly surjective, which is a contradiction.

Sufficient. Firstly, we prove that:

$$\rho := \inf_{\|x\|=1} \| \lambda T(x) - S(x) \| > 0. \tag{3.7}$$

Assume, ad absurdum,

$$\rho = 0. \tag{3.8}$$

With (3.8), we obtain a sequence $(x_n)_{n \in \mathbf{N}}$, $x_n \in X$,

$$\|x_n\| = 1 \tag{3.9}$$

and

$$\lim_{n \to \infty} [\lambda T(x_n) - S(x_n)] = 0. \tag{3.10}$$

The sequence (x_n) being bounded, $(S(x_n))_{n \in \mathbf{N}}$ has a subsequence (x_{k_n}) convergent in Y, and let $\gamma = \lim_{n \to \infty} S(x_{k_n})$. However, T is surjective and $\lambda \neq 0$, so $\exists\, x_0 \in X$ such that $\lambda T(x_0) = \gamma$, and then, from (3.10),

$$\lim_{n \to \infty} \lambda T(x_{k_n}) = \lambda T(x_0). \tag{3.11}$$

From (3.11), T having a continuous inverse, we obtain

$$\lim_{n \to \infty} x_{k_n} = x_0. \tag{3.12}$$

(3.12) imposes, on the one hand, $\|x_0\| \overset{(3.9)}{=} 1$ and, on the other hand, $\lim_{n \to \infty} S(x_{k_n}) = S(x_0)$, which, combined with (3.10) and (3.11), gives $\lambda T(x_0) - S(x_0) = 0$, which is a contradiction, and hence (3.7).

Thus, from (3.7),

$$\left\| \lambda T\left(\frac{x}{\|x\|}\right) - S\left(\frac{x}{\|x\|}\right) \right\| \geq \rho\ \forall x \in X \backslash \{0\},$$

so

$$\rho \|x\|^a \leq \|\lambda T(x) - S(x)\| \ \forall x \in X \backslash \{0\}. \tag{3.13}$$

From (3.13),

$$\lim_{\|x\| \to +\infty} \| \lambda T(x) - S(x) \| = +\infty, \tag{3.14}$$

from which one concludes that $\lambda T - S$ is surjective (see Proposition 2.1).

This surjectivity is regular. Indeed, assuming, ad absurdum, the contrary, we obtain $R > 0$ such that $\forall n \in \mathbf{N}\ \exists x'_n \in X$, $\|x'_n\| > n$ and

$$\| \lambda T(x'_n) - S(x'_n) \| \leq R. \tag{3.15}$$

However, since $\lim\limits_{n\to\infty} \|x'_n\| = +\infty$, we have $\lim\limits_{n\to\infty} \|\lambda T(x'_n) - S(x'_n)\| \overset{(3.14)}{=} +\infty$ and obtain a contradiction with (3.15). □

Proposition 3.6. *Let X be a real reflexive Banach space, smooth and having the property (H), which is compactly embedded in the real Banach space Z, and N: $Z \to Z^*$ an a-homogeneous odd semicontinuous operator. Then the operator $\lambda J_\varphi - N$, with J_φ being the duality map on X with $\varphi(t) = t^a$, $\lambda \neq 0$, is regularly surjective iff λ is not an eigenvalue for the couple (J_φ, N) ([11]).*

Explanation. In the expressions $\lambda J_\varphi - N$ and (J_φ, N), N is actually i' o N o i, i: $X \to Z$ linear compact injection, i': $Z^* \to X^*$ is its adjoint.

Proof ([11]). We apply Proposition 3.5 with $T := J_\varphi$, $S := i'$ o N o i, correctly, as J_φ is (K, L, a) with $K = L = 1$, bijective with continuous inverse (Proposition 2.26), odd and S is odd, a-homogeneous and compact (see the proof of Proposition 2.30). □

3.2. Applications

3.2.1. Application for the p-Laplacian and p-Pseudo-Laplacian

In Proposition 3.6, we now take $(X, \|\cdot\|_X) = (W_0^{1,p}(\Omega), \|\cdot\|_{1,p})$, where $p \in (1, +\infty)$ and Ω is an open bounded set of C^1 class from $\mathbf{R}^n$, $n \geq 2$ (hence $J_\varphi = -\Delta_p$, $\varphi(t) = t^{p-1}$, Proposition 2.39), $(Z, \|\cdot\|_Z) = (L^p(\Omega), \|\cdot\|_{0,p})$, N: $L^p(\Omega) \to L^{p'}(\Omega)$, $\frac{1}{p} + \frac{1}{p'} = 1$, $Nu = |u|^{p-2} u$.

$W_0^{1,p}(\Omega)$ is uniformly convex (Proposition 2.37) and hence also reflexive (Proposition 2.9) with the property (H), with its norm being Gâteaux differentiable (Corollary 2.6) and hence smooth (Proposition 2.3). It is compactly embedded in $L^p(\Omega)$. For the last assertion, we can mention the following:

Theorem 3.1. *Let Ω be a bounded set of the C^1 class. Then*

$$p < n \Rightarrow W^{1,p}(\Omega) \subset L^q(\Omega)\ \forall q \text{ in } [1, p^*],\ \frac{1}{p^*} = \frac{1}{p} - \frac{1}{n},$$

$$p = n \Rightarrow W^{1,p}(\Omega) \subset L^q(\Omega)\ \forall q \text{ in } [1, +\infty),$$

$$p > n \Rightarrow W^{1,p}(\Omega) \subset C(\bar{\Omega}),$$

in all cases with compact injections (Rellich-Kondrashev).

Concerning N, it is the duality map on $L^p(\Omega)$ relative to the weight $t \to t^{p-1}$ (see the following Proposition 3.8); consequently, N is a homeomorphism of $L^p(\Omega)$ on $L^{p'}(\Omega)$ (Corollary 2.5), odd and $(p-1)$-homogeneous.

We apply Proposition 3.6 in order to obtain the following statement [11,13].

Proposition 3.7. *Let p be from* $(1, +\infty)$ *and* $\lambda \neq 0$. *If*

$$\lambda(-\Delta_p u) = |u|^{p-2} u$$

does not have a nonzero solution in $W_0^{1,p}(\Omega)$*, then, for any h from* $W^{-1,p'}(\Omega)$*, the equation*

$$\lambda(-\Delta p\ u) = |u|^{p-2} u + h$$

has solution in $W_0^{1,p}(\Omega)$ *in the sense of* $W^{-1,p'}(\Omega)$.

Explanation. The term $|u|^{p-2} u$ from (3.16) and (3.17) is actually considered to be its image through a compact embedding of $L^{p'}(\Omega)$ in $W^{-1,p'}(\Omega)$ (use Schauder's theorem).

Regarding the operator N, we can complete it with the following result.

Proposition 3.8. *The duality map on* $L^p(\Omega)$*,* $p \in (1, +\infty)$*, of weight* $\varphi(t) = t^{p-1}$ *is*

$$J\varphi\ u = |u|^{p-1} \operatorname{sgn} u,\ u\ \in\ L^p(\Omega)$$

i.e.,

$$\langle J_\varphi\ u,\ h\rangle = \int_\Omega |u|^{p-1}(\operatorname{sgn} u) h dx\ \forall h\ \in\ L^p(\Omega)$$

Proof. Let Ψ: $\Psi(u) = \frac{1}{p}||u||_{0,p}^p$. As $\Psi(u) = \int_0^{||u||_{0,p}} \varphi(t)dt$, we have (Proposition 2.2, 3°)

$$J_\varphi\ (u) = \partial\Psi(u).$$

However, $\Psi'(u)(h) = \int_\Omega |u|^{p-1}(\operatorname{sgn} u)h dx\ \forall h$ from $L^p(\Omega)$ ([46]), and thus the conclusion. □

Proposition 3.9. *In the statement of Proposition 3.7, if* $p \in [2, +\infty)$*, then* $-\Delta_p$ can be replaced by $-\Delta_p^s$ *([11,13]).*

Proof ([11,13]). In Proposition 3.6, we take $(X, ||\cdot||) = (W_0^{1,p}(\Omega), \|\cdot\|_{1,p})$ (see above), and $(Z, ||\cdot||_Z) = (L^p(\Omega), ||\cdot||_{0,p})$, N: $L^p(\Omega) \to L^{p'}(\Omega)$, $\frac{1}{p} + \frac{1}{p'} = 1$, $Nu = |u|^{p-2} u$, and take into account that $(W_0^{1,p}(\Omega), \|\cdot\|_{1,p})$ is uniformly convex (see also Proposition 2.42 and Corollary 2.7 above). The compact embedding of $W_0^{1,p}(\Omega)$ in $L^p(\Omega)$ is given by the equivalence of the norms $\|\cdot\|_{1,p}$ and $||\cdot||_{1,p}$ since $\|\cdot\|_{1,p}$ is equivalent to the norm $|\cdot|_{1,p}$ (see the p-pseudo-Laplacian in Section 2.3.2). □

3.2.2. Another Application for p-Laplacian

Here, in Proposition 3.6, we take $(X, ||\cdot||_X) = (W_0^{1,p}(\Omega), ||\cdot||_{1,p})$, where Ω is an open bounded set of C^1 class in $\mathbf{R}^n$, $n \geq 2$, $(Z, ||\cdot||_Z) = (L^p(\Omega), ||\cdot||_{0,p})$, N: $L^p(\Omega) \to L^{p'}(\Omega)$, $\frac{1}{p}+\frac{1}{p'} = 1$, $Nu = N_f\ u$, N_f is the Nemytskii operator, with f: $\Omega \times \mathbf{R} \to \mathbf{R}$ a Carathéodory function which verifies

1° $|f(x, s)| \leq c_1 |s|^{p-1} + \beta(x)\ \forall s \in \mathbf{R}$, $\forall x \in \Omega \backslash A$, $\mu(A) = 0$, where $c_1 \geq 0$, $\beta \in L^{p'}(\Omega)$;

2° f is odd and $(p-1)$-homogeneous in the second variable.

Then, N_f is odd, $(p-1)$-homogeneous and continuous (Proposition 2.46). We apply Proposition 3.6 (see also Section 3.2.1 above) and obtain the following:

Proposition 3.10. *Let p be from* $(1, +\infty)$ *and* $\lambda \neq 0$*. If*

$$\lambda(-\Delta_p\ u) = N_f\ u$$

has no nonzero solution in $W_0^{1,p}(\Omega)$ *in the sense of* $W^{-1,p'}(\Omega)$*, then, for any h from* $W^{-1,p'}(\Omega)$*, the equation*

$$\lambda(-\Delta_p\ u) = f(\cdot, u(\cdot)) + h,\ x \in \Omega$$

has a solution in $W_0^{1,p}(\Omega)$ in the sense of $W^{-1,p'}(\Omega)$ ([11,13]).

Remark 3.1. *This statement can be compared with Proposition 2.48 above.*

Remark 3.2. *Applications to real phenomena regarding the nonlinear elastic membrane with p-Laplacian and with p-pseudo-Laplacian will be developed in the second part of this article.*

4. Surjectivity to Different Homogeneity Degrees

The propositions in this section originate from another assertion of the author [11,15], which generalizes a theorem of Fučik [42], but they are also based on other propositions obtained by the author. Applications to partial differential equations (weak solutions) are also given.

4.1. Theoretical Results

Proposition 4.1. *Let X and Y be real normed spaces, X complete and reflexive, T: $X \to Y$ (K, L, a) bijection odd with continuous inverse and S: $X \to Y$ odd compact operator b-strongly quasi-homogeneous relative to S_0, $b < a$. For any $\lambda \neq 0$, the operator $\lambda T - S$ is surjective.*

Remark 4.1. *The author proposed this weakened version of the theorem from [42], i.e., with normed space instead of Banach space, and bijection with continuous inverse instead of homeomorphism.*

Proof. According to Corollary 2.2, it is sufficient to prove:

$$\overline{\lim_{||x||\to+\infty}} \frac{||Sx||}{||x||^a} \left(= \lim_{||x||\to+\infty} \frac{||Sx||}{||x||^a} \right) = 0. \tag{4.1}$$

Supposing, ad absurdum, the contrary, we obtain a sequence $(x_n)_{n\in\mathbf{N}}$, $x_n \in X\backslash\{0\}$, $\lim\limits_{n\to\infty} ||x_n||$ = +∞, for which

$$\frac{||S(x_n)||}{||x_n||^a} \geq \varepsilon_0 \; \forall n \text{ in } \mathbf{N}, \tag{4.2}$$

where $\varepsilon_0 > 0$. With X being complete and reflexive, the bounded sequence $(y_n)_{n\in\mathbf{N}}$, $y_n := \frac{x_n}{||x_n||}$ has a weakly convergent subsequence, one denotes this identically, $y_n \overset{w}{\to} y_0$. Then,

$$\lim_{n\to\infty} \frac{S(||x_n||y_n)}{||x_n||^b} = S_0\,(y_0)$$

and as $\lim\limits_{n\to\infty} \frac{||x_n||^b}{||x_n||^a} = 0$, we obtain

$$\lim_{n\to\infty} \frac{||S(x_n)||}{||x_n||^a} = 0,$$

in contradiction with (4.2), and hence (4.1). □

An immediate consequence:

Proposition 4.2. *Let X be a real reflexive Banach space and smooth with the property (H) which is compactly embedded in the real Banach space Z and N: $Z\to Z^*$ odd semicontinuous and b-homogeneous operator.*
Then, for any $\lambda \neq 0$,

$$\lambda J_\varphi - N,$$

J_φ the duality map on X with $\varphi(t) = t^a$, $a > b$, is surjective ([11,15]).

Clarification. In the expression $\lambda J_\varphi - N$, N is actually (abbreviation!) the operator i' o N o i, i' is the adjoint of i.

Proof ([11,15]). Applying Proposition 4.1, with $T = J_\varphi$ ($K = L = 1$ is odd bijective with continuous inverse (Proposition 2.26)), $S := i' \circ N \circ i$ is odd, compact and b-homogeneous. It remains only to prove that S is b-strongly quasi-homogeneous relative to S. Let $t_n \downarrow 0$ and $u_n \overset{w}{\to} u_0$, then $t_n^b S\left(\frac{u_n}{t_n}\right) = S(u_n)$ and $S(u_n) \to S(u_0)$: $u_n \overset{w}{\to} u_0 \overset{i \text{ compact}}{\Rightarrow} i(u_n) \to i(u_0) \overset{N \text{ semicontinuous}}{\Rightarrow} N(i(u_n)) \overset{w}{\to} N(i(u_0))' \overset{i' \text{ compact}}{\Rightarrow} S(u_n) \to S(u_0)$. □

4.2. Applications

4.2.1. First Application

We now take $(X, \|\cdot\|_X) = (W_0^{1,p}(\Omega), \|\cdot\|_{1,p})$ with $p \in (1, +\infty)$ and $(X, \|\cdot\|_X) = (W_0^{1,p}(\Omega), |\cdot|_{1,p})$ with $p \in [2, +\infty)$, respectively, and Ω is open bounded set of C^1 class in $\mathbf{R}^n$, $n \geq 2$, $\varphi(t) = t^{p-1}$; hence $J_\varphi = -\Delta_p$ (Proposition 2.39) and $J_\varphi = -\Delta_p^s$ (Proposition 2.43), respectively, $(Z, \|\cdot\|_Z) = (L^q(\Omega), \|\cdot\|_{0,q})$ with $q \in (1, p)$, N: $L^q(\Omega) \to L^{q'}(\Omega)$, $Nu = |u|^{q-2} u$, $\frac{1}{q} + \frac{1}{q'} = 1$. N is odd, continuous (an even homeomorphism; see Proposition 3.8 and Corollary 2.5 above) and $(q-1)$-homogeneous, $q - 1 < p - 1$. Applying Proposition 4.2, we obtain the following.

Proposition 4.3. *Under the above conditions, for any $\lambda \neq 0$ and for any h from $W^{-1,p'}(\Omega)$, there exists u_0 in $W_0^{1,p}(\Omega)$ such that*

$$\lambda(-\Delta_p)u_0 = (i' \circ N \circ i)u_0 + h$$

and

$$\lambda(-\Delta_p^s)u_0 = (i' \circ N \circ i)u_0 + h$$

respectively ([11,15]).

4.2.2. Second Application

This second application of Proposition 4.2 is made by replacing the operator N from Proposition 4.3 with N_f, the Nemytskii operator. More precisely, we take N: $L^q(\Omega) \to L^{q'}(\Omega)$, $N = N_f$, with $f: \Omega \times \mathbf{R} \to \mathbf{R}$ odd Carathéodory function and $(q-1)$-homogeneous in the second variable, which verifies the growth condition

$$|f(x,s)| \leq c_1 |s|^{q-1} + \beta(x) \ \forall s \text{ in } \mathbf{R}, \forall x \text{ in } \Omega \backslash A, \ \mu(A) = 0,$$

where $c_1 \geq 0$, $\beta \in L^{q'}(\Omega)$.

Then, N_f is odd, $(q-1)$-homogeneous and continuous (Proposition 2.46), and one can apply Proposition 4.2 to obtain:

Proposition 4.4. *Under the above conditions, for any $\lambda \neq 0$ and for any h in $W^{-1,p'}(\Omega)$, there exists u_0 in $W_0^{1,p}(\Omega)$ such that*

$$\lambda(-\Delta_p)u_0 = (i' \circ N_f \circ i)u_0 + h$$

and

$$\lambda(-\Delta_p^s)u_0 = (i' \circ N_f \circ i)u_0 + h$$

respectively ([11,15]).

Remark 4.2. *Applications to models of real phenomena involving a nonlinear elastic membrane and a nonlinear elastic membrane with p-Laplacian and the p-pseudo-Laplacian will be provided in the second part of this work.*

5. Weak Solutions Starting from Ekeland Variational Principle

5.1. Critical Points and Weak Solutions for Elliptic Type Equations

The theoretical results in the following two subsections were obtained by the author in [17].

5.1.1. Theoretical Support

In order to introduce the first result, theoretical support will be given, starting with:

Ekeland Principle. *Let (X, d) be a complete metric space and* $\varphi: X \to (-\infty, +\infty]$ *bounded from below, lower semicontinuous and proper. For any* $\varepsilon > 0$ *and u of X with*

$$\varphi(u) \leq \inf \varphi(X) + \varepsilon$$

and for any $\lambda > 0$, *there exists* v_ε *in X such that*

$$\varphi(v_\varepsilon) < \varphi(w) + \frac{\varepsilon}{\lambda} d(v_\varepsilon, w) \ \forall w \in X \backslash \{v_\varepsilon\}$$

and

$$\varphi(v_\varepsilon) \leq \varphi(u), d(v_\varepsilon, u) \leq \lambda$$

([22,63,64]).

We continue with the following:

Definition 5.1. *Let X be a real normed space,* β *a bornology (Definition 2.3) on X, and let* φ: X $\to$ **R**. *Let c be in* **R** *and F a nonempty subset of X.* φ *verifies the Palais-Smale condition on level c around F (or relative to F),* $(\mathrm{PS})_{c,F}$, *with respect to* β, *when* $\forall (u_n)_{n\geq 1}$ *a sequence of points in X for which*

$$\lim_{n\to\infty} \varphi(u_n) = c, \ \lim_{n\to\infty} ||\nabla_\beta \varphi(u_n)|| = 0 \text{ and } \lim_{n\to\infty} \mathrm{dist}(u_n, F) = 0, \qquad (5.1)$$

this sequence has a convergent subsequence.

To clarify the above notation, see Definition 2.3 regarding the β-derivative.

Let us introduce the definition of the metric gradient in order to provide other observations related to this central notion for the following statement.

Definition 5.2. *In a real normed space X, consider the Gâteaux-differentiable functional* $f: X \to$ **R**. *The metric gradient of f is the multiple-valued mapping:*

$$\nabla f : X \to P(X), \ \nabla f(x) = i^{-1} J_* f'_w(x),$$

where J_*: $X^* \to P(X^{**})$ *is the duality mapping on* X^* *corresponding to the identity, and i is the canonical injection of X into* X^{**}: $i(x) = x^{**}$, $\langle x^{**}, x^* \rangle = \langle x^*, x \rangle$, $\forall x^* \in X^*$.

Consequently, for any $x \in X$: $\nabla f(x) = \{y \in X: i(y) \in J_* f'_w(x)\} = \{y \in X: \langle i(y), f'_w(x)\rangle = \langle f'_w(x), y\rangle = ||f'_w(x)||^2, ||i(y)|| = ||y|| = ||f'_w(x)||\}$. If X is reflexive, for any $x \in X$, $\nabla f(x)$ is nonempty. X^{**} being strictly convex, J_* is single-valued. So, if X is reflexive and strictly convex, then $\nabla f: X \to X$, $\nabla f(x) = i^{-1} J_* f'_w(x)$, and the following equalities hold:

$$\langle f'_w(x), \nabla f(x)\rangle = ||f'_w(x)||^2, \ ||\nabla f(x)|| = ||f'_w(x)||.$$

Through the minimization of a functional on *F* (*minimization with constraints*), its global critical points may be obtained.

As a preliminary, we generalize some results from [65] by introducing Banach space instead of Hilbert space and Gâteaux differentiability instead of C^1-class Fréchet.

Proposition 5.1. *Let X be real reflexive strictly convex Banach space, let φ: $X \to \mathbf{R}$ be lower semicontinuous and Gâteaux differentiable and let F be a closed subset of X such that for every u from F with the metric gradient* $\nabla\varphi(u) \neq 0$, *for sufficiently small* $r > 0$,

$$\left(u - \delta\frac{\nabla\varphi(u)}{||\nabla\varphi(u)||}\right) \in F, \forall\delta \in [0, r]. \tag{5.2}$$

Then, if φ is lower bounded on F, for every $(v_n)_{n\geq 1}$ a minimizing sequence for φ on F, there exists a sequence $(u_n)_{n\geq 1}$ in F such that

$$||\varphi'(u_n)|| \leq \sqrt{\varepsilon_n}, \tag{5.3}$$

$$\varphi(u_n) \leq \varphi(v_n)\ \forall n \tag{5.4}$$

$$\lim_{n\to\infty} ||u_n - v_n|| = 0, \tag{5.5}$$

where $\varepsilon_n > 0$ and $\varepsilon_n \to 0$.

Remark 5.1. *This result is reported in [65] as Lemma 9 in the frame of Hilbert spaces having the function φ of the Fréchet C^1 class, but the condition (5.3) is more complicated due to another condition imposed on the set F.*

Proof. Denote $c := \inf \varphi(F)$ and let n be from $\mathbf{N}$. For $\varepsilon_n := \varphi(v_n) - c + \frac{1}{n}$, hence $\varepsilon_n > 0$, we have $\varphi(v_n) < c + \varepsilon_n$. We apply the enounced *Ekeland principle* with $\lambda = \sqrt{\varepsilon_n}$, $\exists u_n$ in F, with known properties. Thus, we obtain the sequence $(u_n)_{n\geq 1}$ satisfying (5.4), (5.5) ($||u_n - v_n|| \leq \sqrt{\varepsilon_n}$, $\varepsilon_n \to 0$) and

$$\varphi(v) \geq \varphi(u_n) - \sqrt{\varepsilon_n}||v - u_n||\ \forall v \in F. \tag{5.6}$$

Next, we verify (5.3). It is sufficient to work under the assumption that $||\varphi'_w(u_n)|| > 0$ $\forall n$. Thus, we apply the hypothesis made in the statement with respect to F with $u = u_n$ and, denoting, for $\delta \in (0, r]$, $v_\delta := u_n - \delta\frac{\nabla\varphi(u_n)}{||\nabla\varphi(u_n)||}$ ($\in F$), replace v_δ in (5.6) and find

$$\sqrt{\varepsilon_n}||v_\delta - u_n|| \geq \varphi(u_n) - \varphi(v_\delta),$$

multiply this inequality by $\frac{1}{\delta}$, $\delta > 0$, and take the limit for $\delta \to 0+$ in order to keep the sense of the inequality. We remark that $\lim\limits_{\delta\to 0} v_\delta = u_n$; $\lim\limits_{\delta\to 0}\frac{||v_\delta - u_n||}{\delta} = \lim\limits_{\delta\to 0}\frac{\delta\frac{||\nabla\varphi(u_n)||}{||\nabla\varphi(u_n)||}}{\delta} = 1$. Consider that the existence of the limit for $\delta \to 0$ implies the existence of the limit for $\delta \to 0\pm$, together with their equality, $\lim\limits_{\delta\to 0+}\frac{\varphi(u_n) - \varphi(v_\delta)}{\delta} = \lim\limits_{\delta\to 0+}\frac{\varphi\left(u_n - \delta\frac{\nabla\varphi(u_n)}{||\nabla\varphi(u_n)||}\right) - \varphi(u_n)}{-\delta} = \varphi_w'(u_n)\left(\frac{\nabla\varphi(u_n)}{||\nabla\varphi(u_n)||}\right) = \frac{1}{||\nabla\varphi(u_n)||}\langle\varphi_w'(u_n), \nabla\varphi(u_n)\rangle = \frac{1}{||\nabla\varphi(u_n)||}||\varphi'_w(u_n)||^2 = ||\varphi'_w(u_n)||$; taking into account the definition of the Gâteaux derivative and the above considerations on the metric gradient, (5.3) is also fulfilled. □

Remark 5.2. *The Gâteaux derivative from the above statement can be replaced by any β-derivative, and the result remains the same. In the case of the Fréchet derivative, the condition "φ lower semicontinuous" must be removed from the statement.*

Notation. φ: $X \to \mathbf{R}$ is β-differentiable, $c \in \mathbf{R} \Rightarrow$

$$K_c(\varphi) := \{x \in X : \varphi(x) = c,\ \nabla_\beta\varphi(x) = 0\}.$$

Proposition 5.2. *Let X be a real reflexive strictly convex Banach space and φ: $X \to \mathbf{R}$ lower semicontinuous and Gâteaux differentiable and let F be a nonempty convex closed subset such that*

$(I - \nabla\varphi)(F) \subset F$, where I is the identity map. If φ is lower bounded on F, then for every $(v_n)_{n\geq 1}$, a minimizing sequence for φ on F, there is a sequence $(u_n)_{n\geq 1}$ in F such that

$$\varphi(u_n) \leq \varphi(v_n)\ \forall n,\ \lim_{n\to\infty}\|u_n - v_n\| = 0,\ \lim_{n\to\infty}\|\varphi\prime_{w}(u_n)\| = 0.$$

Moreover, if φ satisfies $(\mathrm{PS})_{c,F}$, where $c = \inf \varphi(F)$, then

$$F \cap K_c(\varphi) \neq \varnothing.$$

Proof. Applying Proposition 5.1, (5.2) is satisfied; indeed, if $u \in F$ and $\varphi\prime_{w}(u) \neq 0$, then, F being convex,

$$u - \delta\frac{\nabla\varphi(u)}{||\nabla\varphi(u)||} = \left(1 - \frac{\delta}{||\varphi'_{w}(u)||}\right)u + \frac{\delta}{||\varphi'_{w}(u)||}(I - \nabla\varphi)\ (u) \in F.$$

Let $(u_n)_{n\geq 1}$ be the sequence given by the statement. $c \leq \varphi(u_n) \leq \varphi(v_n)\ \forall n$, hence $\varphi(u_n) \to c$. $||\varphi'_{w}(u_n)|| \overset{(5.3)}{\leq} \sqrt{\varepsilon_n}$, hence $||\varphi'_{w}(u_n)|| \to 0$, clearly dist $(u_n, F) = 0$, and consequently, $(u_n)_{n\geq 1}$ has a convergent subsequence $(u_{k_n})_{n\geq 1}$, $u_{k_n} \to u_0 \in F$. This implies $||\varphi'_{w}(u_{k_n})|| \to ||\varphi'_{w}(u_0)|| = 0$ and thus u_0 is a global critical point of φ contained in F. □

5.1.2. Weak Solutions

Open set of C^1 class in $\mathbf{R}^N$. We use the following notations (the norm is that Euclidean from $\mathbf{R}^{N-1}$): $\mathbf{R}^N_+ = \{x = (x', x_N): x_N > 0\}$, $Q = \{x = (x', x_N) : \|x'\| < 1,\ |x_N| < 1\}$, $Q_+ = Q \cap \mathbf{R}^N_+$, $Q_0 = \{x = (x', x_N): \|x'\| < 1, x_N = 0\}$. Let Ω be an open nonempty set in $\mathbf{R}^N$, $\Omega \neq \mathbf{R}^N$ and $\partial\Omega$ its boundary. By definition, Ω is of *C^1 class* if $\forall x$ from $\partial\Omega$ $\exists U$ is a neighborhood of x in $\mathbf{R}^N$ and $f : Q \to U$ is bijective such that $f \in C^1(\overline{Q}), f^{-1} \in C^1(\overline{U}), f(Q_+) = U \cap \Omega$, and

$$f(Q_0) = U \cap \partial\Omega.$$

Weak solution. Let Ω be an open bounded nonempty set in $\mathbf{R}^N$, $N > 1, f : \Omega \times \mathbf{R}^N \to \mathbf{R}$, and $u_0 \in W_0^{1,p}(\Omega)$. Consider the problems:

$$(*)\begin{cases} -\Delta_p u = f(x,u),\ x \in \Omega \\ u = 0 \text{ on } \partial\Omega, \end{cases}$$

and

$$(**)\begin{cases} -\Delta_p^s u = f(x,u),\ x \in \Omega \\ u = 0 \text{ on } \partial\Omega. \end{cases}$$

The equality $u = 0$ on $\partial\Omega$ for both problems is in the sense of the trace (Definition 2.8). $\overline{u}$ from $X = W_0^{1,p}(\Omega)$ is, by definition, a *weak solution* for $(*)$ and $(**)$ if $\overline{u} = 0$ on $\partial\Omega$ in the sense of the trace and

$$\int_\Omega |\nabla\overline{u}|^{p-2}\nabla\overline{u}\cdot\nabla v dx - \int_\Omega f(x,\overline{u}(x))v dx = 0\ \forall v \in W_0^{1,p} \tag{5.7}$$

and

$$\sum_{i=1}^{n}\int_\Omega \left|\frac{\partial\overline{u}}{\partial x_i}\right|^{p-2}\frac{\partial\overline{u}}{\partial x_i}\frac{\partial v}{\partial x_i}dx - \int_\Omega f(x,\overline{u}(x))v dx = 0\ \forall v \in W_0^{1,p} \tag{5.8}$$

respectively.

Remark 5.3. *Here, ∇w is the weak gradient (see* Section 2.3.1 *here and what follows). $X := W_0^{1,p}(\Omega)$ is endowed in the first case $(*)$ with the norm $\|\cdot\|_{1,p}$ that was defined in Section 2.3.1,* *which is equivalent to the norm* $u \to \left(||u||^{p}_{L^{p}(\Omega)} + \sum_{i=1}^{n}\left\|\frac{\partial u}{\partial x_i}\right\|^{p}_{L^{p}(\Omega)}\right)^{\frac{1}{p}}$ *(also highlighted there). For the second case (∗∗), equip the same vector space with the norm* $u \to \|u\|_{1,p} = \left(\sum_{i=1}^{n}\left\|\frac{\partial u}{\partial x_i}\right\|^{p}_{L^{p}(\Omega)}\right)^{\frac{1}{p}}$, *which is equivalent to* $u \to |u|_{1,p} = \sum_{i=1}^{n}\left\|\frac{\partial u}{\partial x_i}\right\|_{L^{p}(\Omega)}$ *(Section 2.3.2).*

For the *Nemytskii operator*, see also Section 2.3.1 and suppose now that $\mu(\Omega) < +\infty$. Then,

$$u_n(x) \underset{x\in\Omega}{\overset{\mu}{\to}} u_0(x) \Rightarrow N_f u_n(x) \underset{x\in\Omega}{\overset{\mu}{\to}} N_f u_0(x).$$

Assume that f satisfies the *growth condition*:

$$|f(x,s)| \le c\,|s|^{p-1} + b(x),\ \forall x \in \Omega\backslash A \text{ with } \mu(A) = 0, \forall x \in \mathbf{R},$$

where $c \ge 0$, $p > 1$ and $b \in L^q(\Omega)$, $q \in [1, +\infty]$. Then $N_f\,(L^{q(p-1)}(\Omega)) \subset L^q(\Omega)$; N_f is continuous ($q < +\infty$) and bounded on $L^{(p-1)q}(\Omega)$ (Proposition 2.46). If Ω is bounded and $\frac{1}{p} + \frac{1}{q} = 1$, then $N_f(L^p(\Omega)) \subset L^q(\Omega)$ with N_f continuous; moreover, $N_F(L^p(\Omega)) \subset L^1(\Omega)$, with N_F continuous (*ibidem*), where $F(x,s) = \int_0^s f(x,t)dt$, and Φ: $L^p(\Omega) \to \mathbf{R}$, $\Phi(u) = \int_\Omega F(x,u(x))dx$ is of Fréchet C^1 class and $\Phi' = N_f$ [65], so it is also Gâteaux differentiable.

Theorem 5.1. *Let Ω be an open bounded nonempty set in $\mathbf{R}^N$ and $f : \Omega \times \mathbf{R} \to \mathbf{R}$ a Carathéodory function with the growth condition:*

$$|f(x,s)| \le c\,|s|^{p-1} + b(x), \tag{5.9}$$

where $c > 0$, $2 \le p \le \frac{2N}{N-2}$ when $N \ge 3$ and $2 \le p < +\infty$ when $N = 1, 2$, and where $b \in L^q(\Omega)$, $\frac{1}{p} + \frac{1}{q} = 1$.

Then, the energy functional $\varphi : W_0^{1,p}(\Omega) \to \mathbf{R}$, and

$$\varphi(u) = \frac{1}{p}||u||^{p}_{1,p} - \int_\Omega F(x,u(x))dx, \text{ for the problem } (*) \tag{5.10}$$

and

$$\varphi(u) = \frac{1}{p}\|u\|^{p}_{1,p} - \int_\Omega F(x,u(x))dx, \text{ for the problem } (**), \tag{5.11}$$

where $F(x,s) = \int_0^s f(x,t)dt$ is Gâteaux differentiable on $W_0^{1,p}(\Omega)\backslash\{0\}$ and, respectively,

$$\varphi'_w(u)(v) = \int_\Omega |\nabla u|^{p-2}\nabla u \cdot \nabla v dx - \int_\Omega f(x,u(x))v dx, \forall u,v \in W_0^{1,p}(\Omega) \tag{5.12}$$

and

$$\varphi'_w(u)(v) = \sum_{i=1}^{N}\int_\Omega \left|\frac{\partial u}{\partial x_i}\right|^{p-2}\frac{\partial u}{\partial x_i}\frac{\partial v}{\partial x_i}dx - \int_\Omega f(x,u(x))v dx, \forall u,v \in W_0^{1,p}(\Omega). \tag{5.13}$$

Proof. One may consider φ, in both cases, to be the sum of two other functions. The second of these functions being Gâteaux differentiable (see the above considerations), it is sufficient to remark that the maps $u \to \frac{1}{p}||u||^{p}_{1,p}$ and $u \to \frac{1}{p}\|u\|^{p}_{1,p}$ are also Gâteaux differentiable on $W_0^{1,p}(\Omega)\backslash\{0\}$ (Propositions 2.39 and 2.43) and then φ is Gâteaux differentiable on $W_0^{1,p}(\Omega)\backslash\{0\}$. □

Corollary 5.1. *Let Ω and f be as in Theorem 5.1 above. Then the weak solutions of* $(*)$ *and* $(**)$ *are precisely the critical points of the functional $\varphi : W_0^{1,p}(\Omega) \to \mathbf{R}$, respectively:*

$$\varphi(u) = \frac{1}{p}||u||_{1,p}^{p} - \int_{\Omega} F(x,u(x))dx,\ F(x,s) := \int_0^s f(x,t)dt$$

and

$$\varphi(u) = \frac{1}{\mathrm{p}}\|u\|_{1,\mathrm{p}}^{\mathrm{p}} - \int_{\Omega} F(x,u(x))dx,\ F(x,s) := \int_0^s f(x,t)dt.$$

Proof. Indeed, if $\overline{u}$ is a weak solution of $(*)$ and $(**)$, then $\varphi'_{\mathrm{w}}(\overline{u})(v) = 0\ \forall v \in W_0^{1,p}(\Omega)$ ((5.7) and (5.8) respectively (Theorem 5.1)), hence, $\varphi'_{\mathrm{w}}(\overline{u}) = 0$. The inverse assertion is obvious. □

Weak subsolutions and weak supersolutions of $(*)$ and $(**)$. Let Ω be an open bounded set of C^1 class in $\mathbf{R}^N$, $N \geq 3, f : \Omega \times \mathbf{R} \to \mathbf{R}$ a Carathéodory function and let $\overline{u} \in W_0^{1,p}(\Omega)$. $\overline{u}$ is a *weak subsolution* and a *weak supersolution*, respectively, of $(*)$ or $(**)$ if

$$\overline{u} \leq 0 \text{ on } \partial\Omega \text{ and } \overline{u} \geq 0 \text{ on} \partial\Omega, \text{ respectively, and}$$

$$\begin{cases} \int\limits_{\Omega} |\nabla\overline{u}|^{\mathrm{p}-2}\nabla\overline{u} \cdot \nabla v dx \leq \int\limits_{\Omega} f(x,\overline{u}(x))v dx\ \forall v \in W_0^{1,\mathrm{p}}(\Omega),\ v \geq 0 \\ \text{respectively} \\ \int\limits_{\Omega} |\nabla\overline{u}|^{\mathrm{p}-2}\nabla\overline{u} \cdot \nabla v dx \geq \int\limits_{\Omega} f(x,\overline{u}(x))v dx\ \forall v \in W_0^{1,\mathrm{p}}(\Omega),\ v \geq 0. \end{cases} \tag{5.14}$$

or

$$\begin{cases} \sum\limits_{\mathrm{i}=1}^{n}\int\limits_{\Omega} \left|\frac{\partial\overline{u}}{\partial x_{\mathrm{i}}}\right|^{\mathrm{p}-2} \frac{\partial\overline{u}}{\partial x_{\mathrm{i}}}\frac{\partial v}{\partial x_{\mathrm{i}}} dx \leq \int\limits_{\Omega} f(x,\overline{u}(x))v dx\ \forall v \in W_0^{1,\mathrm{p}}(\Omega),\ v \geq 0 \\ \text{respectively} \\ \sum\limits_{\mathrm{i}=1}^{n}\int\limits_{\Omega} \left|\frac{\partial\overline{u}}{\partial x_{\mathrm{i}}}\right|^{\mathrm{p}-2} \frac{\partial\overline{u}}{\partial x_{\mathrm{i}}}\frac{\partial v}{\partial x_{\mathrm{i}}} dx \geq \int\limits_{\Omega} f(x,\overline{u}(x))v dx\ \forall v \in W_0^{1,\mathrm{p}}(\Omega),\ v \geq 0. \end{cases} \tag{5.15}$$

Proposition 5.3. *Let Ω be an open bounded set of C^1 class in $\mathbf{R}^N$, $N \geq 3$, and let $f : \Omega \times \mathbf{R} \to \mathbf{R}$ be a Carathéodory function and u_1 and u_2 from $W_0^{1,p}(\Omega)$ bounded weak subsolution and weak supersolution of* $(*)$*, respectively, with $u_1(x) \leq u_2(x)$ a.e. on Ω. Suppose that f verifies* (5.9) *and there is $\rho > 0$ such that the function g: $g(x, s) = f(x, s) + \rho s$ is strictly increasing in s on* [inf $u_1(\Omega)$, sup$u_2(\Omega)$]. *Then there is a weak solution $\overline{u}$ of* $(*)$ *in $W_0^{1,p}(\Omega)$ with the property*

$$u_1(x) \leq \overline{u}(x) \leq u_2(x) \text{ a.e. on } \Omega.$$

Proof. Taking the equivalent norm on $X = W_0^{1,p}(\Omega)$, we obtain

$$||u|| = \left(\rho||u||_{L^{\mathrm{P}}(\Omega)}^{\mathrm{P}} + \sum_{\mathrm{i}=1}^{n}\left\|\frac{\partial u}{\partial x_{\mathrm{i}}}\right\|_{L^{\mathrm{P}}(\Omega)}^{\mathrm{P}}\right)^{\frac{1}{\mathrm{P}}}.$$

Considering the functional φ: $W_0^{1,p}(\Omega) \to \mathbf{R}$,

$$\varphi(u) = \frac{1}{p}||u||^{\mathrm{P}} - \int\limits_{\Omega} G(x,u(x))dx, G(x,s) := \int\limits_0^s g(x,t)dt. \tag{5.16}$$

where φ is Gâteaux differentiable, and its critical points are the weak solutions of $(*)$ (see Corollary 5.1 above). φ is also lower-bounded, with the norm on $L^p(\Omega)$ actually being of

Fréchet C^1 class (see, for instance, [43], Volume 2). Use Proposition 5.2, $(X, \|\cdot\|)$ being a reflexive strictly convex Banach space (see Section 2). Let

$$F := \{u \in W_0^{1,p}(\Omega) : u_1(x) \le u(x) \le u_2(x) \text{ a.e. on } \Omega\}.$$

F is closed convex. We also obtain

$$(I - \nabla\varphi)F \subset F.$$

Here, $\nabla\varphi$ denotes the metric gradient of φ. Since $(X, \|\cdot\|)$ is reflexive and strictly convex (see in Section 2), $\nabla\varphi$ is thus uni-valued, and it has the above-described properties. Indeed, let u be in F and $v := (I - \nabla\varphi)(u)$. We should prove that $v \in F$. $v = u - \nabla\varphi(u) \in W_0^{1,p}(\Omega)$ and $u_1(x) \le v(x) \le u_2(x)$. Since the definition relation of the subsolution for u_1 actually means $\varphi_w'(u_1)(w) \le 0\ \forall w$ in $W_0^{1,p}(\Omega)$ with $w(x) \ge 0$ almost everywhere (a.e.) on Ω, and that of the supersolution for u_2 is $\varphi_w'(u_2)(w) \ge 0\ \forall w$ in $W_0^{1,p}(\Omega)$, verifying $w(x) \ge 0$ a.e. on Ω, we will prove that $v(x) - u_1(x) \ge 0$ a.e. on Ω and $u_2(x) - v(x) \ge 0$ a.e. on Ω using the Gâteaux derivatives of φ in u_1 and u_2, respectively. $\varphi_w'(u_1)(v - u_1) = \varphi_w'(u_1)(u_1 - u) - \varphi_w'(u_1)(\nabla\varphi(u)) \le -\varphi_w'(u_1)(\nabla\varphi(u)) \le -\varphi_w'(u)(\nabla\varphi(u)) = -\|\varphi_w'(u)\|^2 \le 0$ (take into account that $u_1 \le u$, $\varphi_w'(u_1)$ is a linear map and some properties of the metric gradient). Also $\varphi_w'(u_2)(u_2 - v) = \varphi_w'(u_2)(u_2 - v) + \varphi_w'(u_2)(\nabla\varphi(u)) \ge \varphi_w'(u_2)(\nabla\varphi(u)) \ge \varphi_w'(u)(\nabla\varphi(u)) = \|\varphi_w'(u)\|^2 \ge 0$. φ is lower bounded on F, φ being continuous, actually (for this assertion, see Section 2). Until now, applying Proposition 5.2, for every $(v_n)_{n\ge1}$, a minimizing sequence for φ on F, there is a sequence $(u_n)_{n\ge1}$ in F such that $\varphi(u_n) \le \varphi(v_n)$ $\forall n$, $\lim_{n\to\infty} \|u_n - v_n\| = 0$, $\lim_{n\to\infty} \|\varphi'_w(u_n)\| = 0$. So $\lim_{n\to\infty} \varphi(u_n) = c$ and since $c := \inf \varphi(F)$, we have $\lim_{n\to\infty} \|\varphi'_w(u_n)\| = 0$ already, and the last property from the $(PS)_{c,F}$ condition is verified. To finish the proof, we once again apply Proposition 5.2. □

Example 1. *Consider the problem (Ω is an open bounded set of C^1 class in $\mathbf{R}^N$, $N \ge 3$)*

$$\begin{cases} -\Delta_p u = \alpha(x)\, u\, |u|^{p-2} \text{on } \Omega, \\ u = 0 \text{ on } \partial\Omega, \end{cases} \tag{5.17}$$

where $p = \frac{2N}{N-2}$ and α is continuous with $1 \le \alpha(x) \le a < +\infty$ on Ω. Then $u_1 := 1$ is a weak subsolution, $u_2 := M$, $M > 1$ sufficiently big, is a weak supersolution, $|f(x, s)| \le a|s|^{p-1}$ (condition (5.9)), and $s \to \alpha(x)s|s|^{p-2} + s$ is increasing in s on $[1, M]$; consequently, according to Proposition 5.3, (5.17) has a weak solution $\overline{u}$ with $1 \le \overline{u}(x) \le M$ a.e. on Ω.

Proposition 5.4. *Let Ω be an open bounded set of C^1 class in $\mathbf{R}^N$, $N \ge 3$, and $f: \Omega \times \mathbf{R} \to \mathbf{R}$ a Carathéodory function and u_1, u_2 from $W_0^{1,p}(\Omega)$ bounded weak subsolution and weak supersolution of $(**)$, respectively, with $u_1(x) \le u_2(x)$ a.e. on Ω. Suppose that f verifies (5.9) and there is $\rho > 0$ such that the function g: $g(x, s) = f(x, s) + \rho s$ is strictly increasing in s on $[\inf u_1(\Omega), \sup u_2(\Omega)]$. Then there is a weak solution $\overline{u}$ of $(**)$ in $W_0^{1,p}(\Omega)$ with the property*

$$u_1(x) \le \overline{u}(x) \le u_2(x) \text{ a.e. on } \Omega.$$

Proof. We follow, step by step, the above proof for Proposition 5.3 considering the real reflexive strictly convex Banach space $X = W_0^{1,p}(\Omega)$ endowed with the norm $u \to \|u\|_{1,p} = \left(\sum_{i=1}^{N} \left\|\frac{\partial u}{\partial x_i}\right\|_{L^p(\Omega)}^p\right)^{\frac{1}{p}}$ or the equivalent norm $u \to u_{1,p} = \sum_{i=1}^{N} \left\|\frac{\partial u}{\partial x_i}\right\|_{L^p(\Omega)}$, which are both also equivalent to the other two norms used in Remark 5.3. The function φ is from (5.11), having the weak derivative given in Theorem 5.1. Using similar calculus, we obtain a similar conclusion. □

Example 2. *Consider the problem* (Ω *is an open bounded set of the* C^1 *class in* $\mathbf{R}^N$, $N \geq 3$)

$$\begin{cases} -\Delta_p^s u = \alpha(x)\, u\, |u|^{p-2} \text{on } \Omega, \\ u = 0 \text{ on } \partial\,\Omega\,, \end{cases} \tag{5.18}$$

where $p = \frac{2N}{N-2}$ *and* α *is continuous with* $1 \leq \alpha(x) \leq a < +\infty$ on Ω. *Then,* $u_1 := 1$ *is a weak subsolution,* $u_2 := M$, $M > 1$ *being sufficiently big, is a weak supersolution,* $|f(x, s)| \leq a|s|^{p-1}$ *(condition (5.9)), and* $s \to \alpha(x)s|s|^{p-2} + s$ *is increasing in s on* $[1, M]$*; consequently, according to Proposition 5.8, (5.18) has a weak solution* $\overline{u}$ *with* $1 \leq \overline{u}(x) \leq M$ *a.e. on* Ω.

Remark 5.4. *The results from Sections 5.1.1, 5.1.2 and 5.2.1 have been reported by the author in [17].*

Remark 5.5. *Applications to real phenomena, as well as an application in glaciology, a nonlinear elastic membrane, the pseudo-torsion problem and a nonlinear elastic membrane with the p-pseudo-Laplacian, will be presented in the second part of this article.*

5.2. Critical Points for Nondifferentiable Functionals

5.2.1. Theoretical Results

The meaning of the title is actually "not compulsory differentiable". We start this section with the following:

Definition 5.3. x_0 *is a critical point (in the sense of the Clarke subderivative) for the real function f if* $0 \in \partial f(x_0)$. *In this case,* $f(x_0)$ *is a critical value (in the sense of the Clarke subderivative) for f. To clarify this notion, the Clarke derivative should be introduced. Let X be a real normed space,* $E \subset X$, $f : E \to \mathbf{R}$, $x_0 \in \overset{o}{E}$ *and* $v \in X$. *We set*

$$f^0(x_0;\, v) := \overline{\lim_{\substack{x \to x_0 \\ t \to 0+}}} \frac{f(x + tv) - f(x)}{t}.$$

The upper limit obviously exists. $f^0(x_0; v)$ *is by definition the Clarke derivative (or the generalized directional derivative) of the function f at* x_0 *in the direction v. The functional* ξ *from* X^* *is by definition Clarke subderivative (or generalized gradient) of f in* x_0 *if* $f^0(x_0; v) \geq \xi(v)\ \forall v \in X$. *The set of these generalized gradients is designated as* $\partial f(x_0)$.

Here it is a generalization at p-Laplacian and p-pseudo-Laplacian of an application of this concept from [66].

Let Ω be a bounded domain of $\mathbf{R}^N$ with the smooth boundary $\partial\Omega$ (topological boundary). Consider the nonlinear boundary value problems $(*)$ and $(**)$ from Section 5.1.2 above, where $f : \Omega \times \mathbf{R} \to \mathbf{R}$ is a measurable function with *subcritical growth*, i.e.,

$$\text{(I) } |f(x, s)| \leq a + b|s|^{\sigma}\ \forall s \in \mathbf{R}, x \in \Omega \text{ a.e.},$$

where $a, b > 0$, $0 \leq \sigma < \frac{N+2}{N-2}$ for $N > 2$ and $\sigma \in [0, +\infty)$ for $N = 1$ or $N = 2$.

Set [67]:

$$\underline{f}(x,\, t) = \underline{\lim}_{s \to t} f(x,\, s), \overline{f}(x,\, t) = \overline{\lim}_{s \to t} f(x,\, s).$$

Suppose

(II) $\underline{f}$ and $\overline{f} : \Omega \times \mathbf{R} \to \mathbf{R}$ are measurable with respect to x.

We emphasize that (II) is verified in the following two cases:

$1°$ f is independent of x;

2° f is Baire measurable and $s \to f(x, s)$ is decreasing $\forall x \in \Omega$, in which case we have:

$$\overline{f}(x,t) = \max\{f(x,t+), f(x,t-)\}, \underline{f}(x,t) = \min\{f(x,t+), f(x,t-)\}.$$

Definition 5.4. *u from $W_0^{1,p}(\Omega)$, $p > 1$, is solution of* $(*)$ *and* $(**)$ *if* $u = 0$ on $\partial\,\Omega$ *in the sense of the trace (see in* Section 2.3.2 *above) and*

$$-\Delta_p u(x) \in [\underline{f}(x, u(x)), \overline{f}(x, u(x))] \text{ in } \Omega \text{ a.e.} \tag{5.19}$$

and

$$-\Delta_p^s u(x) \in [\underline{f}(x, u(x)), \overline{f}(x, u(x))] \text{ in } \Omega \text{ a.e.} \tag{5.20}$$

respectively.

Let $X := W_0^{1,p}(\Omega)$, but in the first case $(*)$, the norm endowing X is $\|\cdot\|_{1,p}$ i.e., $\|u\|_{1,p} \overset{\text{notation}}{=} \|u\|_{W_0^{1,p}(\Omega)} = \|u\|_{L^p(\Omega)} + \sum_{i=1}^{N} \left\|\frac{\partial u}{\partial x_i}\right\|_{L^p(\Omega)}$, which is equivalent to the norm $u \to \left(\|u\|_{L^p(\Omega)}^p + \sum_{i=1}^{N} \left\|\frac{\partial u}{\partial x_i}\right\|_{L^p(\Omega)}^p\right)^{\frac{1}{p}}$. For the second case $(**)$, equip (also as previously) the same set X with the norm $u \to \|u\|_{1,p} = \left(\sum_{i=1}^{N} \left\|\frac{\partial u}{\partial x_i}\right\|_{L^p(\Omega)}^p\right)^{\frac{1}{p}}$, which is equivalent to $u \to |u|_{1,p} = \sum_{i=1}^{N} \left\|\frac{\partial u}{\partial x_i}\right\|_{L^p(\Omega)}$.

Associate with $(*)$ the locally Lipschitz functional $\Phi : X \to \mathbf{R}$,

$$\Phi(u) = \frac{1}{p}\|u\|_{1,p}^p - \int_\Omega F(x,u)dx,\ u \in X, \tag{5.21}$$

and associate with $(**)$

$$\Phi(u) = \frac{1}{p}\|u\|_{1,p}^p - \int_\Omega F(x,u)dx,\ u \in X, \tag{5.22}$$

where $F(x,s) = \int_0^s f(x,t)dx$. Set

$$Q(u) := \frac{1}{p}\|u\|_{1,p}^p,\ u \in X,\ \Psi_1(u) := \int_\Omega F(x,u)dx,\ u \in X, \tag{5.23}$$

and

$$Q(u) := \frac{1}{p}\|u\|_{1,p}^p,\ u \in X,\ \Psi_1(u) := \int_\Omega F(x,u)dx,\ u \in X, \tag{5.24}$$

respectively, where F, a map defined on $\Omega \times \mathbf{R}$, taking values in $\mathbf{R}$, is locally Lipschitz (use (I)). The functional Ψ: $L^{\sigma+1}(\Omega) \to \mathbf{R}$, $\Psi(u) = \int_\Omega F(x,u)dx$, is also locally Lipschitz (again (I)). Using the Sobolev embedding $X \subset L^{\sigma+1}(\Omega)$, we find that $\Psi_1 := \Psi \mid X$ is locally Lipschitz on X, which implies that Φ is locally Lipschitz on X, and consequently, according to a local extremum result for Lipschitz functions (if x_0 is a point of local extremum for f, then $0 \in \partial f(x_0)$), the critical points of Φ for Clarke subderivative can be taken into account. One may state:

Proposition 5.5. *Suppose* (I) *and* (II) *are satisfied. Then* Ψ *is locally Lipschitz on* $L^{\sigma+1}(\Omega)$ *and*

(*i*) $\partial\,\Psi\,(u) \subset [\underline{f}(x, u\,(x)), \overline{f}(x, u\,(x))]$ *in* Ω *a.e.*

(*ii*) *If* $\Psi_1 = \Psi \mid X$, *where* $X = W_0^{1,p}(\Omega)$ *endowed with the norm* $\|\cdot\|_{1,p}$ *for the problem* $(*)$ *and* $\|\cdot\|_{1,p}$ *for the problem* $(**)$, *respectively, then*

$$\partial\,\Psi_1\,(u) \subset \partial\,\Psi\,(u)\ \forall u \in X.$$

Proof. The proof for (*i*) can be found in [67], Theorem 2.1, which remains the same here, while the problem was solved for the Laplacian with $X = H_0^1(\Omega)$ only. In order to prove (*ii*), we use 2.2 from [67], observing for both cases (X is endowed with each one from those two norms) that X is reflexive and dense in $L^{\sigma+1}(\Omega)$, as can be seen, for instance, in Section 2, where they are summarized. □

Proposition 5.6. *If* (I) *and* (II) *are verified, every critical point of* Φ *is a solution for* $(*)$ *and* $(**)$, *respectively.*

Proof. *Problem* $(*)$. Let u_0 be a critical point for Φ. We have

$$0 \in \partial\,\Phi(u_0) \subset \partial\,Q(u_0) + \partial\,(-\Psi_1)(u_0) \tag{5.25}$$

since $\Phi \overset{(5.21)}{=} Q - \Psi_1$, and we apply some rules of subdifferential calculus concerning finite sums. $\partial\,Q(u_0) = \{Q'(u_0)\}$, where $Q'(u_0)(v) = \int_\Omega |\nabla u_0|^{p-2}\cdot\nabla v dx = \langle -\Delta_p\, u_0\,, v\rangle$ (Section 2).

Using (5.25) and a specific property of a function f Lipschitz around x_0 ($f^0\,(x_0; v) = \sup_{\xi\in\partial f(x_0)} \xi(v)$, $\forall v \in X$, f^0 the Clarke derivative of f), we find

$$0 \le \int_\Omega |\nabla u_0|^{p-2}\cdot\ \nabla v\mathrm{dx} + (-\Psi_1)0\ (u_0;\ v).$$

However, $(-\Psi_1)^0\,(u_0; v) = \Psi_1^0(u_0; -v)$ (a property of the Clarke derivative; see [22]), and thus,

$$\int_\Omega |\nabla u_0|^{p-2}\cdot\ \nabla(-v)dx\ \le\ \Psi^0(u_0;\ -v)\ \forall v\ \in\ X;$$

that is,

$$\mu_0\ (v) := \int_\Omega |\nabla u_0|^{p-2}\cdot\nabla v dx\ \le\ \Psi_1^0(u_0;\ v)\ \forall v\ \in\ X,$$

$\mu_0 = -\Delta_p\,u_0 \in \partial\,\Psi_1\,(u_0)$ and, using Proposition 5.5, $-\Delta_p\,u_0 \in \partial\,\Psi(u_0)$. Since $\partial\,\Psi(u_0) \subset (L^{\sigma+1}(\Omega))^* = L^{(\sigma+1)/\sigma}(\Omega)$, we obtain $u_0 \in W^{2,(\sigma+1)/\sigma}(\Omega)$ and (5.19):

$$-\Delta_p\,u_0\ (x)\ \in\ [\underline{f}(x,\ u_0(x)), \overline{f}(x,\ u_0(x))] \text{ in } \Omega \text{ a.e.}$$

Problem $(**)$. Let u_0 be a critical point for Φ. We have

$$0 \in \partial\,\Phi(u_0) \subset \partial\,Q(u_0) + \partial(-\Psi_1)(u_0) \tag{5.26}$$

since $\Phi \overset{(5.22)}{=} Q - \Psi_1$, and we apply some rules of subdifferential calculus concerning finite sums (Section 2).

$$\partial\,Q(u_0) = \{Q'(u_0)\},\ \text{where } Q'(u_0)(v) = \sum_{i=1}^N \int_\Omega \left|\frac{\partial u_0}{\partial x_i}\right|^{p-2} \frac{\partial u_0}{\partial x_i}\frac{\partial v}{\partial x_i}dx = \left\langle \Delta_p^s u_0,\ v\right\rangle.$$

Using (5.26) and a mentioned property of a function f Lipschitz around x_0, we find

$$0 \leq \sum_{i=1}^{N} \int_{\Omega} \left| \frac{\partial u_0}{\partial x_i} \right|^{p-2} \frac{\partial u_0}{\partial x_i} \frac{\partial v}{\partial x_i} dx + (-\Psi_1)0\ (u_0;\ v).$$

However, $(-\Psi_1)^0\ (u_0; v) = \Psi_1^0(u_0; -v)$ (a property of the Clarke derivative, see [22]), and thus,

$$\sum_{i=1}^{N} \int_{\Omega} \left| \frac{\partial u_0}{\partial x_i} \right|^{p-2} \frac{\partial u_0}{\partial x_i} \frac{\partial(-v)}{\partial x_i} dx \leq \Psi^0\ (u_0; -v)\ \forall v \in X;$$

that is

$$\mu_0\ (v) := \sum_{i=1}^{N} \int_{\Omega} \left| \frac{\partial u_0}{\partial x_i} \right|^{p-2} \frac{\partial u_0}{\partial x_i} \frac{\partial v}{\partial x_i} dx \leq \Psi_1^0(u_0,\ v)\ \forall v \in X,$$

$\mu_0 = -\Delta_p^s u_0 \in \partial\ \Psi_1(u_0)$ and, using Proposition 5.5, $-\Delta_p^s u_0 \in \partial\ \Psi(u_0)$. Since $\partial\ \Psi(u_0) \subset (L^{\sigma+1}(\Omega))^* = L^{(\sigma+1)/\sigma}(\Omega)$, we obtain $u_0 \in W^{2,\,(\sigma+1)/\sigma}(\Omega)$ and (5.20),

$$-\Delta_p^s u_0\ (x) \in [\underline{f}(x,\ u_0(x)), \overline{f}(x,\ u_0(x))] \text{ in } \Omega \text{ a.e.}$$

□

Remark 5.6. *Some applications to characterize the solution of the modeling given in [68] and solutions using this kind of definition for Dirichlet problems derived from the previously presented problems of the movement of glacier, nonlinear elastic membrane, pseudo-torsion problem or a nonlinear elastic membrane with the p-pseudo-Laplacian will be developed in Part two of this article.*

5.3. Other Solutions

The results from this section have been obtained by the author in [18].

5.3.1. Basic Results

Let us now consider the two problems (∗) and (∗∗) from the above two subsections, but the boundary condition is now by $Bu = 0$ instead of $u = 0$. Once again, we take the function f as in Section 5.2.1 with the corresponding $\underline{f}$ and f, as was performed there.

Definition 5.5. *u from $W^{2,p}(\Omega)$, $p > 1$, is solution of (∗) and (∗∗) from this section if $Bu = 0$ on $\partial\ \Omega$ in the sense of the trace (whose meaning is introduced above) and*

$$-\Delta_p\ u(x) \in [\underline{f}(x,\ u(x)), \overline{f}(x,\ u(x))] \text{ in } \Omega \text{ a.e.} \tag{5.27}$$

and

$$-\Delta_p^s u(x) \in [\underline{f}(x,\ u(x)), \overline{f}(x,\ u(x))] \text{ in } \Omega \text{ a.e.} \tag{5.28}$$

respectively.

We now continue with some necessary results on Lipschitz functions and Palais-Smale type conditions. First, we provide some comments related to the Clarke derivative. From Definition 5.3, the Clarke derivative is:

$$f^0(x_0; v) = \inf_{\substack{V \in V(x_0) \\ r \in (0,+\infty)}} \ \sup_{\substack{x \in V \\ t \in (0,r)}} \frac{f(x+tv) - f(x)}{t}. \tag{5.29}$$

Proposition 5.7. *Let f be Lipschitz around x_0 with the constant L. Then*

$1°$ *the function $v \to f^0(x_0; v)$ has values in* **R**, *is positive homogeneous and subadditive on X and*

$$\left|f^0(x_0; v)\right| \leq L\|v\| \ \forall v \in X;$$

$2°$ $f^0(x_0; -v) = (-f)^0(x_0; v)\ \forall v \in X, \lambda \geq 0 \Rightarrow (\lambda f)^0(x_0; v) = \lambda f^0(x_0; v)\ \forall v \in X;$
$3°$ *$v \to f^0(x_0; v)$ is Lipschitz on X with the constant L [69].*

Proof. $1°$ $f^0(x_0; v) \in \mathbf{R}$. For x near x_0 and with t strictly positive near 0, we have

$$\left|\frac{f(x+tv)-f(x)}{t}\right| \leq \frac{1}{t}L \parallel tv \parallel = L \parallel v \parallel. \tag{5.30}$$

From (5.30), we obtain

$$\left|f^0(x_0; v)\right| \leq L\parallel v \parallel \text{ and so } f^0(x_0; v) \in \mathbf{R}. \tag{5.31}$$

Indeed, suppose ad absurdum that $f^0(x_0; v) > L\|v\|$, for instance. Then, with $\forall V$ from V (x_0) and $\forall r$ from $(0, +\infty)$, we have

$$\sup_{\substack{x \in V \\ t \in (0,r)}} \frac{f(x+tv)-f(x)}{t} > L \parallel v \parallel,$$

in contradiction with (5.30).

$v \to f^0(x; v)$ is positive homogeneous. Since $f^0(x_0; 0) = 0$, let $\lambda > 0$. Then, $f^0(x_0; \lambda v) = \lambda \overline{\lim_{\substack{x \to x_0 \\ \lambda t \to 0+}}} \frac{f(x+t\lambda v)-f(x)}{\lambda t}$, etc.

$v \to f^0(x; v)$ is subadditive.

$$f(x_0; v_1 + v_2) = \overline{\lim_{\substack{x \to x_0 \\ t \to 0+}}}\left[\frac{f((x+tv_1)+tv_2)-f(x+tv_1)}{t} + \frac{f(x+tv_1)-f(x)}{t}\right] \leq$$
$$\overline{\lim_{\substack{x \to x_0 \\ t \to 0+}}} \frac{f((x+tv_1)+tv_2)-f(x+tv_1)}{t} + \overline{\lim_{\substack{x \to x_0 \\ t \to 0+}}} \frac{f(x+tv_1)-f(x)}{t}. \tag{5.32}$$

As $\lim_{\substack{x \to x_0 \\ t \to 0+}} (x+tv_1) = x$, in the third member of (5.32), the first term is equal to $f^0(x_0; v_2)$, and the second is equal to $f^0(x_0; v_1)$.

$2°$ $f^0(x_0; -v) = \overline{\lim_{\substack{x \to x_0 \\ t \to 0+}}} \frac{f(x-tv)-f(x)}{t} \overset{u=x-tv}{=} \overline{\lim_{\substack{u \to x_0 \\ t \to 0+}}} \frac{(-f)(u+tv)-(-f)(u)}{t} = (-f)^0(x_0; v)$, since $\lim_{\substack{x \to x_0 \\ t \to 0+}} (x - tv) = x_0$. For the second statement, we use Formula (5.29).

$3°$ Let v and w be arbitrary in X. For x near x_0 and with t strictly positive near 0, we have

$$f(x_0 + tv) - f(x_0) \leq f(x_0 + tw) - f(x_0) + Lt\|v - w\|.$$

Dividing by t and taking the upper limit for $x \to x_0$ and $t \to 0+$, one finds:

$$f^0(x_0; v) \leq f^0(x_0; w) + L\|v - w\|.$$

Exchanging v with w, we come to the desired conclusion. □

Proposition 5.8. *Let f be locally Lipschitz on X. The function* $\Phi : X \times X \to \mathbf{R}$,

$$\Phi(x; v) = f^0 (x_0; v)$$

is upper semicontinuous [69].

Proof. Let (x_0, v_0) be a point in $X \times X$ and $(x_n, v_n)_{n\geq 1}$ be an arbitrary sequence such that $(x_n, v_n) \to (x_0, v_0)$. We show that

$$\overline{\lim_{n\to\infty}} f^0(x_n, v_n) \leq f^0(x_0; v_0). \tag{5.33}$$

According to (5.29), we have $\forall m, p \in \mathbf{N}$

$$f^0(x_n; v_n) - \frac{1}{n} < \sup_{\substack{x \in B(x_n, \frac{1}{m}) \\ t \in (0, \frac{1}{p})}} \frac{f(x + tv_n) - f(x)}{t}. \tag{5.34}$$

We fix m, p in $\mathbf{N}$ and let k_n be in $\mathbf{N}$, $k_n > n$ such that

$$\frac{1}{m} + \frac{1}{p} < \frac{1}{k_n}. \tag{5.35}$$

With (5.34), we find y_{k_n} and t_{k_n} such that $\|y_{k_n} - x_n\| < \frac{1}{m}$ and $t_{k_n} \in \left(0, \frac{1}{p}\right)$, hence

$$\|y_{k_n} - x_n\| + t_{k_n} \overset{(5.35)}{<} \frac{1}{k_n} \tag{5.36}$$

and moreover (see (5.34)),

$$f^0(x_n; v_n) - \frac{1}{k_n} < \frac{f(y_{k_n} + t_{k_n} v_n) - f(y_{k_n})}{t_{k_n}}. \tag{5.37}$$

The second member of (5.37) is equal to

$$\frac{f(y_{k_n} + t_{k_n} v_0) - f(y_{k_n})}{t_{k_n}} + \frac{f(y_{k_n} + t_{k_n} v_n) - f(y_{k_n} + t_{k_n} v_0)}{t_{k_n}},$$

consequently passing in (5.37) to the upper limit for $n \to \infty$, and taking into account $y_{k_n} \to x_0$, $t_{k_n} \to 0$ (see (5.36)) and $|f(y_{k_n} + t_{k_n} v_n) - f(y_{k_n} + t_{k_n} v_0)| \leq L t_{k_n} \|v_n - v_0\|$, we find even (5.33), since $\overline{\lim_{n\to\infty}} \frac{f(y_{k_n} + t_{k_n} v_0) - f(y_{k_n})}{t_{k_n}} \leq f^0(x_0; v_0)$. □

Proposition 5.9. *If f is Lipschitz around* x_0*, and L is the constant, then*

1° $\partial f(x_0)$ *is nonempty, convex,* $*$*-weakly compact (for X complete) and*

$$\|\xi\| \leq L \, \forall \xi, \in \partial f(x);$$

2° $f^0(x_0; v) = \sup_{\xi \in \partial f(x_0)} \xi(v) \; \forall v \in X$ *([69]).*

Proof. 1° With the function $v \to f^0 (x_0; v)$ being positive homogeneous and subadditive (Proposition 5.7), there is a linear functional ξ such that

$$-f^0 (x_0; -v) \leq \xi(v) \leq f^0 (x_0; v) \; \forall v \in X.$$

However,

$$f^0(x_0;v) \overset{\text{Proposition 5.7}}{\leq} L\|v\|, -f^0(x_0;-v) \geq -L\|-v\|,$$

consequently $|\xi(v)| \leq L\|v\|\ \forall v \in X$, hence $\xi \in X^*$, $\xi \in \partial f\,(x_0)$ and $\|\xi\| \leq L$.

The convexity is obvious according to Definition 5.3.

For the remaining statement, i.e., $\partial f\,(x_0)$ is $*$-weakly compact, it is sufficient to show that $\partial f\,(x_0)$ is $*$-weakly closed (corollary of the Alaoglu-Bourbaki-Kakutani theorem [43], Volume 10, p. 144, 3.37_1). Let $\xi \in \overline{\partial f(x_0)}^{*-\text{weak}}$. Prove

$$f^0\,(x_0;v) \geq \xi(v)\ \forall v \in X. \tag{5.38}$$

Fix v in X and let $\varepsilon > 0$ be arbitrary. There is μ in $\partial f\,(x_0)$ such that $|(\xi - \mu)(v)| < \varepsilon$. Thus $\mu(v) > \xi(v) - \varepsilon$ and we have

$$f^0\,(x_0;v) \geq \mu(v) \geq \xi(v) - \varepsilon.$$

We pass to the limit for $\varepsilon \to 0$ and obtain (5.38).

2° Suppose, ad absurdum, that $\exists\, v_0 \in X$ such that $f^0(x_0;v_0) \neq \sup\limits_{\xi \in \partial f(x_0)} \xi(v_0)$. Since f^0 $(x_0;v_0) \geq \xi(v_0)\ \forall \xi \in \partial f\,(x_0)$, this implies

$$f\,(x_0;v_0) > \xi(v_0)\ \forall \xi \in \partial f\,(x_0). \tag{5.39}$$

We take μ, a linear functional on X, with

$$\mu(v_0) = f^0\,(x_0;v_0) \tag{5.40}$$

and $-f^0\,(x_0;-v) \leq \mu(v) \leq f^0\,(x_0;v)\ \forall v \in X$ ([43], Volume 10, p. 91, 2.2). However, $\mu \in \partial f$ (x_0) (see the beginning of the proof), and consequently, (5.40) contradicts (5.39). □

Proposition 5.10. *Let X be a reflexive or separable Banach space and $f: X \to \mathbf{R}$ locally Lipschitz. For every x_0 from X and $\varepsilon > 0$, there is $\delta > 0$ such that, for every ξ in $\partial f\,(x)$ with $\|x - x_0\| \leq \delta$, there exists ξ' in $\partial f\,(x_0)$ having the property ([67], p. 105)*

$$|(\xi - \xi')(v)| \leq \varepsilon\ \forall v \in X.$$

Proof. Suppose, ad absurdum, the contrary, $\exists\, x_0, v_0 \in X$, $\varepsilon > 0$, and also the sequences $(x_n)_{n\geq 1}$ in X, $(\xi_n)_{n\geq 1}$, ξ_n in $\partial f\,(x_n)$ such that $\forall n \in \mathbf{N}$:

$$\|x_n - x_0\| \leq \frac{1}{n} \text{ and } |(\xi_n - \xi)(v_0)| > \varepsilon_0\ \forall \xi\ \in \partial f\,(x_0). \tag{5.41}$$

According to (5.41), x_n is, for $n \geq N$, in a neighborhood of x_0 as in Proposition 5.9, hence $n \geq N \Rightarrow \|\xi_n\| \leq L$, so there is a subsequence $(\xi_{k_n})_{n\geq 1}$ that is weakly convergent (Šmulian corollary [43], Volume 10, p. 171, 4.29) and, consequently, $*$-weakly convergent (X reflexive $\Leftrightarrow X^*$ reflexive (Pettis [43], Volume 10, p. 151, 4.7)). Let $\xi_{k_n} \overset{*-\text{weak}}{\to} \xi_0$, i.e.,

$$\xi_{k_n}(v) \to \xi_0(v)\ \forall v\ \in\ X \tag{5.42}$$

([43], Volume 10, p. 145, 3.39 or p.145, ex.9 or p. 164, 4.25). However, $\xi_0 \in \partial f\,(x_0)$. Indeed, with u being arbitrarily fixed in X, $\exists\,(h_n)_{n\geq 1}$, $h_n \to 0$ and $(t_n)_{n\geq 1}$, $t_n \downarrow 0$ such that (use Definition 5.3—the Clarke derivative)

$$\forall n\ \frac{1}{t_n}[f(x_{k_n} + h_n + t_n u) - f(x_{k_n} + h_n)] \geq\ \xi_{k_n}(u) - \frac{1}{n},$$

pass to the limit for $n \to \infty$, taking (5.42) into account, $f^0(x_0; u) \geq \xi_0(u)$, i.e., $\xi_0 \in \partial f(x_0)$. Thus, it can take $\xi = \xi_0$ in (5.41), and one obtains a contradiction with (5.42). □

Remark 5.7. *In [67], Proposition 5.10, alias 1, (6), has another formulation. Moreover, X must be reflexive or separable.*

Proposition 5.11. *Let X be a real reflexive space and $f : X \to \mathbf{R}$ be locally Lipschitz.*

1° *For every x_0 in X, there is ξ_0 in $\partial f(x_0)$ such that*

$$\|\xi_0\| = \inf\{\|\xi\| : \xi \in \partial f(x_0)\}.$$

2° *The function μ: $X \to \mathbf{R}$*

$$\mu(x) = \inf\{\|\xi\| : \xi \in \partial f(x)\}$$

is lower semicontinuous ([67], p. 105).

Proof. 1° The application $\xi \to \|\xi\|$ of X^* in $\mathbf{R}$ is weakly lower semicontinuous and hence $*$-weakly lower semicontinuous ([43], vol 10, p. 147, (0)), since X^* is reflexive. On the other hand, $\partial f(x_0)$ is $*$-weakly compact (Proposition 5.9), hence the conclusion.

2° Suppose, ad absurdum, the contrary and let x_0 and x_n, $n \in \mathbf{N}$, be from X, $x_n \to x_0$, with

$$\lim_{n\to\infty} \mu(x_n) < \mu(x_0). \tag{5.43}$$

We take ξ_n in $\partial f(x_n)$ with $\mu(x_n) = \|\xi_n\|$ (see 1°). Proposition 5.10 yields, for every n from $\mathbf{N}$, ξ_n in $\partial f(x_n)$ and ζ_n^0 in $\partial f(x_0)$ such that

$$|(\xi_n - \zeta_n^0)(v)| \leq \frac{1}{n}\ \forall v \in X. \tag{5.44}$$

With $\partial f(x_0)$ being $*$-weakly compact (Proposition 5.9), it is bounded, and hence, $(\xi_n^0)_{n\geq 1}$ has a weakly convergent subsequence and hence is $*$-weakly convergent, $\left(\xi_{k_n}^0\right)_{n\geq 1}$,

$$\xi_{k_n}^0 \overset{*-\text{weak}}{\to} \xi^0 \in \partial f(x_0). \tag{5.45}$$

Since

$$|(\xi_{k_n} - \xi^0)(v)| \leq |(\xi_{k_n} - \xi_{k_n}^0)(v)| + |(\xi_{k_n}^0 - \xi^0)(v)|,$$

from (5.44) and (5.45), we obtain $\xi_{k_n} \overset{*-\text{weak}}{\to} \xi^0$, and this attracts $\lim_{n\to\infty} \|\xi_{k_n}\| \geq \|\xi^0\|$ ([43], Volume 10, p. 145, 3.39, 3°), i.e., $\lim_{n\to\infty} \mu(x_{k_n}) \geq \|\xi^0\| \geq \mu(x_0)$ and we obtain a contradiction with (5.43). □

Remark 5.8. *In [67], 1, (7) (here, Proposition 5.11), the condition "X reflexive" is lacking, and this is an error.*

Definition 5.6. *Let X be a real normed space, $E \subset X$ and $x_0 \in \overline{E}$. The vector v of X is by definition a possible direction for E according to x_0, if there is $\rho > 0$ such that $x_0 + tv \in E\ \forall t$ in $(0, \rho)$. In addition, let be $f : E \to (-\infty, +\infty]$ and $x_0 \in \operatorname{dom} f$. If*

$$\lim_{t\to 0+} \frac{f(x_0 + tv) - f(x_0)}{t}$$

exists and is finite, it is designated by

$$f'(x_0; v),$$

the derivative of f at x_0 *according to the vector* v or *according to the direction* v *(directional derivative)*. Thus

$$f'(x_0;v) = \lim_{t\to 0+} \frac{f(x_0+tv)-f(x_0)}{t}.$$

Remark 5.9. *Suppose E convex, f convex and finite on a neighborhood V of* x_0. *Then there exists* $f'(x_0; v)$. *Indeed, one can suppose V an open ball with the center in* x_0, *let* δ *be its radius,* $\delta \le \rho\|v\|$. *Consider the function* $F : \left[0, \frac{\delta}{\|v\|}\right) \to \mathbf{R}$, $F(t) = f(x_0 + tv)$ *(we supposed* $v \neq 0, f'(x_0; 0) = 0$*). F is convex:* $t_1, t_2 \in \left[0, \frac{\delta}{\|v\|}\right)$ *and* $\lambda_1, \lambda_2 \ge 0$, $\lambda_1 + \lambda_2 = 1 \Rightarrow F(\lambda_1 t_1 + \lambda_2 t_2) = f((\lambda_1 + \lambda_2)x_0 + (\lambda_1 t_1 + \lambda_2 t_2)v) = f(\lambda_1(x_0 + t_1 v) + \lambda_2(x_0 + t_2 v)) \le \lambda_1 f(x_0 + t_1 v) + \lambda_2 f(x_0 + t_2 v) = \lambda_1 F(t_1) + \lambda_2 F(t_2)$. *Thus the function* $\Phi : \left(0, \frac{\delta}{\|v\|}\right) \to \mathbf{R}$, $\Phi(t) = \frac{F(t)-F(0)}{t}$ *is increasing, that is the function* $t \to \frac{f(x_0+tv)-f(x_0)}{t}$ *has this property on* $\left(0, \frac{\delta}{\|v\|}\right)$, *consequently* $\lim_{t\to 0+} \frac{f(x_0+tv)-f(x_0)}{t}$ *is finite.*

Proposition 5.12. *Let E be a convex subset of a real Banach space and* $f : E \to \mathbf{R}$ *be convex. If f is Lipschitz around* $x_0 \in \overset{o}{E}$, *then for every v in X, we have*

$$f^0(x_0; v) = f'(x_0; v)$$

and the set of subderivatives in x_0 *coincides with the set of Clarke subderivatives in* x_0 *([69]).*

Proof. It is sufficient to prove the first statement because the second is obtained by the formulae that are found in Proposition 5.9 and [22], I, 5.5. We obviously suppose that $v \neq 0$ and let $\varepsilon > 0$ be arbitrarily fixed. We set

$$\alpha := \inf_{\substack{V\in V(x_0)\\ r\in(0,+\infty)}} \sup_{\substack{x\in V\\ t\in(0,r)}} \frac{f(x+tv)-f(x)}{t} \left(\overset{(5.29)}{=} f^0(x_0;v)\right),$$

$$\beta := \lim_{r\to 0+} \sup_{\|x-x_0\|<r\varepsilon} \sup_{t\in(0,r)} \frac{f(x+tv)-f(x)}{t}. \tag{5.46}$$

The suppositions $\alpha < \beta$ and $\beta < \alpha$ lead to a contradiction (attention to the definitions: limit, least upper bound and greatest lower bound), therefore $\alpha = \beta$. However, with the function $t \to \frac{f(x+tv)-f(x)}{t}$, x near x_0, increasing on an interval $(0, \eta)$ (see Remark 5.9), we obtain, via (5.46),

$$f^0(x_0; v) = \lim_{r\to 0+} \sup_{\|x-x_0\|<r\varepsilon} \frac{f(x+rv)-f(x)}{r}. \tag{5.47}$$

However, we have

$$\frac{f(x+rv)-f(x)}{r} = \left[\frac{f(x+rv)-f(x)}{r} - \frac{f(x_0+rv)-f(x_0)}{r}\right] + \frac{f(x_0+rv)-f(x_0)}{r}$$

and, via the Lipschitz condition verified on the open ball $B(x_0; r\varepsilon)$ for r near 0, $x \in B(x_0; r\varepsilon) \Rightarrow \left|\frac{f(x+rv)-f(x)}{r} - \frac{f(x_0+rv)-f(x_0)}{r}\right| \le 2\varepsilon L$, and hence, using (5.47),

$$f^0(x_0; v) \le \lim_{r\to 0+} \frac{f(x_0+rv)-f(x_0)}{r} + 2\varepsilon L = f'(x_0; v) + 2\varepsilon L$$

and hence

$$f^0(x_0; v) \le f'(x_0; v).$$

We take the opposite inequality. We have, with $\forall t$ from $(0, r)$,

$$\frac{f(x_0+tv)-f(x_0)}{t} \leq \sup_{\substack{x\in V\\ t\in(0,r)}} \frac{f(x+tv)-f(x)}{t}, \text{ where } V \in \mathrm{V}\,(x_0);$$

hence, $\lim\limits_{t\to 0+} \frac{f(x_0+tv)-f(x_0)}{t} \leq \sup\limits_{\substack{x\in V\\ t\in(0,r)}} \frac{f(x+tv)-f(x)}{t}$ and, consequently, according to (5.29),

$$f'(x_0; v) \leq f^0\,(x_0; v).$$

□

Remark 5.10. *The second part of the proof uses only the hypothesis "there exists $f'(x_0; v)$".*

Proposition 5.13 (Local extremum). *Let f be Lipschitz around x_0. If x_0 is a point of the local extremum for f, we have ([69])*

$$0 \in \partial f\,(x_0).$$

Proof. x_0 *local minimum point*. Let v be arbitrary in X. We must prove that $f^0(x_0; v) \geq 0$. Suppose ad absurdum that $f^0(x_0; v) < 0$. There is, according to (5.29), V in V (x_0) and $r > 0$ such that $\sup\limits_{x\in V} \frac{f(x+tv)-f(x)}{t} < 0$; hence, in particular, we have $t \in (0, r) \Rightarrow f\,(x_0 + tv) - f\,(x_0) < 0$, which prevents x_0 from being a local minimum point for f, which is a contradiction.

x_0 *local maximum point*. In this case, x_0 is a local minimum point for $-f$, and hence $0 \in \partial(-f)(x_0) = -\partial f\,(x_0)$ ([22], *Rules of subdifferential calculus*, 5.26), $0 \in \partial f\,(x_0)$. □

5.3.2. Some Palais-Smale Type Conditions

We now present some results following from some ideas in [67] that are improved and generalized. These results contain conditions of Palais-Smale type suggested by Ekeland principle.

Let X be a complete metric space, φ: X $\to$ **R** and $c \in$ **R**.

φ satisfies the $(\mathrm{PS})^*{}_{c,+}$ *condition* when, for every sequence $(u_n)_{n\geq 1}$, $u_n \in X$, $(\varepsilon_n)_{n\geq 1}$ and $(\delta_n)_{n\geq 1}$, $\varepsilon_n, \delta_n \in \mathbf{R}_+$, $\varepsilon_n \to 0$ and $\delta_n \to 0$, if

$$\varphi(u_n) \to c \tag{5.48}$$

and

$$\forall u \in X\; d(u_n, u) \leq \delta_n \Rightarrow \varphi(u_n) \leq \varphi(u) + \varepsilon_n \mathrm{d}(u_n, u), \tag{5.49}$$

then

$(u_n)_{n\geq 1}$ *has a convergent subsequence.*

By changing u_n and u to each other in (5.49), we obtain the $(\mathrm{PS})^*{}_{c,-}$ *condition*. Finally, $(\mathrm{PS})^*{}_{c}$ *condition* means $(\mathrm{PS})^*{}_{c,+}$ + $(\mathrm{PS})^*{}_{c,-}$.

When, with X being a real Banach space, the conclusion required by the hypothesis

"$(u_n)_{n\geq 1}$ has a convergent subsequence"

is replaced by

"$(u_n)_{n\geq 1}$ *has a weak convergent subsequence*",

we obtain, respectively, the conditions

$$(\mathrm{PS})^*{}_{c,\,w,\,+}, (\mathrm{PS})^*{}_{c,\,w,\,-}, (\mathrm{PS})^*{}_{c,\,w}.$$

Suppose that X is a real Banach space and φ is locally Lipschitz. φ satisfies the $[\mathrm{PS}]^*{}_{\mathrm{c},+}$ *condition* (obvious definition for $[\mathrm{PS}]^*{}_{\mathrm{c},-}$, $[\mathrm{PS}]^*{}_{\mathrm{c}}$) when the properties in (5.48) and (5.49) imply that

c *is a critical value of* φ (for the Clarke subderivative).

The definition is, according to Proposition 5.9, coherent. We have

$$(\mathrm{PS})^*{}_{\mathrm{c},+} \Rightarrow [\mathrm{PS}]^*{}_{\mathrm{c},+},$$

and the reciprocal assertion it is not true (consider φ: $\mathbf{R} \to \mathbf{R}$ Lipschitz, periodic and

$$c = \inf \varphi(\mathbf{R}) \text{ or } c = \sup \varphi(\mathbf{R})).$$

Finally, we provide the last version of the Palais-Smale condition according to Chang [67]. Let X be a real Banach space, φ: $X \to \mathbf{R}$ be locally Lipschitz and $c \in \mathbf{R}$. φ satisfies the $(\mathrm{PS})_{\mathrm{c}}^{\mathrm{ch}}$ *condition* when, for every sequence $(u_n)_{n\geq 1}$ from X, if

$$\varphi(u_n) \to c \tag{5.50}$$

and

$$\mu(u_n) := \inf \{||\xi_n||: \xi_n \in \partial\, \varphi(u_n)\} \to 0, \tag{5.51}$$

then

$(u_n)_{n\geq 1}$ *has a convergent subsequence.*

The definition is correct, $\partial\varphi(u_n) \neq \varnothing\ \forall n$ (Proposition 5.9, see also Proposition 5.10). One can state the following.

Proposition 5.14. *Let X be a real Banach space and φ: $X \to \mathbf{R}$ locally Lipschitz and convex. Then,*

$$\varphi \textit{ verifies } (\mathrm{PS})_{\mathrm{c}}^{\mathrm{ch}} \Rightarrow \varphi \textit{ verifies } (\mathrm{PS})_{\mathrm{c},-}^{*}.$$

Proof. Let (u_n) be a sequence from X and let (ε_n) and (δ_n) be sequences from $\mathbf{R}_+$, $\varepsilon_n \to 0$, $\delta_n \to 0$, such that

$$\varphi(u_n) \to c$$

and

$$||u_n - u|| \leq \delta_n \Rightarrow \varphi(u) \leq \varphi(u_n) + \varepsilon_n\ u_n - u\ \forall u \in X. \tag{5.52}$$

We must prove, for finding a convergent subsequence of (u_n), that

$$\mu(u_n) := \inf \{||\xi_n||: \xi_n \in \partial\, \varphi(u_n)\} \to 0. \tag{5.53}$$

Take $u := u_n + tv$, $||v|| = 1$, $0 < t \leq \delta_n$. Since $||u_n - u|| \leq \delta_n$, (5.52) gives:

$$\frac{\varphi(u_n + tv) - \varphi(u_n)}{t} \leq \varepsilon_n$$

and, passing to the limit for $t \to 0+$, we obtain (Proposition 5.12):

$$\varphi^0(u_n; v) = \varphi'(u_n; v) \leq \varepsilon_n,$$

and consequently, $\xi(v) \leq \varepsilon_n\ \forall \xi \in \partial\, \varphi(u_n)$ (Proposition 5.9); hence, changing v in $-v$,

$$||\xi|| \leq \varepsilon_n\ \forall \xi \in \partial\, \varphi(u_n). \tag{5.54}$$

Let ξ_n be in $\partial\varphi(u_n)$ such that $||\xi_n|| = \mu(u_n)$ (see Proposition 5.9). Then, taking (5.50) into account, we obtain

$$\mu(u_n) \leq \varepsilon_n,$$

which yields (5.49) by passing to the limit. □

Remark 5.11. *The last statement represents what the author recovered from Proposition 5.3 in [67], p. 475. The proof of this ([67], p. 483) contains, among other things, the implicit statement that* $v \to \Phi^0(u_0; v)$ *is not a subnorm, but an even linear functional.*

We now proceed to some propositions of [67].

Proposition 5.15. *Let X be a complete metric space,* φ: $X \to \mathbf{R}$ *lower bounded, lower semicontinuous and* $c := \inf \varphi(X)$. *c is attained when* φ *verifies* $(\mathrm{PS})^*_{c,+}$.

Proof. Let $(v_n)_{n\geq 1}$, $v_n \in X$, be a minimizing sequence for φ such that, for every n, $\varepsilon_n := \varphi(v_n) - c > 0$, and hence $\varepsilon_n \to 0$. Applying Ekeland principle with $\varepsilon = \varepsilon_n$, $\lambda = 1$, one finds $(u_n)_{n\geq 1}$, a sequence in X, with the properties

$$\varphi(u_n) \leq \varphi(v_n),$$
$$\varphi(u_n) \leq \varphi(u) + \varepsilon_n\, d(u_n, u)\ \forall u \in X.$$

Since $c \leq \varphi(u_n)$, we have $\varphi(u_n) \to c$; applying $(\mathrm{PS})^*_{c,+}$ and letting $(u_{k_n})_{n\geq 1}$ be a convergent subsequence, $u_{k_n} \to u_0$. However, $\varphi(u_0) \leq \lim\limits_{n\to\infty} \varphi(u_{k_n}) = c$, and this imposes $\varphi(u_0) = c$. □

Proposition 5.16. *Let X be a real Banach space,* φ: $X \to \mathbf{R}$ *lower bounded, locally Lipschitz and* $c := \inf \varphi(X)$. *If* φ *satisfies* $(\mathrm{PS})^*_{c,+}$, *then* φ *has critical points (for the Clarke subderivative).*

Proof. Apply Proposition 5.15 combined with Proposition 5.13. □

Proposition 5.17. *Let X be a real Banach space,* φ: $X \to \mathbf{R}$ *lower bounded, locally Lipschitz and* $c := \inf \varphi(X)$. *If* φ *verifies* $[\mathrm{PS}]^*_{c,+}$, *then c is a critical value of* φ *(for the Clarke subderivative).*

Proof. Let $(\varepsilon_n)_{n\geq 1}$, $\varepsilon_n > 0$, $\varepsilon_n \to 0$. For every ε_n, take v_n such that $\varphi(v_n) \leq c + \varepsilon_n$ and apply Ekeland principle with $\lambda = 1$. $\exists\, u_n$ such that $\varphi(u_n) \leq \varphi(v_n)$,

$$\varphi(u_n) \leq \varphi(u) + \varepsilon_n\, \|u_n - u\|,\ \forall u \in X. \tag{5.55}$$

Since $\varphi(u_n) \to c$, (5.54) allows the application of the hypothesis $[\mathrm{PS}]^*_{c,+}$, where c is a critical value. □

As an application, we continue with the problems (∗) and (∗∗) in this subsection. However, firstly:

Proposition 5.18. *Let* $X := W^{1,p}(\Omega)$ and Φ: $X \to \mathbf{R}$, $\Phi(u) = \frac{1}{p}\|u\|^p_{1,p} - \int_\Omega G(u)dx - \int_\Omega hudx$ and $\Phi(u) = \frac{1}{p}|\!|\!|u|\!|\!|^p_{1,p} - \int_\Omega G(u)\,dx - \int_\Omega hudx$, *respectively, where* $G : \mathbf{R} \to \mathbf{R}$ *has the period T and is Lipschitz,* $h \in L^{p'}(\Omega)$ and $\int_\Omega huhudx = 0$. *Then, for every c from* $\mathbf{R}$, Φ *verifies* $[\mathrm{PS}]^*_c$.

Clarification. On $X = W^{1,p}(\Omega)$, we can consider for this statement the following norms: $\|u\|_{1,p} = \left(\|u\|^p_{L^p(\Omega)} + \sum\limits_{i=1}^{N}\left\|\frac{\partial u}{\partial x_i}\right\|^p_{L^p(\Omega)}\right)^{\frac{1}{p}}$, which is equivalent to the norm $u \to \|u\|_{L^p(\Omega)} + \sum\limits_{i=1}^{N}\left\|\frac{\partial u}{\partial x_i}\right\|_{L^p(\Omega)}$ for (∗). For the second case (∗∗), we equip the same vector space with the norm $u \to |\!|\!|u|\!|\!|_{1,p} = \left(\sum\limits_{i=1}^{N}\left\|\frac{\partial u}{\partial x_i}\right\|^p_{L^p(\Omega)}\right)^{\frac{1}{p}}$, which is equivalent to $u \to |u|_{1,p} = \sum\limits_{i=1}^{N}\left\|\frac{\partial u}{\partial x_i}\right\|_{L^p(\Omega)}$ (see the considerations in the sections above).

Proof. It is sufficient to prove this for $[PS]^*_{c,+}$. Let $(u_n)_{n\geq 1}$ be a sequence from X, $(\varepsilon_n)_{n\geq 1}$ and $(\delta_n)_{n\geq 1}$ sequences from $\mathbf{R}_+$ convergent to 0. Suppose $\Phi(u_n) \to c$ and

$$\|u_n - u\| \leq \delta_n \Rightarrow \Phi(u_n) \leq \Phi(u) + \varepsilon_n \|u_n - u\|. \tag{5.56}$$

We decompose X into the direct sum

$$X = X_0 \oplus X_1, \tag{5.57}$$

where X_1 is the vector space of constant functions, and $X_0 = X_1{}^{\perp}$, the vector subspace of functions from $W^{1,p}(\Omega)$ having a mean value equal to 0. Let $u_n = v_n + c_n$, $v_n \in X_0$, $c_n \in \mathbf{R}$ and $|G(s)| \leq M$ on $\mathbf{R}$. Hence $\left|\int_\Omega G(u_n)dx\right| \leq \int_\Omega |G(u_n)|dx \leq \int_\Omega M dx = M\mu(\Omega)$, and since $\int_\Omega c_n h\,dx = 0$, we have, in the first case,

$$\Phi(u_n) = \frac{1}{p}\|u_n\|^p_{1,p} - \int_\Omega G(u_n)dx - \int_\Omega hu_n\,dx = \frac{1}{p}\|v_n + c_n\|^p_{1,p} - \int_\Omega G(v_n + c_n)dx -$$
$$\int_\Omega h(v_n + c_n)dx \geq \frac{1}{p}\|v_n + c_n\|^p_p + \frac{1}{p}\sum_{i=1}^N \left\|\frac{\partial v_n}{\partial x_i}\right\|^p_p - M\mu(\Omega) - \int_\Omega hv_n\,dx - c_n\int_\Omega h\,dx \geq$$
$$\frac{1}{p}\|v_n\|^p_p + \frac{1}{p}\sum_{i=1}^N \left\|\frac{\partial v_n}{\partial x_i}\right\|^p_p - M\mu(\Omega) - \|h\|_{p'}\|v_n\|_{1,p} = \frac{1}{p}\|v_n\|^p_{1,p} - M\mu(\Omega) - \|h\|_{p'}\|v_n\|_{1,p}$$
$$\Rightarrow \Phi(u_n) \geq \|v_n\|_{1,p}\left(\frac{1}{p}\|v_n\|^{p-1}_{1,p} - \|h\|_{p'} - M\mu(\Omega)\right) \tag{5.58}$$

since $\int_\Omega hv_n dx \leq \left|\int_\Omega hv_n dx\right| \leq \|h\|_{p'}\,\|v_n\|_p \leq \|h\|_{p'}\,\|v_n\|_{1,p}$, and, similarly, for the second case,

$$\Phi(u_n) = \frac{1}{p}|||u_n|||^p_{1,p} - \int_\Omega G(u_n)dx - \int_\Omega hu_n\,dx = \frac{1}{p}|||v_n + c_n|||^p_{1,p} - \int_\Omega G(v_n + c_n)dx -$$
$$\int_\Omega h(v_n + c_n)dx \geq \frac{1}{p}|||v_n + c_n|||^p_{1,p} - M\mu(\Omega) - \int_\Omega hv_n\,dx - c_n\int_\Omega h\,dx \geq \frac{1}{p}|||v_n|||^p_{1,p} -$$
$$M\mu(\Omega) - \|h\|_{p'}\|v_n\|_p = \frac{1}{p}|||v_n|||^p_{1,p} - M\mu(\Omega) - \alpha|||v_n|||_{1,p} \Rightarrow$$
$$\Phi(u_n) \geq |||v_n|||_{1,p}\left(\frac{1}{p}|||v_n|||^{p-1}_{1,p} - \alpha - M\mu(\Omega)\right) \tag{5.59}$$

since $\int_\Omega hv_n dx \leq \left|\int_\Omega hv_n dx\right| \leq \|h\|_{p'}\,\|v_n\|_p \leq \alpha|||v_n|||_{1,p}$.

As $(\Phi(u_n))_{n\geq 1}$ is bounded, (5.58) and (5.59) impose that $\left(\int_\Omega |\nabla v_n|^2 dx\right)_{n\geq 1}$ is bounded, and hence, $(\|v_n\|_{1,p})_{n\geq 1}$ and $(|||v_n|||_{1,p})_{n\geq 1}$, respectively, are also bounded.

Consider the sequence $(\tilde{u}_n)_{n\geq 1}$, $\tilde{u}_n = v_n + \tilde{c}_n$, where $\tilde{c}_n \equiv c_n$ (modulo T) and $\tilde{c}_n \in [0, T]$. Since Φ has the period T, (5.56) gives

$$\|\tilde{u}_n - (u + \tilde{c}_n - c_n)\| \leq \delta_n \Rightarrow \Phi(\tilde{u}_n) \leq \Phi(u) + \varepsilon_n \|(\tilde{u}_n - u) + (c_n - \tilde{c}_n)\|,$$

i.e.,

$$\|\tilde{u}_n - w\| \leq \delta_n \Rightarrow \Phi(\tilde{u}_n) \leq \Phi(w) + \varepsilon_n \|\tilde{u}_n - w\|. \tag{5.60}$$

However, (v_n) and $(\widetilde{c}_n)$ are bounded, and hence $(\widetilde{u}_n)$ is bounded, consequently, it has a weakly convergent subsequence $(\widetilde{u}_{k_n})_{n\geq 1}$, $\widetilde{u}_{k_n} \overset{weak}{\rightarrow} \widetilde{u}$ (Eberlein–Šmulian), whence the existence of a convergent subsequence of $(\widetilde{u}_{k_n})_{n\geq 1}$, and using the same notation,

$$\widetilde{u}_{k_n} \to \widetilde{u} \tag{5.61}$$

(the same proof as in Proposition 4 [67], p. 484). In (5.60), taking $w = \widetilde{u}_{k_n} + \delta_{k_n} v$, $||v|| = 1$, we obtain $\Phi(\widetilde{u}_{k_n} + \delta_{k_n} v) - \Phi(\widetilde{u}_{k_n}) \geq -\varepsilon_{k_n}\delta_{k_n}$, $-\varepsilon_{k_n} \leq \frac{1}{\delta_{k_n}}[\Phi(\widetilde{u}_{k_n} + \delta_{k_n} v) - \Phi(\widetilde{u}_{k_n})]$, and passing to the limit, we find that, since $(\widetilde{u}_{k_n}, \delta_{k_n}) \overset{(5.61)}{\rightarrow} (\widetilde{u}, 0)$, $0 \leq \overline{\lim_{n\to\infty}} \frac{1}{\delta_{k_n}}[\Phi(\widetilde{u}_{k_n} + \delta_{k_n} v) - \Phi(\widetilde{u}_{k_n})] \leq \Phi^0(\widetilde{u}; v)$, $0 \leq \Phi^0(\widetilde{u}; v)$, $||v|| = 1$, whence $0 \leq \Phi^0(\widetilde{u}; v)\ \forall v \in X$ $(0 \leq \Phi^0(\widetilde{u}; \frac{v}{||v||}) = \frac{1}{||v||}\Phi^0(\widetilde{u}; v))$ (Proposition 5.7), i.e., $0 \in \partial\,\Phi(\widetilde{u})$. Moreover, $c = \Phi(\widetilde{u})$, since $\Phi(\widetilde{u}_{k_n}) = \Phi(\widetilde{u}_{k_n} - \widetilde{c}_{k_n} + c_{k_n}) = \Phi(\widetilde{u}_{k_n}) \to c$, and also $\Phi(\widetilde{u}_{k_n}) \overset{(5.61)}{\rightarrow} \Phi(\widetilde{u})$ (Φ is continuous, being locally Lipschitz), and c is a critical value for Φ. □

Now:

Proposition 5.19. *Nonlinear Neumann problems*

$$(\mathrm{N})\begin{cases} -\Delta_p u = g(u) + h(x), x \in \Omega \\ \mathrm{B}u = 0 \text{ on } \partial\Omega, \end{cases}$$

and

$$(\mathrm{N}')\begin{cases} -\Delta_p^s u = g(u) + h(x), x \in \Omega \\ \mathrm{B}u = 0 \text{ on } \partial\Omega, \end{cases}$$

respectively, with the conditions

$$(\mathrm{III})\ g : \mathbf{R} \to \mathbf{R} \textit{ boundedmeasurable } T-\textit{periodic}, \int_0^T g(s)ds = 0$$

and

$$(\mathrm{IV})\ h \textit{ boundedmeasurable}, \int_\Omega h dx = 0,$$

have solution in $W^{1,p}(\Omega)$ *in the sense of (5.27) and (5.28), respectively.*

Proof. We are in the presence of problems of types (∗) and (∗∗) (this subsection), respectively, with $f(x, u) = g(u) + h(x)$. Conditions III and IV imply (I) ($\sigma = 0$) and (II) from Section 5.2.1. The associated functionals are

$$\Phi(u) = \frac{1}{p}||u||_{1,p}^p - \int_\Omega G(u)\,dx - \int_\Omega hudx,\ u \in W^{1,p}(\Omega),$$

and

$$\Phi(u) = \frac{1}{p}\|u\|_{1,p}^p - \int_\Omega G(u)\,dx - \int_\Omega hudx,\ u \in W^{1,p}(\Omega),$$

respectively, where $G(u(x)) = \int_0^{u(x)} g(t)dt$. G is Lipschitz and has the period T (use (III)). Since (I) and (II) are satisfied, any critical point of Φ is, according to Proposition 2.6, a solution for the problems (N) and (N′), respectively. However, Φ verifies $[PS]^*_c$ for every c in $\mathbf{R}$, particularly for $c = \inf_{u\in W^{1,p}(\Omega)} \Phi(u)$. This is correct since Φ is lower bounded (the same justification as for (5.58) and (5.59), respectively). It only remains to apply Proposition 5.18, c is a critical value, $c = \Phi(u_0)$, u_0 a critical point, u_0 is a solution for (N) or (N′), respectively. □

Remark 5.12. *The series of results in this subsection has been presented by the author in [18].*

Remark 5.13. *Other applications to the velocity problem under the assumption of solid friction, or to the problem studied in [70], for thermal transfer or another pseudo torsion problem are provided in the second part of this work.*

6. Weak Solutions Using a Perturbed Variational Principle

An Application of Ghoussoub-Maurey Linear Principle to p-Laplacian and to p-Pseudo-Laplacian

The results in this section have been partially reported by the author in [17]. We start with the statement of the generalized perturbed variational principle. To clarify the involved notions, we present the following:

Definition 6.1. *Let X be a real normed space, $f : X \to (-\infty, +\infty]$, and C a nonempty subset of X, $x_0 \in C$. f strongly exposes C from below in x_0 when $f(x_0) = \inf f(C) < +\infty$ and $x_n \in C\ \forall n \geq 1$, $f(x_n) \to f(x_0) \Rightarrow x_n \to x_0$. "f strongly exposes C from above in x_0" and has a similar definition. We remark that, taking C = X in the given definition, we fall on the definition of strongly minimum point. And also, a set of G_δ type means a set that is a countable intersection of open sets. A set of the F_σ type means a set that is a countable union of closed sets.*

Ghoussoub-Maurey Linear Principle. *Let X be a reflexive separable space and $\varphi: X \to (-\infty,$ $+\infty]$* lower semicontinuous and proper.

(I) *If φ is bounded from below on the closed bounded nonempty subset C, the set*

$$\{\xi \in X^* : \varphi + \xi \text{ strongly exposes } C \text{ from below}\}$$

is of G_δ type and everywhere dense.

(II) *If, for any ξ from X^*, $\varphi + \xi$ is bounded from below, the set*

$$\{\xi \in X^* : \varphi + \xi \text{ strongly exposes } X \text{ from below}\}$$

is of G_δ type and everywhere dense.

The above linear principle devolves (see the continuation to Theorem 6.1) from the more general Theorem 6.1, and we proceed to its preparation with definitions and some auxiliary propositions.

Definition 6.2. *Let X be a real normed space and C, D with $C \subset D$ nonempty subsets of X^*. C is strict w-H_δ set in D or strict w*-H_δ set in D if*

$$D \backslash C = \bigcup_{n=1}^{\infty} K_n, \tag{6.1}$$

dist $(K_n, C) > 0$, and K_n convex and weakly compact or $*$-weakly compact, respectively.

For instance,

Proposition 6.1. *Any nonempty closed set C of a separable reflexive space X, $C \neq X$, is strict w-H_δ set in X. In particular, if $\varphi: X \to (-\infty, +\infty]$ is l. s. c. (lower semicontinuous) and proper, then the epigraph of φ in $X \times \mathbf{R}$ is strict w-H_δ set in $X \times$* **R**.

Proof. Let $(x_n)_{n\geq 1}$ be a sequence with the set of the terms dense in $X\backslash C$ (open set). Take, for each n from **N**, K_n the closed ball centered in x_n with the radius $r_n := \frac{1}{4}\text{dist}(x_n, C)$. K_n is convex, weakly compact (Kakutani–Šmulian theorem [43], Volume 10, p. 151) and dist(K_n,

C) > r_n : let x be from K_n, dist $(x, C) \geq$ dist (x_n, C) − dist $(x, x_n) \geq 4r_n - r_n = 3r_n$. We take the greatest lower bound. Moreover, $X \backslash C = \bigcup_{n=1}^{\infty} K_n$: let x be from $X \backslash C$, and let $\exists\ (x_{p_n})_{n \geq 1}$ subsequence of $(x_n)_{n \geq 1}$ such that $x_{p_n} \rightarrow x$, which also implies that dist $(x_{p_n}, C) \rightarrow$ dist $(x,$ C), and if u and v are taken such that $0 < u < v <$ dist (x, C), from a rank on, we have 4 dist $(x_{p_n}, x) < u$ but, on the other side, $4r_n$ = dist $(x_{p_n}, C) > v$, and hence $x \in K_{p_n}$. □

Let X be a reflexive space and C, D subsets of X^*, $C \subset D$. We set

$$M\,(C, D) : = \{x \in X : \exists\ \xi \in C \text{ such that } Jx\,(\xi) \geq Jx\,(\eta)\ \forall \eta \in D\},$$

otherwise expressed, $M\,(C, D)$ is the set of x from X for which Jx is upper-bounded on D, and the least upper bound is attained at a point of C, J the Hahn embedding of X in X^{**}. So, with X being reflexive, J is an isomorphism of vector spaces that preserves the norms.

In the following, to abridge the writing, sometimes x designates Jx.

Retain that if C is ∗-weakly compact, $M\,(C, D)$ is closed.

Notations. $B_X\,(x_0, r) \equiv$ the closed ball centered in x_0 of radius r in the normed space X.

$$B_X \equiv B_X\,(0,1).$$

$\overline{E}^{\,*} \equiv$ the closure of the subset E from X^* for the ∗-weak topology.

We proceed to the auxiliary propositions.

Definition 6.3. *Let (X, d) be metric space and* (M, δ) *the metric space of real functions defined on X. For each nonempty subset A of X, we consider*

$$\mathrm{M_A} : = \{f \in \mathrm{M} : f \text{ upper bounded on } A\}$$

and, for each f from $\mathrm{M_A}$ *and t* > 0, *the slice of A,*

$$S(A,\ f,\ t) \stackrel{\text{def}}{=} \{x\ \in\ A :\ f\ (x)\ >\ \sup f(A) - t\},$$

is a set that is obviously nonempty when $\mathrm{M_A} \neq \emptyset$.

Proposition 6.2. *Let X be a reflexive space, D ⊂ X* and K ⊂ D, and K be convex ∗-weakly compact. If*

$$B_X\,(x, \alpha) \subset M(K, D),$$

then, for any $\varepsilon > 0$,

$$S(D,\ Jx,\ \varepsilon)\ \subset\ K + \frac{\varepsilon}{\alpha} Bx*.$$

In particular, when $C \subset D \subset \overline{\text{conv}}^{\,*}C$, we have

$$\text{dist}\,(K, C) = 0.$$

Proof. *First assertion.* This reverts to

$$\xi\ \notin\ K + \frac{\varepsilon}{\alpha} B_{X*}\ \Rightarrow\ \xi\ \notin\ S(D,\ x,\ \varepsilon). \tag{6.2}$$

Suppose ad absurdum that $\xi \in S(D, x, \varepsilon)$, i.e., (see Definition 3.3)

$$x(\xi) > \sup x(D) - \varepsilon\ (x \in M(K, D) \Rightarrow Jx\,(D) \text{ upper bounded}). \tag{6.3}$$

The first member of (6.2) gives

$$||\xi - \eta||_{X*}\ >\ \frac{\varepsilon}{\alpha}\ \forall \eta\ \in\ K. \tag{6.4}$$

Let z be from X such that

$$\|Jz\|_{X^{**}}\ (= \|z\|) = 1 \text{ and } Jz(\xi - \eta) = \|\xi - \eta\|_{X^*} \tag{6.5}$$

(Hahn lemma [43], Volume 10, p. 94).

Combining this with (6.4) and taking the least upper bound, one obtains

$$\sup z(K) \ \leq \ z(\xi) - \frac{\varepsilon}{2}. \tag{6.6}$$

However, $x + \alpha z \overset{(6.5)}{\in} B_X\ (x, \alpha) \subset M(K, D)$, hence $\exists \eta_0$ is in K such that

$$(x + \alpha z)(\eta_0) \geq (x + \alpha z)(\xi). \tag{6.7}$$

However,

$$(x + \alpha z)(\xi) = x(\xi) + \alpha z(\xi) \overset{(6.3),(6.6)}{>} [\sup x(D) - \varepsilon] + \alpha[\sup z(K) + \frac{\varepsilon}{\alpha}] \ \geq \ x(\eta_0) + z(\eta_0)$$

and we obtain a contradiction with (6.7); thus, (6.2) is validated.

Second assertion. This results from

$$\bigcap_{\varepsilon>0} S(D, x, \varepsilon) \subset \ K, \tag{6.8}$$

$$\bigcap_{\varepsilon>0} S(D, x, \varepsilon) \cap \ C \ \neq \ \varnothing. \tag{6.9}$$

For (6.8): $\xi \in \bigcap_{\varepsilon>0} S(D, x, \varepsilon) \overset{(6.2)}{\Rightarrow} \xi = \eta_\varepsilon + \frac{\varepsilon}{\alpha} u_\varepsilon, \eta_\varepsilon \in K, \|u_\varepsilon\| \leq 1$, and hence $\| \xi - \eta_\varepsilon \| \leq \frac{\varepsilon}{\alpha}$, ξ is strong adherent point of K, and the strong closure of K is included in the $*$-weak closure of this, which is in K. □

Proposition 6.3. *Let X be reflexive space, $C \subset X^*$ nonempty and $U \subset X$ nonempty open having the property*

$$\sup Jx\ (C) < +\infty\ \forall x \in U.$$

Then Jx, for any x from U, is upper bounded on $\overline{\text{conv}}\ ^*C$ and attains its least upper bound.

Proof. Set $D := \overline{\text{conv}}\ ^*C$. We have

$$\sup Jx\ (C) = \sup Jx\ (D)$$

$[\xi \in \text{conv } C \Rightarrow \xi = \lambda_1 \xi_1 + \lambda_2 \xi_2, \xi_1, \xi_2 \in C, \lambda_1 + \lambda_2 = 1, \lambda_1, \lambda_2 \geq 0 \Rightarrow Jx\ (\xi) = \lambda_1\ Jx\ (\xi_1) + \lambda_2\ Jx(\xi_2) \leq \sup Jx\ (C)$; $\xi \in D \Rightarrow \exists\ \xi_n \in \text{conv } C, \xi_n \overset{*-\text{weak}}{\rightarrow} \xi \Rightarrow \xi_n\ (x) \rightarrow \xi(x), \xi_n\ (x) \leq \sup Jx\ (C)$ $\forall n \geq 1$, hence $\xi(x) \leq \sup Jx\ (C)]$, and so,

$$\sup Jx\ (D) < +\infty\ \forall x \in U, \tag{6.11}$$

and the first assertion is proved.

We proceed to the second assertion. We fix x from U, $\exists \varepsilon > 0$ with $x + \varepsilon z \in U\ \forall z$ in B_X. Then

$$\sup J(x + \varepsilon z)(D) = \sup\ (Jx + \varepsilon Jz)(D) < +\infty\ \forall z \in B_X\ ((6.11)),$$

consequently, once again using (6.11),

$$\sup Jz\ (D) < +\infty\ \forall z \in B_X, \tag{6.12}$$

which implies

$$\sup Jz\ (D) < +\infty\ \forall z \in X \tag{6.13}$$

(for any fixed z, $z \neq 0$, replace z in (6.12) with $\frac{z}{\|z\|}$, $Jy(\xi) = \xi(y)$). Replacing z with $-z$ in (6.13), one finds

$$\inf Jz\,(D) > -\infty \;\forall z \in X. \tag{6.14}$$

However, X is reflexive, hence (6.13) and (6.14) express that D is weakly bounded, and consequently, D is even bounded. With D also being $*$-weakly closed, it is $*$-weakly compact ([43], Volume 10, p. 144), hence the conclusion by applying Weierstrass theorem. □

Remark 6.1. *Proposition 6.3 is Lemma 2.7 from [65], Ch.2. Here, an improved proof is proposed.*

Proposition 6.4. *Let X be a reflexive space, $C \subset X^*$ nonempty and U nonempty open from X such that*

$$\sup Jx\,(C) < +\infty \;\forall x \in U.$$

If C is a strict w^*-H_δ set in $D{:} = \overline{\text{conv}}^{\,*}C$, then the set

$$V := \{x \in U\text{: } Jx \text{ attains } \sup Jx\,(D) \text{ in } C\}$$

includes a set of G_δ type that is dense in U.

Proof. According to the definition

$$D \backslash C = \bigcup_{n=1}^{\infty} K_n, \tag{6.15}$$

K_n is convex $*$-weakly compact and dist $(K_n, C) > 0$. Every Jx, $x \in U$ is upper bounded on D and attains its supremum on this (Proposition 6.3). As dist $(K_n, C) > 0$, Proposition 6.2 prevents $M(K_n, D)$ from including any nonempty ball; in other words, $\forall n \geq 1$ int $M(K_n, D) = \varnothing$, and so $M(K_n, D)$, being also closed, is thin, and $U_n := X \backslash M(K_n, D)$ is open and dense in X. Then $\bigcap_{n=1}^{\infty} U_n$ is dense in X (Baire theorem), hence $\bigcap_{n=1}^{\infty} (U \cap U_n)$, a set of the G_δ type, is dense in U. We see that if $x \in \bigcap_{n=1}^{\infty} (U \cap U_n)$, then Jx, which is upper bounded on D, attains a fortiori its least upper bound on C, as $x \notin M(K_n, D)\; \forall n \geq 1$ and one takes into account (6.13). □

Proposition 6.5. *Let X be a reflexive space, C subset of X^* and separable, $D := \overline{\text{conv}}^{\,*}C$ and U nonempty open subset of X such that $\sup Jx\,(C) < +\infty\; \forall x \in U$. Suppose that $M(C, D)$ includes a dense and of G_δ-type subset of U. Then, for any $K \subset D$ $*$-weakly compact with $K \cap C = \varnothing$ and for any $\varepsilon > 0$, the set*

$$G(K, \varepsilon) := \left\{x \in U :\, \exists r > 0 \text{ such that } S^*(D, Jx, r) \cap K = \varnothing \text{ and } \operatorname{diam} S^*(D, Jx, r) < \varepsilon\right\}$$

is open and dense in U.

Proof. *$G(K, \varepsilon)$ is open.* We use the fact that, D being bounded (proof for Proposition 6.3), the subset $S(D, Jx, r)$ is also bounded.

$G(K, \varepsilon)$ is dense in U. Let $V \subset U$, V nonempty open arbitrary. C being separable, we can find a sequence $(C_n)_{n \geq 1}$, $C_n \subset D$, with C_n being convex $*$-weakly compact, with the properties

$$C \subset \bigcup_{n=1}^{\infty} C_n, \tag{6.16}$$

$$\text{dist}\,(C_n, K) > 0\; \forall n, \tag{6.17}$$

$$\text{diam } Cn \leq \frac{\varepsilon}{2}\; \forall n. \tag{6.18}$$

We obviously have $V \supset \bigcap \bigcup_{n=1}^{\infty} M(C_n, D) \cap V \overset{(6.16)}{\supset} M(C, D) \cap V$. However, the last member includes, according to the hypothesis, a set of the G_δ type that is dense in V, which forces, via the Baire theorem, the second member to have at least one term, let this term be $M(C_{n_0}, D) \cap V$, with a nonempty interior. From this interior, we take a point x. It remains to show

$$x \in G(K, \varepsilon). \tag{6.19}$$

Applying Proposition 6.2, for every $\rho > 0$, there exists $r > 0$ such that

$$S(D, Jx, r) \subset C_{n_0} + \rho B_{X^*} \tag{6.20}$$

($\exists\, \alpha > 0$ such that $B_X(x, \alpha) \subset M(C_{n_0}, D)$, taking $r = \alpha\rho$). We take

$$\rho < \min\left\{\frac{\varepsilon}{4}, \operatorname{dist}(C_{n_0}, K)\right\}. \tag{6.21}$$

(6.20) gives

$$\overline{S}^*(D, Jx, r) \subset \overline{C_{n_0} + \rho B_{X^*}}^* = C_{n_0} + \rho B_{X^*} \tag{6.22}$$

because the last term, being $*$-weakly compact, is also $*$-weakly closed. However,

$$(C_{n_0} + \rho B_{X^*}) \cap K = \varnothing: \tag{6.23}$$

let, ad absurdum, $\xi + \rho u = \zeta$, $\xi \in C_{n_0}$, $u \in B_{X^*}$, $\zeta \in K$, then $\rho = \|\xi - \zeta\| \geq \operatorname{dist}(C_{n_0}, K)$, and we obtain a contradiction with (6.21). So, (6.22) and (6.23) give $\overline{S}^*(D, Jx, r) \cap K = \varnothing$. Moreover,

$$\operatorname{diam} \overline{S}^*(D, Jx, r) \overset{(6.22)}{\leq} \operatorname{diam} C_{n_0} + 2\rho \overset{(6.18),(6.21)}{<} \frac{\varepsilon}{2} + \frac{\varepsilon}{2} = \varepsilon,$$

which finishes the proof. □

Now:

Theorem 6.1. *Let X be a reflexive space, C separable subset of X^*, which is a strict w^*-H_δ set in $D := \overline{\operatorname{conv}}^* C$, and U be open subset of X such that* $\sup Jx(C) < +\infty\ \forall x \in U$. *Then*
(I) *The set*

$$\{x \in U: Jx \text{ strongly exposes } D \text{ from above at a point of } C\}$$

is of the G_δ type and dense in U.

(II) *If $\varphi: C \to (-\infty, +\infty]$ is proper lower semicontinuous and $\varphi + Jx$ is, $\forall x$ from X, bounded from below on C, then the set*

$$\{x \in X: \varphi + Jx \text{ strongly exposes } C \text{ from below}\}$$

is of G_δ type and dense in X (N. Ghoussoub, B. Maurey [65]).

Proof. (I). According to the hypothesis, $D \backslash C = \bigcup_{n=1}^{\infty} K_n$, K_n is convex $*$-weakly compact, $\operatorname{dist}(K_n, D) > 0$. $M(C, D)$ includes a subset of the G_δ type dense in U (Proposition 6.4), but then, for each n from $\mathbf{N}$, the set $V_n := G(K_1 \cup K_2 \cup \ldots \cup K_n, \frac{1}{n})$ is open and dense in U (Proposition 6.5), consequently $\bigcap_{n=1}^{\infty} V_n$ is dense in U (relativized Baire theorem) and it remains only to observe that $\bigcap_{n=1}^{\infty} V_n = \{x \in X: Jx$ strongly exposes D from above at a point of $C\}$.

(II). $C \times \mathbf{R}$, separable subset of $X^* \times \mathbf{R}$, is a strict w^*-H_δ set in $D \times \mathbf{R}$ and then, φ being l. s. c., the epigraph epi φ in $C \times \mathbf{R}$ (nonempty set, φ is proper) is a strict w^*-H_δ set in $D \times \mathbf{R}$ and hence also in $\overline{\text{conv}}^*$epi φ. $W := \{(x, \alpha): x \in X, \alpha < 0\}$ is open in $X \times \mathbf{R}$, and sup (Jx, α)(epi $\varphi) < +\infty$ $\forall(x, \alpha) \in W$ [(Jx, α), continuous linear functional, acts on $C \times \mathbf{R}$ by the rule $(Jx, \alpha)(\xi, \lambda) = Jx(\xi) + \alpha\lambda$]. Indeed, $Jx(\xi) + \alpha\lambda \le Jx(\xi) + \alpha\varphi(\xi)$, $\exists\, a$ in $\mathbf{R}$, such that $(J\frac{x}{\alpha})(\xi) + \varphi(\xi) \ge a$ $\forall \xi \in C$ (the hypothesis), hence $Jx(\xi) + \alpha\varphi(\xi) \le \alpha a$ $\forall \xi \in C$. We show that for each $\varepsilon > 0$, $\exists\, y_0$ with $\|y_0\| \le 2\varepsilon$ and $\varphi + Jy_0$ strongly exposes C from below, which is enough to validate (II). Applying (I), $\exists\, (x_\varepsilon, \alpha_\varepsilon)$ in W such that

$$\|(x_\varepsilon, \alpha_\varepsilon) - (0, -1)\| \le \varepsilon \tag{6.24}$$

($(0, -1) \in W$!) and $(Jx_\varepsilon, \alpha_\varepsilon)$ strongly exposes epi φ from above at a point (ξ_0, λ_0). Then, $\forall$ (ξ, λ) from epi φ with $\xi \neq \xi_0$, we have

$$Jx_\varepsilon\,(\xi_0) + \alpha_\varepsilon\,\lambda_0 > Jx_\varepsilon\,(\xi) + \alpha_\varepsilon\,\lambda,$$

consequently, taking $y_0 := \frac{x_\varepsilon}{\alpha_\varepsilon}$, we have, in particular,

$$\varphi(\xi_0) + Jy_0\,(\xi_0) < \varphi(\xi) + Jy_0\,(\xi)\ \forall\, \xi \in C\backslash\{\xi_0\},$$

ξ_0 is a strict global minimum point for $\varphi + Jy_0$. Moreover, as $\varepsilon < \frac{1}{2}$ can be supposed, we have $\|y_0\| = \frac{\|x_\varepsilon\|}{|\alpha_\varepsilon|} \le 2\varepsilon$, because, via (6.24), $\|x_\varepsilon\| \le \varepsilon$ and $|\alpha_\varepsilon + 1| \le \varepsilon$, hence, $\alpha_\varepsilon \in \left(-\frac{3}{2}, -\frac{1}{2}\right)$.

Finally, let $(\xi_n)_{n\ge1}$ be a minimizing sequence for $\varphi + Jy_0$ on C, then $(\xi_n, \varphi(\xi_n))_{n\ge1}$ is maximizing sequence for $(Jx_\varepsilon, \alpha_\varepsilon)$ which strongly exposes epi φ in (ξ_0, λ_0), which imposes $\xi_n \to \xi_0$. □

Proof of Ghoussoub-Maurey linear principle

Proof. (I). Set $Y := X^*$, a separable reflexive space ([43], Volume 10, p. 162). Then, $Y^* = X$ (identification via the Hahn embedding; X is reflexive). C is separable and strict w^*-H_δ set in Y^* (Proposition 6.1, the weak and $*$-weak topologies coincide) and hence also in $D := \overline{\text{conv}}^*C$ ($X\backslash C = \bigcup_{n=1}^{\infty} K_n$ with the properties from (6.1), take the intersection with D). Apply (II), Theorem 6.1 transcribed with Y replaced by X; this is correct, as $\varphi + \xi$, $\xi \in X^* = Y^{**}$, is bounded from below $|(\xi(x)| \le \|\xi\|\,\|x\|$ and C is bounded).

(II). The epigraph epi φ of φ in $X \times \mathbf{R}$ is strict w-H_δ set in $X \times \mathbf{R}$ (Proposition 6.1). In the following, using the proof for (II), Theorem 6.1 beginning from (6.24), epi φ is that considered above. □

Corollary 6.1. *Let X be reflexive space, C a subset of X^* separable bounded strict w^*-H_δ set in $D := \overline{\text{conv}}^*C$ and φ: $X \to (-\infty, +\infty]$ bounded from below, l. s. c. and proper. For any $\varepsilon > 0$, there exists x_0 in X with $\|x_0\| \le \varepsilon$ and ξ_0 in C such that*

$1°$ $(\varphi + Jx_0)(\xi_0) < (\varphi + Jx_0)(\xi)$ $\forall \xi \in C\backslash\{\xi_0\}$;

$2°$ *Any minimizing sequence from C for $\varphi + Jx_0$ converges to ξ_0 ([65]).*

Proof. C bounded implies that $\varphi + Jx$ bounded from below $\forall x \in X$, consequently (II), Theorem 6.1 can intercede to obtain $1°$ and $2°$. □

We imply this theorem in two generalizations of a minimization problem of the form [71]:

$$C_f := \min\{\int_\Omega \left[\frac{1}{p}\left(|u|^p + \sum_{i=1}^{N}\left|\frac{\partial u}{\partial x_i}\right|^p\right) - f(u)\right]dx:\ u \in W_0^{1,p}(\Omega), \|\,u\,\|\,2* = 1\}, \tag{6.25}$$

and

$$C_f := \min\{\int_{\Omega}\left(\frac{1}{p}\sum_{i=1}^{N}\left|\frac{\partial u}{\partial x_i}\right|^p - f(u)\right)dx\colon\ u\ \in\ W_0^{1,p}(\Omega), \|\ u\ \|\ 2* = 1\}, \tag{6.26}$$

where Ω is open set of C^1 class in $\mathbf{R}^N$, $N \geq 3, f \in W^{-1,p\prime}(\Omega)$ (= $(W_0^{1,p}(\Omega))^*$), $\frac{1}{p}+\frac{1}{p'} = 1$, $2^* = \frac{2N}{N-2}$—the critical exponent for the Sobolev embedding (for the necessary explanations, here and in the following, see Section 2).

Let Ω be an open bounded set of the C^1 class in $\mathbf{R}^N$, $N \geq 3$. Consider the problems ($*$) and ($**$) from Section 5.1.2, where $f : \Omega \times \mathbf{R} \to \mathbf{R}$ is a Carathéodory function with the growth condition

$$|f\ (x,\ s)|\ \leq\ c|s|^{p-1}\ + b(x),\ >\ 0,\ 2\ \leq\ p\ \leq \frac{2N}{N-2},\ b\ \in\ L^{p'}(\Omega),\ \frac{1}{p}+\frac{1}{p'} = 1. \tag{6.27}$$

The functionals φ: $W_0^{1,p}(\Omega) \to \mathbf{R}$,

$$\varphi(u) = \int_{\Omega}\left[\frac{1}{p}\left(|u|^p + \sum_{i=1}^{N}\left|\frac{\partial u}{\partial x_i}\right|^p\right) - F(x, u(x))\right] dx \tag{6.28}$$

and

$$\varphi(u) = \int_{\Omega}\left(\frac{1}{p}\sum_{i=1}^{N}\left|\frac{\partial u}{\partial x_i}\right|^p - F(x, u(x))\right) dx, \tag{6.29}$$

with $F(x, s) : = \int_0^s f(x,t)\, dt$, are of the Fréchet C^1 class and their critical points are the weak solutions of the problems ($*$) and ($**$), respectively.

Problem ($*$). Let λ_1 be the first eigenvalue of $-\Delta_p$ in $W_0^{1,p}(\Omega)$ with a homogeneous boundary condition. We have (see, for instance, Section 2)

$$\lambda_1\ = \inf\{\frac{||u||_{1,p}^p}{|i(u)|_{0,p}^p}\colon\ u \in\ W_0^{1,p}(\Omega)\backslash\{0\}\}\ (\text{the Rayleigh} - \text{Ritz quotient}). \tag{6.30}$$

Now, we provide an answer to (6.25). We use the norm $\|\cdot\|_{1,p}$ on $W_0^{1,p}(\Omega)$ (see above). We denote the dual of $(W_0^{1,p}(\Omega), \|\cdot\|_{1,p})$ by $W^{-1,p\prime}(\Omega)$, where p' is the conjugate of p (i.e., $\frac{1}{p}+\frac{1}{p'}= 1$).

Proposition 6.6. *Under the above assumptions and, in addition, the growth condition*

$$F(x,\ s)\ \leq\ c_1\frac{s^p}{p}\ +\ \alpha(x)s, \tag{6.31}$$

with $0 < c_1 < \lambda_1$, $\alpha \in L^{q\prime}(\Omega)$ *for some* $2 \leq q \leq \frac{2N}{N-2}$ *and* $f\,(x, -s) = -f\,(x, s)$, $\forall x$ *from* Ω, *the following assertions hold:*

(i) The set of functions h from $W^{-1,p\prime}(\Omega)$, *having the property that the functional* $\varphi_h : W_0^{1,p}(\Omega) \to \mathbf{R}$,

$$\varphi h\ (u) = \frac{1}{p}||u||_p^p - \int_{\Omega}(F(x,u(x)) + h(u(x)))\,dx \tag{6.32}$$

has an attained minimum in only one point and includes a G_δ *set that is everywhere dense.*

(ii) The set of functions h from $W^{-1,p'}(\Omega)$, having the property

$$\text{the problem} \begin{cases} -\Delta_p u = f(x,u) + h(u) \text{ in } \Omega \\ u = 0 \text{ on } \partial\Omega \end{cases} \text{has solutions,}$$

includes a G_δ set that is everywhere dense.

(iii) Moreover, if $s \to f(x, s)$ is increasing, then the set of functions h from $W^{-1,p'}(\Omega)$, having the property

$$\text{the problem} \begin{cases} -\Delta_p u = f(x,u) + h(u) \text{ in } \Omega \\ u = 0 \text{ on } \partial\Omega \end{cases} \text{has a unique solution,}$$

includes a G_δ set that is everywhere dense.

Remark 6.2. *This is a generalization applied to the p-Laplacian and at $W_0^{1,p}(\Omega)$ of Theorem 2.13 from [65].*

Proof. It is sufficient to justify (*i*). Consider, for each *h* from $W^{-1,p'}(\Omega)$, the functional ξ_h from $W^{-1,p'}(\Omega)$,

$$\xi_h(u) = -\int_\Omega h(u(x))\,dx. \tag{6.33}$$

One may see that $\varphi_h = \varphi + \xi_h$ (see (6.28)). Consequently, according to the Ghoussoub-Maurey linear principle, (II), if we show that φ_h is bounded from below for any *h* from $W^{-1,p'}(\Omega)$, then (*i*) is proven. However, taking into account the Sobolev embedding and (6.31), we have $\forall u \in W_0^{1,p}(\Omega)$,

$$(\varphi + \xi_h)(u) = \frac{1}{p}\|u\|_{1,p}^p - \int_\Omega F(x,u(x))\,dx - \int_\Omega h(u(x))\,dx \geq \frac{1}{p}\|u\|_{1,p}^p - c_1\int_\Omega \frac{|u(x)|^p}{p}\,dx -$$

$$\int_\Omega \alpha(x)u(x)\,dx - \int_\Omega h(u(x))\,dx \geq \frac{1}{p}\|u\|_{1,p}^p - \frac{c_1}{\lambda_1 p}\|u\|_{1,p}^p - \|\alpha\|_{q'}\|u\|_q - \|h\|_{W^{-1,p'}}\|u\|_{1,p} \geq$$

$$\frac{1}{p}\left(1 - \frac{c_1}{\lambda_1}\right)\|u\|_{1,p}^p - r\|u\|_{1,p} = \|u\|_{1,p}\left[\frac{1}{p}\left(1 - \frac{c_1}{\lambda_1}\right)\|u\|_{1,p}^{p-1} - r\right],$$

$r \in \mathbf{R}$, and hence the conclusion since $1 - \frac{c_1}{\lambda_1} > 0$. To prove some of these inequalities,

$$\int_\Omega F(x,u(x))\,dx \leq \int_\Omega\left(\frac{|u(x)|^p}{p} + \alpha(x)u(x)\right)dx = \frac{1}{p}\|i(u)\|_{0,p}^p + \int_\Omega \alpha(x)u(x)\,dx \leq$$

$$\frac{1}{p\lambda_1}\|u\|_{1,p}^p + \|\alpha\|_{0,q'}\|u\|_q \leq \frac{1}{p\lambda_1}\|u\|_{1,p}^p + K\|u\|_{1,p}$$

(see *q* and properties of Sobolev spaces in Section 2) and

$\int_\Omega h(u(x))\,dx = \langle h, u\rangle \leq \|h\|_{W^{-1,p'}}\|u\|_{1,p}$ (the norm of the linear continuous map).

□

Problem (∗∗). Let λ_1 be the first eigenvalue of $-\Delta_p^s$ in $W_0^{1,p}(\Omega)$ with a homogeneous boundary condition. We have (see Section 2)

$$\lambda_1 = \inf \left\{ \frac{\| u \|_{1,p}^p}{|i(u)|_{0,p}^p} : u \in W_0^{1,p}(\Omega)\backslash\{0\}\right\} \text{ (the Rayleigh – Ritz quotient).}$$

Now, we provide an answer to (6.26). We use the norm $\| \cdot \|_p$ on $W_0^{1,p}(\Omega)$ (see above). We denote the dual of $(W_0^{1,p}(\Omega), \| \cdot \|_p)$ also by $W^{-1,p'}(\Omega)$, where p' is the conjugate of p (i.e., $\frac{1}{p}+\frac{1}{p'} = 1$).

Proposition 6.7. *Under the above assumptions and, in addition, the growth condition*

$$F(x, s) \leq c1 \frac{s^p}{p} + \alpha(x)s,$$

with $0 < c_1 < \lambda_1$, $\alpha \in L^{q'}(\Omega)$ *for some* $2 \leq q \leq \frac{2N}{N-2}$ *and* $f(x, -s) = -f(x, s)$, $\forall x$ *from* Ω, *the following assertions hold.*

(i) The set of functions h from $W^{-1,p'}(\Omega)$*, having the property that the functional* $\varphi_h : W_0^{1,p}(\Omega) \to \mathbf{R}$,

$$\varphi h\ (u) = \frac{1}{p}\| u \|_p^p - \int_\Omega (F(x, u(x)) + h(u(x)))\, dx$$

has an attained minimum in only one point and includes a G_δ *set that is everywhere dense.*

(ii) The set of functions h from $W^{-1,p'}(\Omega)$*, having the property*

$$\text{the problem} \begin{cases} -\Delta_p^s u = f(x, u) + h\ (u) \text{ in } \Omega \\ u = 0 \text{ on } \partial\,\Omega \end{cases} \text{has solutions,}$$

includes a G_δ *set that is everywhere dense.*

(iii) Moreover, if $s \to f(x, s)$ *is increasing, then the set of functions h from* $W^{-1,p'}(\Omega)$*, having the property*

$$\text{the problem} \begin{cases} -\Delta_p^s u = f(x, u) + h(u) \text{ in } \Omega \\ u = 0 \text{ on } \partial\Omega \end{cases} \text{has a unique solution,}$$

includes a G_δ *set that is everywhere dense.*

Remark 6.3. *This is a generalization applied to the p-pseudo-Laplacian and at* $W_0^{1,p}(\Omega)$ *of Theorem 2.13 from [65].*

Proof. The proof and the afferent calculus follow, step by step, those for Proposition 6.6. There, one replaces the norm $\|\cdot\|_p$ on $W_0^{1,p}(\Omega)$ with the norm $\| \cdot \|_p$, and the inequalities and considerations remain the same. □

Remark 6.4. *For the above results, there are some applications for particular problems from [72–74], together with others for the pseudo torsion problem.*

7. Conclusions

Seven methods to obtain and/or characterize weak solutions for some problems of mathematical physics equations involving Dirichlet or Neumann problems for the p-Laplacian and the p-pseudo-Laplacian have been developed. They were presented starting from the most general abstract framework, together with detailed proofs, and numerous auxiliary propositions are highlighted. The aim of this unfolding is to be applied to problems derived from the modeling of real phenomena.

The first three ways use surjectivity results (obtained from three generalizations due to the author of three surjectivity theorems of Fučik and Nečas) and they are applied to duality maps and Nemytskii operators. The novelty of this work consists of the presentation of all the proof details, together with examples, to use this theory to solve mathematical physics problems describing real phenomena. Many demonstration details are explained in accordance with the aim of this journal. We proposed solving methods, and the characterization of the solutions for problems derived from glaciology, a nonlinear elastic membrane either with the p-Laplacian or with the p-pseudo-Laplacian and the pseudo torsion problem will be provided in Part two of this work.

The fourth sequence of results starts with Ekeland variational principle to obtain theoretical propositions that generalize two statements given by Ghoussoub, in which the author replaced the real Hilbert space with a real reflexive uniformly convex Banach space and the Fréchet C^1 class of the goal function with the condition imposed that it be lower semicontinuous and Gâteaux differentiable. It is also worthwhile to underline that Gâteaux differentiability can be replaced by the property of β-differentiability, with β being a bornology any. These theoretical statements have been used to characterize weak solutions for the p-Laplacian and for the p-pseudo-Laplacian. Some adequate examples will be also given in Part two of this work. The novelty consists in using these results for the targeted modeling of real phenomena problems solved for glaciology, nonlinear elastic membrane with p-Laplacian and p-pseudo-Laplacian and pseudo torsion problem.

The fifth succession of statements establishes results for nondifferentiable functionals using the Clarke gradient and critical points for this type of map and other specific notions until their insertion for the characterization of weak solutions for Dirichlet problems with the p-Laplacian and the p-pseudo-Laplacian, respectively, in $W_0^{1,p}(\Omega)$. Applications in thermal transfer, for Dirichlet problems derived from previously presented problems of the movement of a glacier, nonlinear elastic membrane, the pseudo torsion problem or nonlinear elastic membrane with the p-Laplacian and p-pseudo-Laplacian will be presented in Part two.

The sixth series of results, using properties of the Clarke subderivative, conditions of the Palais-Smale type and Ekeland principle, are results for Neumann or mixed problems. They are involved in the solution of corresponding problems for the p-Laplacian and the p-pseudo-Laplacian. The novelty resides in applications to solutions for the velocity of solid friction, the study of glacier flow, injection molding, thermal transfer and the pseudo-torsion problem.

The last sequence of assertions starts from the Ghoussoub-Maurey linear principle, which is used in order to solve some minimization problems. Generalizations of the minimization problem for the Laplacian given by Brezis and Nirenberg have been obtained in conjunction with the characterization of weak solutions of Dirichlet problems for the p-Laplacian and for the p-pseudo-Laplacian.

We are particularly interested in these applications, and this work is a necessary study for our future developments since our final goal is to obtain a mathematical model for a specific process involving transfer phenomena for the targeted environmental engineering application. The role of the reactor (in nanofabrication) in nano-liquid-liquid dispersed systems, in which micro- or nano-droplets play this role, and the determinant parameters are related to surface phenomena as a result of special intermolecular forces at the interface. In this context, some innovative mathematical modeling methods have to be proposed and tested in order to properly simulate the physical-chemical interactions and processes specific to nanofabrication. However, one may stress that there are no models available that can be applied for describing the diffusion phenomena involved in the micro-emulsification of dispersed systems in connection with surface properties at the interface in self-organized systems, and this will be the subject of future research.

Funding: This research received no external funding.

Data Availability Statement: Not applicable.

Conflicts of Interest: The author declares no conflict of interest.

References

1. Diaz, J.I.; Hernandez, J.; Tello, L. On the multiplicity of equilibrium solutions to a nonlinear diffusion equation on a manifold arising in climatology. *J. Math. Anal. Appl.* **1997**, *216*, 593–613. [CrossRef]
2. Diaz, J.I.; Thelin, F. On a nonlinear parabolic problem arising in some models related to turbulent flows. *SIAM J. Math. Anal.* **1994**, *25*, 1085–1111. [CrossRef]
3. Glowinski, R.; Rappaz, J. Approximation of a nonlinear elliptic problem arising in a non-Newtonian fluid model in glaciology. *Modél. Math. Anal. Numér.* **2003**, *37*, 175–186. [CrossRef]
4. King, J.R.; McCue, S.W. Quadrature domains and p-Laplacian growth. *Complex Anal. Oper. Theory* **2009**, *3*, 453–469. [CrossRef]
5. Aronsson, G.; Janfalk, U. On Helle-Shaw flow of power-law fluids. *Eur. J. Appl. Math.* **1992**, *3*, 343–366. [CrossRef]
6. Schowalter, R.E.; Walkington, N.J. Diffusion of fluid in a fissured medium with microstructure. *SIAM J. Math. Anal.* **1991**, *22*, 1702–1722. [CrossRef]
7. Péllissier, M.C.; Reynaud, M.L. Étude d'un modèle mathématique d'écoulement de glacier, R.C. *Acad. Sci. Paris Sér. I Math.* **1974**, *279*, 531–534.
8. Bhattacharya, T.; Dibenedetto, E.; Manfredi, J. Limits as $p \to \infty$ of $\Delta_p u_p = f$ and related extremal problems. *Rend. Sem. Math. Univ. Pol. Torino Fasc. Spec.* **1989**, *47*, 15–68.
9. Kawohl, B. A family of torsional creep problems. *J. Reine Angew. Math.* **1990**, *410*, 1–22.
10. Benci, V.; Fortunato, D.; Pisani, L. Solitons like solutions of a Lorenz invariant equation in dimension 3. *Rev. Math. Phys.* **1998**, *10*, 315–344. [CrossRef]
11. Meghea, I. Minimax theorems in β-differentiability and theorems of surjectivity and of Fredholm alternative type for operators of the form $J_\varphi - \lambda S$. Ph.D. Thesis, University of Bucharest, Bucharest, Romania, 1999.
12. Meghea, I. Two solutions for a problem of partial differential equations. *UPB Sci. Bull. Ser. A* **2010**, *72*, 41–58.
13. Meghea, I. Some results of Fredholm alternative type for operators of the form $\lambda J_\varphi - S$ with applications. *UPB Sci. Bull. Ser. A* **2010**, *72*, 21–32.
14. Meghea, I. Weak solutions for p-pseudo-Laplacian Δ_p^s using a perturbed variational principle and via surjectivity results. *BSG Proc.* **2010**, *17*, 140–150.
15. Meghea, I. Weak solutions for p-Laplacian and for p-pseudo-Laplacian using surjectivity theorems. *BSG Proc.* **2011**, *18*, 67–76.
16. Meghea, I. On some perturbed variational principles: Connexions and applications. *Rev. Roum. Math. Pure Appl.* **2009**, *54*, 493–511.
17. Meghea, I. Variational approaches to characterize weak solutions for some problems of mathematical physics equations. *Abstr. Appl. Anal.* **2016**, *2016*, 2071926. [CrossRef]
18. Meghea, I.; Stamin, C.S. On a problem of mathematical physics equations. *Bull. Transilv. Univ. Bras. Ser. III Math. Inform. Phys.* **2018**, *11*, 169–180.
19. Meghea, I. Application of a Variant of Mountain Pass Theorem in Modeling Real Phenomena. *Mathematics* **2022**, *10*, 3476. [CrossRef]
20. Meghea, I. Applications of a perturbed linear variational principle via p-Laplacian. *UPB Sci. Bull. Ser. A* **2022**, *84*, 141–152.
21. Meghea, I. Applications for a generalization of two fundamental variational principles. *UPB Sci. Bull. Ser. A* **2020**, *82*, 57–68.
22. Meghea, I. *Ekeland Variational Principles with Generalizations and Variants;* Old City Publishing: Philadelphia, PA, USA; Éditions des Archives Contemporaines: Paris, France, 2009.
23. Burrage, K.; Hale, N.; Kay, D. An efficient FEM scheme for fractional-in-space reaction-diffusion equations. *SIAM J. Sci. Comput.* **2012**, *34*, A2145–A2172. [CrossRef]
24. Dang, J.; Hu, Q.; Xia, S.; Zhang, H. Exponential growth of solution for a reaction-diffusion equation with memory and multiple nonlinearities. *Res. Appl. Math.* **2017**, *1*, 101258. [CrossRef] [PubMed]
25. Fayolle, P.A.; Belyaev, A.G. p-Laplace diffusion for distance function estimation, optimal transport approximation, and image enhancement. *Comput. Aided Geom. Des.* **2018**, *67*, 1–20. [CrossRef]
26. Mukherjee, T.; Sreenadh, K. On Dirichlet problem for fractional p-Laplacian wirh singular non-linearity. *Adv. Nonlinear Anal.* **2019**, *8*, 52–72. [CrossRef]
27. Zhang, L.; Wang, F.; Ru, Y. Existence of nontrivial solutions for fractional differential equations with p-Laplacian. *J. Funct. Spaces* **2019**, *2019*, 3486410. [CrossRef]
28. Benedikt, J.; Girg, P.; Kotrla, L.; Takáč, P. Origin of the p-Laplacian and A. Missbach. *Electron. J. Differ. Equ.* **2018**, *2018*, 16.
29. Lafleche, L.; Salem, S. p-Laplacian Keller-Segel Equation: Fair Competition and Diffusion Dominated Cases. 2018. Available online: https://hal.archives-ouvertes.fr/hal-01883785 (accessed on 1 February 2022).
30. Cellina, A. The regularity of solutions of some variational problems, including the p-Laplace equation for $3 \leq p < 4$. *AIMS* **2018**, *38*, 4071–4085.

31. Khan, H.; Li, Y.; Sun, H.; Khan, A. Esistence of solution and Hyers-Ulam stability for a coupled system of fractional differential equations with p-Laplacian operator. *J. Nonlinear Sci. Appl.* **2017**, *10*, 5219–5229. [CrossRef]
32. Xu, X. Existence theorems for a crystal surface model involving the p-Laplace operator. *SIAM J. Math. Anal.* **2017**, *50*, 1–21. [CrossRef]
33. Akagi, G.; Matsuura, K. Nonlinear diffusion equations driven by the $p(\cdot)$-Laplacian. *Nonlinear Differ. Equ. Appl.* **2013**, *20*, 37–64. [CrossRef]
34. Gulsen, T.; Yilmaz, E. Inverse nodal problem for p-Laplacian diffusion equation with polynomoally dependent spectral parameter. *Commun. Fac. Sci. Univ. Ank. Sér. A1 Math. Stat.* **2016**, *65*, 23–36.
35. Lee, Y.S.; Chung, S.Y. Extiction and positivity of solutions of the p-Laplacian evolution equation on networks. *J. Math. Anal. Appl.* **2012**, *386*, 581–592. [CrossRef]
36. Rasouli, S.H. An ecological model with the p-Laplacian and diffusion. *Int. J. Biomath.* **2016**, *9*, 1650008. [CrossRef]
37. Yang, Y.; Deng, J. Qualitative properties of a p-Laplacian population model with delay. *Adv. Differ. Equ.* **2017**, *2017*, 13. [CrossRef]
38. Elmoataz, A.; Toutain, M.; Tenbrinck, D. On the p-Laplacian and ∞-Laplacian on graphs with applications in image and data processing. *SIAM J. Imaging Sci.* **2015**, *8*, 2412–2451. [CrossRef]
39. Gupta, S.; Kumar, D.; Singh, J. Analytical solutions of convection-diffusion problems by combining Laplace transform method and homotopy perturbation method. *Alex. Eng. J.* **2015**, *54*, 645–651. [CrossRef]
40. Liero, M.; Koprucki, T.; Fischer, A.; Scholz, R.; Glitzki, A. p-Laplace thermistor modeling of electrothermal feedback in organic semiconductors devices. *Z. Angew. Math. Phys.* **2015**, *66*, 2957–2977. [CrossRef]
41. Silva, M.A.J. On a viscoelastic plate equation with history setting and perturbation of p-Laplacian type. *IMA J. Appl. Math. Adv. Access* **2012**, *78*, 1130–1146.
42. Fučik, S.; Nečas, J.; Souček, J. *Spectral Analysis of Nonlinear Operators*; Springer: Berlin/Heidelberg, Germany; New York, NY, USA, 1973.
43. Meghea, C.; Meghea, I. *Treatise on Differential Calculus and Integral Calculus for Mathematicians, Physicists, Chemists and Engineers in Ten Volumes*; Old City Publishing: Philadelphia, PA, USA; Éditions des Archives Contemporaines: Paris, France, 2015.
44. Dinca, G.; Jebelean, P. Some existence results for a class of nonlinear equations involving a duality mapping. *Nonlinear Anal.* **2001**, *46*, 347–363. [CrossRef]
45. Lions, J.L. *Quelques Méthodes des Résolution des Problèmes Aux Limites Non Linéaires*; Dunod, Gauthier-Villard: Paris, France, 1969.
46. Vainberg, M.M. *Variational Methods for the Study of Nonlinear Operators*; Holden Day Inc.: San Francisco, CA, USA, 1964.
47. Glowinski, R.; Marocco, A. Sur l'approximation, par éléments finis d'ordre un, et la résolution, par pénalisation—Dualité, d'une classe de problèmes de Dirichlet non linéaires. *Rev. Française D'autom. Inform. Rech. Opérationnelle* **1975**, *9*, 41–76. [CrossRef]
48. Mazur, S. Über schwache Konvergenz in den Räumen (L^p). *Stud. Math.* **1933**, *4*, 128–133. [CrossRef]
49. Stein, E. *Singular Integrals and Differentiability Properties of Functions*; Princeton University Press: Princeton, NJ, USA, 1970.
50. Dinca, G.; Jebelean, P.; Mawhin, J. *Variational and Topological Methods for Dirichlet Problems with p-Laplacian*; Catholic University of Louvain: Louvain-la-Neuve, Belgium, 1999.
51. Adams, R.A. *Sobolev Spaces*; Academic Press: New York, NY, USA, 1975.
52. Jebelean, P. Classical and Generalized Solutions for p-Laplacian; Ph.D. Thesis, University of Bucharest, Bucharest, Romania, 1994.
53. Figueiredo, G. *Topics in Nonlinear Functional Analysis*; The University of Maryland: College Park, MD, USA, 1967.
54. Ambrosetti, A.; Prodi, G. *Analisi Nonlineare*; Editrice Tecnico Scientifica: Pisa, Italy, 1973.
55. Lliboutry, L. *Traité de Glaciologie*; Masson & Cie: Paris, France, 1965; Book II.
56. Pélissier, M.C. *Sur Quelques Problèmes non Linéaires en Glaciologie*; Publications Mathèmatiques d'Orsay, no. 110, U.E.R. Mathèmatique; Université Paris IX: Paris, France, 1975.
57. Lindquist, P. Stability for the solutions of div $(|\nabla u|^{p-2}\nabla u) = f$ with varying p. *J. Math. Anal. Appl.* **1987**, *127*, 93–102. [CrossRef]
58. Cuccu, F.; Emamizadeh, B.; Porru, G. Nonlinear elastic membranes involving the p-Laplacian operator. *Electron. J. Differ. Equ.* **2006**, *2006*, 1–10.
59. Cuccu, F.; Emamizadeh, B.; Porru, G. Optimization or the best eigenvalue in problems involving the p-Laplacian. *Proc. Am. Math. Soc.* **2009**, *137*, 1677–1687. [CrossRef]
60. Belloni, M.; Kawohl, B. The pseudo-p-Laplace eigenvalue problem and viscosity solutions as $p \to \infty$. *ESAIM Control Optim. Calc. Var.* **2004**, *10*, 28–52. [CrossRef]
61. Nečas, J. Sur l'alternative de Fredholm pour les opérateurs nonlinéaires avec applications aux problèmes aux limites. *Ann. Sc. Norm. Sup. Pisa* **1969**, *23*, 331–345.
62. Brezis, H. *Analyse Fonctionnelle. Théorie et Applications*; Masson: Paris, France; Milan, Italy; Barcelone, Spain; Bonn, Germany, 1992.
63. Ekeland, I. *On the variational principle. Cahiers de Mathematique de la Décision*; Université Paris: Paris, France, 1972.
64. Ekeland, I. On the variational principle. *J. Math. Anal. Appl.* **1974**, *47*, 324–353. [CrossRef]
65. Ghoussoub, N. *Duality and Perturbation Methods in Critical Point Theory*; Cambridge University Press: Cambridge, UK, 1993.
66. Costa, D.G.; Gonçalves, J.V. Critical point theory for nondifferentiable functionals and applications. *J. Math. Anal. Appl.* **1990**, *153*, 470–485. [CrossRef]
67. Chang, K.C. Variational methods for non-differentiable functionals and their applications to partial differential equations. *J. Math. Anal. Appl.* **1981**, *80*, 102–129. [CrossRef]

68. Lanchon-Ducauquois, H.; Tulita, C.; Meuris, C. *Modélisation du Transfert Thermique Dans l'He II*; Congrès Français du Thermique: Lyon, France, 2000.
69. Clarke, F.H. *Optimization and Non-Smooth Analysis*; Canadian Mathematical Society: Otawa, ON, Canada, 1983.
70. Aronsson, G. On p-hrmonic functions, convex duality and an asymptotic formula for injection mould filing. *Eur. J. Appl. Math.* **1996**, *7*, 417–437. [CrossRef]
71. Brezis, H.; Nirenberg, L. A minimization problem with critical exponent and non-zero data. *Symmetry Nat. Sc. Norm. Sup. Pisa* **1989**, *1*, 129–140.
72. Lee, C.; Folgar, F.; Tucker, C.L. Simulation of compression molding for fiber-reinforced thermosetting polymers. *Trans. ASME* **1984**, *106*, 114–125. [CrossRef]
73. Bergwall, A. A geometric evolution problem. *Q. Appl. Math.* **2002**, *60*, 37–73. [CrossRef]
74. Janfalk, U. On a minimization problem for vector fields in L^1. *Bull. Lond. Math. Soc.* **1996**, *28*, 165–176. [CrossRef]

axioms

MDPI

Article

Solutions for Some Specific Mathematical Physics Problems Issued from Modeling Real Phenomena: Part 2

Irina Meghea

Department of Mathematical Methods and Models, Faculty of Applied Sciences, University Politehnica of Bucharest, 060042 Bucharest, Romania; irina.meghea@upb.ro or i_meghea@yahoo.com; Tel.: +40-756575418

Abstract: This paper brings together methods to solve and/or characterize solutions of some problems of mathematical physics equations involving p-Laplacian and p-pseudo-Laplacian. Using the widely debated results of surjectivity or variational approaches, one may obtain or characterize weak solutions for Dirichlet or Newmann problems for these important operators. The relevance of these operators and the possibility to be involved in the modeling of an important class of real phenomena is once again revealed by their applications. The use of certain variational methods facilitates the complete solution of the problem using appropriate numerical methods and computational algorithms. Some theoretical results are involved to complete the solutions for a sequence of models issued from real phenomena drawing.

Keywords: modeling real phenomena; p-Laplacian; p-pseudo-Laplacian; surjectivity methods; variational methods; Dirichlet problem; Neumann problem

MSC: 35A01; 35A15; 35J35; 35J40; 47J30

1. Introduction

This paper is devoted to obtaining some solutions for special problems of mathematical physics equations involving p-Laplacian and p-pseudo-Laplacian for models issued from real phenomena. This is still a current topic that is very widely debated, as is proven in papers [1–4] considering the p-Laplacian where the accent falls on the applications and the importance of the models. Positive solutions for boundary value problems with p-Laplacian are obtained and discussed in [5–7].

Global weak solutions for evolution problems with logarithmic nonlinearities involving the p-pseudo-Laplacian are presented in [7–10], and those with p-Laplacian are studied in [11]. The existence of periodic solution [12], radial symmetry [13], symmetry [14], or principal eigenvalues [15] for fractional p-Laplacian, minimizers [16], and Picone type identities for p-Laplacian [17] or p-pseudo-Laplacian [18], regularity, and multiplicity results [19] represent interesting and topical issues that have important implications.

This paper is the requisite continuation of the work under the same title, part one [20]. The theoretical framework is constructed and correspondingly extended in [20] in order to understand the entire abstract background, while the next step towards the real problems is made by applying the main results to propose solutions and/or their characterizations for real phenomena models. In this work, problems for partial differential equations involving the p-Laplacian and p-pseudo-Laplacian are studied considering Dirichlet problems derived from glaciology, nonlinear elastic membrane with p-Laplace or p-pseudo-Laplace equation, vibration of a nonhomogeneous membrane fixed along the boundary, and pseudo torsion problems are solved using propositions from [20] obtained *via* surjectivity results. Fredholm alternative type results are used to solve applications for nonlinear elastic membrane with p-Laplacian and p-pseudo-Laplacian. Surjectivity to different homogeneity degrees also provides some statements which are involved here to provide the formulation of the existence of the solution for nonlinear elastic membrane for both operators, but under different conditions. Critical points and weak solutions for elliptic type equations prove existing propositions applied for real models issued from glaciology, nonlinear elastic membrane, and the pseudo torsion problem. Critical points for nondifferentiable functionals provided the appropriate frame to characterize the solution in modeling the thermal transfer, and also some of the problems mentioned above. Other results obtained through the Ekeland variational principle and some conditions of the Palais-Smale type provide solving methods for some problems from glaciology, injection mold filling, thermal transfer, or the pseudo torsion problem. Finally, the last frame, which originated in a perturbed variational principle, was provided to intervene in the study of a generalized Helle-Show flow of a power-law fluid, and also for the pseudo torsion problem. For some of the problems derived from real phenomena modeling presented in this work, the author proposed different solving methods to those reported in the paper [21]. Starting from theoretical results based on a namely version of Mountain Pass Theorem, the study [21] aimed to gain a better understanding of the passage from the high abstract frame to characterize the solution, with designing new models for special physical phenomena being the final goal. Some other applications for problems involving the p-Laplacian having the theoretical background in a perturbed variational principle have been presented by the author in [22].

For these problems that resulted from the mathematical modeling, we came up with original solving methods following the abstract frame from [20]. The novelty of this work stems from these original approaches, as it represents one of the preliminary studies for future developments to find a mathematical model (there are none available) to be applied for describing diffusion phenomena involved in micro-emulsification of disperse systems in tight connection with surface properties at the interface in self-organized systems.

This paper is organized in the following manner: the propositions or the theorems which are directly related to the discussed problems are briefly remembered, followed by the model derived from the real phenomenon considered. For any theoretical detail, the paper [20] can be consulted.

2. Surjectivity for the Operators $\lambda J_\phi - S$. Applications to Partial Differential Equations

2.1. Theoretical Results

We start this section displaying the (final) theoretical results widely presented in [20] which are directly involved in solving some types of mathematical physics problems and characterization of their solutions for a few models drawing real phenomena.

The role of surjectivity in solving problems of the following types was highlighted in [20], and one can cite recent papers such as [23] where new surjectivity (based on Ekeland variational principle) results are discussed and involved in applications for Dirichlet problems for p-Laplacian.

Statement for the Problem

$$(*)\begin{cases} -\lambda\,\Delta_p\, u = f(\cdot\,,\ u(\cdot)) + h, x \in \Omega, \lambda \in \mathbf{R} \\ u \mid \partial\Omega = 0 \end{cases}$$

Proposition 1. *Let Ω be an open bounded set of C^1class from $\mathbf{R}^N$, $N \geq 2$, $p \in (1, +\infty)$, h from $W^{-1,p'}(\Omega)$ and f: $\Omega \times \mathbf{R} \to \mathbf{R}$ a Carathéodory function with the properties*

$1^0\ f(x, -s) = -f(x, s)\ \forall s$ *from* $\mathbf{R}$, $\forall x$ *from* Ω,

$2^0\ |f(x, s)| \leq c_1|s|^{q-1} + \beta(x)\ \forall s$ *from* $\mathbf{R}$, $\forall x$ *from* $\Omega \setminus A$, $\mu(A) = 0$,

where $c_1 \geq 0$, $q \in (1, p)$, $\beta \in L^{q'}(\Omega), \frac{1}{q} + \frac{1}{q'} = 1$.

Then, for any $\lambda \neq 0$, the problem $(*)$ has solution in $W_0^{1,p}(\Omega)$ in the sense of $W^{-1,p'}(\Omega)$.

Proposition 2. *Let Ω be an open bounded set of C^1 class from $\mathbf{R}^N$, $N \geq 2$, $p \in (1, +\infty)$, h from $W^{-1,p'}(\Omega)$ and $f : \Omega \times \mathbf{R} \to \mathbf{R}$ Carathéodory function having the properties*

1^0 $f(x, -s) = -f(x, s)$ $\forall x$ *from* Ω, $\forall s$ *from* $\mathbf{R}$,
2^0 $| f(x, s) | \leq c_1 |s|^{p-1} + \beta(x)$ $\forall s$ *from* $\mathbf{R}$, $\forall x$ *from* $\Omega \setminus A$, $\mu(A) = 0$,

where $c_1 \geq 0$, $\beta \in L^{p'}(\Omega)$, $\frac{1}{p} + \frac{1}{p'} = 1$.

Finally, let $i : W_0^{1,p}(\Omega) \to L^p(\Omega)$ *be linear compact embedding. Then, for any* λ, *if*

$$|\lambda| > c_1 \lambda_1^{-1},\ \lambda_1 := \inf\left\{ \frac{||u||_{1,p}^p}{||i(u)||_{0,p}^p} : u \in W_0^{1,p}(\Omega)\backslash\{0\} \right\},$$

the problem $(*)$ *has solution in* $W_0^{1,p}(\Omega)$ *in the sense of* $W^{-1,p'}(\Omega)$.

Statement for the Problem

$$(**)\begin{cases} -\lambda\,\Delta_p^s u = f(\cdot, u(\cdot)) + h,\ x \in \Omega,\ \lambda \in \mathbf{R} \\ u \mid \partial\Omega = 0 \end{cases}$$

Proposition 3. *Let Ω be an open bounded of C^1 class set from $\mathbf{R}^N$, $N \geq 2$, $p \in [2, +\infty)$, h from $W^{-1,p'}(\Omega)$ and $f : \Omega \times \mathbf{R} \to \mathbf{R}$ Carathéodory function with the properties*

1^0 $f(x, -s) = -f(x, s)$ $\forall x$ *from* Ω, $\forall s$ *from* $\mathbf{R}$,
2^0 $| f(x, s) | \leq c_1 |s|^{q-1} + \beta(x)$ $\forall s$ *from* $\mathbf{R}$, $\forall x$ *from* $\Omega \setminus A$, $\mu(A) = 0$,

where $c_1 \geq 0$, $q \in (1, p)$, $\beta \in L^{q'}(\Omega)$, $\frac{1}{q} + \frac{1}{q'} = 1$.

Then, for any $\lambda \neq 0$, *the problem* $(**)$ *has solution in* $W_0^{1,p}(\Omega)$ *in the sense of* $W^{-1,p'}(\Omega)$.

Proposition 4. *Let Ω be an open bounded set of C^1class from $\mathbf{R}^N$, $N \geq 2$, $p \in [2, +\infty)$, h from $W^{-1,p'}(\Omega)$ and $f : \Omega \times \mathbf{R} \to \mathbf{R}$ Carathéodory function having the properties*

1^0 $f(x, -s) = -f(x, s)$ $\forall x$ *from* Ω, $\forall s$ *from* $\mathbf{R}$,
2^0 $|f(x, s)| \leq c_1 |s|^{p-1} + \beta(x)$ $\forall s$ *from* $\mathbf{R}$, $\forall x$ *from* $\Omega \setminus A$, $\mu(A) = 0$,

where $c_1 \geq 0$, $\beta \in L^{p'}(\Omega)$, $\frac{1}{p} + \frac{1}{p'} = 1$.

Finally, let $i : W_0^{1,p}(\Omega) \to L^p(\Omega)$ *be linear compact embedding. Then, for any* λ, *if*

$$|\lambda| > c_1 \lambda_1^{-1},\ \lambda_1 := \inf\left\{ \frac{\| u \|_{1,p}^p}{||i(u)||_{0,p}^p} : u \in W_0^{1,p}(\Omega)\backslash\{0\} \right\},$$

the problem $(**)$ *has solution in* $W_0^{1,p}(\Omega)$ *in the sense of* $W^{-1,p'}(\Omega)$.

2.2. *Applications in Solving some Real Models*

Apply propositions 1, 2, 3, and 4 to solve problems issued from real phenomena mo-deling.

2.2.1. Application in Glaciology

Elliptic partial differential equations with the principal part $\Delta_p u$ are applied in physics, for instance, the description of phenomena in glaciology as the sliding of glaciers, see [24–26]. In [27], a Dirichlet problem is formulated:

$$-\ \Delta_p u = 1 \mathrm{on} \Omega,$$

$$u = \varphi \text{ on } \partial\Omega,$$

with $p = 1+\frac{1}{g}$, g being the Glen exponent, where $0 < g < +\infty$, hence $0 < p < +\infty$ and, for a real glacier, $g \geq 3$, and usually taken, $g = 3$, so $p = \frac{4}{3}$. Replacing u by $v = u - \varphi$ on the boundary of Ω in the sense of the trace and $u \equiv v$ on the interior of Ω, one can apply Proposition 1 in the particular case $f \equiv 0$, $h \equiv 1$, $\lambda = 1$ (hence $\lambda \neq 0$) to give another proof for the existence of the solution of the above problem.

Novel and interesting applications, completely solved *via* special variational and numerical methods, can be consulted in [28].

2.2.2. Nonlinear Elastic Membrane

I. To describe a nonlinear elastic membrane under the load f, we can use the mathematical model:

$$-\Delta_p u = f \text{on} \Omega$$
$$u = 0 \text{ on } \partial\Omega.$$

The solution u stands for the deformation of the membrane from the rest position [29,30]. The nonlinearity of the p-Laplacian is often used to reflect the impact of non-ideal material to the usual vibrating homogeneous elastic membrane modeled by Laplace operator. In this case, the deformation energy is given by $\int_\Omega |\nabla u|^{\mathrm{P}} dx$. Therefore, the greatest lower bound on $W_0^{1,p}(\Omega)\backslash\{0\}$, λ_1, of the Rayleigh quotients from the above Proposition 2 is usually referred to as the principal frequency of the vibrating nonlinear elastic membrane.

Consider the problem:

$$-\lambda\Delta_p u = |u|^{p-2}u, \ x \in \Omega, \ \lambda \in \mathbf{R}$$
$$u \mid \partial\Omega = 0.$$

This can be considered as $(*)$ with $f(\cdot, u(\cdot)) = |u|^{p-2}u$ and $h \equiv 0$. f having this form fulfills the two conditions – properties of Carathéodory function from Proposition 2 taking $c_1 = 1$ and $\beta \equiv 0$ in 2^0. Therefore, for any λ, e.g., $|\lambda| \geq \lambda_1^{-1}$, the last problem has a solution in $W_0^{1,p}(\Omega)$ in the sense of $W^{-1,p'}(\Omega)$.

II. In the paper [31], a model was proposed for the vibration of a nonhomogeneous membrane which is fixed along the boundary. Several materials (with different densities) were investigated there, following the location of these materials inside Ω by studying the first mode in the vibration of the membrane. Ω is a bounded smooth domain in $\mathbf{R}^N$ and g is a Lebesgue measurable function verifying the condition $0 \leq g(x) \leq H$, $\forall x \in \Omega$, where H is a positive constant, $g \not\equiv 0$ and H. g can be replaced by any Lebesgue measurable function, equal to it almost everywhere. Consider the eigenvalue Dirichlet problem:

$$-\Delta_p u = \lambda g(x)|u|^{p-1}u, \ x \in \Omega,$$
$$u \mid \partial\Omega = 0.$$

To superpose our theory, it is sufficient to replace λ by $\frac{1}{\lambda}$ since this is made with the equation: $-\lambda\Delta_p u = f(\cdot, u(\cdot)) + h(\cdot)$. Take in Proposition 2: $f(x, s) = g(x)|s|^{p-1}$, so $|f(x,s)| = |g(x)||s|^{p-1} \leq H|s|^{p-1}$, hence 2^0 is fulfilled with $h \equiv 0$, $c_1 = H$, and, for any λ with $\left|\frac{1}{\lambda}\right| \geq H\lambda_1^{-1}$, equivalent $|\lambda| \leq \frac{\lambda_1}{H}$, $\lambda_1 := \inf\left\{\frac{\|u\|_{1,p}^p}{\|i(u)\|_{0,p}^p} : u \in W_0^{1,p}(\Omega)\backslash\{0\}\right\}$, the above problem has a solution in $W_0^{1,p}(\Omega)$ in the sense of $W^{-1,p'}(\Omega)$. in the sense of $W^{-1,p'}(\Omega)$.

III. Using Proposition 2, we can propose a proof for the existence of the solution of the nonlinear problem of elastic membrane under the load $f + h$, in the general case when f is a Carathéodory function which fulfills the conditions 1^0 and 2^0, h from $W^{-1,p'}(\Omega)$ and λ such that

$$|\lambda| > c_1\lambda_1^{-1},\ \lambda_1 := \inf\left\{ \frac{\left\|u\right\|_{1,p}^{p}}{\left\|i(u)\right\|_{0,p}^{p}} : u \in W_0^{1,p}(\Omega)\backslash\{0\} \right\}$$

from the cited result.

The nonlinear elastic membrane treated with variational methods is another actual research field, as the papers [32–35] prove.

2.2.3. The Pseudo Torsion Problem

In [36], we found the pseudo torsion problem:

$$-\Delta_p^s u = 1$$

$$u \mid \partial\Omega = 0$$

for which we applied Proposition 3 in the particular case $f \equiv 0, h \equiv 1, \lambda = 1$ (hence $\lambda \neq 0$) to provide another proof for the existence of the solution of the above problem.

The torsion problem has been treated as a Dirichlet eigenvalue problem in [37], with the bounded reaction (free term of the fractional differential equation) involved in a Dirichlet problem in [38], and the asymptotic behavior for solutions of some torsional-creep type problems is studied in [39].

2.2.4. Nonlinear Elastic Membrane with p-Pseudo-Laplacian

I. In [40], the expression $\int_\Omega \sum_{i=1}^{n} \left|\frac{\partial u}{\partial x_i}\right|^p dx$ was proposed for the deformation energy of the membrane and was woven out of elastic strings in a rectangular form. The phenomenon can be modelled with a Dirichlet problem for the p-pseudo-Laplacian:

$$-\lambda\Delta_p^s u = |u|^{p-2} u,\ x \in \Omega,\ \lambda \in \mathbf{R}$$

$$u \mid \partial\Omega = 0.$$

Under the above notation, $\frac{1}{\lambda}$ is the eigenvalue for such a problem. One can apply Proposition 4, taking $f(\cdot, u(\cdot)) = |u|^{p-2}u$, $h \equiv 0$ and with $c_1 = 1$ and $\beta \equiv 0$ in 2^0, to obtain that the last exposed problem has a solution in $W_0^{1,p}(\Omega)$ in the sense of $W^{-1,p'}(\Omega)$, for any λ, with

$$\left|\lambda\right| > \lambda_1^{-1},\ \lambda_1 := \inf\left\{ \frac{\left\|u\right\|_{1,p}^{p}}{\left\|i(u)\right\|_{0,p}^{p}} : u \in W_0^{1,p}(\Omega)\backslash\{0\} \right\}.$$

II. Take in **I** the load $f + h$, in the general case when f is a Carathéodory function, which fulfills the conditions 1^0 and 2^0 from Proposition 4, h from $W^{-1,p'}(\Omega)$ and λ e.g., $|\lambda| > c_1\lambda_1^{-1}$,

$$\lambda_1 := \inf\left\{ \frac{\left\|u\right\|_{1,p}^{p}}{\left\|i(u)\right\|_{0,p}^{p}} : u \in W_0^{1,p}(\Omega)\backslash\{0\} \right\}$$

from the cited result.

Nonlinear elastic membrane is one of the wide subjects which also benefits the eigenvalues and eigenfunctions. An extended theoretical study exploited to model such a kind of phenomenon is presented in [41] by the extension through the numerical simulation.

3. Applications for Results of the Fredholm Alternative Type for Operators $\lambda J_\phi - S$

3.1. Results

Proposition 5. *Let p be from* $(1, +\infty)$ *and* $\lambda \neq 0$. *If*

$$\lambda(-\Delta_p u) = |u|^{p-2} u$$

does not have a nonzero solution in $W_0^{1,p}(\Omega)$, *then, for any h from* $W^{-1,p'}(\Omega)$, *the equation*

$$\lambda(-\Delta_p u) = |u|^{p-2} u + h$$

has a solution in $W_0^{1,p}(\Omega)$ *in the sense of* $W^{-1,p'}(\Omega)$.

Proposition 6. *In the statement of Proposition 5, if* $p \in [2, +\infty)$, *then* $-\Delta_p$ *can be replaced by* $-\Delta_p^s$.

Proposition 7. *Let p be from* $(1, +\infty)$ *and* $\lambda \neq 0$. *If*

$$\lambda(-\Delta_p u) = N_f u$$

has no nonzero solution in $W_0^{1,p}(\Omega)$ *in the sense of* $W^{-1,p'}(\Omega)$, *then, for any h from* $W^{-1,p'}(\Omega)$, *the equation:*

$$\lambda(-\Delta_p u) = f(\cdot, u(\cdot)) + h, \ x \in \Omega$$

has a solution in $W_0^{1,p}(\Omega)$ *in the sense of* $W^{-1,p'}(\Omega)$.

Statements of the Fredholm alternative type represent an important theoretical instrument to solve fractional evolution problems having a certain kind of boundary conditions as the paper [42] provides, and they can also be involved in optimization and evaluation of the process performance, as the recent work [43] proves.

3.2. Applications for Real Phenomena

3.2.1. Nonlinear Elastic Membrane

Take the nonlinear elastic membrane under the load *f*, for which the mathematical model can be considered:

$$-\Delta_p u = f \text{on} \Omega$$

$$u = 0 \text{ on } \partial\Omega.$$

In the case of the homogeneous problem:

$$-\lambda \Delta_p u = |u|^{p-2} u, \ x \in \Omega, \ \lambda \in \mathbf{R}$$

$$u \,|\, \partial\Omega = 0.$$

has no nonzero solution. By applying Proposition 5, for any h from $W^{-1,p'}(\Omega)$, the pro-blem:

$$\lambda(-\Delta_p u) = |u|^{p-2} u + h, \ x \in \Omega, \ \lambda \in \mathbf{R}$$

$$u \,|\, \partial\Omega = 0.$$

has a solution in the sense of $W^{-1,p'}(\Omega)$.

Remark. For the load *f* being a Carathéodory function, one can obtain a similar result using Proposition 7.

3.2.2. Nonlinear Elastic Membrane with p-Pseudo-Laplacian

When the membrane is woven out of elastic strings in a rectangular form, then the phenomenon can be modelled with a Dirichlet problem for the p-pseudo-Laplacian and the load f has another form as in Section 2.2.4, and if the homogeneous problem:

$$-\lambda\, \Delta_p^s u = |u|^{p-2}u,\ x \in \Omega,\ \lambda \in \mathbf{R}$$

$$u \mid \partial\Omega = 0.$$

has no nonzero solution, therefore, applying Proposition 6 for $p \in [2, +\infty)$,

$$-\lambda\, \Delta_p^s u = |u|^{p-2}u + h,\ x \in \Omega,\ \lambda \in \mathbf{R}$$

$$u \mid \partial\Omega = 0$$

has a solution in the sense of $W^{-1,p'}(\Omega)$, for any h from $W^{-1,p'}(\Omega)$.

4. Problems Solved Using Surjectivity to Different Homogeneity Degrees

4.1. Theoretical Results

Proposition 8. *Under the above conditions, for any $\lambda \neq 0$ and for any h from $W^{-1,p'}(\Omega)$, there exists u_0 in $W_0^{1,p}(\Omega)$ such that*

$$\lambda(-\Delta_p)u_0 = (i' \text{ o } N \text{ o } i)u_0 + h$$

respectively,

$$\lambda(-\Delta_p^s)u_0 = (i' \text{ o } N \text{ o } i)u_0 + h.$$

Proposition 9. *Under the above conditions, for any $\lambda \neq 0$ and for any h in $W^{-1,p'}(\Omega)$, there exists u_0 in $W_0^{1,p}(\Omega)$ such that*

$$\lambda(-\Delta_p)u_0 = \left(i' \text{ o } N_f \text{ o } i\right)u_0 + h$$

respectively,

$$\lambda(-\Delta_p^s)u_0 = \left(i' \text{ o } N_f \text{ o } i\right)u_0 + h.$$

The association of homogeneity and fractional problems remains a very current topic, as the rich development of results from the paper [44] demonstrates.

4.2. Applications to Real Phenomena Models

4.2.1. Nonlinear Elastic Membrane

I. Use Proposition 8 to prove the existence of the solution for the problem of a nonlinear elastic membrane under the load $f + h$, where we can use the mathematical model:

$$\lambda(-\Delta_p u) = |u|^{q-2}\, u + h \text{on} \Omega$$

$$u = 0 \text{ on } \partial\,\Omega,$$

with $q \in (1, p), \frac{1}{q} + \frac{1}{q'} = 1$, $\forall\lambda \neq 0$ and $\forall h$ in $W^{-1,p'}(\Omega)$.

II. Similarly, for the problem:

$$\lambda(-\Delta_p)u = f + h \text{on} \Omega$$

$$u = 0 \text{ on } \partial\Omega,$$

with $f : \Omega \times \mathbf{R} \to \mathbf{R}$ an odd Carathéodory function and $(q - 1)$ - homogeneous in the second variable, which verifies the growth condition:

$$|f(x,s)| \le c_1|s|^{q-1} + \beta(x)\forall s \text{ in } \mathbf{R},\ \forall x \text{ in } \Omega \backslash A, \mu(A) = 0,$$

where $c_1 \ge 0$, $\beta \in L^{q'}(\Omega)$ by applying Proposition 9.

4.2.2. Nonlinear Elastic Membrane with p-Pseudo-Laplacian

I. Demonstrate the existence of the solution from $W_0^{1,p}(\Omega)$ in the sense of $W^{-1,p'}(\Omega)$ for the problem:

$$\lambda(-\Delta_p^s u) = |u|^{q-2}u + h,\ x \in \Omega,\ \lambda \in \mathbf{R},$$
$$u \mid \partial\Omega = 0,$$

with $q \in (1,p), \frac{1}{q} + \frac{1}{q'} = 1, \lambda \neq 0$ and h in $W^{-1,p'}(\Omega)$ by applying Proposition 8.

II. For a similar problem:

$$\lambda(-\Delta_p^s u) = f + h,\ x \in \Omega,\ \lambda \in \mathbf{R},$$
$$u \mid \partial\Omega = 0,$$

with $f : \Omega \times \mathbf{R} \to \mathbf{R}$ an odd Carathéodory function and $(q - 1)$ - homogeneous in the second variable, which verifies the growth condition:

$$|f(x,s)| \le c_1|s|^{q-1} + \beta(x)\forall s \text{ in } \mathbf{R},\ \forall x \text{ in } \Omega \backslash A, \mu(A) = 0,$$

where $c_1 \ge 0$, $\beta \in L^{q'}(\Omega)$ and we have the existence of the solution by applying Proposition 9.

5. Problems Having Weak Solutions Starting from Ekeland Variational Principle

There are three groups of results. The first two are based on critical point notion and the last one, which is of a different kind, will be involved in the construction of the solutions of some mathematical physics problems. Many methods use critical points theory to find or characterize solutions for fractional boundary problems as in [45]. Both highly theoretical and extremely applicative approaches involving critical points and fractional calculus were performed in [46] to draw solutions for several real models and obtain the concrete solution *via* specific numerical methods.

5.1. Critical Points and Weak Solutions for Elliptic Type Equations — Applications

5.1.1. Theoretical Support

Let Ω be an open bounded nonempty set in $\mathbf{R}^N$ and let $f : \Omega \times \mathbf{R} \to \mathbf{R}$ be a Carathéodory function with the growth condition:

$$| f(x, s)| \le c|s|^{p-1} + b(x), \tag{1}$$

where $c > 0$, $2 \le p \le \frac{2N}{N-2}$ when $N \ge 3$ and $2 \le p < +\infty$ when $N = 1, 2$, and where $b \in L^q(\Omega)$,

$$\frac{1}{p} + \frac{1}{q} = 1.$$

Consider the problems:

$$(*)\begin{cases} -\Delta_p u = f(x,u),\ x \in \Omega \\ u = 0 \text{ on } \partial\Omega, \end{cases}$$

and

$$(**)\begin{cases} -\Delta_p^s u = f(x,u),\ x \in \Omega \\ u = 0 \text{ on } \partial\Omega. \end{cases}$$

Proposition 10. *Let Ω be an open bounded of C^1 class set in $\mathbf{R}^N$, $N \geq 3$, $f : \Omega \times \mathbf{R} \to \mathbf{R}$ a Carathéodory function and u_1, u_2 from $W_0^{1,p}(\Omega)$ bounded weak subsolution and weak supersolution of $(*)$, respectively, with $u_1(x) \leq u_2(x)$ a.e. on Ω. Suppose that f verifies* (1) *and there is $\rho > 0$ such that the function g: $g(x, s) = f(x, s) + \rho s$ is strictly increasing in s on* $[\inf u_1(\Omega), \sup u_2(\Omega)]$. *Then there is a weak solution $\overline{u}$ of $(*)$ in $W_0^{1,p}(\Omega)$ with the property*

$$u_1(x) \leq \overline{u}(x) \leq u_2(x) \text{ a.e.on } \Omega$$

Proposition 11. *Let Ω be an open bounded of C^1 class set in $\mathbf{R}^N$, $N \geq 3$ and $f : \Omega \times \mathbf{R} \to \mathbf{R}$ a Carathéodory function and u_1, u_2 from $W_0^{1,p}(\Omega)$ bounded weak subsolution and weak supersolution of $(**)$, respectively, with $u_1(x) \leq u_2(x)$ a.e. on Ω. Suppose that f verifies* (1) *and there is $\rho > 0$ such that the function g: $g(x, s) = f(x, s) + \rho s$ is strictly increasing in s on* $[\inf u_1(\Omega), \sup u_2(\Omega)]$. *Additionally, there is a weak solution $\overline{u}$ of $(**)$ in $W_0^{1,p}(\Omega)$ with the property:*

$$u_1(x) \leq \overline{u}(x) \leq u_2(x) \text{ a.e.on } \Omega.$$

5.1.2. Applications to Real Phenomena

I. *Application in Glaciology*

Consider once again the problem presented in Section 2.2.1:

$$-\ \Delta_p u = 1 \text{ on } \Omega,$$

$$u = 0 \text{ on } \partial\Omega,$$

and remark that we can characterize the weak solution for this using Proposition 10. Observe that all the conditions from the cited result are fulfilled here by combining it, for instance, with the above example.

II. *Nonlinear Elastic Membrane*

Take once again the problem describing a nonlinear elastic membrane under the load f, for which we use the mathematical model:

$$-\ \Delta_p u = f \text{ on } \Omega$$

$$u = 0 \text{ on } \partial\Omega.$$

When the free term of the equation fulfills the conditions from Proposition 10, one obtains a characterization of the solution of the considered problem.

III. *The Pseudo Torsion Problem*

Consider once again the pseudo torsion problem discussed in Section 2.2.3:

$$-\ \Delta_p^s u = 1 \text{ on } \Omega,$$

$$u \mid \partial\Omega = 0.$$

By applying Proposition 11, one obtains a characterization of the weak solution of this (remark that the conditions from the cited result are fulfilled combining, for instance, with the above example).

IV. *Nonlinear Elastic Membrane with p-Pseudo-Laplacian*

When the phenomenon can be modelled with a Dirichlet problem for the p-pseudo-Laplacian:

$$-\Delta_p^s u = |u|^{p-2}u,\ x \in \Omega,$$

$$u \mid \partial\Omega = 0,$$

by applying Proposition 11, one gives a characterization of the solution for the above pro-blem.

Furthermore, the right-hand term f of the last equation is as in Proposition 11, then one obtains a more general characterization of the solution of such a problem.

5.2. *Applications of Critical Points for Nondifferentiable Functionals*

5.2.1. Theoretical Results

Let Ω be a bounded domain of $\mathbf{R}^N$ with the smooth boundary $\partial\Omega$ (topological boundary). Consider the nonlinear boundary value problems (∗) and (∗∗) from Section 5.1.2 above, where $f : \Omega \times \mathbf{R} \to \mathbf{R}$ is a measurable function with *subcritical growth*, i.e.,

$$\text{(I) } |f(x, s)| \leq a + b|s|^{\sigma} \ \forall s \in \mathbf{R}, x \in \Omega \ a.e.,$$

where $a, b > 0$, $0 \leq \sigma < \frac{N+2}{N-2}$ for $N > 2$ and $\sigma \in [0, +\infty)$ for $N = 1$ or $N = 2$.

Set:

$$\underline{f}(x, t) = \underline{\lim}_{s \to t} f(x, s), \overline{f}(x, t) = \overline{\lim}_{s \to t} f(x, s)$$

Suppose

$$\text{(II)} \underline{f}, \overline{f} : \Omega \times \mathbf{R} \to \mathbf{R} \text{ are measurable with respect to } x.$$

Associate to (∗) the locally Lipschitz functional Φ: $X \to \mathbf{R}$,

$$\Phi(u) = \frac{1}{p}||u||_{1,p}^{p} - \int_{\Omega} F(x,u)\, dx,\ u \in X,$$

and associate to (∗∗)

$$\Phi(u) = \frac{1}{p}\| u \|_{1,p}^{p} - \int_{\Omega} F(x,u)\, dx,\ u \in X,$$

where $F(x, s) = \int_0^s f(x,t)dx$.

Proposition 12. *If* (I) *and* (II) *are verified, every critical point of* Φ *is a solution for* (∗) *and* (∗∗), *respectively*.

5.2.2. Applications — Real Phenomena Modeling

I. We propose here an immediate application to characterize the solution of the modeling given in [47] for thermal transfer. Among cryogenic fluids used in industrial or laboratory applications, helium II offers remarkable properties. However, its behavior, both mechanical and thermal, appears particularly complex. Regarding the heat transfer at the heart of this fluid and through the interface with a solid, the two phenomenological laws have been used in [47] in order to obtain a mathematical model which should make it possible to optimally ensure the desired temperature in the problems associated with cooling by helium II; this goal is particularly crucial for multifilamentary superconductors.

The mathematical model proposed in the last cited work aims to determine u: $\Omega \to (0, c)$ (the value of c is experimentally obtained as 2.4844×10^{-3}) such that:

$$- \Delta_p u = r \text{ on } \Omega,$$

where r is a source term for a given $p \geq 1$, and the second time the value $p = \frac{4}{3}$ is established there, together with a boundary condition of Dirichlet type $u = \varphi$ on $\partial\Omega$ in the sense of the trace. If $\varphi \equiv 0$, one can replace u by $v = u - \varphi$. When the conditions from Proposition 12 are fulfilled, conclude that one can characterize the solution of this problem to be a critical point for the corresponding Φ functional.

II. One can give characterizations of the solutions using this kind of definition for the Dirichlet problems issued from the already-presented problems of the movement of the glacier, nonlinear elastic membrane, pseudo torsion problem, or nonlinear elastic membrane with p-pseudo-Laplacian.

5.3. Other Solutions Starting from Ekeland Principle

5.3.1. Theoretical Results

Definition 1. u from $W^{2,p}(\Omega)$, $p > 1$ is *solution* of $(*)$ and $(**)$, respectively, from this section if $Bu = 0$ on $\partial\Omega$ in the sense of trace (meaning introduced above) and

$$-\Delta_p u(x) \in \left[\underline{f}(x, u(x)), \overline{f}(x, u(x))\right] \text{ in } \Omega \text{ a.e.} \tag{2}$$

and

$$-\Delta_p^s u(x) \in \left[\underline{f}(x, u(x)), \overline{f}(x, u(x))\right] \text{ in } \Omega \text{ a.e.} \tag{3}$$

respectively.

Proposition 13. *Nonlinear Neumann problems*

$$(N)\begin{cases} -\Delta_p u = g(u) + h(x), x \in \Omega \\ Bu = 0 \text{ on } \partial\Omega, \end{cases}$$

and

$$(N')\begin{cases} -\Delta_p^s u = g(u) + h(x), x \in \Omega \\ Bu = 0 \text{ on } \partial\Omega, \end{cases}$$

respectively, with the conditions

(III) g: $\mathbf{R} \to \mathbf{R}$ *bounded measurable T-periodic,*

$$\int_0^T g(s)ds = 0 \textit{ and}$$

(IV) h *bounded measurable,*

$$\int_\Omega h dx = 0,$$

have a solution in $W^{1,p}(\Omega)$ *in the sense of* (2) and (3) respectively.

5.3.2. Related Applications

I. We can apply Proposition 13 with $g \equiv 1$ and $h \equiv 0$ to prove that there exists a solution for the velocity problem under the assumption of solid friction, see [26],

$$-\Delta_p u = \text{sgn } u \text{ on } \Omega,$$

$$|\nabla u|^{p-2}\frac{\partial u}{\partial n} = \begin{cases} 0, \text{ on } \Gamma_0 \\ -f, \text{ on } \Gamma_1 \end{cases},$$

where $p = 1 + \frac{1}{n}$, $1 < p < 2$, u in $W^{2,p}(\Omega)$.

This problem appears when the flow of glaciers is studied [26], i.e., to determine the velocity under the Weertman hypothesis:

$$-\Delta_p u = \text{sgn } u \text{ on } \Omega,$$

$$|\nabla u|^{p-2}\frac{\partial u}{\partial n} = 0 \text{ on } \Gamma_0,$$

$$|\nabla u|^{p-2}\frac{\partial u}{\partial n}+c_1|u|^{\pi-2}\text{u}=0 \text{ on } \Gamma_1,$$

where $p = 1 + \frac{1}{n}$ and $\pi = 1 + \frac{2}{n+1}$, $c_1 > 0$ is a constant, and n is the exponent from the Glen law.

II. Involve Proposition 13 to give another solution for the problem studied in [48]. According to [42], the physical problem is as follows: the polymer is injected, over a period of time, $t_0 < t < t_1$ at some point $x_1 \in \Omega$. It is not necessary to have the domain Ω simply connected. Some notations: Ω_t = the part of Ω which is filled by fluid at time t; φ = pressure; v = fluid velocity (averaged over $-h \le z \le h$); $\Gamma_0 = \partial\Omega_t \cap \Omega$, and $\Gamma_1 = \partial\Omega_t \cap \partial\Omega$. Γ_0 is the flow front. It is assumed that $\partial\Omega$ is solid (except for air vents). The equation for φ is:

$$\Delta_p\varphi = 0 \text{ on } \Omega_t \setminus \{x_1\},$$

where $p = \frac{1}{n} + 1$, n is a material constant. Further, φ = constant (chosen 0) on Γ_0 and $\frac{\partial\varphi}{\partial n} = 0$ on Γ_1. It follows that the fluid front Γ_0 meets $\partial\Omega$ at right angles (provided that φ is smooth up to the boundary and $\nabla\varphi \neq 0$). Also note that φ must have a singularity at x_1. In this approach, the development with time of the domain Ω_t filled by fluid is controlled by φ, which is determined from an elliptic partial differential equation. Note that, in this physically oriented description, all considered curves, functions, and vector fields are assumed "smooth", such that each of the crucial expressions has a well-defined pointwise meaning. Following [48], the mathematical problem means to obtain the solution φ of the instantaneous flow problem which can be obtained as the solution φ^* of a convex extremum problem by an appropriate and rather obvious choice of that problem. Taking $g \equiv 1$ and $h \equiv 0$, Ω_t instead of Ω in (N), we are placed under the conditions of Proposition 13 and give, *via* this result, another proof for the existence of the solution for the mentioned problem.

III. We can add here the example of the solution of the modeling given in [47] for thermal transfer described at Section 5.2.2 with the same equation under Neumann boundary conditions (flux imposed): $|\nabla u|^{p-2}\frac{\partial u}{\partial n} = \psi$ on $\partial\Omega$. Proposition 13 establishes the existence of the solution.

IV. Consider the pseudo torsion problem:

$$-\Delta_p^s u = \text{sgn}\, u \text{ on } \Omega,$$
$$\left.\frac{\partial u}{\partial n}\right|_{\partial\Omega} = 0$$

for which we applied Proposition 13 in order to establish an existence result.

6. Weak Solutions Using a Perturbed Variational Principle

6.1. Theoretical Results

Let Ω be an open bounded set of C^1 class in $\mathbf{R}^N$, $N \ge 3$. Consider the problems $(*)$ and $(**)$ from Section 5.1.1, where $f : \Omega \times \mathbf{R} \to \mathbf{R}$ is a Carathéodory function with the growth condition

$$|f\ (x,\ s)| \le c|s|^{p-1} + b(x), c > 0,\ 2 \le p \le \frac{2N}{N-2},\ b \in L^{p\prime}(\Omega), \frac{1}{p} + \frac{1}{p\prime} = 1.$$

The functionals φ: $W_0^{1,p}(\Omega) \to \mathbf{R}$,

$$\varphi(u) = \int_\Omega \left[\frac{1}{p}\left(|u|^p + \sum_{i=1}^N \left|\frac{\partial u}{\partial x_i}\right|^p\right) - F(x, u(x))\right] dx$$

and

$$\varphi(u) = \int_{\Omega} \left(\frac{1}{p} \sum_{i=1}^{N} \left| \frac{\partial u \partial}{x_i} \right|^p - F(x, u(x)) \right) dx,$$

with $F(x, s) : = \int_0^s f(x,t)\, dt$, are of Fréchet C^1 class and their critical points are the weak solutions of the problems (∗) and (∗∗), respectively.

Problem (∗). Let λ_1 be the first eigenvalue of $-\Delta_p$ in $W_0^{1,p}(\Omega)$ with a homogeneous boun-dary condition. We have (see, for instance, in the Section 2)

$$\lambda_1 = \inf\left\{ \frac{||u||_{1,p}^p}{||i(u)||_{0,p}^p} : u \in W_0^{1,p}(\Omega)\backslash\{0\} \right\} \text{ (the Rayleigh-Ritz quotient)}.$$

Proposition 14. *Under the above assumptions and, in addition, the growth condition*

$$F(x,\ s) \leq c_1 \frac{s^p}{p} + \alpha(x)s,$$

with $0 < c_1 < \lambda_1$, $\alpha \in L^{q'}(\Omega)$ *for some* $2 \leq q \leq \frac{2N}{N-2}$ *and* $f\ (x, -s) = -f\ (x, s)$, $\forall x$ *from* Ω, *the following assertions hold*:

(*i*) *The set of functions h from* $W^{-1,p'}(\Omega)$, *having the property that the functional* φ_h: $W_0^{1,p}(\Omega) \to \mathbf{R}$,

$$\varphi_h(u) = \frac{1}{p} \left|\left|u\right|\right|_p^p - \int_{\Omega} (F(x,u(x)) + h(u(x)))\, dx$$

has in only one point an attained minimum, includes a G_δ *set everywhere dense;*

(*ii*) *The set of functions h from* $W^{-1,p'}(\Omega)$, *having the property*

$$\text{the problem} \begin{cases} -\Delta_p u = f(x,u) + h(u) \text{ in } \Omega \\ u = 0 \text{ on } \partial\Omega \end{cases} \text{has solutions,}$$

includes a G_δ *set everywhere dense;*

(*iii*) *Moreover, if* $s \to f\ (x, s)$ *is increasing, then the set of functions h from* $W^{-1,p'}(\Omega)$, having *the property*

$$\text{the problem} \begin{cases} -\Delta_p u = f(x,u) + h(u) \ in\ \Omega \\ u = 0\ on\ \partial\Omega \end{cases} \text{has a unique solution,}$$

includes a G_δ *set everywhere dense.*

Problem (∗∗). Let λ_1 be the first eigenvalue of $-\Delta_p^s$ in $W_0^{1,p}(\Omega)$ with a homogeneous boundary condition. We have (see in Section 2)

$$\lambda_1 = \inf\left\{ \frac{\| u \|_{1,p}^p}{||i(u)||_{0,p}^p} : u \in W_0^{1,p}(\Omega)\backslash\{0\} \right\} \text{ (the Rayleigh-Ritz quotient)}.$$

Proposition 15. *Under the above assumptions and, in addition, the growth condition*

$$F(x,\ s) \leq c_1 \frac{s^p}{p} + \alpha(x)s,$$

with $0 < c_1 < \lambda_1$, $\alpha \in L^{q'}(\Omega)$ *for some* $2 \leq q \leq \frac{2N}{N-2}$ *and* $f\ (x, -s) = -f\ (x, s)$, $\forall x$ *from* Ω, *the following assertions hold.*

(i) The set of functions h from $W^{-1,p'}(\Omega)$*, having the property that the functional* φ_h: $W_0^{1,p}(\Omega) \to \mathbf{R}$,

$$\varphi_h(u) = \frac{1}{p}\|u\|_p^p - \int_\Omega (F(x,u(x)) + h(u(x)))\, dx$$

has in only one point an attained minimum, includes a G_δ *set everywhere dense;*

(ii) The set of functions h from $W^{-1,p'}(\Omega)$*, having the property*

$$\text{theproblem}\begin{cases} -\Delta_p^s u = f(x,u) + h(u) \text{ in } \Omega \\ u = 0 \text{ on } \partial\Omega \end{cases} \text{has solutions,}$$

includes a G_δ *set everywhere dense;*

(iii) Moreover, if $s \to f(x, s)$ *is increasing, then the set of functions h from* $W^{-1,p'}(\Omega)$*, having the property*

$$\text{theproblem}\begin{cases} -\Delta_p^s u = f(x,u) + h(u) \ in\ \Omega \\ u = 0\ on\ \partial\Omega \end{cases} \text{has a uniquesolutions,}$$

includes a G_δ *set everywhere dense.*

Both unconstrained and constrained minimization problems for the energy functional, involving a special kind of Dirichlet problem with *p*-Laplacian, have been studied in [49], where the existence and the uniqueness of some types of solution have been obtained. One of the most important characteristics of the application of variational principles is the possibility to conduct the solving of the problem until the visualization of the result of the real-world model *via* an appropriate numerical method as the work [50] successfully sustains.

6.2. Applications

I. As the first application, we propose characterizing the solution of the Dirichlet problem which models the compression molding of polymers. This means to study a generalized Helle-Show flow of a power-law fluid which leads to the *p*-Poisson equation for the instantaneous pressure in the fluid. Therefore, this pressure *u* is the solution of:

$$-\ \Delta_p u = 1 \text{ on } \Omega,$$

$$u = 0 \text{ on } \partial\Omega,$$

where $p = \frac{1}{n} + 1$, *n* being the power-law index of the polymer, a typical value going over the interval (0.3, 0.5) [51,52]. Observe that the conditions from Proposition 6, *(iii)* are fulfilled when we take $f \equiv 0$, as in the equation above. One can consider $h \equiv 1$ to obtain that the pressure Dirichlet problem has a unique solution using the cited result. One can also apply Proposition 14, *(ii)* or *(iii)*, considering the same *f* and *h* fulfilling either the conditions from *(ii)* or those from *(iii)* to prove either the existence only or the existence and the uniqueness of the minimum for the corresponding functional for pressure, and hence one can discuss about its dual problem which has as solution (maximum) the flow function [53].

II. We can also prove the existence and the uniqueness of the solution of the pseudo torsion problem:

$$-\ \Delta_p^s u = 1$$

$$u \mid \partial\Omega = 0,$$

for which we apply Proposition 15. For the right-hand member of the equation of the form $f + h$, as in Proposition 15 *(ii)* or *(iii)*, we can obtain either the existence only or the existence and the uniqueness of the solution.

7. Conclusions

In this paper, some methods to solve different problems issued from real phenomena models have been presented. The theoretical results widely developed and debated in the paper under the same name, part one, are applied in order to draw the solutions and to characterize them. This is the natural step towards an appropriate numerical method, hence the validation of the model.

The novelty of this work consists in the presentation of detailed applications invol-ving the obtained theory in solving mathematical physics problems describing real phenomena. We proposed solving methods and characterization of the solutions for problems issued from glaciology, nonlinear elastic membrane either with p-Laplacian or with p-pseudo-Laplacian and for the pseudo torsion problem, those starting from some surjectivity statements for a special kind of operators, or *via* theorems of Fredholm alternative types, or surjectivity at different homogeneity degrees.

Weak solutions starting from the Ekeland variational principle, applied to critical points and weak solutions for elliptic type equations, critical points for nondifferentiable functionals applied for glaciology problems, pseudo torsion problems, nonlinear elastic membrane with p-Laplacian and p-pseudo-Laplacian, thermal transfer models, Neumann problems issued from injection mold filling, and other Neumann problems with p-pseudo-Laplacian have been presented. In the end, using a result obtained *via* a perturbed variational principle, the solution for a Dirichlet problem studying a generalized Helle-Show flow of a power-law fluid and the existence and the uniqueness of the solution for a pseudo torsion problem are obtained.

We are particularly interested in these applications, and this work is a necessary study in our future developments, as our final goal is to obtain a mathematical model for a specific process involving transfer phenomena for targeted environmental engineering applications. The role of the reactor (in nanofabrication) in nano-liquid-liquid dispersed systems is played by micro- or nano-droplets, and the determinant parameters are related to surface phenomena as a result of special intermolecular forces at interface. In this context, some innovative modeling mathematical methods have to be proposed and tested in order to properly simulate the physical-chemical interactions and processes specific to nanofabrication. However, one may stress that there is no model available to be applied for describing diffusion phenomena involved in the micro-emulsification of disperse systems in connection with surface properties at the interface in self-organized systems. Moreover, such disperse systems can be successfully applied for the removal of organic or inorganic pollutants from wastewater, and this is the subject of future research.

Funding: This research was funded by the University POLITEHNICA of Bucharest.

Data Availability Statement: Not applicable.

Conflicts of Interest: The author declares no conflict of interest.

References

1. Su, Y.; Feng, Z. Lions-type theorem of the p-Laplacian with applications. *Adv. Nonlinear Anal.* **2021**, *10*, 1178–1200. [CrossRef]
2. Kaushik, B.; Garain, P. Weighted anisotropic Sobolev inequality with extremal and associated singular problems. *Differ. Integral Equ.* **2023**, *36*, 59–92. [CrossRef]
3. Ávarez-Caudevilla, P. Asymptotic behavior of cooperative systems involving p-Laplacian operators. *Electron. J. Differ. Equ.* **2022**, *2022*, 1–23.
4. Palencia, J.L.D.; Otero, A. Oscillatory solutions and smoothing of a high-order p-Laplacian operator. *AIMS Electron. Res. Arch.* **2022**, *30*, 3527–3547. [CrossRef]
5. Dong, X.; Bai, Z.; Zhang, S. Positive solutions to boundary value problems of p-Laplacian with fractional derivative. *Bound. Value Probl.* **2017**, *2017*, 5. [CrossRef]
6. Sankar, R.R.; Sreedhar, N.; Prasad, K.R. Existence of positive solutions for $3n^{\text{th}}$ order boundary value problems involving p-Laplacian. *Creat. Math. Inform.* **2022**, *31*, 101–108. [CrossRef]
7. Wei, L.; Ma, R. Global continuum and multiple positive solutions to one-dimensional p-Laplacian boundary value problem. *Adv. Differ. Equ.* **2020**, *2020*, 204. [CrossRef]

8. Nhang, L.C.; Truong, L.X. Global solution and blow-up for a class of pseudo p-Laplacian evolution equations with logarithmic nonlinearity. *Comput. Math. Appl.* **2017**, *73*, 2076–2091.
9. He, Y.; Gao, H.; Wang, H. Blow-up and decay of pseudo-parabolic p-Laplacian equation with logarithmic nonlinearity. *Comput. Math. Appl.* **2018**, *75*, 459–469. [CrossRef]
10. Jayachandran, S.; Soundararajan, G. p-biharmonic pseudo-parabolic equation with logarithmic nonlinearity. *3C TIC* **2022**, *11*, 108–122. [CrossRef]
11. Chu, Y.; Wu, Y.; Cheng, L. Blow up and decay for a class of p-Laplacian hyperbolic equation with logarithmic nonlinearity. *Taiwan J. Math.* **2022**, *26*, 741–763. [CrossRef]
12. Xin, Y.; Liu, H. Existence of periodic solution for fourth-order generalized neutral p-Laplacian differential equation with attractive and repulsive singularities. *J. Inequal. Appl.* **2018**, *2018*, 259. [CrossRef] [PubMed]
13. Hou, W.; Zhang, L.; Agarwal, R.P.; Wang, G. Radial symmetry for a generalized nonlinear fractional p-Laplacian problem. *Nonlinear Anal. Model. Control* **2021**, *26*, 349–362. [CrossRef]
14. Wu, L.; Niu, P. Symmetry and nonexistence of positive solution to fractional p-Laplacian equations. *D.C.D.S.* **2018**, *39*, 1573–1583. [CrossRef]
15. Asso, O.; Cuesta, M.; Doumaté, J.T.; Leadi, L. Principal eigenvalues for the fractional p-Laplacian with unbounded sign-changing weights. *Electron. J. Differ. Equ.* **2023**, *2023*, 1–29. [CrossRef]
16. Iannizzotto, A.; Mosconi, S.; Squassina, M. Sobolev *versus* Hölder minimizers for the degenerate fractional p-Laplacian. *Nonlinear Anal.* **2020**, *191*, 111635. [CrossRef]
17. Dwivedi, G. Generalized Picone identity for the Finsler p-Laplacian and its applications. *Ukr. Math. J.* **2022**, *73*, 1674–1685. [CrossRef]
18. Feng, T.; Yu, M. Nonlinear Picone identities to pseudo p-Lapalce operator and applications. *Bull. Iranian Math. Soc.* **2017**, *43*, 2517–2530.
19. Goel, D.; Kumar, D.; Sreenadh, K. Regularity and multiplicity results for fractional (p, q)-Laplacian equations. *Commun. Contemp. Math.* **2020**, *22*, 1950065. [CrossRef]
20. Meghea, I. Solutions for some mathematical physics problems issued from modeling real phenomena: Part 1. *Axioms* **2023**, *12*, 532. [CrossRef]
21. Meghea, I. Application of a Variant of Mountain Pass Theorem in Modeling Real Phenomena. *Mathematics* **2022**, *10*, 3476. [CrossRef]
22. Meghea, I. Applications of a perturbed variational principle *via* p-Laplacian. *U.P.B. Sci. Bull. Ser. A* **2022**, *84*, 141–152.
23. Chiappinelli, R.; Edmunds, D. Remarks on Surjectivity of Gradient Operators. *Mathematics* **2020**, *8*, 1538. [CrossRef]
24. Lliboutry, L. *Traité de Glaciologie*; (I); Masson & Cie: Paris, France, 1964.
25. Lliboutry, L. *Traité de Glaciologie*; (II); Masson & Cie: Paris, France, 1965.
26. Pélissier, M.C. *Sur Quelques Problèmes non Linéaires en Glaciologie*; Publications Mathèmatiques d'Orsay, no. 110, U.E.R. Mathématique; Université Paris IX: Paris, France, 1975.
27. Lindquist, P. Stability for the solutions of $\mathrm{div}(|\nabla u|^{p-2}\nabla u) = f$ with varying p. *J. Math. Anal. Appl.* **1987**, *127*, 93–102. [CrossRef]
28. de Diego, G.; Farrell, P.; Hewitt, I. On the finite element approximation of a semicoercive stokes variational inequality arising in glaciology. *SIAM J. Numer. Anal.* **2023**, *61*, 1–25. [CrossRef]
29. Cuccu, F.; Emamizadeh, B.; Porru, G. Nonlinear elastic membranes involving the p-Laplacian operator. *Electron. J. Diff. Equ.* **2006**, *2006*, 1–10.
30. Silva, M.A.J. On a viscoelastic plate equation with history setting and perturbation of p-Laplacian type. *IMA J. Appl. Math. Adv. Access* **2012**, *78*, 1130–1146.
31. Cuccu, F.; Emamizadeh, B.; Porru, G. Optimization or the best eigenvalue in problems involving the p-Laplacian. *Proc. Am. Math. Soc.* **2009**, *137*, 1677–1687. [CrossRef]
32. Nair, V.; Sharma, I. Equilibria of liquid drops on pre-stretched nonlinear elastic membranes through a variational approach. *Phys. Fluids* **2023**, *35*, 047111. [CrossRef]
33. Yousfi, Y.; Hadi, I.; Benbrik, A. Optimal Form for Compliance of Membrane Boundary Shift in Nonlinear Case. *Int. J. Math. Math. Sci.* **2018**, *2018*, 1689269. [CrossRef]
34. Zhu, L. Complete quenching phenomenon for a parabolic p-Laplacian equation with a weighted absorption. *J. Inequal. Appl.* **2018**, *2018*, 248. [CrossRef]
35. Merah, A.; Mesloub, F. Elastic Membrane Equation with Dynamic Boundary Conditions and Infinite Memory. *Bol. Soc. Parana. Matemática* **2022**, *40*, 1–15. [CrossRef]
36. Kawohl, B. A family of torsional creep problems. *J. Reine Angew. Math.* **1990**, *410*, 1–22.
37. Della Pietra, F.; di Blasio, G.; Gavitone, N. Sharp estimates on the first Dirichlet eigenvalue of nonlinear elliptic operators via maximum principle. *Adv. Nonlinear Anal.* **2020**, *9*, 278–291. [CrossRef]
38. Iannizzotto, A.; Mosconi, S.; Squassina, M. Fine boundary regularity for the degenerate fractional p-Laplacian. *J. Funct. Anal.* **2020**, *279*, 108659. [CrossRef]
39. Mihăilescu, M.; Pérez-Llanos, M. Inhomogeneous torsional creep problems in anisotropic Orlicz Sobolev spaces. *J. Math. Phys.* **2018**, *59*, 071513. [CrossRef]

40. Belloni, M.; Kawohl, B. The pseudo-p-Laplace eigenvalue problem and viscosity solutions as $p \to \infty$. *ESAIM Control Optim. Calc. Var.* **2004**, *10*, 28–52. [CrossRef]
41. Balogh, A.; Varlamov, V. Analysis of Nonlinear Elastic Membrane Oscillations by Eigenfunction Expansion. *WSEAS Trans. Syst.* **2004**, *4*, 1430–1435.
42. Wang, J.R.; Zhou, Y.; Fečkan, M. Alternative Results and Robustness for Fractional Evolution Equations with Periodic Boundary Conditions. *Electron. J. Qual. Theory Differ. Equ.* **2011**, *97*, 1–15. [CrossRef]
43. Rak, J.; Tucek, J. Solving magnetic induction heating problem with multidimensional Fredholm integral equation methods: Alternative approach for optimization and evaluation of the process performance. *AIP Adv.* **2022**, *12*, 105110. [CrossRef]
44. Cholewa, J.; Rodriguez-Bernal, A. Self-similarity in homogeneous stationary and evolution problems. *J. Evol. Equ.* **2023**, *23*, 42. [CrossRef]
45. Jiao, F.; Zhou, Y. Existence of solutions for a class of fractional boundary value problems *via* critical point theory. *Comput. Math. Appl.* **2011**, *62*, 1181–1199.
46. Atangana, A. Mathematical model of survival of fractional calculus, critics and their impact: How singular is our world? *Adv. Differ. Equ.* **2021**, *2021*, 403. [CrossRef]
47. Lanchon-Ducauquois, H.; Tulita, C.; Meuris, C. *Modélisation du Transfert Thermique Dans l'He II*; Congrès Français du Thermique: Lyon, France, 2000.
48. Aronsson, G. On p-hrmonic functions, convex duality and an asymptotic formula for injection mould filing. *Eur. J. Appl. Math.* **1996**, *7*, 417–437. [CrossRef]
49. Emamizadeh, B.; Liu, Y. Constrained and unconstrained rearrangement minimization problems related to p-Laplace operator. *Isr. J. Mat.* **2014**, *206*, 281–298. [CrossRef]
50. Takahashi, K. Mean-field theory of turbulence from the variational principle and its application to the rotation of a thin fluid disk. *Prog. Theor. Exp. Phys.* **2017**, *2017*, 083J01. [CrossRef]
51. Lee, C.; Folgar, F.; Tucker, C.L. Simulation of compression molding for fiber-reinforced thermosetting polymers. *Trans. ASME* **1984**, *106*, 114–125. [CrossRef]
52. Bergwall, A. A geometric evolution problem. *Q. Appl. Math.* **2002**, *LX*, 37–73. [CrossRef]
53. Janfalk, U. On a minimization problem for vector fields in L^1. *Bull. Lond. Math. Soc.* **1996**, *28*, 165–176. [CrossRef]

axioms

MDPI

Article

Ekeland Variational Principle and Some of Its Equivalents on a Weighted Graph, Completeness and the OSC Property

Basit Ali [1], Ştefan Cobzaş [2,*] and Mokhwetha Daniel Mabula [3]

1 Department of Mathematics, School of Science, University of Management and Technology, C-II, Johar Town, Lahore 54770, Pakistan
2 Faculty of Mathematics and Computer Science, Babeş-Bolyai University, 400 084 Cluj-Napoca, Romania
3 Department of Mathematics, University of Pretoria, 0002 Pretoria, South Africa
* Correspondence: scobzas@math.ubbcluj.ro

Abstract: We prove a version of the Ekeland Variational Principle (EkVP) in a weighted graph G and its equivalence to Caristi fixed point theorem and to the Takahashi minimization principle. The usual completeness and topological notions are replaced with some weaker versions expressed in terms of the graph G. The main tool used in the proof is the OSC property for sequences in a graph. Converse results, meaning the completeness of weighted graphs for which one of these principles holds, are also considered.

Keywords: Ekeland variational principle; Takahashi minimization principle; Caristi fixed point theorem; weighted graph; partially ordered metric space; completeness; the OSC property

MSC: 58E30; 47H10; 05C22; 06F30; 54E50

1. Introduction

Ekeland Variational Principle (EkVP) [1] is one of the most important tools in nonlinear analysis that is used to minimize lower semicontinuous (LSC for short) and bounded from below functions on a metric space. To date, it has been applied in various contexts, see [2–7], and the references therein. For instance, in [7], it was applied to the so-called "end problem" in behavioral sciences, that is, to know when and where a human dynamic, which starts from an initial position and follows a transition, ends somewhere. On the other hand, another important issue is the "Completeness problem", meaning to know under what circumstances the validity of some result implies the completeness of the underlying space. Notice that a thorough analysis of various situations when the validity of a result (variational principle, fixed point) on a metric space forces its completeness was given in [8].

Due to its usefulness and applicability in mathematics and other related disciplines, EkVP has been studied in different contexts. Not so long ago, Alfuraidan, and Khamsi [9], following the approach taken by Jachymski [10], obtained a version of EkVP in metric spaces endowed with a graph, via the OSC property for sequences. In the present paper we follow this line by proving a version of Ekeland Variational Principle (EkVP) in a weighted graph G and its equivalence to Caristi fixed point theorem and to Takahashi minimization principle. The usual completeness and topological notions are replaced with some weaker versions expressed in terms of the graph G (called G-completeness, G-LSC, etc). Converse results, meaning the completeness of weighted graphs for which one of these principles holds, are also considered.

We start by recalling Ekeland Variational Principle, both the weak and the full version.

Theorem 1 (Ekeland Variational Principle—weak form (wEkVP)). *Let (X,d) be a complete metric space and $f : X \to \mathbb{R} \cup \{+\infty\}$ an LSC and bounded from below proper function. Then for every $\varepsilon > 0$ there exists an element $y_\varepsilon \in X$ such that*

$$f(y_\varepsilon) \le \inf f(X) + \varepsilon, \tag{1}$$

and

$$f(y_\varepsilon) < f(y) + \varepsilon d(y, y_\varepsilon), \quad \forall y \in X \setminus \{y_\varepsilon\}. \tag{2}$$

The full version of EkVP is the following.

Theorem 2 (Ekeland Variational Principle—EkVP). *Let (X,d) be a complete metric space and $f : X \to \mathbb{R} \cup \{+\infty\}$ an LSC bounded below proper function. Let $\varepsilon > 0$ and $x_0 \in \operatorname{dom} f$.*

Then, given $\lambda > 0$, there exists $z = z_{\varepsilon,\lambda} \in X$ such that

$$\begin{aligned} &(\text{a}) \quad f(z) + \frac{\varepsilon}{\lambda} d(z, x_0) \le f(x_0); \\ &(\text{b}) \quad \forall x \in X,\ x \ne z,\ \ f(z) < f(x) + \frac{\varepsilon}{\lambda} d(z, x). \end{aligned} \tag{3}$$

If further, x_0 satisfies the condition

$$f(x_0) \le \inf f(X) + \varepsilon, \tag{4}$$

then

$$(\text{c}) \quad d(z, x_0) \le \lambda.$$

A function $f : X \to \mathbb{R} \cup \{\infty\}$ is called *proper* if $\operatorname{dom}(f) := \{x \in X : f(x) \in \mathbb{R}\}$ is nonempty.

Remark 1. *Notice that condition (a) in the above theorem implies $f(z) \le f(x_0)$. Sometimes EkVP is formulated with this condition instead of (a).*

An important consequence of the full version of EkVP is obtained by taking $\lambda = \sqrt{\varepsilon}$ in Theorem 2.

Corollary 1. *Under the hypotheses of Theorem 2, for every $\varepsilon > 0$ and $x_0 \in X$ with $f(x_0) \le \inf f(X) + \varepsilon$ there exists $y_\varepsilon \in X$ such that*

$$\begin{aligned} &(\text{a})\ f(y_\varepsilon) + \sqrt{\varepsilon} d(y_\varepsilon, x_0) \le f(x_0); \\ &(\text{b})\ \forall x \in X,\ x \ne y_\varepsilon,\ \ f(y_\varepsilon) < f(x) + \sqrt{\varepsilon} d(y_\varepsilon, x); \\ &(\text{c})\ d(y_\varepsilon, x_0) \le \sqrt{\varepsilon}. \end{aligned} \tag{5}$$

Taking further $\varepsilon_n = 1/n$, one obtains a sequence (y_n) approximating the minimum point of the function f.

Note that the validity of Ekeland Variational Principle (in its weak form) implies the completeness of the metric space X. This was discovered by Weston [11] in 1977 and rediscovered by Sullivan [12] in 1981 (see also the survey [13]).

More exactly, the following result holds.

Theorem 3. *For a metric space (X,d) the following statements are equivalent.*

1. *The metric space (X,d) is complete.*
2. *If for every Lipschitz function $f : X \to [0,\infty)$ there exists a point $z \in X$ such that*

$$f(z) \le f(x) + \rho(z, x) \quad \text{for all } x \in X, \tag{6}$$

Notice that the class of Lipschitz functions considered in 2 is smaller than that of LSC functions considered in Theorem 1.

Ekeland Variational Principle is equivalent to many results in fixed point theory, geometry of Banach spaces (the drop theorem) and optimization. We mention only two of these, namely Caristi fixed point theorem and Takahashi minimization principle.

We start with Caristi fixed point theorem [14] (see also [15]), presented both in single-valued and set-valued versions.

Theorem 4 (Caristi fixed point theorem). *Let (X,d) be a complete metric space and $\varphi : X \to [0,\infty)$ be an LSC function.*

1. *If $T : X \to X$ is a mapping satisfying the condition*
$$\forall x \in X,\ \ d(T(x),x) \le \varphi(x) - \varphi(T(x))\,, \tag{7}$$
then T has a fixed point, i.e., there exists $z \in X$ such that $z = T(z)$.
2. *If $T : X \rightrightarrows X$ is a set-valued mapping satisfying the condition*
$$\forall x \in X,\ \ \exists y \in T(x),\ \ d(y,x) \le \varphi(x) - \varphi(y)\,, \tag{8}$$
then T has a fixed point, i.e., there exists $z \in X$ such that $z \in T(z)$.
3. *If $T : X \rightrightarrows X$ is a set-valued mapping with nonempty values satisfying the condition*
$$\forall x \in X,\ \ \forall y \in T(x),\ \ d(y,x) \le \varphi(x) - \varphi(y)\,, \tag{9}$$
then there exists $z \in X$ such that $T(z) = \{z\}$.

Notice that both 2 and 3 are extensions of 1—if the mapping T is single-valued, then each of them agrees with 1.

Another result is Takahashi minimization principle [16] (see also [17]).

Theorem 5 (Takahashi minimization principle). *Let (X,d) be a complete metric space and let $\varphi : X \to [0,\infty)$ be an LSC function.*

If for every $x \in X$ satisfying the condition $\varphi(x) > \inf \varphi(X)$ there exists $y \in X \setminus \{x\}$ such that
$$\varphi(y) + d(x,y) \le \varphi(x)\,, \tag{10}$$
then φ attains its infimum on X, i.e., there exists $z \in X$ such that $\varphi(z) = \inf \varphi(X)$.

Remark 2. *Replacing φ with $\tilde{\varphi} = \varphi - \inf \varphi(X)$, the above results can be automatically extended to a bounded from below LSC function $\varphi : X \to \mathbb{R}$. Considering an extended proper LSC function $\varphi : X \to \mathbb{R} \cup \{\infty\}$, then the results hold on $\operatorname{dom}(\varphi) := \{x \in X : \varphi(x) \in \mathbb{R}\}$.*

Recall that a function $\varphi : X \to \mathbb{R} \cup \{\infty\}$ is called proper if $\operatorname{dom}(\varphi) \neq \emptyset$.

2. Preliminaries

In this section, we present some notions and results on partially ordered metric spaces and graph theory, needed for the main results of the paper.

A *partial order* on a nonempty set X is a reflexive, transitive and antisymmetric relation $\preceq$ on X. One also says that $(X,\preceq)$ is a *partially ordered set*. We consider orders $\preceq$ on a metric space (X,d) in which case we shall say that $(X,d,\preceq)$ is a partially ordered metric space. Initially, no relation between the order $\preceq$ and the metric d is supposed to hold but, in order to make the things to work, some connections are needed (see Definition 1).

We present now some preliminary notions from graph theory. A good introductory text, with many examples, is [18], Chapter 8, (see also [19] or [20]).

A *directed graph* (*digraph* for short) G is formed by a set $V(G)$, called the set of *vertices* of the graph G, and a set $E(G)$ of *edges* corresponding to ordered pairs $(u,v) \in V(G) \times V(G)$.

The graph will be denoted by $G = (V(G), E(G))$. Two edges e_1, e_2 are called *parallel* if they correspond to the same pair (u, v). In this paper, we shall always suppose that the graph G has no parallel edges, so that the set $E(G)$ can be viewed as a subset of $V(G) \times V(G)$. A *path* in the graph G connecting two points $u, v \in V(G)$ is a succession $(u, u_1), (u_1, u_2), \ldots, (u_n, v)$ of edges, where $n \geq 1$ and the points $u, u_1, \ldots, u_n, v$ are pairwise distinct. A path with $v = u$ is called a *cycle*. A graph without cycles is called *acyclic*.

A graph $G = (V(G), E(G))$ is called:

- *reflexive* if $(u, u) \in E(G)$ for all $u \in V(G)$;
- *transitive* if $(u, v), (v, w) \in E(G)$ implies $(u, w) \in E(G)$.

A *weight* on a graph $G = (V(G), E(G))$ is a function (usually non-negative) $d : E(G) \to \mathbb{R}$. We say that $G = (V(G), E(G), d)$ is a *weighted graph*. In this paper, we shall suppose that the graph is contained in a metric space (X, d) and that the weight is the metric d.

The next remark emphasizes the tight connection between graphs and partial orders.

Remark 3. *Let $(X, \preceq)$ be a partially ordered set. Put $V(G) = X$ and $E(G) = \{(x, y) \in X \times X : x \preceq y\}$. Then $G = (V(G), E(G))$ is a reflexive transitive acyclic directed graph.*

Conversely, given a reflexive transitive acyclic directed graph $G = (V(G), E(G))$ put

$$x \leq_G y \iff (x, y) \in E(G)\,. \tag{11}$$

Then $\leq_G$ is a partial order on $V(G)$ and the graph $\tilde{G}$ associated with the order $\leq_G$ in the way described above agrees with G.

Consequently, there is a one-to-one correspondence between reflexive transitive acyclic directed graphs and partial orders.

Only the relation between acyclicity and antisymmetry needs some explanation, the others (reflexivity, transitivity) being obvious.

Suppose that G is the graph corresponding to a partial order $\preceq$ in the way described in Remark 3. If $u, u_1, \ldots, u_n, u$ is a loop in G, then, by the definition of $E(G)$, $u \preceq u_1 \preceq u$ with $u_1 \neq u$, in contradiction to the antisymmetry of $\preceq$. This shows that the graph G is acyclic.

Conversely, let $\leq_G$ be the partial order associated with a graph G (having the properties mentioned in Remark 3). If $u \leq_G v$ and $v \leq_G u$, for some $u \neq v$ in $V(G)$, then $(u, v), (v, u) \in E(G)$, i.e., u, v, u is a loop in G, in contradiction to the acyclicity of G.

We introduce now some notions in weighted graphs and their analogs in partially ordered metric spaces.

Definition 1.

- *A weighted digraph $G = (V(G), E(G), d)$, where d is a metric on $V(G)$, is said to satisfy the OSC property if $(x, x_n) \in E(G)$ for all $n \in \mathbb{N}$, for every sequence (x_n) in $V(G)$ such that $x_n \xrightarrow{d} x$ and $(x_{n+1}, x_n) \in E(G)$ for all $n \in \mathbb{N}$.*
- *A partially ordered metric space $(X, d, \preceq)$ is said to satisfy the OSC condition if $x \preceq x_n$ for all $n \in \mathbb{N}$, for every sequence (x_n) in X such that $x_n \xrightarrow{d} x$ and $x_{n+1} \preceq x_n$ for all $n \in \mathbb{N}$.*

Remark 4. *In [9], the OSC property for graphs is defined with the supplementary condition that $(y, x_n) \in E(G)$, $n \in \mathbb{N}$, implies $(y, x) \in E(G)$. In a partially ordered metric space this corresponds to the condition that $x = \inf_n x_n$.*

The condition OSC, as given in Definition 1, is also used by Jachymski [10].

For partially ordered metric spaces the OSC condition was introduced in [21] in the study of fixed points for contractions on ordered metric spaces. Some authors consider a weakened version of the OSC, where one asks that the conclusion holds only for a subsequence $(x_{n_k})_{k \in \mathbb{N}}$ of (x_n). As remarked Jachymski [10], the transitivity of $\preceq$ implies the equivalence of these conditions. Furthermore, if $\preceq$ is a reflexive relation on the metric space (X, d) satisfying the OSC property, then $\preceq$ is transitive.

We introduce now the definitions of completeness and of some topological notions expressed in terms of the graph and of the partial order.

Definition 2. *Let $G = (V(G), E(G), d)$ be a weighted digraph, where d is a metric on $V(G)$.*

- *A sequence (x_n) in $V(G)$ is called a G-sequence if $(x_{n+1}, x_n) \in E(G)$ for all $n \in \mathbb{N}$.*
- *A G-Cauchy sequence is a G-sequence that is Cauchy with respect to d.*
- *A subset Y of $V(G)$ is called G-closed if $y \in Y$ for every G-sequence (y_n) in Y, d-convergent to $y \in V(G)$.*
- *A function $f : V(G) \to \mathbb{R}$ is called G-continuous (G-LSC) if $\lim_n f(x_n) = f(x)$ (resp. $f(x) \le \liminf_n f(x_n)$) for every G-sequence (x_n) in $V(G)$ d-convergent to x.*

In a partially ordered metric space $(X, d, \preceq)$ the notions of decreasingly Cauchy sequence, decreasingly closed set, decreasingly continuous (or LSC) function, can be defined in a similar way by replacing the condition $(x_{n+1}, x_n) \in E(G)$ with $x_{n+1} \preceq x_n$.

Let (X, d) be a metric space and $\varphi : X \to [0, \infty)$ be a function. We define a partial order $\le_\varphi$ on X by

$$\begin{aligned} x \le_\varphi y &\iff d(x,y) \le \varphi(y) - \varphi(x) \\ &\iff \varphi(x) + d(x,y) \le \varphi(y). \end{aligned} \tag{12}$$

Remark 5. *The relation (12) is a partial order on X, called by some authors the Brønsted order (see [22,23]). It is related to the Bishop-Phelps theorem on the denseness of the support functionals of a closed bounded convex subset of a Banach space, see [24,25].*

The following proposition contains some simple remarks about $\le_\varphi$.

Proposition 1. *Let (X, d) be a metric space, $\varphi : X \to [0, \infty)$ and let $\le_\varphi$ be defined by (12).*

1. *The relation $\le_\varphi$ is a partial order on X.*
2. *Every $\le_\varphi$-decreasing sequence in X is Cauchy.*
3. *If φ is LSC, then $y \le_\varphi x$ for every sequence (y_n) in X satisfying $y_n \le_\varphi x$ and $y_n \xrightarrow{d} y$. Furthermore, the partial order $\le_\varphi$ satisfies the OSC.*

Proof.

1. The proof is a straightforward verification.

2. Let (x_n) be a sequence in X such that $x_{n+1} \le_\varphi x_n$ for all $n \in \mathbb{N}$. The inequality

$$0 \le d(x_n, x_{n+1}) \le \varphi(x_n) - \varphi(x_{n+1})$$

shows that $(\varphi(x_n))_{n\in\mathbb{N}}$ is a decreasing sequence in $\mathbb{R}_+$, so convergent and, hence, Cauchy. The transitivity of $\le_\varphi$ implies $x_{n+k} \le_\varphi x_n$, that is,

$$d(x_n, x_{n+k}) \le \varphi(x_n) - \varphi(x_{n+k}),$$

an inequality which shows that (x_n) is d-Cauchy.

3. We have

$$y_n \le_\varphi x \iff \varphi(y_n) + d(y_n, x) \le \varphi(x).$$

Taking into account the LSC of the function φ, one obtains

$$\varphi(y) + d(y,x) \le \liminf_n [\varphi(y_n) + d(y_n, x)] \le \varphi(x),$$

that is, $y \le_\varphi x$.

Let now (y_n) be a sequence in X such that $y_{n+1} \le_\varphi y_n$, $n \in \mathbb{N}$, and $y_n \xrightarrow{d} y$. By transitivity $y_{n+k} \le_\varphi y_n$, $n, k \in \mathbb{N}$, which, fixing n and letting $k \to \infty$, yields $y \le_\varphi y_n$ for all $n \in \mathbb{N}$. □

Remark 6. *Supposing φ only decreasingly LSC, then 3 holds for convergent decreasing sequences only. A similar result holds for G-sequences in a weighted graph G.*

3. Ekeland Variational Principle in Metric Spaces Endowed with a Graph

The following theorem is an extension of a result proved in [9], Theorem 3.3, (see also [26]). The main modification consists of the replacement of topological and completeness conditions with their G-versions. A property $\mathcal{P}$ on a set X can be interpreted as a function $\mathcal{P} : X \to \{0,1\}$, where $\mathcal{P}(x) = 1$ means that x has property $\mathcal{P}$, while $\mathcal{P}(x) = 0$ means that x does not have it. Let $\text{Dom}(\mathcal{P}) := \{x \in X : \mathcal{P}(x) = 1\}$. If X is a topological space, then we say that $\mathcal{P}$ is closed if $\text{Dom}(\mathcal{P})$ is closed.

The following example will be used to prove the equivalence of EkVP in weighted graphs to that in ordered metric spaces (see Theorem 7).

Example 1. *Let $G = (V(G), E(G), d)$ be a weighted digraph, where d is a metric on $V(G)$ and let $\varphi : X \to [0,\infty)$ be a function. For $\varepsilon > 0$ we define a property $\mathcal{P}_\varepsilon$ on X by*

$$\mathcal{P}_\varepsilon \text{ holds for } x \in V(G) \iff \varphi(x) \le \inf \varphi(X) + \varepsilon\,.$$

Then

$$\text{Dom}(\mathcal{P}_\varepsilon) = \{x \in X : \varphi(x) \le \inf \varphi(X) + \varepsilon\}\,.$$

The set $\text{Dom}(\mathcal{P}_\varepsilon)$ is closed (G-closed) provided the function φ is LSC (G-LSC).

The closedness property of $\text{Dom}(\mathcal{P}_\varepsilon)$ follows from the fact that a function φ is LSC (G-LSC) if and only if the set $\{x \in X : \varphi(x) \le \alpha\}$ is closed (G-closed) for every $\alpha \in \mathbb{R}$.

Theorem 6. *Let $G = (V(G), E(G), d)$ be a reflexive transitive acyclic weighted digraph, where d is a G-complete metric on $V(G)$ having the OSC property for G-sequences. Consider a G-closed property $\mathcal{P}$ on $V(G)$ such that $\text{Dom}(\mathcal{P})$ is nonempty and a G-lower semi-continuous function $\varphi : V(G) \to [0,\infty)$. For any given $\varepsilon > 0$ and $\lambda > 0$ let $x_0 \in \text{Dom}(\mathcal{P})$ be such that*

$$\varphi(x_0) \le \inf \varphi(\text{Dom}(\mathcal{P})) + \varepsilon\,. \tag{13}$$

Then there exists $z \in \text{Dom}(\mathcal{P})$ such that

$$\begin{aligned} &\text{(i)} \quad \varphi(z) + \lambda^{-1}\varepsilon\, d(x_0,z), \le \varphi(x_0),\\ &\text{(ii)} \quad d(x_0,z) \le \lambda,\\ &\text{(iii)} \quad \varphi(z) < \varphi(x) + \lambda^{-1}\varepsilon\, d(x,z), \end{aligned} \tag{14}$$

for all $x \in \text{Dom}(\mathcal{P})$ such that $x \ne z$ and $(x,z) \in E(G)$.

Proof. Put, for convenience, $Y = \text{Dom}(\mathcal{P})$. Let also $\gamma = \varepsilon/\lambda$ and $d_\gamma = \gamma \cdot d$. Then d_γ is a metric on $V(G)$, Lipschitz equivalent to d, so that all the properties holding for d holds for d_γ too. Define the partial order $\le_\gamma$ by (12) with d_γ instead of d. For $x \in Y$ let

$$S(x) = \{y \in Y : y \le_\gamma x \text{ and } (y,x) \in E(G)\}\,. \tag{15}$$

Claim I. *The sets $S(x)$ have the following properties:*

$$\begin{aligned} &\text{(i)} \quad y \in S(x) \text{ implies } S(y) \subseteq S(x) \text{ and } \varphi(y) + d_\gamma(y,x) \le \varphi(x);\\ &\text{(ii)} \quad S(x) \text{ is G-closed.} \end{aligned} \tag{16}$$

Indeed, let $y \in S(x)$ and $z \in S(y)$. Then

$$\begin{aligned} y &\leq_\gamma x \text{ and } (y,x) \in E(G), \\ z &\leq_\gamma y \text{ and } (y,z) \in E(G), \end{aligned}$$

so that, by the transitivity of $\leq_\gamma$ and of $E(G)$,

$$z \leq_\gamma x \text{ and } (z,x) \in E(G),$$

that is, $z \in S(x)$.

Let (y_n) be a G-sequence in $S(x)$, d-convergent to some $y \in Y$. Then $y_n \leq_\gamma x$ for all $n \in \mathbb{N}$, so that, by the G-LSC of φ, $y \leq_\gamma x$ (see Proposition 1 and Remark 6). Furthermore, $(y_n,x) \in E(G)$ and, by the OSC, $(y,y_n) \in E(G)$, so that, by transitivity, $(y,x) \in E(G)$.

Consequently, $y \in S(x)$, showing that $S(x)$ is G-closed.

Let $J(x) = \inf \varphi(S(x))$. We define now inductively a sequence of sets in Y.

Choose $x_1 \in S(x_0)$ such that

$$\varphi(x_1) \leq J(x_0) + \frac{1}{2},$$

and let $x_{n+1} \in S(x_n)$ be such that

$$\varphi(x_{n+1}) \leq J(x_n) + \frac{1}{2^{n+1}}, \ n \in \mathbb{N}.$$

Then (x_n) satisfies

$$x_{n+1} \leq_\gamma x_n \quad \text{and} \quad (x_{n+1},x_n) \in E(G),$$

for all $n \geq 0$, so that, By Proposition 1, it is a G-Cauchy sequence. Since Y is a G-closed subset of $V(g)$, it follows that it is also G-complete, so that the sequence (x_n) is d-convergent to some $z \in Y$.

Since $x_{n+k} \in S(x_{n+k}) \subseteq S(x_n)$ and $S(x_n)$ is G-closed, it follows $z \in S(x_n)$ for all $n \geq 0$. From $z \in S(x_0)$ and Claim I, $\varphi(z) + \lambda^{-1}\varepsilon\, d(x_0,z) \leq \varphi(x_0)$, i.e., the inequality (i) from (14) holds true.

Let us show that

$$S(z) = \{z\}. \tag{17}$$

Let $x \in S(z)$. We have $S(z) \subseteq S(x_n)$ for all $n \geq 0$, so that, taking into account the choice of the elements x_n, one obtains

$$\varphi(x_{n+1}) - \frac{1}{2^{n+1}} \leq J(x_n) \leq \varphi(x),$$

implying $\varphi(x_{n+1}) - \varphi(x) \leq \frac{1}{2^{n+1}}$. Since $x \leq_\gamma x_{n+1}$, we have

$$d_\gamma(x,x_{n+1}) \leq \varphi(x_{n+1}) - \varphi(x) \leq \frac{1}{2^{n+1}},$$

for all $n \geq 0$. Letting $n \to \infty$, one obtains $d_\gamma(x,z) = 0$ and so $x = z$.

Suppose now that $x \in Y$ is such that $x \neq z$ and $(x,z) \in E(G)$. Then, by (17), $x \notin S(z)$, so that the inequality $x \leq_\gamma z$ fails, that is

$$\gamma d(x,z) > \varphi(z) - \varphi(x),$$

which is equivalent to the inequality (iii) in (14).

Since $z \in S(x_0)$ we have $z \leq_\gamma x_0$, so that, by (13),

$$\frac{\varepsilon}{\lambda} d(z, x_0) \leq \varphi(x_0) - \varphi(z) \leq \varphi(x_0) - \inf \varphi(Y) \leq \varepsilon .$$

Hence $d(z, x_0) \leq \lambda$. □

Taking $\mathcal{P}$ on X with $\mathrm{Dom}(\mathcal{P}) = X$ one obtains the following weak form of EkVP in weighted graphs.

Corollary 2. *Let $G = (V(G), E(G), d)$ be a weighted graph satisfying the hypotheses of Theorem 6. Then for every $\varepsilon, \lambda > o$ there exists $z \in X$ such that*

$$\varphi(z) < \varphi(x) + \lambda^{-1} \varepsilon\, d(x, z), \tag{18}$$

for all $x \in X \setminus \{z\}$ with $(x, z) \in E(G)$.

Remark 7. *Similar results for equilibrium versions of Ekeland Variational Principle were obtained by Alfuraidan and Khamsi [2].*

Theorem 7. *Consider the following statements.*

1. *For every reflexive transitive acyclic weighted digraph $G = (V(G), E(G), d)$, where d is a G-complete metric on $V(G)$ such that the OSC property for G-sequences is satisfied, the following property holds.*

   (A_1) *For any G-closed property $\mathcal{P}$ on $V(G)$ such that $\mathrm{Dom}(\mathcal{P})$ is nonempty, every G-lower semi-continuous function $\varphi : V(G) \to [0, \infty)$, any given $\varepsilon > 0$ and $\lambda > 0$ and $x_0 \in \mathrm{Dom}(\mathcal{P})$ such that*

   $$\varphi(x_0) \leq \inf \varphi(\mathrm{Dom}(\mathcal{P})) + \varepsilon,$$

   there exists $z \in \mathrm{Dom}(\mathcal{P})$ such that

   $$\begin{array}{ll} \text{(i)} & \varphi(z) + \lambda^{-1}\varepsilon\, d(x_0, z) \leq \varphi(x_0), \\ \text{(ii)} & d(z, x_0) \leq \lambda, \\ \text{(iii)} & \varphi(z) < \varphi(x) + \lambda^{-1}\varepsilon\, d(x, z), \end{array} \tag{19}$$

   for all $x \in \mathrm{Dom}(\mathcal{P})$ with $x \neq z$ and $(x, z) \in E(G)$.

2. *For every partially ordered decreasingly complete metric space $(X, d, \preceq)$ with the OSC property for decreasing sequences, the following property holds.*

   (A_2) *For any decreasingly lower semi-continuous function $\varphi : X \to [0, \infty)$, any $\varepsilon > 0$, any $\lambda > 0$, and any $x_0 \in X$ satisfying*

   $$\varphi(x_0) \leq \inf \varphi(X) + \varepsilon$$

   there exists $z \in X$ such that

   $$\begin{array}{ll} \text{(i)} & \varphi(z) + \lambda^{-1}\varepsilon\, d(x_0, z) \leq \varphi(x_0), \\ \text{(ii)} & d(z, x_0) \leq \lambda, \\ \text{(iii)} & \varphi(z) < \varphi(x) + \varepsilon\lambda^{-1} d(x, z), \end{array} \tag{20}$$

   for all $x \in X$ with $x \neq z$ and $x \preceq z$.

3. *For every complete metric space (X, d) the following property holds.*

   (A_3) *For any LSC function $\varphi : X \to [0, \infty)$, any $\varepsilon > 0$ and any $x_0 \in X$ satisfying*

   $$\varphi(x_0) \leq \inf \varphi(X) + \varepsilon$$

there exists $x_\varepsilon \in X$ *such that*

$$\begin{aligned} &\text{(i)} \quad \varphi(x_\varepsilon) + \varepsilon\, d(x_\varepsilon, z) \leq \varphi(x_0), \\ &\text{(ii)} \quad d(x_\varepsilon, x_0) \leq 1, \\ &\text{(iii)} \quad \varphi(x_\varepsilon) < \varphi(x) + \varepsilon\, d(x, x_\varepsilon), \end{aligned} \tag{21}$$

for all $x \in X$ *with* $x \neq x_\varepsilon$.

4. *For every complete metric space* (X, d) *the following property holds.*
   (A_4) *For any LSC function* $\phi : X \to [0, \infty)$ *and for any* $\varepsilon > 0$ *there exists* $x_\varepsilon \in X$ *such that*

$$\phi(x_\varepsilon) \leq \inf \phi(X) + \varepsilon$$

and

$$\varphi(x_\varepsilon) < \varphi(x) + \varepsilon\, d(x, x_\varepsilon),$$

for all $x \in X$ *with* $x \neq x_\varepsilon$.

Then

$$1 \iff 2 \Rightarrow 3 \Rightarrow 4.$$

Proof. $1 \Rightarrow 2$. Take $V(G) = X$ and

$$E(G) = \{(x, y) \in X \times X : x \preceq y\}.$$

Then $G = (V(G), E(G))$ is a reflexive transitive acyclic digraph (see Remark 3). The completeness of $(X, d, \preceq)$ for decreasing Cauchy sequences implies the G-completeness of $(V(G), d)$.

Furthermore, by the definition of the graph G, the OSC property for decreasing sequences in $(X, d, \preceq)$ implies the OSC property for G-sequences of the graph G.

Define now $\mathcal{P}$ as in Example 1, i.e., $\mathcal{P}(x)$ holds if and only if $\varphi(x) \leq \inf \varphi(X) + \varepsilon$. Then $\mathrm{Dom}(\mathcal{P})$ is nonempty as φ is bounded below (by 0) and decreasingly closed (because φ is decreasingly LSC), hence $\mathrm{Dom}(\mathcal{P})$ is G-closed in G.

Now, a direct application of 1 yields the first two inequalities in (20) as well as the third one, but only for $x \in \mathrm{Dom}(\mathcal{P})$ with $x \neq z$ and $x \preceq z$. If $x \notin \mathrm{Dom}(\mathcal{P})$, then

$$\varphi(x) > \inf \varphi(X) + \varepsilon \geq \varphi(x_0) \geq \varphi(z),$$

so that

$$\varphi(z) < \varphi(x) < \varphi(x) + \varepsilon \lambda^{-1} d(x, z),$$

(no matter x satisfies $x \preceq z$ or not).

Consequently, the third inequality holds for all $x \in X$ with $x \neq z$ and $x \preceq z$.

$2 \Rightarrow 1$. Suppose that we are given a weighted graph $G(V(G), E(G), d)$, a function $\varphi : V(G) \to [0, \infty)$ and a property $\mathcal{P}$ on $V(G)$ such that the hypotheses from 1 hold for these data.

Define $X = \mathrm{Dom}(\mathcal{P})$ and the partial order $\preceq$ by

$$x \preceq y \iff (x, y) \in E(G),$$

for $x, y \in X$. Again, the G-closedness of X and the G-completeness of G, imply the G-completeness of (X, d), and so the completeness of (X, d) for decreasing Cauchy sequences. The fact that φ is decreasingly LSC is a direct consequence of G-lower smicontinuity of φ.

Now, the conclusions from (A_1) follows from those in (A_2).

$2 \Rightarrow 3$. Define an order on X by

$$x \preceq y \iff d(x, y) \leq \varphi(x) - \varphi(y).$$

Then $\preceq$ is a partial order on X which, by Proposition 1, satisfies the OSC. The result follows now from 2 with $\lambda = 1$.

Indeed, by 2, the third inequality in (23) holds for all $x \in X \setminus \{x_\varepsilon\}$ with $x \preceq x_\varepsilon$ and, by the definition of the order $\preceq$, it is automatically satisfied for all $x \in X$ for which the inequality $x \preceq x_\varepsilon$ fails.

$3 \Rightarrow 4$. Notice that 4 is a particular case of 3. □

Theorem 8. *The following properties hold.*

1. *Let $G = (V(G), E(G), d)$ be a reflexive transitive acyclic digraph, where d is a metric on G such that the OSC property holds on G. The following statements are equivalent:*
   (i) *The metric space $(V(G), d)$ is complete.*
   (ii) *For any lower semi-continuous function $\varphi : V(G) \to [0, \infty)$ and any $\varepsilon > 0$ there exists $x_\varepsilon \in V(G)$ such that*
   $$\varphi(x_\varepsilon) < \varphi(x) + \varepsilon\, d(x, x_\varepsilon), \tag{22}$$
   for all $x \in V(G)$ with $x \neq x_\varepsilon$ and $(x, x_\varepsilon) \in E(G)$.
2. *Let now (X, d) be a metric space. The following statements are equivalent:*
   (i) *The metric space (X, d) is complete.*
   (ii) *For any partial order $\preceq$ on X satisfying the OSC property, any continuous function $\varphi : X \to [0, \infty)$ and any $\varepsilon > 0$ there exists $x_\varepsilon \in X$ such that*
   $$\varphi(x_\varepsilon) < \varphi(x) + \varepsilon\, d(x, x_\varepsilon), \tag{23}$$
   for all $x \in X$ with $x \neq x_\varepsilon$ and $x \preceq x_\varepsilon$.
3. *For a metric space (X, d) the following statements are equivalent:*
   (i) *The metric space (X, d) is complete.*
   (ii) *For any continuous function $\varphi : X \to [0, \infty)$, any $\varepsilon > 0$, $\lambda > 0$ and any $x_0 \in X$ satisfying*
   $$\varphi(x_0) \leq \inf \varphi(X) + \varepsilon$$
   there exists $z \in X$ such that
   $$\begin{aligned} &\varphi(z) + \lambda^{-1}\varepsilon \leq \varphi(x_0), \\ &d(x_\varepsilon, x_0) \leq \lambda, \\ &\varphi(z) < \varphi(x) + \lambda^{-1}\varepsilon d(x, z), \end{aligned} \tag{24}$$
   for all $x \in X$ with $x \neq z$.
   (iii) *For any continuous function $\varphi : X \to [0, \infty)$ and for any $\varepsilon > 0$ there exists $x_\varepsilon \in X$ such that*
   $$\varphi(x_\varepsilon) < \varphi(x) + \varepsilon d(x, x_\varepsilon),$$
   for all $x \in X$ with $x \neq x_\varepsilon$.

Proof. 3. (i) $\Rightarrow$ (ii) is Ekeland Variational principle, while (ii) $\Rightarrow$ (iii) is trivial. The implication (iii) $\Rightarrow$ (i) is Sullivan's result [12] (see Theorem 3).

2. We suppose that (ii) from 2 holds for the metric space (X, d) and show that, in this case, statement (iii) from 3 holds, which will imply the completeness of (X, d).

Let $\varphi : X \to [0, \infty)$ be a continuous function and $\varepsilon > 0$.

On the metric space (X, d) consider the order

$$x \preceq y \iff d(x, y) \leq \varphi(y) - \varphi(x).$$

Since φ is continuous, the OSC property holds in $(X, d, \preceq)$ (by Proposition 1). It follows that there exists $x_\varepsilon \in X$ such that the inequality (23) holds. Since $d(x, x_\varepsilon) > \varphi(x_\varepsilon) - \varphi(x)$ for all $x \in X$ for which $x \preceq x_\varepsilon$ fails, it follows that the inequality (23) holds for all $x \in X \setminus \{x_\varepsilon\}$

with $x \neq x_\varepsilon$. Consequently, the statement (ii) from 3 holds, implying the completeness of (X,d).

1. The relation

$$x \preceq y \iff (x,y) \in E(G)$$

establishes a one-to-one correspondence between reflexive transitive acyclic weighted graphs and partially ordered metric spaces (see Remark 3) as well as the equivalence between the properties expressed in terms of the graph and those expressed in terms of the order. Consequently, 1 is a rephrasing of 2 in terms of graphs. □

4. Caristi Fixed Point Theorem and Takahashi Minimization Principle on Weighted Graphs

In this section, we present versions of Caristi fixed point theorem (Theorem 4) and Takahashi minimization principle (Theorem 5) on weighted graphs.

We start with Caristi fixed point theorem.

Theorem 9. *Let $G = (V(G), E(G), d)$ be a reflexive transitive acyclic digraph, where d is a G-complete metric on $V(G)$ such that the OSC property for G-sequences holds on G and let $\varphi : X \to [0, \infty)$ be a G-LSC function.*

1. *If $T : X \to X$ is a mapping satisfying the condition*

$$\forall x \in X, \ (T(x), x) \in E(G) \ \text{and} \ d(T(x), x) \leq \varphi(x) - \varphi(T(x)), \tag{25}$$

then T has a fixed point, i.e., there exists $z \in X$ such that $z = T(z)$.

2. *If $T : X \rightrightarrows X$ is a set-valued mapping such that for every $x \in X$ there exists $y \in T(x)$ satisfying the condition*

$$(y, x) \in E(G) \ \text{and} \ d(y, x) \leq \varphi(x) - \varphi(y), \tag{26}$$

then T has a fixed point, i.e., there exists $z \in X$ such that $z \in T(z)$.

3. *Suppose that $T : X \rightrightarrows X$ is a set-valued mapping with nonempty values such that $T(X) \times X \subseteq E(G)$ and for every $x \in X$ and all $y \in T(x)$,*

$$d(y, x) \leq \varphi(x) - \varphi(y). \tag{27}$$

Then there exists $z \in X$ such that $T(z) = \{z\}$.

Proof. Consider again the order $\leq_\varphi$ given by

$$x \leq_\varphi y \iff d(x,y) \leq \varphi(y) - \varphi(x),$$

and for $x \in V(G)$ let

$$S(x) = \{y \in V(G) : y \leq_\varphi x \ \text{and} \ (y,x) \in E(G)\}.$$

Since a single-valued mapping $T : X \to X$ can be viewed as a set-valued one $x \mapsto \{T(x)\}$, $x \in X$, conditions (25) and (26) can be expressed as

$$\forall x \in X, \ S(x) \cap T(x) \neq \emptyset,$$

implying that 1 is a particular case of 2.

To prove 2 we appeal to Corollary 2. Observe that condition (18) for $\lambda = \varepsilon - 1$ can be expressed as: there exists $z \in X$ such that

$$S(z) = \{z\}.$$

But the condition $S(z) \cap T(z) \neq \emptyset$ means that $z \in T(z)$, i.e., z is a fixed point for T.

3. Observe that

$$T(X) \times X \subseteq E(G) \iff \forall x \in X,\ T(x) \times \{x\} \subseteq E(G)$$
$$\iff \forall x \in X,\ \forall y \in T(x),\ (y,x) \in E(G).$$

Let $z \in X$ satisfying (18).

Since the mapping T has nonempty values and $T(X) \times X \subseteq E(G)$, it follows that condition (27) implies (26). Hence, the proof of statement 2 shows that $z \in F(z)$. If it would exists and element $x \neq z$ in $F(z)$, then $(x,z) \in E(G)$ so that, by (18),

$$\varphi(z) < \varphi(x) + d(x,z),$$

in contradiction to (27). □

A point z satisfying $T(z) = \{z\}$ is called a stationary point (or a strict fixed point) of T.
A point z satisfying $T(z) = \{z\}$ is called a stationary point (or a strict fixed point) of T.
A point z satisfying $T(z) = \{z\}$ is called a stationary point (or a strict fixed point) of T.
We present now a version of Takahashi minimization principle in weighted graphs.

Theorem 10. *Let $G = (V(G), E(G), d)$ be a reflexive transitive acyclic digraph, where d is a G-complete metric on $V(G)$ such that the OSC property for G-sequences holds on G and let $\varphi : X \to [0, \infty)$ be a G-LSC function.*

If for every $x \in V(G)$ satisfying the condition $\varphi(x) > \inf \varphi(X)$ there exists $y \in V(G) \setminus \{x\}$ such that

$$(y,x) \in E(G) \ \text{ and } \ \varphi(y) + d(x,y) \leq \varphi(x), \tag{28}$$

then φ attains its infimum on $V(G)$, i.e., there exists $z \in V(G)$ such that $\varphi(z) = \inf \varphi(V(G))$.

Proof. Considering again the order $\leq_\varphi$ and the sets $S(x)$ as given in the proof of Theorem 9, condition (28) can be expressed as

$$S(x) \setminus \{x\} \neq \emptyset,$$

for every $x \in V(G)$ with $\varphi(x) > \inf \varphi(V(G))$. By Corollary 2 there exists $z \in V(G)$ with $S(z) = \{z\}$. It follows that this z must satisfy

$$\varphi(z) = \inf \varphi(V(G)).$$

□

5. The Equivalence of Principles

We prove in this section the equivalence of Ekekand, Caristi and Takahashi principles. We formulate them in terms of the order $\leq_\phi$ and the sets $S(x)$.

Theorem 11. *Let $G = (V(G), E(G), d)$ be a reflexive transitive acyclic digraph, where d is a metric on $V(G)$ and let $\varphi : X \to [0, \infty)$ be a function. Let $\leq_\varphi$ be the partial order on $V(G)$ given for $x, y \in V(G)$ by*

$$y \leq_\varphi x \iff d(x,y) \leq \varphi(x) - \varphi(y),$$

and, for $x \in V(G)$, put

$$S(x) = \{y \in X : y \leq_\varphi x \ \text{ and } \ (y,x) \in E(G)\}.$$

Then the following statements are equivalent.

(wEk) *The following holds*

$$\exists z \in V(G) \ \text{ such that } \ S(z) = \{z\}. \tag{29}$$

(Car) *Any mapping $T : X \to X$ satisfying*

$$T(x) \in S(x) \text{ for all } x \in V(G), \tag{30}$$

has a fixed point, i.e., there exists $z \in V(G)$ such that $T(z) = z$.

(Tak) *If*

$$S(x) \setminus \{x\} \neq \emptyset, \tag{31}$$

for every $x \in V(G)$ with $\varphi(x) > \inf \varphi(V(G))$, then there exists $z \in V(G)$ such that $\varphi(z) = \inf \varphi(V(G))$.

Proof. The implication (wEk) $\Rightarrow$ (Car) is contained in the proof of Theorem 9.

(Car) $\Rightarrow$ (wEk).

We prove the equivalent implication $\neg$(wEk) $\Rightarrow$ $\neg$(Car).

Observe that $\neg$(wEk) means that

$$S(x) \setminus \{x\} \neq \emptyset \text{ for all } x \in V(G). \tag{32}$$

Let $T : V(G) \to V(G)$ be defined for $x \in V(G)$ by $T(x) = y_x$, where $y_x \in S(x) \setminus \{x\}$. Then T satisfies (30), but, by the choice of y_x, $T(x) \neq x$ for all $x \in V(G)$, i.e., (Car) fails.

(Tak) $\Longleftrightarrow$ (wEk).

We prove the equivalent assertion $\neg$(Tak) $\Longleftrightarrow$ $\neg$(wEk).

Observe that (Tak) can be formally written as

$$\begin{aligned} &[\forall x \in V(G), \quad \varphi(x) > \inf \varphi(X) \Rightarrow S(x) \setminus \{x\} \neq \emptyset] \\ &\Rightarrow [\exists z \in V(G), \quad \varphi(z) = \inf \varphi(V(G))], \end{aligned}$$

so that, its negation $\neg$(Tak) is given by

$$\begin{aligned} &\neg(\text{Tak}) \\ &\Longleftrightarrow [\forall x \in V(G), \quad \varphi(x) > \inf \varphi(X) \Rightarrow S(x) \setminus \{x\} \neq \emptyset] \\ &\wedge [\forall z \in V(G), \quad \varphi(z) > \inf \varphi(V(G)] \\ &\Longleftrightarrow \forall x \in V(G), \quad S(x) \setminus \{x\} \neq \emptyset \\ &\Longleftrightarrow \neg(\text{wEk}). \end{aligned}$$

(The last equivalence from above follows from (32)). □

These equivalences and Theorem 8 show that the completeness of $(V(G), d)$ is also equivalent to the fulfillment of each of these principles.

Corollary 3. *Let $G = (V(G), E(G), d)$ be a reflexive transitive acyclic digraph, where d is a metric on $V(G)$ such that the OSC property for G-sequences holds on G. Then the following statements are equivalent.*

1. *The metric space $(V(G), d)$ is G-complete.*
2. (wEk) *For every G-LSC function $\varphi : V(G) \to [0, \infty)$ there exists $z \in V(G)$ such that*

$$S(z) = \{z\}. \tag{33}$$

3. (Car) *For every G-LSC function $\varphi : V(G) \to [0, \infty)$ and any mapping $T : V(G) \to V(G)$ satisfying*

$$T(x) \in S(x) \text{ for all } x \in V(G), \tag{34}$$

there exists $z \in V(G)$ such that $T(z) = z$.

4. (Tak) *For every G-LSC function $\varphi : V(G) \to [0, \infty)$ such that*

$$S(x) \setminus \{x\} \neq \emptyset, \tag{35}$$

for all $x \in V(G)$ *with* $\varphi(x) > \inf \varphi(V(G))$, *there exists* $z \in V(G)$ *with* $\varphi(z) = \inf \varphi(V(G))$.

Remark 8. *In the proof of Theorem 11 we have used some rules from Mathematical Logic (calculus of propositions and calculus of predicates). The sign* $\neg$ *stands for negation,* $\vee$ *is for "or", while* $\wedge$ *is for "and".*

$$\begin{aligned}
&\neg(\neg p) \leftrightarrow p, \qquad &&\neg(p \vee q) \leftrightarrow (\neg p \wedge \neg q), \qquad &&\neg(p \wedge q) \leftrightarrow (\neg p \vee \neg q),\\
&(p \to q) \leftrightarrow (\neg p \vee q), &&\neg(p \to q) \leftrightarrow (p \wedge \neg q), &&(p \to q) \leftrightarrow (\neg q \to \neg p),\\
&\neg(\forall x,\ P(x)) \leftrightarrow (\exists x,\ \neg P(x)),\\
&\neg(\exists x,\ P(x)) \leftrightarrow (\forall x,\ \neg P(x)).
\end{aligned}$$

6. Conclusions

There are many extensions of Ekeland Variational Principles and its equivalences obtained either relaxing the conditions on the function φ (e.g., by considering functions with values in an ordered vector space) or considering spaces more general than the metric ones (uniform spaces, quasi-metric spaces, w-metric spaces, partial-metric spaces, etc.), or both.

In the present paper such an extension is given within the framework of metric spaces endowed with a graph and for a function φ satisfying a weaker notion of lower semi-continuity as well as a weaker notion of completeness, all expressed in terms of the graph, completing in this way the results obtained by Alfuraidan and Khamsi [2] and Jachymski [10].

Author Contributions: Conceptualization, A.B., Ş.C. and M.D.M.; investigation, A.B., Ş.C. and M.D.M.; writing–original draft preparation, A.B., Ş.C. and M.D.M.; review and editing, A.B., Ş.C. and M.D.M. All authors have read and agreed to the published version of the manuscript.

Funding: This research received no external funding.

Data Availability Statement: Not applicable.

Acknowledgments: The authors express their thanks to reviewers for their remarks and suggestions that led to a substantial improvement of the presentation.

Conflicts of Interest: The authors declare no conflict of interest.

References

1. Ekeland, I. On the variational principle. *J. Math. Anal. Appl.* **1974**, *47*, 324–353. [CrossRef]
2. Alfuraidan, M.R.; Khamsi, M. Graphical Ekeland's principle for equilibrium problems. *Proc. Am. Math. Soc. Ser. B* **2022**, *9*, 33–40. [CrossRef]
3. Al-Homidan, S.; Ansari, Q.H.; Yao, J.-C. Some generalizations of Ekeland-type variational principle with applications to equilibrium problems and fixed point theory. *Nonlinear Anal.* **2008**, *69*, 26–139. [CrossRef]
4. De Figueiredo, D.G. *Lectures on the Ekeland Variational Principle with Applications and Detours*; Lectures on Mathematics and Physics, Mathematics, Tata Institute of Fundamental Research 81; Springer: Berlin/Heidelberg, Germany, 1989.
5. Ekeland, I. Nonconvex minimization problems. *Bull. Am. Math. Soc.* **1979**, *1*, 443–474. [CrossRef]
6. Qiu, J.-H. An equilibrium version of vectorial Ekeland variational principle and its applications to equilibrium problems. *Nonlinear Anal. Real World Appl.* **2016**, *27*, 26–42. [CrossRef]
7. Bao, T.Q.; Cobzaş, S.; Soubeyran, A. Variational principles, completeness and the existence of traps in behavioral sciences. *Ann. Oper. Res.* **2018**, *269*, 53–79. [CrossRef]
8. Cobzaş, S. Fixed points and completeness in metric and generalized metric spaces. *J. Math. Sci.* **2020**, *250*, 475–535. (Translated from Russian: *Fundam. Prikl. Mat.* **2018**, *22*, 127–215). [CrossRef]
9. Alfuraidan, M.R.; Khamsi, M. Ekeland variational principle on weighted graphs. *Proc. Am. Math. Soc.* **2019**, *147*, 5313–5321. [CrossRef]
10. Jachymski, J. The contraction principle for mappings on a metric space with a graph. *Proc. Am. Math. Soc.* **2008**, *136*, 1359–1373. [CrossRef]
11. Weston, J.D. A characterization of metric completeness. *Proc. Am. Math. Soc.* **1977**, *64*, 186–188. [CrossRef]
12. Sullivan, F. A characterization of complete metric spaces. *Proc. Am. Math. Soc.* **1981**, *83*, 345–346. [CrossRef]

13. Sullivan, F. Ordering and completeness of metric spaces. *Nieuw Arch. Wisk.* **1981**, *29*, 178–193.
14. Caristi, J. Fixed point theorems for mappings satisfying inwardness conditions. *Trans. Am. Math. Soc.* **1976**, *215*, 241–251. [CrossRef]
15. Caristi, J.; Kirk, W.A. Geometric fixed point theory and inwardness conditions. In *Geometry of Metric and Linear Spaces;* Lecture Notes in Mathematics 490; Springer: Berlin/Heidelberg, Germany, 1975; pp. 74–83.
16. Takahashi, W. Existence theorems generalizing fixed point theorems for multivalued mappings. In *Fixed Point Theory and Applications (Marseille, 1989);* Pitman Research Notes in Mathematics Series; Longman Scientific and Technical: Harlow, UK, 1991; Volume 252, pp. 397–406.
17. Takahashi, W. *Nonlinear Functional Analysis—Fixed Point Theory and Its Applications;* Yokohama Publishers: Yokohama, Japan, 2000.
18. Johnsonbaugh, R. *Discrete Mathematics*, 7th ed.; Prentice Hall: Upper Saddle River, NJ, USA, 2009.
19. Bollobás, B. *Graph Theory: An Introductory Course*, 3rd ed.; Springer: Berlin/Heidelberg, Germany, 1990.
20. Wallis, W.D. *A Beginner's Guide to Graph Theory*, 2nd ed.; Birkhäuser: Boston, MA, USA, 2007.
21. Nieto J.J.; Rodríguez-López, R. Contractive mapping theorems in partially ordered sets and applications to ordinary differential equations. *Order* **2005**, *22*, 223–239. [CrossRef]
22. Brøndsted, A. On a lemma of Bishop and Phelps. *Pac. J. Math.* **1974**, *55*, 335–341. [CrossRef]
23. Brøndsted, A. Fixed points and partial orders. *Proc. Am. Math. Soc.* **1976**, *60*, 365–366. [CrossRef]
24. Bishop, E.; Phelps, R.R. The support functionals of a convex set. In *Proceedings of Symposia in Pure Mathematics VII*; American Mathematical Society: Providence, RI, USA, 1963; pp. 27–35.
25. Phelps, R.R. *Convex Functions, Monotone Operators and Differentiability*, 2nd ed.; Lecture Notes in Mathematics 1364; Springer: Berlin/Heidelberg, Germany, 1993.
26. Alfuraidan, M.R.; Khamsi, M.A. Caristi fixed point theorem in metric spaces with a graph. *Abstr. Appl. Anal.* **2014**, *2014*, 303484. [CrossRef]

axioms

MDPI

Article

Unfolding a Hidden Lagrangian Structure of a Class of Evolution Equations

Philip Rosenau

School of Mathematical Sciences, Tel Aviv University, Tel Aviv 69978, Israel; rosenau@tauex.tau.ac.il

Abstract: It is shown that a simple modification of the standard Lagrangian underlying the dynamics of Newtonian lattices enables one to infer the hidden Lagrangian structure of certain classes of first order in time evolution equations which lack the conventional Lagrangian structure. Implication to other setups is outlined and exemplified.

Keywords: inverse variational problem; Lagrangian; non-linear dispersion PDE

MSC: 35A15; 37K06; 70H03

1. The Problem

Unlike the Roman Deity Janus enshrined with two equal faces, in the calculus of variations most of the attention is given to the direct venue which emerges naturally when a scientific problem is ab initio introduced via the variational principle. However, in many scientific endeavors, in particular when the underlying problem is partially phenomenological, models are derived on the level of differential equations, thus raising a natural quest for an underlying Lagrangian structure which apart from "scientific beauty" would carry many advantages, with conservation laws being one of them. The 'upstream' path from Equations to the underlying variational structure is known as an inverse problem of calculus of variations. Unfortunately, our ability to tackle the inverse problem and thus deduce the underlying Lagrangian structure from a given dynamical system is far more modest in spite of the long-standing attempts, c.f., [1–5], which date back to Helmholtz, as those efforts, rather than provide us with a definite algorithm to construct the Lagrangian, provide us the conditions for its existence or statements of equivalence rather than with a specific 'how' (notably, there is a far richer literature on Hamiltonian structures than on Lagrangians, though a more balanced approach may be found in texts on dispersive waves. c.f., [6–8]).

In the present communication, we unfold the algorithm to determine the underlying Lagrangian of a particular dynamical system as it relates to the $K(n,n)$ equations

$$K(n,m) \quad u_t = (u^m)_x + (u^n)_{xxx}, \quad 1 < n, m, \tag{1}$$

and a variety of their extensions. Equation (1) were introduced by us some time ago, refs. [9,10] and for $1 < n$ beget the compaction, solitary wave with a finite span. In the particular case $m = n$, its compactons take a simple trigonometric form. For instance, when $n = 2$

$$u = \frac{4\lambda}{3}\cos^2\Big(\frac{x+\lambda t}{4}\Big)H(2\pi - |x+\lambda t|), \tag{2}$$

with H being the Heaviside function. However, besides compactons, the $K(m,n)$ equations had many other fascinating features; at the time the model was introduced, Lagrangian structure did not seem to be one of them. The apparent lack of a Lagrangian structure was the main critique directed at the $K(m,n)$ models by Cooper et al. [11], who introduced an alternative, compacton-supporting model derived from an ab initio assumed Lagrangian. In what follows, for the $m = n$ and $m = n + 1$ cases we shall construct the seemingly 'missing' Lagrangian and thus, at least in part, refute their critique, but first let us note that to account for other physically relevant cases [12], the $K(m, n)$ model was extended to the $C(m; a, b)$ setup [10]

$$C(m;a,b) \quad u_t = (u^m)_x + \left[u^a (u^b)_{xx}\right]_x, \quad and \quad n \doteq a + b, \tag{3}$$

which conserves

$$I_1 = \int u dx \quad and \quad I_\omega = \int u^\omega dx, \tag{4}$$

where $\omega \doteq b + 1 - a$. For $a = 0$, Equation (3) reduces to the $K(m, n)$ setup and with model in [11] being a particular $b = a + 1$ case.

As shown in [10], for $\omega = 2$, i.e., $b = a + 1$, the $C(m; a, a + 1)$ equations follow from a conventional Lagrangian which in terms of $u = \psi_x$ reads

$$\mathcal{L} = \int dt \int \Big\{\frac{1}{2}\psi_t\psi_x + \frac{{\psi_x}^{m+1}}{m+1} - \frac{1}{2}\psi_x^{n-1}\psi_{xx}^2\Big\}dx, \tag{5}$$

adding to the conservation roster the conservation of energy. However, since in the $K(m, n)$ equations $a = 0$, in this setup only the semi-linear, Korteveg–deVries-like sub-cases are endowed with the Lagrangian structure (5).

Yet, insofar as the $m = n$ and $m = n + 1$ cases are concerned, i.e., for the $K(n, n)$ and $K(n + 1, n)$ cases, the claim in [11] was too sweeping as it *refers only to the conventional Lagrangian structure (5). We have recently demonstrated* [13], that both setups *admit a Lagrangian structure* which, however, is 'hidden from sight' and, as we shall see shortly, quite different from the conventional one (5). Consequently, the two conservation laws in (4) were appended with an additional, non-local, conservation law.

As we shall see shortly, in both $K(n, n)$ and $K(n + 1, n)$ setups, the derivation of the non-standard Lagrangian was based on non-obvious steps/tricks. The present communication aims to re-derive the underlying Lagrangian of the $K(n, n)$ setup via a more algorithmic approach, which exploits a certain formal affinity between the $K(n, n)$ equations and a dynamical system describing the motion of a Newtonian mass-spring chain which is not only easily deduced from a Lagrangian setup, but is often ab initio formulated via its Lagrangian. Although tying two very different setups may seem at first to be yet another ad hoc trick, as we shall see the idea may be easily extended to other dynamical systems, and thus has potentially a much wider scope. To avoid misunderstanding, we note that we assume the considered problems to be stated on the whole line with solutions vanishing at infinity and thus satisfying the natural boundary conditions implied by the variational derivation.

Let us first briefly summarize the derivation in [13]; see also [10]. To this end, the $K(n, n)$ equations are rewritten as a Hamiltonian system

$$u_t = \partial_x L^2 \frac{\delta}{\delta u} I_\omega \quad where \quad L^2 = 1 + \frac{\partial^2}{\partial x^2}. \tag{6}$$

This step is deductive. The maneuver which leads to the breakthrough is to introduce a new variable v via

$$u = L[v], \tag{7}$$

with L understood in a pseudo-differential sense. In terms of L, we have

$$v_t = \partial_x \frac{\delta}{\delta v} \int \frac{1}{1+n} \big(L[v]\big)^{1+n} dx = \partial_x L\big(L[v]\big)^n. \tag{8}$$

The next, final step consists of introducing a 'potential' variable ψ [7–9], where $v = \psi_x$ that casts Equation (8) into a form which, as per ref. [4], is akin to the Lagrangian

$$\mathcal{L} = \int dt \int \left\{ \frac{1}{2}\psi_t\psi_x - \frac{1}{n+1}\big(L[\psi_x]\big)^{n+1} \right\} dx \tag{9}$$

of what, prior to their map, were $K(n,n,)$ equations.

Two remarks are in order:

(1) As noted, in the preceding discussion we have tacitly assumed that our system is given on a line with all data vanishing at infinity, thus the natural boundary conditions assumed tacitly in the variational derivation hold trivially. If non-trivial boundary conditions are at play, the issue may become more evolved. However, recalling the very recent work of Olver [14] who further developed the old observation [1–5] that one may modify the variational problem without altering the corresponding Euler–Lagrange equations by adding a null Lagrangian to the integrand, we note that since this modification changes the associated natural boundary conditions, it enables one to enlarge the range of boundary value problems akin to variational techniques. Thus, the core difficulty remains to find the underlying Lagrangian, whereas its extension to handle non-natural boundary conditions may be delegated to the unfolding of a proper null Lagrangian.

(2) Note that the last step of introducing a potential in (5) is well known and apart from its more recent use in dispersive systems [6–8], it could be found in the classical textbooks in electrodynamics., c.f., [15], or continuum [16,17].

With a Lagrangian and its invariant properties at hand, in addition to the conservation of mass and energy, we now also have conservation of the momentum $\int v^2 dx$, which in terms of the original variables, turns into the conservation of

$$I_2 = \int u L^{-2}[u] dx.$$

It is easily seen that though the presented approach was applied to a very particular problem it may be quite naturally extended. Thus, for instance, one may consider

$$u_t = \partial_x L_*^2(F(u)), \tag{10}$$

where L_*^2 is any 'reasonable' linear operator and $F(u)$ any nice function [4]. For instance, in Ref. [18] addressing synchronisation of oscillators $F(u) = \cos u$ was assumed. Using the previous notation, in terms of v we have

$$v_t = \partial_x L_*\big(F(L_* v)\big). \tag{11}$$

In terms of ψ, $v = \psi_x$, the underlying Lagrangian reads,

$$\mathcal{L} = \int dt \int \{ \frac{1}{2}\psi_t\psi_x - G\big(L_*[\psi_x]\big) \} dx, \quad and \;\; F = G'. \tag{12}$$

As another extension, consider the *second order in time system* (c.f., Equation (27))

$$u_{tt} = \partial_x^2 L_*^2(F(u)). \tag{13}$$

In terms of ψ, $v = \psi_x$, its Lagrangian reads,

$$\mathcal{L} = \int dt \int \{ \frac{1}{2}\psi_t^2 - G\big(L_*[\psi_x]\big) \} dx, \tag{14}$$

and $F = G'$.

In the next section, we take a detour needed to tie our problem with the obvious Lagrangian structure of a Newtonian mass-spring lattice which will render a more natural path toward the deduction of a Lagrangian structure of the $K(n,n)$ equations. Yet another take on the lattice–Lagrangian relations is briefly discussed in the Appendix A.

2. The Newtonian Chain

We start with the Hamiltonian of an unrelated mass-particle chain [19,20],

$$\mathcal{H} = \sum_{N}^{+N} \Big\{ \frac{m}{2}(y_n)^2 + P\big(\frac{y_{n+1} - y_n}{h}\big) \Big\}. \tag{15}$$

Let $y_n = y(t, nh)$, $\ell = h/2$, $m = \rho h$, $\rho \downarrow 1$, and $D_x \doteq \ell\partial_x$, then expansion of the potential P yields

$$P\big(\frac{y_{n+1} - y_n}{h}\big) = P(y_x) - \frac{h^2}{24}(y_{xx})^2 P''(y_x) + \mathcal{O}(h^4).$$

To this order of expansion and the standard discrete-continuum association, the ab initio available Lagrangian density becomes

$$\mathcal{L} = \int\int \Big\{ \frac{1}{2}(y_t)^2 - P(y_x) + \frac{h^2}{24}(y_{xx})^2 P''(y_x) \Big\} dtdx, \tag{16}$$

with its equations of motion

$$y_{tt} = \frac{\partial}{\partial x}\Big[P'(y_x) + \frac{h^2}{12}\sqrt{P''(y_x)}\frac{\partial}{\partial x}\big(\sqrt{P''(y_x)}y_{xx}\big) \Big]. \tag{17}$$

Thus, if $P(s) = s^4/4$ and $u = y_x$, then after one differentiation the resulting PDE reads

$$u_{tt} = \big[u^3 + \frac{h^2}{8}u(u^2)_{xx}\big]_{xx}. \tag{18}$$

However, we shall also need an alternative description. Let

$$M(\ell) \doteq \frac{2\ell\partial_x}{e^{\ell\partial_x} - e^{-\ell\partial_x}}, \quad \mathcal{L}_{\mathcal{D}} \doteq M^{-1}, \tag{19}$$

and v a new variable defined *via*

$$y = M(\ell)[v] \quad or \quad v = \mathcal{L}_{\mathcal{D}}[y], \tag{20}$$

then in terms of v, the Hamiltonian (13) reads

$$\mathcal{H} = \int\int \Big\{ \frac{1}{2}(Mv_t)^2 + P(v_x) \Big\} dtdx, \tag{21}$$

which yields

$$M^2 v_{tt} = \big[P'(v_x)\big]_x. \tag{22}$$

Acting on (20) with $\mathcal{L}_{\mathcal{D}}{}^2$ and ∂_x we obtain

$$u_{tt} = \mathcal{L}_{\mathcal{D}}^2\big[P'(u)\big]_{xx} \quad where \quad u = v_x. \tag{23}$$

Actually, without invoking v, we may use y ab initio and rewrite the Hamiltonian (13) in terms of y

$$\mathcal{H} = \int\int \Big\{ \frac{1}{2}(y_t)^2 + P(\mathcal{L}_{\mathcal{D}}y_x) \Big\} dtdx, \tag{24}$$

with its Lagrangian density

$$\mathcal{L} = \int\int \Big\{ \frac{1}{2}(y_t)^2 - P(\mathcal{L}_{\mathcal{D}}y_x) \Big\} dtdx, \tag{25}$$

which yields

$$y_{tt} = \Big[\mathcal{L}_{\mathcal{D}}P'(\mathcal{L}_{\mathcal{D}}y_x)\Big]_x. \tag{26}$$

Of course, since $u = v_x = \mathcal{L}_\mathcal{D} y_x$, acting with $\mathcal{L}_\mathcal{D} \partial x$, turns Equation (24) into (21).

Note that if, say, $P'(u) = u^3$ and $\mathcal{L}_\mathcal{D} = 1 + \frac{h^2}{12}\partial_x^2$, obtained after carrying the expansion of $\mathcal{L}_\mathcal{D}$ to fourth order, Equation (21) turns into a second order in time variant of the $K(n,n)$ equation

$$u_{tt} = \left[u^n + \frac{h^2}{12}(u^n)_{xx}\right]_{xx}. \tag{27}$$

With its Lagrangian structure given via (14). Both Equations (18) and (27) and their underlying Lagrangians provide a quasi-continuum rendition of the same lattice, with expansions centering around different nodal locations.

Bridging between the Two Systems

The Newtonian system is second order in time. To turn it into a structurally analogous, but of first order in time system, we modify the kinetic part in (23)

$$y_t^2 \to y_t y_x \tag{28}$$

with the resulting Lagrangian becoming

$$\mathcal{L} = \int\int \left\{\frac{1}{2} y_t y_x - P(\mathcal{L}_\mathcal{D} y_x)\right\} dt dx. \tag{29}$$

Identifying P with G and ψ with y, begets a Lagrangian form identical to (12), with a related dynamical system which is first order in time. Setting $u = \mathcal{L}_\mathcal{D} y_x$ yields Equation (11). In particular, $P(s) = \frac{1}{n+1}s^n$ yields the $K(n,n)$ setup with the resulting sought-after Lagrangian structure.

Finally, consider again the direct expansion of the lattice and its underlying standard Lagrangian (14). Assuming again that $P(s) = \frac{1}{n+1}s^{n+1}$, $m = n$ and repeating the $y_t^2 \to y_t y_x$ association, we recover module normalizable coefficients, the Lagrangian (5) and the underlying Equation (3); $C(m; a, a+1)$, with $2a = n - 1$.

Thus, as with Equations (21) and (25), with each of the expansions being based on a different nodal location on the lattice, we obtain a different equation of motion and a different corresponding Lagrangian: one which is conventional and readily available, and the other hidden and subject of the present exploration.

3. Closing Comments

The present note is a modest take on the inverse problem of the calculus of variations to seek from a particular partial differential system its variational antecedent. At the present state of affairs, the statements regarding the underlying Lagrangian structure of a given dynamical system are affirmative rather than constructive. Every success is ad hoc and relies on certain intuitive steps which have to be inferred independently for each problem.

Exploiting a formal structural affinity between two different physico-mathematical entities wherein one, being second order in time, is endowed with a natural Lagrangian structure, the Lagrangian of the other is constructed via a natural modification. What saves the presented approach from being yet another ad hoc spiel is the fact that the approach carries to a wider set of problems wherein the first order in time dynamical system lacks an obvious underlying Lagrangian, but a better chance may await us looking at structurally similar second-order equations in time endowed with an obvious Lagrangian structure.

Funding: The research was funded in part by the ISF contract 1983/22.

Data Availability Statement: Not applicable.

Acknowledgments: The author thanks P. Olver for his constructive comments.

Conflicts of Interest: The author declares no conflict of interest.

Appendix A

Another take on the discussed problem is provided by the following first-order system [8]

$$\frac{d}{dt}u_n = \sum_{-N}^{+N} \frac{f(u_{n+1}) - f(u_{n-1})}{2\ell}. \tag{A1}$$

Let $D_x = \ell\partial_x$ and $\mathcal{L}_+^2 \doteq \mathcal{L}_D$, then

$$u_t = \partial_x \mathcal{L}_+^2 f(u). \tag{A2}$$

If $u = \mathcal{L}_+ v$, then

$$v_t = \partial_x \mathcal{L}_+ f(\mathcal{L}_+ v). \tag{A3}$$

As before, let $v = \psi_x$, then the desired Lagrangian is

$$\mathcal{L} = \int\int \Big\{\frac{1}{2}\psi_t\psi_x - Q(\mathcal{L}_+\psi_x)\Big\} dtdx, \tag{A4}$$

where $f(u) = Q'(u)$.

We may approximate $\mathcal{L}_+$ in two ways. In the standard approach we utilize the first two terms $\mathcal{L}_+^2 \simeq \mathcal{L}_a^2 \doteq 1 + \frac{D_x^2}{6}$ of the exact expression

$$\mathcal{L}_+^2 = 1 + \frac{D_x^2}{3!} + \frac{D_x^4}{5!} + \ldots \tag{A5}$$

which renders $\mathcal{L}_a$ a pseudo differential operator. But if instead we adopt

$$\mathcal{L}_+^2 \simeq \mathcal{L}_b^2 \doteq (1 + \frac{D_x^2}{12})^2, \tag{A6}$$

with $\mathcal{L}_b = 1 + \frac{D_x^2}{12}$ being a nice differential operator, and within small error covering the first three terms in (A5).

References

1. Anderson I.A. Aspects of the inverse problem to the calculus of variations. *Arch. Math.* **1988**, *24*, 181–202.
2. Tonti, E. Inverse problem: Its general solution. In *Lecture Notes in Pure and Applied Mathematics No. 100: Differential Geometry, Calculus of Variations and Their Applications*; Marcel Decker: New York, NY, USA, 1985; pp. 497–510.
3. Giaquinta, M.; Hildebrandt, S. *Calculus of Variations I. The Lagrangian Formalism*; Springer: New York, NY, USA, 1996.
4. Olver, P.J. Dirac's theory of constraints in field theory and the canonical form of Hamiltonian differential operators. *J. Math. Phys.* **1986**, *27*, 2495. [CrossRef]
5. Olver, P.J. On the Hamiltonian structure of evolution equations. *Math. Proc. Camb. Philos. Soc.* **1980**, *88*, 71. [CrossRef]
6. Whitham, G.B. *Linear and Nonlinear Waves*; John Wiley and Sons: Cambridge, MA, USA, 1974.
7. Infeld, E.; Rowlands, G. *Nonlinear Waves, Solitons and Chaos*; Cambridge Univesity Press: Cambridge, UK, 1990.
8. Drazin, P.G.; Johnson, R.S. *Solitons: An Introduction*; Cambridge Univesity Press: Cambridge, UK, 1990.
9. Rosenau, P.; Hyman, J.M. Solitons with finite wavelength. *Phys. Rev. Letts.* **1993**, *70*, 564. [CrossRef] [PubMed]
10. Rosenau, P.; Zilburg, A. Compactons. *J. Phys. A Math. Theor.* **2018**, *51*, 343001. [CrossRef]
11. Cooper, F.; Shepard, H.; Sodano, P. Solitary waves in a class of generalized Korteweg–de Vries equations. *Phys. Rev. E* **1993**, *48*, 4027. [CrossRef] [PubMed]
12. Rubinstein, J. Evolution equations for stratified dilute suspensions. *Phys. Fluids A Fluid Dyn.* **1990**, *2*, 3. [CrossRef]
13. Zilburg, A.; Rosenau, P. On Hamiltonian formulations of the C1(m, a, b) equations. *Phys. Letts.* **2017**, *A381*, 1557. [CrossRef]
14. Olver, P.J. Boundary Conditions and Null Lagrangians in the Calculus of Variations and Elasticity. *J. Elast.* **2022**. [CrossRef]
15. Stratton, J.A. *Electromagnetic Theory*; McGraw Hill: New York, NY, USA, 1941.
16. Sieniutycz, S. *Conservation Laws in Variational Thermo-Hydrodynamics*; Kluwer: Dordrecht, The Netherlands, 1994.
17. Sieniutycz, S.; Berry, R.S. Canonical formalism, fundamental equation, and generalized thermomechanics for irreversible fluids with heat transfer. *Phys. Rev. E* **1993**, *47*, 1765. [CrossRef] [PubMed]
18. Rosenau, P.; Pikovsky, A. Solitary phase waves in a chain of autonomous oscillators. *Chaos* **2020**, *30*, 053119. [CrossRef] [PubMed]

19. Rosenau, P. Hamiltonian dynamics of dense chains and lattices: Or how to correct the continuum. *Phys. Letts.* **2003**, *A311*, 39. [CrossRef]
20. Rosenau, P.; Schochet, S. Compact and almost compact breathers: A bridge between an anharmonic lattice and its continuum limit. *Chaos* **2005**, *15*, 015111. [CrossRef] [PubMed]

axioms

MDPI

Article

A Systematic Approach to Standard Dissipative Continua

Sebastian Stark

Fraunhofer Institute for Ceramic Technologies and Systems IKTS, Winterbergstr. 28, 01277 Dresden, Germany; sebastian.stark@ikts.fraunhofer.de

Abstract: Many isothermal dissipative continuum problems can be formulated in a variational setting using the concept of "standard dissipative continua". A major advantage of this approach is that complex problems can be cast into a compact, thermodynamically consistent formulation based on a single space–time continuous functional together with a corresponding variational principle. Formulating the problem in terms of a functional provides an immediate avenue for performing spatial and temporal discretization, which are the prerequisites for a numerical solution. Within the present contribution, a novel systematic approach to standard dissipative formulations is proposed, with the main goal being the development and implementation of generic procedures and algorithms for the formulation as well as the computational solution of a subset of isothermal dissipative continuum problems. In order to demonstrate the capabilities of the approach, its application to example problems is discussed.

Keywords: standard dissipative continua; variational principles; finite element method

MSC: 35A15; 49S05; 49-04; 65M60; 74F99; 68V99

1. Introduction

Starting from classical continuum theories, recent decades have seen substantial developments towards the modeling of nonlinear dissipative multi-physics phenomena. Examples include electromechanical coupling in ferroelectric materials [1], magnetoelectromechanical coupling in multiferroic materials [2] as well as electrochemomechanical coupling in batteries [3] and hydrogels [4]. Although most continuum concepts are, in principle, readily extended to account for such multiphysics effects, the formulation of thermodynamically consistent theories and their solution by numerical methods becomes an increasingly tedious task as the number of coupled physics and, therefore, unknown variables increases. This is particularly of concern for:

1. The model formulation in terms of a number of partial differential (or differential algebraic) equations, which may often be combined in many different ways to form a final set of space–time continuous equations;
2. The mathematical analysis of the space–time continuous equations, e.g., with regard to the well posedness of the problem and stability properties;
3. The development of consistent, robust and efficient spatial and temporal discretization schemes;
4. The numerical solution of the space–time discrete problem.

An established approach to reduce the mentioned difficulties is to formulate continuum models in terms of *variational principles* based on a single functional of the unknowns instead of *partial differential equations*, so that the solution of the problem furnishes an extremum or a saddle point of the functional. This approach often provides a compact statement of the problem, which clearly exposes its structure, and thereby facilitates the mathematical analysis as well as the development of robust and efficient discretization and numerical solution procedures. The latter has, e.g., been demonstrated by Simo and Honein [5],

Ortiz and Stainier [6], and Hackl and Fischer [7] in the context of plasticity and viscoplasticity, by Yang et al. [8] in the context of thermomechanically coupled problems, and by Carstensen et al. [9] and Ortiz and Repetto [10] in the context of micro-structure formation. Of particular interest in this regard is the concept of "standard dissipative continua" (see, e.g., Halphen and Nguyen [11], Germain et al. [12]), which effectively involves minimum or saddle point formulations, with thermodynamic consistency being ensured by choosing a so-called dissipation functional to satisfy certain conditions. Examples illustrating the wide applicability of this concept are, e.g., the early work of Biot [13] on fluid transport in porous media as well as a multitude of contributions covering the homogenization of inelastic micro-structures [14,15], gradient-enhanced plasticity [16–20], rate-dependent ferroelectricity [21], magnetostriction with hysteresis [22], electro-magneto-mechanics [2], fluid transport in porous media [23], Cahn–Hilliard-type and classical diffusion [24,25], and fracture in lithium-ion batteries [26].

Regardless of whether differential (algebraic) equations or a functional together with a variational principle are chosen as the point of departure, the mere implementation effort required to obtain validated numerical software remains a substantial obstacle, especially in the case of multiphysics problems. Due to this aspect, many sophisticated continuum formulations are often only demonstrated for highly simplified situations (e.g., one-dimensional problems), while their application to real-world examples remains elusive. This aspect provides the main motivation for the present contribution. In particular, a systematic approach to standard dissipative formulations is proposed, which covers the steps from problem formulation in the space–time continuous setting through its discretization to implementation.

The plan of the paper is as follows: Firstly, the standard dissipative space–time continuous problem formulation is formalized without reference to particular physics. Secondly, simple approaches for the spatial and temporal discretization of the space–time continuous problem are described. Thirdly, a preliminary implementation based on the open source finite element library deal.II (Alzetta et al. [27], Bangerth et al. [28]) is briefly discussed. Finally, the usefulness of the approach is shown by the application to two multiphysics examples. The first example addresses the buckling behavior of a viscoelastic dielectric elastomer subjected to an electric voltage, while the second example concerns the swelling/shrinking of a hydrogel upon a change of exterior ion concentrations. Both examples include numerical convergence studies with regard to spatial and temporal discretization in order to show that the expected numerical properties indeed translate to practical computations.

2. Formalization of the Space–Time Continuous Problem

In this section, a generic formulation for standard dissipative continua is proposed, with the scope being limited to isothermal problems with elliptic or parabolic structure. It is emphasized in this context that more general standard dissipative formulations than the one presented below are possible. However, certain simplifications are unavoidable in view of implementation aspects. The proposed formulation essentially represents a trade-off between the generality of the formulation and complexity of the implementation into numerical software. Furthermore, it is remarked that most of the theoretical developments are, at least as far as the general ideas are concerned, in some form already available in the pertinent literature. Here, the intended contribution is to compile the theory in a form suitable for subsequent implementation.

The contents of this section are summarized as follows: Firstly, the computational domain including subdomains, boundaries and interfaces is described together with the notation required for bookkeeping purposes. Secondly, the notions of "generalized fields" and "dependent fields" are introduced, and the form of the functionals considered in this work is specified. Despite the fact that these aspects are of subordinate importance from a physical standpoint, they are indispensable with regard to the desired problem-independent implementation of the approach into computer code. Thirdly, the unknowns involved in the statement of the problem are grouped into several categories based on their role in the variational formulation. Fourthly, the space–time continuous incremental potential is introduced, followed by a statement of the space–time continuous incremental variational principle assumed in the present work. Finally, ways to systematically reduce the number of unknowns involved in the problem formulation are described.

2.1. Computational Domain

The Euclidean d-space $\mathcal{R}^d$ with $d = 2$ or $d = 3$ is considered for a range of time $\mathcal{T} = [t_0, t_e)$, with t_0 and t_e being the initial and the final times, respectively. In what follows, $\mathbf{X} \in \mathcal{R}^d$ denotes a spatial location and $t \in \mathcal{T}$ an instant of time. As illustrated in Figure 1, $\mathcal{R}^d$ is assumed to be split into (i) the "environment" Ω^0; (ii) the bounded domain Ω, which is further subdivided into N^Ω "domain portions" Ω^α labeled by α; and (iii) the bounded, sufficiently smooth $d-1$ dimensional interface Σ, which is further subdivided into N^Σ "interface portions" Σ^γ labeled by γ. It is generally assumed that the boundary of each domain portion Ω^α is a part of Σ. This means that $\partial\Omega^\alpha \cap \Sigma = \partial\Omega^\alpha$. Moreover, it is understood that Ω and Σ have no points in common, i.e., $\Sigma \cap \Omega = \emptyset$. In the sequel, the union of Σ and Ω will be referred to as the "computational domain". This computational domain is generally assumed to be kept fixed. This means that it does not change with time. Together with the interface Σ, a piece-wise continuous unit normal field $\mathbf{N}(\mathbf{X})$ is introduced. Using this unit normal field, the '+' and '−' sides of the interface at a location $\mathbf{X} \in \Sigma$ are defined such that $\mathbf{N}(\mathbf{X})$ points from the − to the + side.

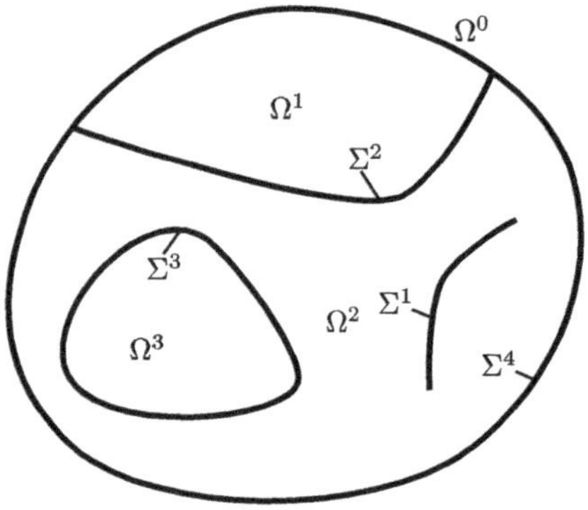

Figure 1. Domain under consideration.

Remark 1.

- *An interface portion Σ^γ need not necessarily be aligned with an interface between different domain portions Ω^α or an interface between a domain portion Ω^α and the environment Ω^0. This means that a "slit" within a domain portion is permissible, as can be seen in the interface portion Σ^1 in Figure 1.*
- *A more complete description would also involve lower-dimensional entities (lines, line portions, and points in three dimensions; points in two dimensions). However, these are firstly rarely relevant to practical examples, and secondly, these are more difficult to implement. Therefore, they are ignored below.*
- *The introduction of different domain and interface portions concerns in particular multiphysics phenomena, with different physics being operative in different regions, and, possibly, combined with interfacial effects.*
- *Keeping the domain of computation fixed does not imply that a Lagrangian or Eulerian viewpoint is adopted. In fact, even arbitrary Lagrangian Eulerian formulations are possible.*

2.2. Generalized Fields, Dependent Fields and the Form of Functionals

Before discussing the standard dissipative formulation considered in this work,

(i) the notions of "generalized fields" and "dependent fields" are introduced, and
(ii) the form a functional can take within this work is narrowed down.

2.2.1. Generalized Fields

A generalized field $\mathbf{G} = \mathbf{G}(\mathbf{X}, t)$ comprises:

1. A number of $N^{\mathbf{G},\Omega}$ time-dependent scalar fields, which are formally defined on the entire computational domain, but which may only be non-zero on Ω. These fields are collected in the vector $\mathbf{G}^{\Omega} = \mathbf{G}^{\Omega}(\mathbf{X}, t)$ and will be referred to as "domain-related fields". The latter may represent, e.g., mechanical displacements, velocities, pressures, electric fields, etc.
2. A number of $N^{\mathbf{G},\Sigma}$ time-dependent scalar fields, which are formally defined on the entire computational domain, but which may only be non-zero on Σ. These fields are collected in the vector $\mathbf{G}^{\Sigma} = \mathbf{G}^{\Sigma}(\mathbf{X}, t)$ and will be referred to as "interface-related fields". The latter may represent, e.g., curvatures, electrical surface charges, interfacial reaction rates, etc.
3. A number of $N^{\mathbf{G},C}$ time-dependent scalars. These scalars are collected in the vector $\mathbf{G}^{C} = \mathbf{G}^{C}(t)$; and they may represent quantities such as integral electric currents, displacements and rotations of rigid domain portions, etc.

With these definitions,

$$\mathbf{G} = \begin{pmatrix} \mathbf{G}^{\Omega} \\ \mathbf{G}^{\Sigma} \\ \mathbf{G}^{C} \end{pmatrix} \tag{1}$$

is as a vector of dimension $N^{\mathbf{G}} = N^{\mathbf{G},\Omega} + N^{\mathbf{G},\Sigma} + N^{\mathbf{G},C}$.

The derivative of $\mathbf{G}$ with respect to $\mathbf{X}$, i.e., the gradient, is introduced according to

$$\nabla\mathbf{G} = \begin{pmatrix} \nabla\mathbf{G}^{\Omega} \\ \nabla_{\Sigma}\mathbf{G}^{\Sigma} \\ \mathbf{0} \end{pmatrix}, \tag{2}$$

with ∇_{Σ} indicating the surface gradient, and $\nabla\mathbf{G}^{\Omega} = \mathbf{0}$ if $\mathbf{X} \in \Sigma$ and $\nabla_{\Sigma}\mathbf{G}^{\Sigma} = \mathbf{0}$ if $\mathbf{X} \in \Omega$. It is noted that $\nabla\mathbf{G}$ may be interpreted as an $N^{\mathbf{G}} \times d$ matrix.

The derivative of $\mathbf{G}$ with respect to t, i.e., the rate, is denoted by

$$\dot{\mathbf{G}} = \begin{pmatrix} \dot{\mathbf{G}}^{\Omega} \\ \dot{\mathbf{G}}^{\Sigma} \\ \dot{\mathbf{G}}^{C} \end{pmatrix}. \tag{3}$$

Two generalized fields $\mathbf{A}$ and $\mathbf{B}$ may be concatenated to form a single generalized field $\mathbf{C}$. In this case, it is understood that the components are rearranged such that the domain-related fields, the interface-related fields and the scalars are contiguous again. This means that:

$$\mathbf{C} = \begin{pmatrix} \mathbf{A} \\ \mathbf{B} \end{pmatrix} = \begin{pmatrix} \mathbf{A}^{\Omega} \\ \mathbf{B}^{\Omega} \\ \mathbf{A}^{\Sigma} \\ \mathbf{B}^{\Sigma} \\ \mathbf{A}^{C} \\ \mathbf{B}^{C} \end{pmatrix} = \begin{pmatrix} \mathbf{C}^{\Omega} \\ \mathbf{C}^{\Sigma} \\ \mathbf{C}^{C} \end{pmatrix}. \tag{4}$$

This procedure can be applied recursively to concatenate more than two generalized fields.

Remark 2. *Vector/tensor fields are considered to be represented by an appropriate number of scalar fields, with the individual scalar fields typically representing vector/tensor coordinates with regard to a particular basis system.*

2.2.2. Dependent Fields

For each generalized field $\mathbf{G}$, a number of $N^{\mathbf{g},\Omega}$ "domain-related dependent fields" and a number of $N^{\mathbf{g},\Sigma}$ "interface-related dependent fields" are introduced. These dependent fields are collected in the vectors $\mathbf{g}^{\Omega}$ and $\mathbf{g}^{\Sigma}$, respectively. In this section, the convention will be followed that upper case letters denote generalized fields, while the corresponding lower case letters denote the associated dependent fields.

The purpose of the dependent fields is the introduction of variables, in terms of which the functionals governing the standard dissipative formulation can be conveniently expressed without direct use of spatial derivatives. A typical example for a dependent field is the mechanical strain field, which is used to introduce the strain energy density in continuum mechanics.

The dependent fields $\mathbf{g}^{\Omega}$ and $\mathbf{g}^{\Sigma}$ are assumed to be linearly related to the generalized field $\mathbf{G}$. In particular,

$$(\mathbf{g}^{\Omega})_{\lambda} = \sum_{\epsilon=1}^{N^{\mathbf{G},\Omega}} \left[a_{\lambda\epsilon}^{\mathbf{G},\Omega} (\mathbf{G}^{\Omega})_{\epsilon} + \mathbf{b}_{\lambda\epsilon}^{\mathbf{G},\Omega} \cdot (\nabla \mathbf{G}^{\Omega})_{\epsilon} \right] + \sum_{\iota=1}^{N^{\mathbf{G},C}} c_{\lambda\iota}^{\mathbf{G},\Omega} (\mathbf{G}^{C})_{\iota} + d_{\lambda}^{\mathbf{G},\Omega} \tag{5}$$

if $\mathbf{X} \in \Omega$ and $(\mathbf{g}^{\Omega})_{\lambda} = 0$ otherwise, with $a_{\lambda\epsilon}^{\mathbf{G},\Omega}$, $c_{\lambda\iota}^{\mathbf{G},\Omega}$ and $d_{\lambda}^{\mathbf{G},\Omega}$ being constants, $\mathbf{b}_{\lambda\epsilon}^{\mathbf{G},\Omega}$ constant vectors of dimension d, and $(\mathbf{Y})_{\lambda}$ denoting the component λ of a vector $\mathbf{Y}$. Similarly,

$$\begin{aligned}(\mathbf{g}^{\Sigma})_{\nu} = & \sum_{\eta=1}^{N^{\mathbf{G},\Sigma}} \left[a_{\nu\eta}^{\mathbf{G},\Sigma} (\mathbf{G}^{\Sigma})_{\eta} + \mathbf{b}_{\nu\eta}^{\mathbf{G},\Sigma} \cdot (\nabla_{\Sigma} \mathbf{G}^{\Sigma})_{\eta} \right] \\ & + \sum_{\epsilon=1}^{N^{\mathbf{G},\Omega}} \left[a_{\nu\epsilon}^{\mathbf{G}+} (\mathbf{G}^{\Omega}|^{+})_{\epsilon} + \mathbf{b}_{\nu\epsilon}^{\mathbf{G}+} \cdot (\nabla \mathbf{G}^{\Omega}|^{+})_{\epsilon} \right] \\ & + \sum_{\epsilon=1}^{N^{\mathbf{G},\Omega}} \left[a_{\nu\epsilon}^{\mathbf{G}-} (\mathbf{G}^{\Omega}|^{-})_{\epsilon} + \mathbf{b}_{\nu\epsilon}^{\mathbf{G}-} \cdot (\nabla \mathbf{G}^{\Omega}|^{-})_{\epsilon} \right] \\ & + \sum_{\iota=1}^{N^{\mathbf{G},C}} c_{\nu\iota}^{\mathbf{G},\Sigma} (\mathbf{G}^{C})_{\iota} + d_{\nu}^{\mathbf{G},\Sigma}\end{aligned} \tag{6}$$

if $\mathbf{X} \in \Sigma$ and $(\mathbf{g}^{\Sigma})_{\nu} = 0$ otherwise, with $a_{\nu\eta}^{\mathbf{G},\Sigma}$, $a_{\nu\epsilon}^{\mathbf{G}+}$, $a_{\nu\epsilon}^{\mathbf{G}-}$, $c_{\nu\iota}^{\mathbf{G},\Sigma}$ and $d_{\nu}^{\mathbf{G},\Sigma}$ being constants, and $\mathbf{b}_{\nu\eta}^{\mathbf{G},\Sigma}$, $\mathbf{b}_{\nu\epsilon}^{\mathbf{G}+}$, $\mathbf{b}_{\nu\epsilon}^{\mathbf{G}-}$ constant vectors of dimension d. In the latter equation as well as in the following, the notation $|^{+/-}$ indicates that reference is made to the limit value as points $\mathbf{X} \in \Sigma$ are approached from the $+$ and the $-$ side of the interface Σ, respectively.

Remark 3.

- *The restriction of $\mathbf{g}^{\Omega}$ and $\mathbf{g}^{\Sigma}$ to a dependence on first spatial derivatives of the generalized field $\mathbf{G}$ may seem rather limiting. However, the formulation to be described does enable the effective incorporation of higher-order derivatives through the introduction of auxiliary quantities. In fact, including higher spatial derivatives would, in a finite element context, require higher-order continuous finite elements; and the latter are rarely used in practice due to the superiority of mixed formulations eliminating the higher spatial derivatives through auxiliary quantities.*
- *The choice of the dependent fields is usually subject to a substantial degree of freedom and will typically be determined by what is most convenient for the definition of the governing functionals.*
- *The constants and constant vectors appearing in (5) and (6) may be made dependent upon $\mathbf{X}$ without affecting the discussion below. Furthermore, nonlinear dependencies of the dependent fields on the generalized fields and derivatives thereof may be allowed for . However, such dependencies are omitted here as they have not yet been implemented (nonetheless, they can be incorporated through constraints, which can be implemented using Lagrangian multipliers).*

2.2.3. Form of Functionals

Let $H[\mathbf{A}^\alpha;\mathbf{B}^\beta,t]$ be a functional of a number of generalized fields $\mathbf{A}^\alpha$ indexed by α and a number of generalized fields $\mathbf{B}^\beta$ indexed by β, with the semicolon indicating that the quantities to the right are regarded as parameters when the variations of the functional H are computed. In the sequel it is assumed that every such functional is of the specific form

$$H[\mathbf{A}^\alpha;\mathbf{B}^\beta,t] = \int_\Omega h^\Omega(\mathbf{a}^{\alpha,\Omega};\mathbf{b}^{\beta,\Omega},\mathbf{X},t)\,\mathrm{d}V + \int_\Sigma h^\Sigma(\mathbf{a}^{\alpha,\Sigma};\mathbf{b}^{\beta,\Sigma},\mathbf{X},t)\,\mathrm{d}S + h^{\mathrm{C}}(\mathbf{A}^{\alpha,\mathrm{C}};\mathbf{B}^{\beta,\mathrm{C}},t), \quad (7)$$

where $\mathrm{d}V$ is the volume element, $\mathrm{d}S$ the interface element, and h^Ω, h^Σ and h^{C} are functions.

Remark 4. *The previous assumption regarding the form of a functional will eventually ensure that the incremental variational principle to be stated below implies a set of partial differential (algebraic) equations and equations without spatial dependency (which may, however, involve integrals).*

2.3. *Unknown Variables*

Conceptually, three different types of unknowns are considered, leading to the definition of the three following generalized fields:

1. A generalized "state variable" $\mathbf{Q}$, which is used to describe the state within the computational domain. $\mathbf{Q}$ may, besides classical "thermodynamic state variables", also comprise a number of "auxiliary state variables", which will be used in the usual way as Lagrangian multipliers enforcing constraints on the admissible thermodynamic states (incompressibility constraints, electroneutrality constraints, etc.). In particular, $\mathbf{Q}$ is assumed to be of the format

$$\mathbf{Q} = \begin{pmatrix}\mathbf{U}\\ \mathbf{P}\end{pmatrix}, \quad (8)$$

where $\mathbf{U}$ comprises the thermodynamic state variables, while $\mathbf{P}$ comprises the auxiliary state variables/Lagrangian multipliers. $\mathbf{Q}$ is subject to an initial condition of the form

$$\mathbf{Q}(\mathbf{X},t_0) = \mathbf{Q}_0(\mathbf{X}), \quad (9)$$

where $\mathbf{Q}_0$ may need to satisfy certain consistency requirements as will be remarked later.

2. A generalized "process variable" $\mathbf{V}$, which may be interpreted as an auxiliary quantity used to constrain the ways the thermodynamic state can change in that only certain combinations of the rates $\dot{\mathbf{Q}}$ and $\dot{\mathbf{V}}$ are admissible. $\mathbf{V}$ is, without loss of generality, subjected to the initial condition

$$\mathbf{V}(\mathbf{X},t_0) = \mathbf{V}_0(\mathbf{X}) = \mathbf{0}. \quad (10)$$

3. A generalized Lagrangian multiplier $\mathbf{M}$, which will be used to actually incorporate constraints for $\dot{\mathbf{Q}}$ and $\dot{\mathbf{V}}$.

Remark 5.

- *The explicit distinction between state variables and process variables appears to be a feature distinguishing the present standard dissipative formulation from what is available in the literature to date, although it is acknowledged that, e.g., the works of Biot [13] and Miehe et al. [23,24,25] implicitly contain such a distinction. Physically, the introduction of process variables may, e.g., be motivated by the following two simple examples: (i) diffusion processes, in which molar concentrations are changed by species fluxes; and (ii) chemical reactions, in which the amounts of the substances involved are changed by chemical reaction processes.*

- *Ultimately, only the rate of the process variable, $\dot{\mathbf{V}}$, will enter the formulation. Hence, it would seem more natural to directly introduce the rate as an unknown. However, the viewpoint adopted here proves beneficial from the implementation point of view.*

2.4. Space–Time Continuous Incremental Potential

The space–time continuous problem formulation in terms of an incremental variational principle (herein, the term "incremental" refers to a formulation in terms of rate-type quantities, and does not refer to a time-discrete formulation as it is often the case in the literature) is based on

1. A Helmholtz free energy functional $\Psi[\mathbf{Q}]$. Specifically, the Helmholtz free energy functional is assumed to be of the form

$$\Psi[\mathbf{Q}] = \Psi^{\mathrm{U}}[\mathbf{U}] + \Psi^{\mathrm{P}}[\mathbf{P}, \mathbf{U}], \tag{11}$$

   with Ψ^{P} being linear in its first argument. In general, Ψ will be assumed to be Fréchet differentiable. It is remarked in this context that the constraints for the thermodynamic states $\mathbf{U}$ are obtained by requiring the first variation of Ψ^{P} with respect to $\mathbf{P}$ to be zero; and Ψ^{U} represents the physical Helmholtz free energy for all thermodynamic states consistent with these constraints.
2. A power functional $P[\dot{\mathbf{U}}, \dot{\mathbf{V}}; \mathbf{U}, t]$ accounting for the influence of the environment on the computational domain under consideration. P is assumed to be linear in the pair $(\dot{\mathbf{U}}, \dot{\mathbf{V}})$.
3. A dissipation functional $\mathring{\Delta}[\dot{\mathbf{U}}, \dot{\mathbf{V}}; \mathbf{U}, t]$, which is related to the description of dissipative effects. It is assumed that $\mathring{\Delta}$ is (i) non-negative; (ii) convex in the pair $(\dot{\mathbf{U}}, \dot{\mathbf{V}})$; and (iii) satisfies the condition $\mathring{\Delta}[\mathbf{0}, \mathbf{0}; \mathbf{U}, t] = 0$. The latter conditions are, within the standard dissipative framework, sufficient for the satisfaction of the second law of thermodynamics as will be remarked later.
4. A Lagrangian multiplier functional $L[\mathbf{M}, \dot{\mathbf{U}}, \dot{\mathbf{V}}; \mathbf{U}, t]$ incorporating constraints for $\dot{\mathbf{U}}$ and $\dot{\mathbf{V}}$. L is assumed to be of the form

$$L = L_1[\mathbf{M}, \dot{\mathbf{U}}, \dot{\mathbf{V}}; \mathbf{U}, t] + L_2[\mathbf{M}; \mathbf{U}, t], \tag{12}$$

   where L_1 is bilinear with regard to $\mathbf{M}$ and the pair $(\dot{\mathbf{U}}, \dot{\mathbf{V}})$ and L_2 is linear in $\mathbf{M}$.

Finally, the space–time continuous incremental potential

$$\Pi[\dot{\mathbf{Q}}, \dot{\mathbf{V}}, \mathbf{M}; \mathbf{Q}, t] = \dot{\Psi}[\mathbf{Q}, \dot{\mathbf{Q}}] + \Gamma[\dot{\mathbf{U}}, \dot{\mathbf{V}}, \mathbf{M}; \mathbf{U}, t] \tag{13}$$

is introduced, where

$$\Gamma[\dot{\mathbf{U}}, \dot{\mathbf{V}}, \mathbf{M}; \mathbf{U}, t] = -P[\dot{\mathbf{U}}, \dot{\mathbf{V}}; \mathbf{U}, t] + \mathring{\Delta}[\dot{\mathbf{U}}, \dot{\mathbf{V}}; \mathbf{U}, t] + L[\mathbf{M}, \dot{\mathbf{U}}, \dot{\mathbf{V}}; \mathbf{U}, t]. \tag{14}$$

2.5. Space–Time Continuous Incremental Variational Principle

Using the previously introduced functionals, the space–time continuous incremental variational principle now requires that $\dot{\mathbf{Q}}, \dot{\mathbf{V}}, \mathbf{M}$ furnishes a stationary point of Π at every instant of time. This means that the problem can be formulated as

> Find the unknowns $(\mathbf{Q}, \mathbf{V}, \mathbf{M})$ such that $\mathbf{Q}(\mathbf{X}, t_0) = \mathbf{Q}_0$, and $\mathbf{V}(\mathbf{X}, t_0) = \mathbf{0}$, and
>
> $$\begin{aligned} 0 &= \delta\Pi[\dot{\mathbf{Q}}, \dot{\mathbf{V}}, \mathbf{M}, \delta\dot{\mathbf{Q}}, \delta\dot{\mathbf{V}}, \delta\mathbf{M}; \mathbf{Q}, t] \\ &= \delta\dot{\Psi}[\mathbf{Q}, \delta\dot{\mathbf{Q}}] + \delta\Gamma[\dot{\mathbf{U}}, \dot{\mathbf{V}}, \mathbf{M}, \delta\dot{\mathbf{U}}, \delta\dot{\mathbf{V}}, \delta\mathbf{M}; \mathbf{U}, t] \end{aligned} \tag{15}$$
>
> for all $[\delta\dot{\mathbf{Q}}, \delta\dot{\mathbf{V}}, \delta\mathbf{M}]$ and all $t \in (\mathcal{T} \setminus t_0)$,

where the notation is used here and henceforth that the first variation of a functional $I[x_1, \ldots, x_n; y_1, \ldots, y_n]$ is $\delta I[x_1, \ldots, x_n, \delta x_1, \ldots, \delta x_n; y_1, \ldots, y_n]$.

Remark 6.

- *Equation* (15) *may be seen as an extension of Biot's equation, cf. Equation (2.14) in Biot [29] and Equation (2.14) in Biot [30].*
- *For the general case, partial differential algebraic equations are involved and, therefore,* (15) *cannot generally be used as a "point-wise" equation to determine the rates* $\dot{\mathbf{Q}}$, $\dot{\mathbf{V}}$ *based on the current thermodynamic state* $\mathbf{Q}$. *Rather, neighboring instants of time need to be taken into consideration by differentiating the equations implied by* (15) *with respect to time. This aspect becomes particularly evident when considering the example of elasticity (which does not involve dissipative processes). In this case,* (15) *implies the mechanical equilibrium condition, which only involves the mechanical displacement and not the rate of the mechanical displacement. Therefore, differentiation with respect to time is necessary in order to obtain an equation in the rates.*
- *In order for the problem to be well posed, further conditions need to be satisfied. Although a general discussion of this aspect without reference to a particular problem appears to be difficult, a few further remarks are made in the following:*
  - *The constraints represented by the functionals* Ψ^{P} *and* L *must be consistent in that they are neither redundant nor contradictory.*
  - *Non-convex* Ψ^{U} *and/or domains of admissible thermodynamic states may be a severe issue with regard to unique solvability and stability, as can be seen in the discussion in Abed-Meraim and Nguyen [31].*
  - *The initial conditions need to be consistent in that* $\mathbf{Q}_0$ *must be such that a stationary point of* Π *exists at* $t = t_0$.
- *The problem formulation in terms of the first variation of* Π *implies the assumption of sufficient regularity of the functionals involved. This becomes a crucial aspect in the case of problems including rate-independent processes. In this case, the dissipation functional* $\mathring{\Delta}$ *contains contributions which are positively homogeneous of degree one in the rates. The associated non-differentiability of* $\mathring{\Delta}$ *invalidates* (15)*, and hence it may appear that the formulation cannot be used for these cases. However, the situation can be remedied by employing the techniques of convex analysis and, in particular, replacing regular differentiation by the use of subdifferentials (as can be seen, e.g., in Rockafellar [32], pp. 213 ff.), thus extending the formulation to rate-independent processes.*
- *The above formulation in terms of an incremental variational principle is motivated by the description of reversible isothermal processes, in which case the concepts of equilibrium thermodynamics apply and the free energy of the system under consideration is minimized at all times. In order to account for the actual dissipative nature of the problem under consideration, "generalized dissipative forces" are included into the formulation, which are mathematically characterized by the Fréchet derivative of* $\mathring{\Delta}$ *with respect to* $\dot{\mathbf{U}}$ *and* $\dot{\mathbf{V}}$. *These generalized dissipative forces may be interpreted as those external loads, which would have to be applied by an external agency at a certain instant of time* t *to bring the system instantaneously into equilibrium. This approach is abstract in that these external loads are fictitious and cannot be applied in reality. However, accepting the approach based on the experience that it has been succesfully applied to a wide range of problems in the past, the situation is formally transformed from a problem of non-equilibrium thermodynamics into one of equilibrium thermodynamics, so that the well-known concepts of equilibrium thermodynamics can be used, and a mathematically sound formulation results, as can also be seen in Germain et al. [12]. Moreover, by ensuring that* $\delta\mathring{\Delta}(\dot{\mathbf{U}}, \dot{\mathbf{V}}, \dot{\mathbf{U}}, \dot{\mathbf{V}}; \mathbf{U}, t) \geq 0$ *for any choice of* $(\dot{\mathbf{U}}, \dot{\mathbf{V}})$, *it is guaranteed that the generalized dissipative forces are always associated with a negative power (i.e., a positive dissipation), such that the second law of thermodynamics is satisfied a priori and need not be discussed further. The assumptions made above (*$\mathring{\Delta}$ *is non-negative, convex with respect to the pair* $(\dot{\mathbf{U}}, \dot{\mathbf{V}})$ *and satisfies the condition* $\mathring{\Delta}[\mathbf{0}, \mathbf{0}; \mathbf{U}, t] = 0$*) indeed imply that* $\delta\mathring{\Delta}(\dot{\mathbf{U}}, \dot{\mathbf{V}}, \dot{\mathbf{U}}, \dot{\mathbf{V}}; \mathbf{U}, t) \geq 0$.

2.6. Reduced Space–Time Continuous Incremental Variational Principles

In the following, two straightforward possibilities to reduce the set of unknown variables are described. It is emphasized that further possibilities exist, which are not discussed here. Furthermore, it is noted that the space–time discretization methods as well as the implementation discussed in the next sections are equally applicable to both, the original and the reduced formulations.

2.6.1. Reduction of the Set of Process Variables and Lagrangian Multipliers

The introduction of the generalized process variable $\mathbf{V}$ and the generalized Lagrangian multiplier $\mathbf{M}$ often leads to an excessive number of unknown fields. However, in many cases, it is possible to systematically eliminate $\mathbf{V}$ and $\mathbf{M}$, or rather subsets thereof, before actually numerically solving the problem. In particular, the space–time continuous incremental functional Π only depends on $\dot{\mathbf{V}}$, but not on $\mathbf{V}$ itself. Furthermore, Π depends on $\dot{\mathbf{V}}$ and $\mathbf{M}$ only through the contribution Γ. Thus, a reduced functional

$$\Gamma^{\text{red}}[\dot{\mathbf{U}}, \dot{\mathbf{V}}^0, \mathbf{M}^0; \mathbf{U}, t] = \inf_{\dot{\mathbf{V}}^1} \sup_{\mathbf{M}^1} \Gamma[\dot{\mathbf{U}}, \dot{\mathbf{V}}, \mathbf{M}; \mathbf{U}, t] \tag{16}$$

may be introduced by joint partial minimization and maximization, where

$$\mathbf{V} = \begin{pmatrix} \mathbf{V}^0 \\ \mathbf{V}^1 \end{pmatrix} \qquad \mathbf{M} = \begin{pmatrix} \mathbf{M}^0 \\ \mathbf{M}^1 \end{pmatrix}. \tag{17}$$

Then, $\delta\Gamma$ can be replaced by $\delta\Gamma^{\text{red}}$ in (15) to obtain an equivalent formulation in the reduced set of variables $(\mathbf{Q}, \mathbf{V}^0, \mathbf{M}^0)$.

Remark 7. *The selection of the variables $\mathbf{V}^0$ and $\mathbf{M}^0$ typically depends on the properties of the dissipation functional $\mathring{\Delta}$. However, numerical considerations (e.g., with respect to the choice of finite elements) may also be important in this regard.*

2.6.2. Reduction of the Set of State Variables

Another possibility to reduce the set of variables exists if certain state variables factor into Ψ, while Γ is independent of these variables. In order to discuss this case, it is assumed that

$$\mathbf{Q} = \begin{pmatrix} \mathbf{U}^1 \\ \mathbf{U}^0 \\ \mathbf{P}^0 \end{pmatrix} = \begin{pmatrix} \mathbf{U}^1 \\ \mathbf{Q}^0 \end{pmatrix}, \tag{18}$$

and that Γ neither depends on $\mathbf{U}^1$ nor on $\dot{\mathbf{U}}^1$, meaning that there exists a functional Γ^{red} such that

$$\Gamma[\dot{\mathbf{U}}, \dot{\mathbf{V}}, \mathbf{M}; \mathbf{U}, t] = \Gamma^{\text{red}}[\dot{\mathbf{U}}^0, \dot{\mathbf{V}}, \mathbf{M}; \mathbf{U}^0, t]. \tag{19}$$

Then, if Ψ is additionally convex in $\mathbf{U}^1$, a reduced thermodynamic potential

$$\Psi^{\text{red}}[\mathbf{Q}^0] = \inf_{\mathbf{U}^1} \Psi[\mathbf{Q}] \tag{20}$$

may be introduced; and $\delta\Psi$ and $\delta\Gamma$ can be replaced by $\delta\Psi^{\text{red}}$ and $\delta\Gamma^{\text{red}}$ in (15) to obtain an equivalent formulation in the reduced set of variables $(\mathbf{Q}^0, \mathbf{V}, \mathbf{M})$.

Remark 8. *Using this approach, the linearity of Ψ with regard to $\mathbf{P}$ may be lost, which does, however, not have consequences for the applicability of* (15).

3. Space–Time Discrete Formulation

The spatial discretization of the fields involved in $\mathbf{Q}$, $\mathbf{V}$ and $\mathbf{M}$ is assumed to be performed using the finite element method in this work. In this regard, standard methods can be used, which will not be further discussed here. However, it is pointed out that the satisfaction of the inf − sup condition is typically the most difficult part of spatial discretization if the variational problem to be solved is of saddle point type, see, e.g., Bathe [33] and Auricchio et al. [34].

With regard to temporal discretization, a number of simple and straightforward-to-implement one step schemes have been discussed and analyzed in a somewhat narrower context in a previous work [35]. These methods can be readily extended to the current formulation; and for the self-containedness of the present work, these will be briefly described below, although the reader is referred to [35] for details.

In the following, it is assumed throughout that the time interval $[t_0, t_e]$ is divided by the discrete time points $t_n = t_0 + n\Delta t$, where $n = 0, 1, \dots N$ and $\Delta t = (t_e - t_0)/N$ (however, the formulations are not restricted to uniform time increments). The numerically approximated values of $\mathbf{Q}$, $\mathbf{V}$ and $\mathbf{M}$ at time t_n are denoted by $\mathbf{Q}_n$, $\mathbf{V}_n$ and $\mathbf{M}_n$, respectively; and the initial values at time t_0 are given by $\mathbf{Q}_0(\mathbf{X})$ and $\mathbf{V}_0(\mathbf{X}) = \mathbf{0}$.

3.1. Variationally Consistent Method

The "variationally consistent method" is based on a straightforward discretization of the space–time continuous incremental functional Π. In particular, a time-discrete counterpart $\Delta\Pi^{n\to n+1}$ of Π is introduced according to

$$\begin{aligned}\Delta\Pi^{n\to n+1}[\mathbf{Q}_{n+1}, \mathbf{V}_{n+1}, \mathbf{M}_{n+1}] &= \Psi[\mathbf{Q}_{n+1}] - \Psi[\mathbf{Q}_n] \\ &\quad + \Delta t \Gamma\left[\frac{\mathbf{U}_{n+1} - \mathbf{U}_n}{\Delta t}, \frac{\mathbf{V}_{n+1} - \mathbf{V}_n}{\Delta t}, \mathbf{M}_{n+1}; \mathbf{U}_n, t_{n+1}\right]. \end{aligned} \tag{21}$$

Then, the stationary point of $\Delta\Pi^{n\to n+1}$ is searched during each time step to obtain $\mathbf{Q}_{n+1}$, $\mathbf{V}_{n+1}$ and $\mathbf{M}_{n+1}$ based on the solution of the previous time step. The corresponding stationarity condition leads to the time-discrete variational formulation

Find the unknowns $(\mathbf{Q}_{n+1}, \mathbf{V}_{n+1}, \mathbf{M}_{n+1})$ such that

$$\begin{aligned} 0 = \delta\Psi[\mathbf{Q}_{n+1}, \delta\mathbf{Q}_{n+1}] + \delta\Gamma\Bigg[&\frac{\mathbf{U}_{n+1} - \mathbf{U}_n}{\Delta t}, \frac{\mathbf{V}_{n+1} - \mathbf{V}_n}{\Delta t}, \mathbf{M}_{n+1}, \\ &\delta\mathbf{U}_{n+1}, \delta\mathbf{V}_{n+1}, \Delta t\delta\mathbf{M}_{n+1}; \mathbf{U}_n, t_{n+1}\Bigg] \end{aligned} \tag{22}$$

for all $(\delta\mathbf{Q}_{n+1}, \delta\mathbf{V}_{n+1}, \delta\mathbf{M}_{n+1})$ and all $n \in \{0, 1, \dots N-1\}$,

which is a consistent approximation of (15). According to the analysis in [35], the method represents a first-order accurate time integrator, provided that the the problem is sufficiently regular.

Remark 9. *As a result of discretizing Π, the variational structure of the space–time continuous problem is preserved, which makes the method particularly attractive from the mathematical point of view. This concerns, e.g., the fact that the resulting finite element systems are symmetric.*

3.2. The α-Family

The "α-family" is based on the introduction of a real parameter $\alpha \in [0, 1]$, where $\alpha = 0$ corresponds to a forward Euler type scheme, $\alpha = 1/2$ to a Crank–Nicolson type scheme, and $\alpha = 1$ to a backward Euler type scheme. Moreover, the following quantities are defined:

$$\mathbf{Q}_n^\alpha = (1-\alpha)\mathbf{Q}_n + \alpha\mathbf{Q}_{n+1} \tag{23}$$
$$\mathbf{M}_n^\alpha = (1-\alpha)\mathbf{M}_n + \alpha\mathbf{M}_{n+1} \tag{24}$$
$$t_n^\alpha = (1-\alpha)t_n + \alpha t_{n+1}. \tag{25}$$

Then, the time-discrete version of (15) reads

Find the unknowns $(\mathbf{Q}_{n+1}, \mathbf{V}_{n+1}, \mathbf{M}_n^\alpha)$ such that

$$0 = (1-\alpha)\delta\Psi[\mathbf{Q}_n, \delta\mathbf{Q}_{n+1}] + \alpha\delta\Psi[\mathbf{Q}_{n+1}, \delta\mathbf{Q}_{n+1}] + \delta\Gamma\left[\frac{\mathbf{U}_{n+1}-\mathbf{U}_n}{\Delta t}, \frac{\mathbf{V}_{n+1}-\mathbf{V}_n}{\Delta t}, \mathbf{M}_n^\alpha, \delta\mathbf{U}_{n+1}, \delta\mathbf{V}_{n+1}, \Delta t\delta\mathbf{M}_n^\alpha; \mathbf{U}_n^\alpha, t_n^\alpha\right] \tag{26}$$

for all $(\delta\mathbf{Q}_{n+1}, \delta\mathbf{V}_{n+1}, \delta\mathbf{M}_n^\alpha)$ and all $n \in \{0, 1, \dots N-1\}$.

For a sufficiently regular problem, the method is second-order accurate for $\alpha = 1/2$ or otherwise first-order accurate [35]. However, the method is non-convergent for $\alpha < 1/2$ if the system of equations implied by (15) is of differential algebraic nature. Furthermore, no associated time-discrete incremental potential exists for the method if Γ exhibits a parametric dependence on $\mathbf{U}$, so that the finite element systems are unsymmetric in this case.

3.3. The Modified α-Family

The "modified α-family" is a "predictor-corrector" method. In particular, the quantities $\hat{\mathbf{Q}}^{n+1}$, $\hat{\mathbf{V}}^{n+1}$, $\hat{\mathbf{M}}_n^\alpha$ are introduced, which are "predictions" of $\mathbf{Q}^{n+1}$, $\mathbf{V}^{n+1}$ and $\mathbf{M}_n^\alpha$. During the predictor step, the problem

Find the unknowns $(\hat{\mathbf{Q}}_{n+1}, \hat{\mathbf{V}}_{n+1}, \hat{\mathbf{M}}_n^\alpha)$ such that

$$0 = (1-\alpha)\delta\Psi[\mathbf{Q}_n, \delta\hat{\mathbf{Q}}_{n+1}] + \alpha\delta\Psi[\hat{\mathbf{Q}}_{n+1}, \delta\hat{\mathbf{Q}}_{n+1}] + \delta\Gamma\left[\frac{\hat{\mathbf{U}}_{n+1}-\mathbf{U}_n}{\Delta t}, \frac{\hat{\mathbf{V}}_{n+1}-\mathbf{V}_n}{\Delta t}, \hat{\mathbf{M}}_n^\alpha, \delta\hat{\mathbf{U}}_{n+1}, \delta\hat{\mathbf{V}}_{n+1}, \Delta t\delta\hat{\mathbf{M}}_n^\alpha; \mathbf{U}_n, t_n^\alpha\right] \tag{27}$$

for all $(\delta\hat{\mathbf{Q}}_{n+1}, \delta\hat{\mathbf{V}}_{n+1}, \delta\hat{\mathbf{M}}_n^\alpha)$

is solved. Based on the resulting predicted values, the time-discrete problem is then

Find the unknowns $(\mathbf{Q}_{n+1}, \mathbf{V}_{n+1}, \mathbf{M}_n^\alpha)$ such that

$$0 = (1-\alpha)\delta\Psi[\mathbf{Q}_n, \delta\mathbf{Q}_{n+1}] + \alpha\delta\Psi[\mathbf{Q}_{n+1}, \delta\mathbf{Q}_{n+1}] + \delta\Gamma\left[\frac{\mathbf{U}_{n+1}-\mathbf{U}_n}{\Delta t}, \frac{\mathbf{V}_{n+1}-\mathbf{V}_n}{\Delta t}, \mathbf{M}_n^\alpha, \delta\mathbf{U}_{n+1}, \delta\mathbf{V}_{n+1}, \Delta t\delta\mathbf{M}_n^\alpha; \hat{\mathbf{U}}_n^\alpha, t_n^\alpha\right] \tag{28}$$

for all $(\delta\mathbf{Q}_{n+1}, \delta\mathbf{V}_{n+1}, \delta\mathbf{M}_n^\alpha)$ and all $n \in \{0, 1, \dots N-1\}$, where $\hat{\mathbf{U}}_n^\alpha = (1-\alpha)\mathbf{U}_n + \alpha\hat{\mathbf{U}}_{n+1}$.

For many (but not all) cases, the method provides the same accuracy as the α-family, while retaining the symmetric and variational structure, so that corresponding time-discrete incremental potentials exist for both steps.

4. Implementation

In order to show the feasibility of the approach, the space time discrete formulation described above has been preliminarily implemented in two and three dimensions for both sequential and distributed memory parallel computations. In particular, the open source C++ libraries GalerkinTools and IncrementalFE have been developed. The library GalerkinTools allows for the definition of weak forms corresponding to functionals of the generic form (7) (in fact, the library covers slightly more general weak forms including those unsymmetric weak forms required for the α-family of methods for temporal discretization). Furthermore, GalerkinTools provides methods for the automatic assembly of the corresponding finite element systems based on the functionalities of the open source finite element library deal.II (Alzetta et al. [27], Bangerth et al. [28]). In addition, interfaces for the solution of the resulting linear systems of equations are included. For this purpose, the unsymmetric sparse direct UMFPACK solver (Davis [36]), the symmetric and unsymmetric sparse direct PARDISO solvers (Schenk and Gärtner [37,38], Karypis and Kumar [39]), the symmetric and unsymmetric sparse direct MUMPS solvers (Amestoy et al. [40,41]) and the symmetric sparse direct MA57 solver (HSL, a collection of Fortran codes for large-scale scientific computation, see http://www.hsl.rl.ac.uk/ (accessed on 5 January 2023)) can currently be used. Based on the library GalerkinTools, the library IncrementalFE then encapsulates the special functionality required for the solution of problems formulated within the standard dissipative framework. In particular, this involves functionalities for the definition of the functionals Ψ and Γ, together with the temporal discretization schemes described in the previous section. Furthermore, IncrementalFE implements a simple Newton–Raphson scheme, optionally combined with a line search, to solve the nonlinear finite element problems arising in each time step. For details regarding the functionalities and implementation of the libraries GalerkinTools and IncrementalFE, the reader is referred to the documentation bundled with these libraries. However, the general sequence of steps needed to define and solve a particular problem is briefly described in the following:

1. Setup of the finite element mesh, which corresponds to the definition of the computational domain. During this step, the domain Ω is first meshed using either the built-in functionalities of deal.II or by importing a mesh from an external mesh generator. Subsequently, the domain is partitioned into domain portions by assigning "material IDs" to the individual cells of the mesh. This is followed by the definition of the interface Σ based on faces of the previously defined volume-related cells, which also goes along with the definition of the $-$ and $+$ sides of the interface as well as a partitioning of the interface by assigning "material IDs". As a final step of mesh generation, local mesh refinement may be performed.
2. Definition of the unknowns $\mathbf{Q}$, $\mathbf{V}$ and $\mathbf{M}$ of the problem and the corresponding finite element spaces. During this step, the domain-related unknown fields, the interface-related unknown fields and the scalars are defined. This includes the definition of the finite elements to be used for the discretization of the domain-related and interface-related unknowns as well as Dirichlet-type constraints. Furthermore, for each unknown field, the domain portions and interface portions, respectively, are defined where the respective field may be non-zero. In order to allow for the use of vector-valued finite elements, several unknown fields of a particular type may be defined at once.
3. Definition of the domain-related dependent fields $\mathbf{q}^{\Omega}$, $\mathbf{v}^{\Omega}$, $\mathbf{m}^{\Omega}$ and the interface-related dependent fields $\mathbf{q}^{\Sigma}$, $\mathbf{v}^{\Sigma}$, $\mathbf{m}^{\Sigma}$ based on the previously defined unknowns $\mathbf{Q}$, $\mathbf{V}$ and $\mathbf{M}$ according to Equations (5) and (6), respectively.
4. Definition of Ψ and Γ as functionals of the form (7). It is noted in this context that the definition of the integrals over Ω and Σ, respectively, may be split into several integrals, which are summed up subsequently. This split (i) facilitates the re-usability of the implementation of certain terms (e.g., a Neo-Hookean strain energy density) and thus makes the definition of Ψ and Γ "modular"; (ii) allows for using different numerical quadrature schemes for different terms; and (iii) allows for a better structuring of the problem, which can be internally exploited by the library GalerkinTools to determine which entries in the finite element system matrix are non-zero. The actual definition of a single integral typically involves (i) the implementation of the integrand (which is expressed in terms of the dependent fields relevant to the integral) and its first and second derivatives; (ii) the specification of domain and interface portions, respectively, where the integrand is non-zero; (iii) the definition of the quadrature scheme to be used for evaluating the integral; (iv) the definition of the temporal integration scheme to be used (in fact, one may use different schemes for different terms, although this has not been discussed above); and (v) the definition of parameters (particularly constitutive parameters).

5. Solving the problem. Currently, time-stepping needs to be implemented manually, although single time steps are automatically handled by the library IncrementalFE.

Remark 10.

- *The entire problem definition is facilitated by the use of C++ as an object-oriented language. As a result, e.g., each unknown field is a separate object, which leads to a rather natural structuring of the code in that it closely resembles the underlying mathematical statement of the problem under study in terms of formulae.*
- *Typically, the most time-consuming step of the problem definition is, besides in some cases the mesh generation, the implementation of the integrands for the definition of Ψ and Γ. However, due to the mentioned modular design, the implementation of certain integrands can be re-used. This does, in principle, allow for a library of integrands covering a multitude of situations. Furthermore, automatic differentiation schemes may be used in order to simplify the implementation of the first and second derivatives of the integrands, which are required for the solution of the problem.*
- *The library GalerkinTools also allows for the definition of "hidden variables" for each integrand, so that, in principle, classical rate-independent plasticity approaches are covered. For example, for the variationally consistent method, the latter may easily be achieved by locally "pre-minimizing" the time-discrete incremental potential $\Delta\Pi^{n\to n+1}$ with respect to the plastic deformation variables. However, proper testing of classical plasticity approaches is yet to be performed. Therefore, a discussion of these is not included in the present contribution.*
- *Implementation-wise, the main difficulties are the definition of functionals of the generic form (7) and the assembly procedures for the associated finite-element systems. These functionalities are provided by GalerkinTools; and, on this basis, the implementation of particular temporal discretization schemes and iterative algorithms for the solution of the nonlinear problems arising in each time step is straightforward. Hence, the library IncrementalFE is rather slim; and if temporal discretization schemes and/or iterative algorithms other than those discussed in this work need to be considered, these can be implemented with little effort (provided that the temporally discretized versions are compatible with the assumed form for functionals). The same applies to the use of other linear solvers than those mentioned above, and, in particular, iterative linear solvers.*

5. Examples

In this section, (i) the buckling behavior of a viscoelastic dielectric elastomer subjected to an electric voltage, and (ii) the swelling/shrinking of a hydrogel subjected to a change in exterior ion concentrations are discussed as examples. It is emphasized that the main objective is to demonstrate the feasibility and practicability of the approach, and not to give a detailed exposition of particular physical effects. Therefore, the statement of the problems will be kept concise; and a discussion of the differential (algebraic) equations implied by the formulations is omitted.

It is emphasized that the discussion of the example problems mostly follows the sequence of steps described in Section 4, which highlights the systematic approach to standard dissipative problems proposed in this work. The equations are written using the symbolic vector/tensor notation; and it is tacitly assumed that each vector/tensor field is represented by an appropriate number of domain-related/interface-related scalar fields, which embody vector/tensor coordinates with regard to the standard basis of $\mathcal{R}^3$.

Moreover, it is noted that both example problems have been chosen to be axisymmetric in order to reduce the computational cost and, therefore, facilitate numerical convergence studies. Despite this fact, the problems will be described in the fully three-dimensional setting for the sake of simplicity. The steps necessary for reduction to the axisymmetric setting should be sufficiently obvious and are, therefore, not described in detail.

5.1. Example 1: Buckling of a Viscoelastic Dielectric Elastomer

The first example problem is illustrated in Figure 2. A circular disc of incompressible viscoelastic dielectric elastomer with radius L and thickness H is considered. The constitutive behavior is assumed to be described by the relations proposed by Hong [42]. The radial displacement is constrained to zero on the entire lateral surface of the disc. Furthermore, the average axial displacement is constrained to zero on the lateral surface. The latter constraint was chosen instead of a homogeneous constraint on the entire surface in order to avoid stress/strain singularities, which would complicate the convergence studies due to the need for excessive local mesh refinement. The bottom surface and the top surface are assumed to be electrodes, with a transient voltage $U(t)$ applied across these electrodes. As a result of Maxwell stress, the disc shrinks in the axial direction; and due to the incompressibility of the material, this leads to buckling and large deformations of the disc in the axial direction. In order to induce the "imperfection" needed for a well-defined buckling behavior, the gravitational acceleration g is taken into account and assumed to point downwards in the figure. Fringing fields at the edges of the electrodes are neglected for simplicity.

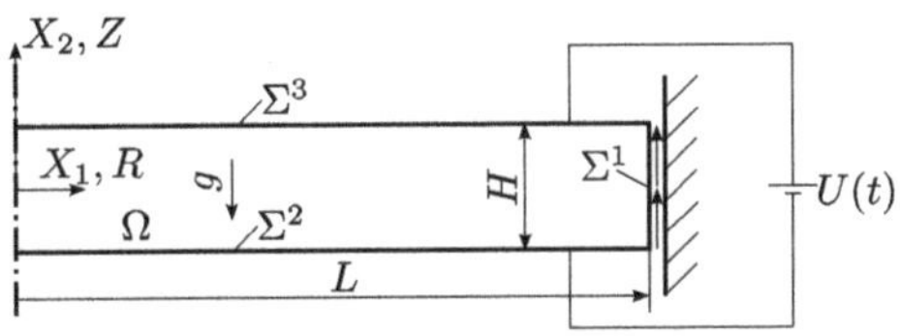

Figure 2. Illustration of example problem 1.

5.1.1. Computational Domain

The computational domain Ω shown in Figure 2 represents the reference configuration of the disc, which is assumed to be stress-free. It is noted that this reference configuration is not actually assumed at any instant of time due to the action of the gravitational acceleration. The in-plane Cartesian coordinates in Figure 2 are X_1 and X_2, while the out-of-plane coordinate is X_3. If a radial coordinate R and an axial coordinate Z of a cylindrical coordinate system are introduced as shown in the figure, the body occupies the region described by $0 \le R \le L$ and $-H/2 \le Z \le H/2$. The lateral surface of this disc is Σ^1, the bottom surface Σ^2 and the top surface Σ^3.

5.1.2. Unknown Variables

State Variables

The thermodynamic state variables

$$\mathbf{u} : \begin{cases} \Omega \times \mathcal{T} \to \mathcal{R}^3 \\ (\mathbf{X}, t) \mapsto \mathbf{u}(\mathbf{X}, t) \end{cases} \tag{29}$$

$$\mathbf{D} : \begin{cases} \Omega \times \mathcal{T} \to \mathcal{R}^3 \\ (\mathbf{X}, t) \mapsto \mathbf{D}(\mathbf{X}, t) \end{cases} \tag{30}$$

$$\mathbf{U}^{\mathrm{i}} : \begin{cases} \Omega \times \mathcal{T} \to \mathcal{R}^6 \\ (\mathbf{X}, t) \mapsto \mathbf{U}^{\mathrm{i}}(\mathbf{X}, t) \end{cases} \tag{31}$$

are introduced together with the corresponding initial conditions

$$\mathbf{u}(\mathbf{X}, t_0) = \mathbf{u}_0(\mathbf{X}) \tag{32}$$

$$\mathbf{D}(\mathbf{X}, t_0) = \mathbf{D}_0(\mathbf{X}) \tag{33}$$

$$\mathbf{U}^{\mathrm{i}}(t_0) = \mathbf{I}, \tag{34}$$

with $\mathbf{I}$ being the identity tensor of rank 2. The thermodynamic state variables have the following significance:

- $\mathbf{u}$ is the mechanical displacement field. It describes how the placements of material points in the reference configuration are mapped onto their placements in the current configuration. In particular, $\mathbf{x}(\mathbf{X},t) = \mathbf{X} + \mathbf{u}(\mathbf{X},t)$, with $\mathbf{x}(\mathbf{X},t)$ being the placement of the material point $\mathbf{X}$ at time t.
- $\mathbf{D}$ is the referential electric displacement field.
- $\mathbf{U}^{\mathrm{i}}$ is the (symmetric) inelastic stretch tensor.

The thermodynamic state variables are supplemented by the auxiliary state variables

$$\varphi : \begin{cases} \Omega \times \mathcal{T} \to \mathcal{R} \\ (\mathbf{X},t) \mapsto \varphi(\mathbf{X},t) \end{cases} \tag{35}$$

$$p : \begin{cases} \Omega \times \mathcal{T} \to \mathcal{R} \\ (\mathbf{X},t) \mapsto p(\mathbf{X},t) \end{cases} \tag{36}$$

$$p^{\mathrm{i}} : \begin{cases} \Omega \times \mathcal{T} \to \mathcal{R} \\ (\mathbf{X},t) \mapsto p^{\mathrm{i}}(\mathbf{X},t) \end{cases} \tag{37}$$

$$l^{uz} : \begin{cases} \mathcal{T} \to \mathcal{R} \\ t \mapsto l^{uz}(t) \end{cases} \tag{38}$$

together with the corresponding initial conditions

$$\varphi(\mathbf{X},t_0) = \varphi_0(\mathbf{X}) \tag{39}$$

$$p(\mathbf{X},t_0) = p_0(\mathbf{X}) \tag{40}$$

$$p^{\mathrm{i}}(\mathbf{X},t_0) = p^{\mathrm{i}}_0(\mathbf{X}) \tag{41}$$

$$l^{uz}(t_0) = l^{uz}_0. \tag{42}$$

The auxiliary state variables have the following significance:

- φ is the electric scalar potential, which acts as a Lagrangian multiplier enforcing the condition that there is no free space charge density in the interior of the domain.
- p is a pressure type variable, which acts as a Lagrangian multiplier enforcing the condition that the elastomer does not exhibit any overall local volume change.
- p^{i} is a further pressure type variable, which acts as a Lagrangian multiplier enforcing the condition that the elastomer does not exhibit any inelastic local volume change.
- l^{uz} is used to constrain the average axial displacement of the disc on the lateral surface Σ^1 to zero.

The practical determination of the initial values $\mathbf{u}_0(\mathbf{X})$, $\mathbf{D}_0(\mathbf{X})$, $\varphi_0(\mathbf{X})$, $p_0(\mathbf{X})$, $p^{\mathrm{i}}_0(\mathbf{X})$ and l^{uz}_0 will be discussed later.

Process Variables and Lagrangian Multipliers

For this first example, neither process variables nor Lagrangian multipliers are needed.

Dirichlet Constraints

The state variables $\mathbf{u}$ and $\mathbf{D}$ are constrained by the Dirichlet conditions

$$\mathbf{u} \cdot \mathbf{N} = 0 \quad \text{on} \quad \Sigma^1 \tag{43}$$

$$\mathbf{D} \cdot \mathbf{N} = 0 \quad \text{on} \quad \Sigma^1. \tag{44}$$

5.1.3. Dependent Fields

Here and in the following, only those dependent fields are listed explicitly, which are "non-trivial" in that they are not equal to an unknown field itself or the gradient/divergence/curl of an unknown field (the divergence actually involves three unknown scalar fields in three dimensions since a vector field is formally represented by an appropriate number of scalar fields; and the curl involves three unknown scalar fields and three dependent fields). In particular, the only non-trivial domain-related dependent fields used below represent the mechanical deformation gradient

$$\mathbf{F} = \nabla \mathbf{u} + \mathbf{I}, \tag{45}$$

where the latter equation must be expanded into coordinate-wise relations in order to be consistent with the generic form of domain-related dependent fields according to Equation (5).

5.1.4. The Functionals

As noted above, the functionals describing the variational problem are chosen such that the constitutive behavior of the viscoelastic dielectric elastomer is described by the constitutive model of Hong [42].

Helmholtz Free-Energy Functional Ψ

The Helmholtz free energy functional $\Psi[\mathbf{Q}] = \Psi^{\mathrm{U}}[\mathbf{U}] + \Psi^{\mathrm{P}}[\mathbf{P}, \mathbf{U}]$ is composed of the contributions

$$\Psi^{\mathrm{U}}[\mathbf{U}] = \int\limits_{\Omega} \Big\{ \frac{1}{2\epsilon} \mathbf{D} \cdot \mathbf{F}^{\top} \cdot \mathbf{F} \cdot \mathbf{D} + \frac{\mu^{\mathrm{e}}}{2} \Big[\mathrm{tr}\Big(\mathbf{F}^{\top} \cdot \mathbf{F} \Big) - 2\ln(J) - 3 \Big] + \frac{\mu^{\mathrm{i}}}{2} \Big[\mathrm{tr}\Big(\mathbf{U}^{\mathrm{i}^{-1}} \cdot \mathbf{F}^{\top} \cdot \mathbf{F} \cdot \mathbf{U}^{\mathrm{i}^{-1}} \Big) - 2\Big(J - J^{\mathrm{i}} \Big) - 3 \Big] + \rho_0 g (\mathbf{u})_Z \Big\} \, \mathrm{d}V \tag{46}$$

and

$$\Psi^{\mathrm{P}}[\mathbf{P}, \mathbf{U}] = \int\limits_{\Omega} \Big[-\varphi \nabla \cdot \mathbf{D} + p(1 - J) + p^{\mathrm{i}}\Big(1 - J^{\mathrm{i}}\Big) \Big] \, \mathrm{d}V - \int\limits_{\Sigma^1} l^{uz} (\mathbf{u})_Z \, \mathrm{d}S. \tag{47}$$

In these equations, $J = \det \mathbf{F}$, $J^{\mathrm{i}} = \det \mathbf{U}^{\mathrm{i}}$, $(\mathbf{u})_Z$ is the axial displacement, g is the gravitational acceleration, ρ_0 is the mass density of the elastomer in the reference state, ϵ is the permittivity of the material and μ^{e} and μ^{i} are elastic constants.

Power Functional P

The power functional takes the form

$$P[\dot{\mathbf{U}}, \dot{\mathbf{V}}; \mathbf{U}, t] = -\int\limits_{\Sigma^3} U(t) \dot{\mathbf{D}} \cdot \mathbf{N} \, \mathrm{d}S. \tag{48}$$

In the following, the ramp loading

$$U(t) = U_{\mathrm{e}} \frac{t - t_0}{t_{\mathrm{e}} - t_0} \tag{49}$$

with the maximum voltage U_{e} will be considered.

Dissipation Functional $\mathring{\Delta}$

For the dissipation functional, the form

$$\mathring{\Delta}[\dot{\mathbf{U}}, \dot{\mathbf{V}}; \mathbf{U}, t] = \int\limits_{\Omega} \eta \mathrm{tr}(\mathbf{d} \cdot \mathbf{d}) \, \mathrm{d}V \tag{50}$$

is assumed, where η is the viscosity and $\mathbf{d} = \mathrm{sym}\Big(\mathbf{F} \cdot \mathbf{U}^{\mathrm{i}^{-1}} \cdot \dot{\mathbf{U}}^{\mathrm{i}} \cdot \mathbf{F}^{-1} \Big)$ is the inelastic stretching.

5.1.5. Reduced Formulations

Variant 1: Vector Potential Formulation

A first possibility to reduce the set of variables is to express $\mathbf{D}$ in terms of a vector potential $\mathbf{A}$ according to

$$\mathbf{D} = -\nabla \times \mathbf{A}. \tag{51}$$

By doing so, $\mathbf{D}$ becomes a dependent field, while

$$\mathbf{A} : \begin{cases} \Omega \times \mathcal{T} \to \mathcal{R}^3 \\ (\mathbf{X}, t) \mapsto \mathbf{A}(\mathbf{X}, t) \end{cases} \tag{52}$$

becomes a state variable. As a consequence of the identity $\nabla \cdot (\nabla \times \mathbf{A}) = 0$, the Lagrangian multiplier term $-\varphi \nabla \cdot \mathbf{D}$ drops out in (47), such that φ is no longer required as an unknown variable. Furthermore, the Dirichlet constraint $\mathbf{D} \cdot \mathbf{N} = 0$ on Σ^1 is transformed to

$$\mathbf{A} = A^{\mathrm{S}} \mathbf{N} \times \mathbf{e}_2 \quad \text{on} \quad \Sigma^1, \tag{53}$$

where $\mathbf{e}_2$ is the unit normal vector in the axial direction, and

$$A^{\mathrm{S}} : \begin{cases} \mathcal{T} \to \mathcal{R} \\ t \mapsto A^{\mathrm{S}}(t) \end{cases} \tag{54}$$

is another state variable. For details regarding this boundary condition, the reader is referred to [43]. In general, gauging is required for the uniqueness of the vector potential in three dimensions, as can also be seen in [43]. However, for the axisymmetric case considered herein, gauging can be achieved by requiring that only the circumferential component of $\mathbf{A}$ is non-zero, which is assumed henceforth.

Variant 2: Scalar Potential Formulation

Another possibility is to apply the procedure described in Section 2.6.2 to eliminate $\mathbf{D}$. A technical difficulty occurring in this context is that the normal electric displacement $\mathbf{D} \cdot \mathbf{N}$ on the surfaces Σ^2 and Σ^3 cannot be eliminated. To resolve this issue, the additional state variable

$$\omega : \begin{cases} (\Sigma^2 \cup \Sigma^3) \times \mathcal{T} \to \mathcal{R} \\ (\mathbf{X}, t) \mapsto \omega(\mathbf{X}, t) \end{cases} \tag{55}$$

is introduced, which represents $\mathbf{D} \cdot \mathbf{N}$. Then,

$$\begin{aligned} \Psi^{\mathrm{U,red}}[\mathbf{U}] = \int_\Omega \Big\{ & -\frac{\epsilon}{2} \nabla \varphi \cdot \mathbf{F}^{-1} \cdot \mathbf{F}^{-\top} \cdot \nabla \varphi + \frac{\mu^{\mathrm{e}}}{2} \Big[\mathrm{tr}\Big(\mathbf{F}^\top \cdot \mathbf{F}\Big) - 2\ln(J) - 3 \Big] \\ & + \frac{\mu^{\mathrm{i}}}{2} \Big[\mathrm{tr}\Big(\mathbf{U}^{\mathrm{i}^{-1}} \cdot \mathbf{F}^\top \cdot \mathbf{F} \cdot \mathbf{U}^{\mathrm{i}^{-1}} \Big) - 2\Big(J - J^{\mathrm{i}}\Big) - 3 \Big] + \rho_0 g (\mathbf{u})_Z \Big\} \, \mathrm{d}V, \end{aligned} \tag{56}$$

$$\Psi^{\mathrm{P,red}}[\mathbf{P}, \mathbf{U}] = \int_\Omega \Big[p(1 - J) + p^{\mathrm{i}}\Big(1 - J^{\mathrm{i}}\Big) \Big] \, \mathrm{d}V - \int_{\Sigma^1} l^{u_Z} (\mathbf{u})_Z \, \mathrm{d}S - \int_{\Sigma^2 \cup \Sigma^3} \varphi \omega \, \mathrm{d}S, \tag{57}$$

and

$$P[\dot{\mathbf{U}}, \dot{\mathbf{V}}; \mathbf{U}, t] = -\int_{\Sigma^3} U(t) \dot{\omega} \, \mathrm{d}S, \tag{58}$$

while $\mathring{\Delta}$ remains unchanged. In this formulation, $\dot{\omega}$ acts as a Lagrange multiplier enforcing the boundary conditions

$$\varphi = 0 \qquad \text{on} \quad \Sigma^2 \tag{59}$$
$$\varphi = U(t) \qquad \text{on} \quad \Sigma^3. \tag{60}$$

By imposing the latter conditions directly as Dirichlet constraints for φ, the state variable ω is eliminated from the set of unknown variables.

5.1.6. Normalization

In order to improve the conditioning of the finite element system matrices and to remove units from the simulations, it is advantageous to normalize the equations. Here, the normalization proposed by Hong [42] is used:

$$\begin{aligned}
&\tilde{\mathbf{X}} = \frac{\mathbf{X}}{H}, \quad \tilde{t} = \frac{t\mu^{\mathrm{i}}}{\eta}, \quad \tilde{\nabla}() = \nabla()H, \quad \tilde{\dot{()}} = \dot{()}\frac{\eta}{\mu^{\mathrm{i}}}, \\
&\tilde{\mathbf{u}} = \frac{\mathbf{u}}{H}, \quad \tilde{\mathbf{D}} = \frac{\mathbf{D}}{\sqrt{\mu\epsilon}}, \quad \tilde{\mathbf{U}}^{\mathrm{i}} = \mathbf{U}^{\mathrm{i}}, \quad \tilde{\mathbf{A}} = \frac{\mathbf{A}}{H\sqrt{\mu\epsilon}}, \\
&\tilde{\varphi} = \frac{\varphi}{H}\sqrt{\frac{\epsilon}{\mu}}, \quad \tilde{p} = \frac{p}{\mu}, \quad \tilde{p}^{\mathrm{i}} = \frac{p^{\mathrm{i}}}{\mu}, \quad \tilde{l}^{\mathrm{uz}} = \frac{l^{\mathrm{uz}}}{\mu}, \\
&\tilde{t}_0 = \frac{t_0\mu^{\mathrm{i}}}{\eta}, \quad \tilde{t}_{\mathrm{e}} = \frac{t_{\mathrm{e}}\mu^{\mathrm{i}}}{\eta}, \quad \tilde{U}_{\mathrm{e}} = \frac{U_{\mathrm{e}}}{H}\sqrt{\frac{\epsilon}{\mu}}, \\
&\tilde{H} = 1, \quad \tilde{L} = \frac{H}{L}, \\
&\tilde{\mu}^{\mathrm{e}} = \frac{\mu^{\mathrm{e}}}{\mu}, \quad \tilde{\mu}^{\mathrm{i}} = \frac{\mu^{\mathrm{i}}}{\mu}, \quad \tilde{\epsilon} = 1, \quad \tilde{\eta} = \frac{\mu^{\mathrm{i}}}{\mu}, \quad \tilde{\rho}_0\tilde{g} = \frac{\rho_0 g H}{\mu},
\end{aligned} \tag{61}$$

where $\mu = \mu^{\mathrm{e}} + \mu^{\mathrm{i}}$.

5.1.7. Parameters

The parameters used in the numerical example below are listed in Table 1.

Table 1. Parameters used for example 1.

Quantity	Value
$\tilde{t}_0$	0
$\tilde{t}_{\mathrm{e}}$	2.25
$\tilde{U}_{\mathrm{e}}$	0.45
$\tilde{L}$	30
$\tilde{\mu}^{\mathrm{e}}$	0.5
$\tilde{\mu}^{\mathrm{i}}$	0.5
$\tilde{\eta}$	0.25
$\tilde{\rho}_0\tilde{g}$	$1 \cdot 10^{-5}$

5.1.8. Spatial Discretization, Temporal Discretization

The α-family with $\alpha = 1/2$ is used for temporal discretization. The spatial discretization is done in the two-dimensional axisymmetric setting, thus reducing the number of scalar fields required for the representation of $\mathbf{u}$ and $\mathbf{D}$ to two each, and for $\mathbf{U}^{\mathrm{i}}$ to four. In the case of the vector potential $\mathbf{A}$, only a single scalar field is required since only the circumferential component is non-zero. The particular quadrilateral finite elements employed for the analysis are compiled in Table 2. In this table, the nomenclature of the deal.II library [44] is used. It is noted that the use of the pair $\mathrm{RT}_1 - \mathrm{DGQ}_1$ for $\mathbf{D} - \varphi$ is empirical since the usual proof of stability cannot be readily extended to the axisymmetric case. In contrast, positive results concerning the stability of the pair $\mathrm{Q}_2 - \mathrm{P}_1$ for $\mathbf{u} - p$ for the axisymmetric Stokes problem are available in the literature [45]. Moreover, it is noted that the support points of the elements used for $\mathbf{U}^{\mathrm{i}}$ and p^{i} have been chosen to coincide with the quadrature points; and, as a consequence, these variables become "local" variables similar to the plastic strain in classical elastoplasticity (in fact, these variables can be eliminated at the quadrature point level, although this was not performed herein).

Table 2. Finite elements used for example 1.

Variable	Finite Element
$\mathbf{u}$	Q_2
$\mathbf{D}$	RT_1
$\mathbf{U}^{\mathrm{i}}$	DGQ_2
$\mathbf{A}$	Q_2
φ	DGQ_1 (Q_2 for scalar potential formulation)
p	DGP_1
p^{i}	DGQ_2

5.1.9. Initial Values

As mentioned earlier, the initial values for the state variables and auxiliary state variables need to be determined before the calculation. Due to the action of the gravitational acceleration, the initial state is inhomogeneous and must, therefore, be determined numerically. This has for simplicity been achieved by taking a very small time step of $1 \cdot 10^{-8} \tilde{t}_{\mathrm{e}}$ with $\alpha = 1$ before the actual computation, such that any increments in $\mathbf{U}^{\mathrm{i}}$ remain negligibly small. A more rigorous approach would be to explicitly constrain $\dot{\mathbf{U}}^{\mathrm{i}}$ to zero for determining the initial values. This has, however, not been implemented yet.

5.1.10. Example Calculations and Results

The implementation of the constitutive equations and the numerical procedures were first validated against the results obtained by Hong [42], as can be seen in Appendix A. Subsequently, spatial and temporal convergence studies have been performed for the formulations in terms of $\mathbf{D} - \varphi$ ("mixed formulation"), $\mathbf{A}$ ("vector potential formulation") and φ ("scalar potential formulation"). The starting point for these simulations is to take $N^t = 16$ equally spaced time increments for the entire simulation together with a coarse finite element mesh consisting of five rectangular cells in the radial direction and a single rectangular cell in the axial direction, see Figure 3 for an illustration of the coarse finite element mesh. Then, the number of time increments is increased to $N^t = 16 \cdot 2^{m^t}$, where m^t is the refinement cycle. Similarly, the finite element mesh is uniformly refined m^h times (in this work, the term "uniform refinement" refers to splitting a rectangular cell into four equally shaped rectangular cells by introducing new vertices at the midpoints of the edges and at the center of the cell). In particular, calculations with $m^t = 0, 1, \ldots, m^{t,\max}$ ($m^{t,\max} = 6$) and $m^h = 0$ were performed to study the convergence behavior in time; and calculations with $m^h = 0, 1, \ldots, m^{h,\max}$ ($m^{h,\max} = 6$) and $m^t = 0$ were performed to study the spatial convergence behavior. For the finest mesh with $m^h = 6$, this results in 1,231,108 degrees of freedom for the scalar potential formulation, 1,395,075 degrees of freedom for the mixed formulation, and 1,231,109 degrees of freedom for the vector potential formulation. However, it is emphasized that the computational cost cannot be directly related to the number of unknowns, since the system structure as well as the linear solver employed also play a major role in this regard; and the study of these aspects is beyond the scope of the present contribution.

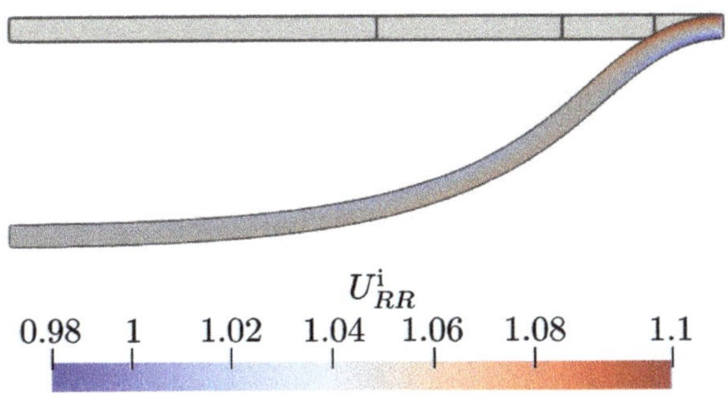

Figure 3. Coarse finite element mesh in the reference configuration together with radial inelastic stretch in the deformed configuration at $t = t_e$ (result obtained with $m_t = 0$ and $m_h = 6$).

With regard to the convergence behavior in time, the error e_{m^t} is, for each $m^t = 0, 1, \ldots, m^{t,\max} - 1$, evaluated according to

$$e_{m^t} = \|\tilde{\nabla}\tilde{\mathbf{u}}_{m^t} - \tilde{\nabla}\tilde{\mathbf{u}}_{m^{t,\max}}\|_{\mathcal{L}^2}. \tag{62}$$

For simplicity, no other unknowns are included into the error. However, it has also been checked that the other unknowns show the expected convergence behavior.

An analogous approach is utilized to assess the spatial convergence behavior. In particular, the error e_{m^h} is, for each $m^h = 0, 1, \ldots, m^{h,\max} - 1$, evaluated according to

$$e_{m^h} = \|\tilde{\nabla}\tilde{\mathbf{u}}_{m^h} - \tilde{\nabla}\tilde{\mathbf{u}}_{m^{h,\max}}\|_{\mathcal{L}^2}. \tag{63}$$

The deformed shape of the disc is shown in Figure 3 together with the radial inelastic stretch. It can be noticed that substantial inelastic deformation of approximately 10% takes place at the lateral surface of the body. Figure 4 shows the results of the convergence studies. In particular, Figure 4a shows the temporal convergence behavior, while Figure 4b shows the spatial convergence behavior. It is seen that in both cases the expected rates of convergence of $k^t = 2$ and $k^h = 2$ are observed for all three formulations, which confirms the validity of the approach. It is interesting that all three formulations essentially exhibit the same convergence behavior, a fact which is likely to be attributed to the relatively simple electric field distribution in the disc.

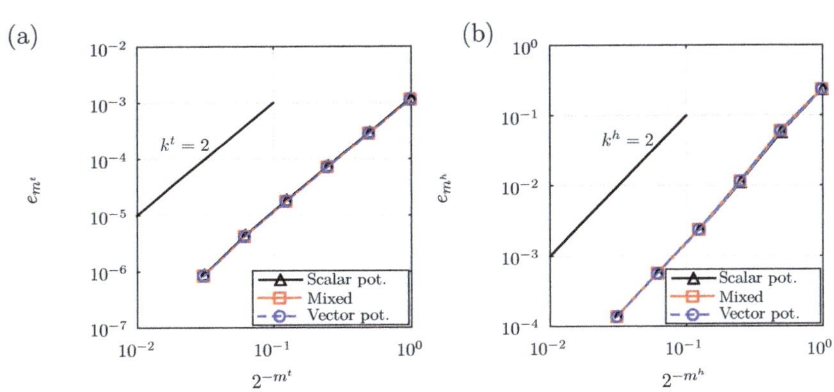

Figure 4. Convergence results for example 1: **(a)** temporal convergence; and **(b)** spatial convergence.

5.2. Example 2: Swelling/Shrinking of a Hydrogel

The second example problem is illustrated in Figure 5. A circular cylinder of hydrogel material with radius H and height H is considered. The hydrogel is assumed to consist of a polymeric backbone material with charged groups attached to it, and an electrolyte composed of water and the ions of a fully dissociated monovalent salt. The polymeric backbone material and water are assumed to be incompressible, and the volume change associated with a change in the concentrations of cations and anions is neglected. It is further assumed that there are no voids in the hydrogel and, hence, the volume fractions of polymeric backbone material and water must locally add up to 1. The constitutive behavior of the hydrogel is assumed to be described by the relations proposed by Acartürk [4], with the simplification of local electroneutrality (i.e., the local net space charge density is assumed to be zero). The displacement is fixed to zero at the center of the bottom surface of the cylinder, while all other surfaces are mechanically free. No matter is allowed to flow across the bottom and lateral surfaces. In contrast, water and ions may be exchanged across the top surface, which is in contact with an external electrolytic solution. The latter is composed of water and a fully dissociated monovalent salt of the same type as in the hydrogel, with a prescribed transient homogeneous molar concentration of both cations and anions, of $\bar{c}^{\text{ext}}(t)$. Starting from equilibrium, the external ion concentration is changed and the response of the hydrogel in terms of swelling/shrinking deformation and change in local water and ion concentrations is tracked.

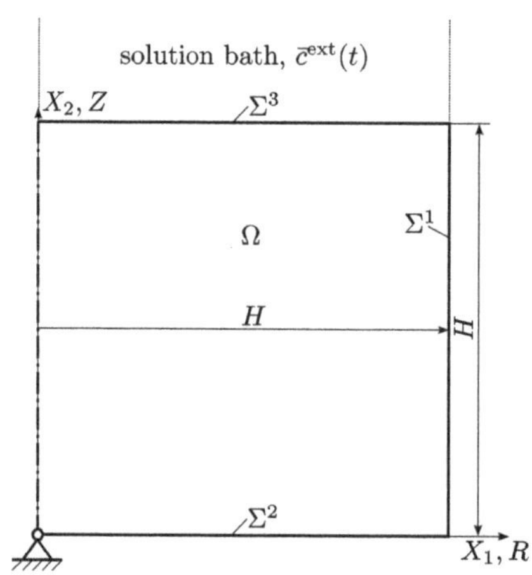

Figure 5. Illustration of example problem 2.

5.2.1. Computational Domain

The computational domain Ω shown in Figure 5 represents the reference configuration of the cylinder, which coincides with the configuration at the initial time $t = t_0$. The in-plane Cartesian coordinates in Figure 2 are again X_1 and X_2, while the out-of-plane coordinate is X_3. In terms of the radial coordinate R and the axial coordinate Z of a cylindrical coordinate system, the body occupies the region described by $0 \leq R \leq H$ and $0 \leq Z \leq H$. The lateral surface of the cylinder is Σ^1, the bottom surface Σ^2, and the top surface Σ^3.

5.2.2. Unknown Variables

State Variables

The thermodynamic state variables

$$\mathbf{u}: \begin{cases} \Omega \times \mathcal{T} \to \mathcal{R}^3 \\ (\mathbf{X}, t) \mapsto \mathbf{u}(\mathbf{X}, t). \end{cases} \tag{64}$$

$$c^{\mathrm{H_2O}}: \begin{cases} \Omega \times \mathcal{T} \to \mathcal{R} \\ (\mathbf{X}, t) \mapsto c^{\mathrm{H_2O}}(\mathbf{X}, t) \end{cases} \tag{65}$$

$$c^{i}: \begin{cases} \Omega \times \mathcal{T} \to \mathcal{R} \\ (\mathbf{X}, t) \mapsto c^{i}(\mathbf{X}, t) \end{cases} \tag{66}$$

are introduced, where $i \in \{\mathrm{A}^+, \mathrm{B}^-\}$. The corresponding initial conditions read

$$\mathbf{u}(\mathbf{X}, t_0) = \mathbf{0} \tag{67}$$

$$c^{\mathrm{H_2O}}(\mathbf{X}, t_0) = c_0^{\mathrm{H_2O}} \tag{68}$$

$$c^{i}(\mathbf{X}, t_0) = c_0^{i}, \tag{69}$$

with $c_0^{\mathrm{H_2O}}$ and c_0^{i} being constants since the initial state is homogeneous. The thermodynamic state variables have the following significance:

- $\mathbf{u}$ is the mechanical displacement field.
- $c^{\mathrm{H_2O}}$ is the referential molar concentration of water (with regard to the total volume in the reference state).
- c^{i} are the referential molar concentrations of the A^+ and B^- ions (with regard to the total volume in the reference state).

These thermodynamic state variables are supplemented by the auxiliary state variables

$$p: \begin{cases} \Omega \times \mathcal{T} \to \mathcal{R} \\ (\mathbf{X}, t) \mapsto p(\mathbf{X}, t) \end{cases} \tag{70}$$

$$\varphi: \begin{cases} \Omega \times \mathcal{T} \to \mathcal{R} \\ (\mathbf{X}, t) \mapsto \varphi(\mathbf{X}, t) \end{cases} \tag{71}$$

together with the corresponding initial conditions

$$p(\mathbf{X}, t_0) = p_0 \tag{72}$$

$$\varphi(\mathbf{X}, t_0) = \varphi_0, \tag{73}$$

where p_0 and φ_0 are constants. The auxiliary state variables have the following significance:

- p is a pressure type variable, which acts as a Lagrangian multiplier enforcing the condition that the volume fractions of water and polymeric backbone material must add up to 1 everywhere.
- φ is the electric scalar potential, which enforces the local electroneutrality condition.

It is noted that the constants $c_0^{\mathrm{H_2O}}$, c_0^{i}, p_0, and φ_0 cannot be chosen independently. Rather, they are interrelated through the assumption that the initial state at time $t = t_0$ is equilibrated.

Process Variables

The process variables involved in the problem are

$$\mathbf{I}^{\mathrm{H_2O}}: \begin{cases} \Omega \times \mathcal{T} \to \mathcal{R}^3 \\ (\mathbf{X}, t) \mapsto \mathbf{I}^{\mathrm{H_2O}}(\mathbf{X}, t) \end{cases} \tag{74}$$

$$\mathbf{I}^{i}: \begin{cases} \Omega \times \mathcal{T} \to \mathcal{R}^3 \\ (\mathbf{X}, t) \mapsto \mathbf{I}^{i}(\mathbf{X}, t) \end{cases} \tag{75}$$

These have the following significance:

- $\mathbf{I}^{\mathrm{H_2O}}$ is the time-integrated referential flux of water in the hydrogel.
- $\mathbf{I}^{i}$ are the time-integrated referential fluxes of the ionic species $i \in \{\mathrm{A}^+, \mathrm{B}^-\}$.

Lagrangian Multipliers

The Lagrangian multipliers

$$\eta^{\mathrm{H_2O}} : \begin{cases} \Omega \times (\mathcal{T} \setminus t_0) \to \mathbb{R} \\ (\mathbf{X}, t) \mapsto \eta^{\mathrm{H_2O}}(\mathbf{X}, t) \end{cases} \tag{76}$$

$$\eta^{i} : \begin{cases} \Omega \times (\mathcal{T} \setminus t_0) \to \mathbb{R} \\ (\mathbf{X}, t) \mapsto \eta^{i}(\mathbf{X}, t) \end{cases} \tag{77}$$

$$\varphi^{\mathrm{s}} : \begin{cases} \Sigma^3 \times (\mathcal{T} \setminus t_0) \to \mathbb{R} \\ (\mathbf{X}, t) \mapsto \varphi^{\mathrm{s}}(\mathbf{X}, t) \end{cases} \tag{78}$$

are introduced. These have the following significance:

- $\eta^{\mathrm{H_2O}}$ and η^{i} are used to incorporate the respective balance equations for water and the ionic species A^+ and B^-.
- φ^{s} is used to ensure that no net charge flows locally across Σ^3. It is noted in this context that the assumption of no local net charge flow implies a certain behavior of the external solution bath. Other assumptions are possible (e.g., no global net charge flow), however, these are in any case only an approximation to the real behavior; and for the proper resolution of the behavior at the boundary, the exterior solution bath needs to be explicitly modeled.

Dirichlet Constraints

The unknowns $\mathbf{u}$, $\mathbf{I}^{\mathrm{H_2O}}$, $\mathbf{I}^{i}$ and η^{B^-} are subject to the following Dirichlet type constraints

$$\mathbf{u} = 0 \qquad \text{at} \quad \mathbf{X} = (0,0,0) \tag{79}$$

$$\mathbf{I}^{\mathrm{H_2O}} \cdot \mathbf{N} = 0 \qquad \text{on} \quad \Sigma^1 \cup \Sigma^2 \tag{80}$$

$$\mathbf{I}^{i} \cdot \mathbf{N} = 0 \qquad \text{on} \quad \Sigma^1 \cup \Sigma^2 \tag{81}$$

$$\eta^{\mathrm{B}^-} = \eta_0^{\mathrm{B}^-} \qquad \text{at} \quad \mathbf{X} = (0,0,0). \tag{82}$$

Here, η^{B^-} is constrained to the arbitrary constant $\eta_0^{\mathrm{B}^-}$ at the origin in order to ensure the uniqueness of the involved scalar potential type quantities, which are only determined up to a constant by the model.

5.2.3. Dependent Fields

As before, only the "non-trivial"-dependent fields are listed; and the mechanical deformation gradient

$$\mathbf{F} = \nabla \mathbf{u} + \mathbf{I} \tag{83}$$

is the only field of this type.

5.2.4. The Functionals

Helmholtz Free Energy Functional Ψ

The part Ψ^{U} of the Helmholtz free energy functional is assumed to take the form

$$\Psi^{\mathrm{U}}[\mathbf{U}] = \int_{\Omega} \psi^{\mathrm{el}}(\mathbf{F})\,\mathrm{d}V + \int_{\Omega} c^{\mathrm{H_2O}} \psi^{\mathrm{fl}}\left(\frac{c^{i}}{c^{\mathrm{H_2O}}}\right) \mathrm{d}V, \tag{84}$$

with the first integral representing the elastic-free energy contribution of the polymeric backbone and the second integral the free energy contributions of the fluid. In particular,

$$\psi^{\mathrm{el}} = \frac{\mu}{2}\Big[\mathrm{tr}\Big(\mathbf{F}^{\top}\cdot\mathbf{F}\Big) - 2\ln(J) - 3\Big] + \lambda(1-n_0)^2\left(\frac{J-1}{1-n_0} - \ln\frac{J-n_0}{1-n_0}\right), \tag{85}$$

$$\psi^{\mathrm{fl}} = \sum_i \frac{c^i}{c^{\mathrm{H_2O}}} RT\left[\ln\left(\frac{c^i}{c^{\mathrm{H_2O}}}\right) - 1\right] \tag{86}$$

are assumed. Here, $J = \det \mathbf{F}$ again, λ and μ are Lamé's constants, $n_0 = 1 - c_0^{\mathrm{H_2O}} V_{\mathrm{m}}^{\mathrm{H_2O}}$ is the volume fraction of polymeric backbone material in the reference state, where $V_{\mathrm{m}}^{\mathrm{H_2O}}$ denotes the molar volume of water, R is the gas constant and T is the temperature.

The part Ψ^{P} of the Helmholtz free energy functional reads

$$\Psi^{\mathrm{P}}[\mathbf{P},\mathbf{U}] = \int\limits_{\Omega} p\Big(n_0 + c^{\mathrm{H_2O}} V_{\mathrm{m}}^{\mathrm{H_2O}} - J\Big)\,\mathrm{d}V + \int\limits_{\Omega} F\varphi\left(\sum_i z^i c^i + z^{\mathrm{C}^-} c^{\mathrm{C}^-}\right)\mathrm{d}V, \tag{87}$$

where the first integral enforces the condition that the volume fractions of fluid and polymeric backbone material add up to 1, and the second integral incorporates the electroneutrality condition. In the latter term, F is Faraday's constant, z^i and z^{C^-} are the respective charges of the ionic species A^+, B^- and the charged groups C^- attached to the backbone polymer in multiples of the elementary charge, and c^{C^-} is the (constant) referential molar concentration of the charged groups.

Power Functional P

For the power functional, the form

$$P[\dot{\mathbf{U}},\dot{\mathbf{V}};\mathbf{U},t] = \int\limits_{\Sigma^3}\left[\bar{\mu}^{\mathrm{H_2O}}(t)\,\mathbf{I}^{\mathrm{H_2O}}\cdot\mathbf{N} + \sum_i \bar{\mu}^i(t)\,\mathbf{I}^i\cdot\mathbf{N}\right]\mathrm{d}S \tag{88}$$

is assumed, where

$$\bar{\mu}^{\mathrm{H_2O}}(t) = 2RT\frac{\bar{c}^{\mathrm{ext}}(t)}{V_{\mathrm{m}}^{\mathrm{H_2O}}} \tag{89}$$

$$\bar{\mu}^i(t) = -RT\ln\left(\frac{\bar{c}^{\mathrm{ext}}(t)}{V_{\mathrm{m}}^{\mathrm{H_2O}}}\right). \tag{90}$$

For the purposes of this example, the ramp function

$$\bar{c}^{\mathrm{ext}}(t) = \bar{c}_0^{\mathrm{ext}} + \left(\bar{c}_{\mathrm{e}}^{\mathrm{ext}} - \bar{c}_0^{\mathrm{ext}}\right)\frac{t-t_0}{t_{\mathrm{e}}-t_0} \tag{91}$$

is used for $\bar{c}^{\mathrm{ext}}(t)$, where $\bar{c}_0^{\mathrm{ext}}$ is the initial concentration of ions in the external solution at time $t = t_0$, and $\bar{c}_{\mathrm{e}}^{\mathrm{ext}}$ the final concentration at time $t = t_{\mathrm{e}}$.

Lagrangian Multiplier Functional L

The Lagrangian multiplier functional is assumed to take the form

$$\begin{aligned} L[\mathbf{M},\dot{\mathbf{U}},\dot{\mathbf{V}};\mathbf{U},t] = &\int\limits_{\Omega} \eta^{\mathrm{H_2O}}\Big(-\nabla\cdot\mathbf{I}^{\mathrm{H_2O}} - \dot{c}^{\mathrm{H_2O}}\Big)\,\mathrm{d}V \\ &+ \int\limits_{\Omega}\sum_i \eta^i\Big(-\nabla\cdot\mathbf{I}^i - \dot{c}^i\Big)\,\mathrm{d}V \\ &+ \int\limits_{\Sigma^3} F\varphi^{\mathrm{s}}\sum_i z^i\,\mathbf{I}^i\cdot\mathbf{N}\,\mathrm{d}S. \end{aligned} \tag{92}$$

where the first two integrals incorporate the respective balance equations for water and the two ion species, and the third integral enforces the condition that the local net charge flow across Σ^3 is zero.

Dissipation Functional $\mathring{\Delta}$

For the dissipation functional, the form

$$\mathring{\Delta}[\dot{\mathbf{U}}, \dot{\mathbf{V}}; \mathbf{U}, t] = \int_{\Omega} \mathring{\delta}\left(\dot{\mathbf{I}}^{\mathrm{H_2O}}, \dot{\mathbf{I}}^i; \mathbf{F}, c^i, c^{\mathrm{H_2O}}\right) \mathrm{d}V \tag{93}$$

is assumed. In this relation,

$$\mathring{\delta} = \frac{c^{\mathrm{H_2O}} V_{\mathrm{m}}^{\mathrm{H_2O}}}{J} \left[\sum_i \frac{RT}{2D^i c^i} \left(\dot{\mathbf{I}}^i - \frac{c^i}{c^{\mathrm{H_2O}}} \dot{\mathbf{I}}^{\mathrm{H_2O}} \right) \cdot \mathbf{F}^\top \cdot \mathbf{F} \cdot \left(\dot{\mathbf{I}}^i - \frac{c^i}{c^{\mathrm{H_2O}}} \dot{\mathbf{I}}^{\mathrm{H_2O}} \right) \right.$$
$$\left. + \frac{RT}{2D^{\mathrm{H_2O}} c^{\mathrm{H_2O}}} \dot{\mathbf{I}}^{\mathrm{H_2O}} \cdot \mathbf{F}^\top \cdot \mathbf{F} \cdot \dot{\mathbf{I}}^{\mathrm{H_2O}} \right] \tag{94}$$

is the local dissipation function, where D^i are the respective diffusivities of the ionic species in water, and $D^{\mathrm{H_2O}}$ is a material parameter characterizing the Darcy type "resistance" associated with the motion of water through the polymeric backbone material.

For later use, the dual local dissipation function is introduced according to

$$\phi(\nabla\eta^{\mathrm{H_2O}}, \nabla\eta^i; \mathbf{F}, c^i, c^{\mathrm{H_2O}})$$
$$= - \inf_{\dot{\mathbf{I}}^{\mathrm{H_2O}}, \dot{\mathbf{I}}^i} \left[\nabla\eta^{\mathrm{H_2O}} \cdot \dot{\mathbf{I}}^{\mathrm{H_2O}} + \sum_i \nabla\eta^i \cdot \dot{\mathbf{I}}^i + \mathring{\delta}\left(\dot{\mathbf{I}}^{\mathrm{H_2O}}, \dot{\mathbf{I}}^i; \mathbf{F}, c^i, c^{\mathrm{H_2O}}\right) \right]$$
$$= \frac{J}{c^{\mathrm{H_2O}} V_{\mathrm{m}}^{\mathrm{H_2O}}} \left[\sum_i \frac{D^i c^i}{2RT} \nabla\eta^i \cdot \mathbf{F}^{-1} \cdot \mathbf{F}^{-\top} \cdot \nabla\eta^i + \frac{D^{\mathrm{H_2O}} c^{\mathrm{H_2O}}}{2RT} \right.$$
$$\left. \times \left(\nabla\eta^{\mathrm{H_2O}} + \sum_i \frac{c^i}{c^{\mathrm{H_2O}}} \nabla\eta^i \right) \cdot \mathbf{F}^{-1} \cdot \mathbf{F}^{-\top} \cdot \left(\nabla\eta^{\mathrm{H_2O}} + \sum_i \frac{c^i}{c^{\mathrm{H_2O}}} \nabla\eta^i \right) \right]. \tag{95}$$

5.2.5. Reduced Formulation

By using the procedure described in Section 2.6.1, the variables $\mathbf{I}^{\mathrm{H_2O}}$ and $\mathbf{I}^i$ can be eliminated on Ω. This leads to the reduced sets of variables

$$\mathbf{V}^0 = \begin{pmatrix} I_{\mathrm{N}}^{\mathrm{H_2O}} \\ I_{\mathrm{N}}^i \end{pmatrix} \qquad \mathbf{M}^0 = \mathbf{M}, \tag{96}$$

where

$$I_{\mathrm{N}}^{\mathrm{H_2O}} : \begin{cases} \Sigma^3 \times \mathcal{T} \to \mathcal{R} \\ (\mathbf{X}, t) \mapsto I_{\mathrm{N}}^{\mathrm{H_2O}}(\mathbf{X}, t) \end{cases} \tag{97}$$

$$I_{\mathrm{N}}^i : \begin{cases} \Sigma^3 \times \mathcal{T} \to \mathcal{R} \\ (\mathbf{X}, t) \mapsto I_{\mathrm{N}}^i(\mathbf{X}, t) \end{cases} \tag{98}$$

represent $\mathbf{I}^{\mathrm{H_2O}} \cdot \mathbf{N}$ and $\mathbf{I}^i \cdot \mathbf{N}$, respectively, on Σ^3. The corresponding reduced functional is obtained from Equation (16) using the dual local dissipation function (95). It reads

$$\Gamma^{\mathrm{red}}[\dot{\mathbf{U}}, \dot{\mathbf{V}}^0, \mathbf{M}^0; \mathbf{U}, t] = - \int_{\Omega} \left(\eta^{\mathrm{H_2O}} \dot{c}^{\mathrm{H_2O}} + \sum_i \eta^i \dot{c}^i \right) \mathrm{d}V$$
$$- \int_{\Omega} \phi(\nabla\eta^{\mathrm{H_2O}}, \nabla\eta^i; \mathbf{F}, c^i, c^{\mathrm{H_2O}}) \, \mathrm{d}V$$

$$
\begin{aligned}
&- \int_{\Sigma^3} \left[\eta^{\mathrm{H_2O}} - \bar{\mu}^{\mathrm{H_2O}}(t) \right] I_{\mathrm{N}}^{\mathrm{H_2O}} \, \mathrm{d}S \\
&- \int_{\Sigma^3} \sum_i \left[\eta^i - F \varphi^{\mathrm{s}} z^i - \bar{\mu}^i(t) \right] I_{\mathrm{N}}^i \, \mathrm{d}S. \qquad (99)
\end{aligned}
$$

Similarly to example 1, $I_{\mathrm{N}}^{\mathrm{H_2O}}$ and I_{N}^i can be eliminated by imposing appropriate Dirichlet conditions for $\eta^{\mathrm{H_2O}}$ and η^i. However, due to the involvement of φ^{s} in these conditions, the resulting equations are more complicated to implement and hence, $I_{\mathrm{N}}^{\mathrm{H_2O}}$ and I_{N}^i are kept as variables.

5.2.6. Normalization

All quantities are normalized using the reference values $c^* = 1$ mol/L, $D^* = 1 \cdot 10^{-4}\,\mathrm{cm^2/s}$, $R^* = 8.3144$ J/(mol K), $T^* = 298$ K, $F^* = 96{,}485.33$ C/mol and $L^* = 1$ mm. In particular, the normalized quantities are

$$
\begin{aligned}
&\tilde{\mathbf{X}} = \frac{\mathbf{X}}{L^*}, \quad \tilde{t} = \frac{tD^*}{L^{*2}}, \quad \tilde{\nabla}() = \nabla()L^*, \quad \tilde{\dot{()}} = \dot{()}\frac{L^{*2}}{D^*}, \\
&\tilde{\mathbf{u}} = \frac{\mathbf{u}}{L^*}, \quad \tilde{c}^{\mathrm{H_2O}} = \frac{c^{\mathrm{H_2O}}}{c^*}, \quad \tilde{c}^i = \frac{c^i}{c^*}, \quad \tilde{p} = \frac{p}{R^*T^*c^*}, \quad \tilde{\varphi} = \frac{\varphi F^*}{R^*T^*}, \\
&\tilde{\mathbf{I}}^{\mathrm{H_2O}} = \frac{\mathbf{I}^{\mathrm{H_2O}}}{c^*L^*}, \quad \tilde{\mathbf{I}}^i = \frac{\mathbf{I}^i}{c^*L^*}, \quad \tilde{I}_{\mathrm{N}}^{\mathrm{H_2O}} = \frac{I_{\mathrm{N}}^{\mathrm{H_2O}}}{c^*L^*}, \quad \tilde{I}_{\mathrm{N}}^i = \frac{I_{\mathrm{N}}^i}{c^*L^*}, \\
&\tilde{\eta}^{\mathrm{H_2O}} = \frac{\eta^{\mathrm{H_2O}}}{R^*T^*}, \quad \tilde{\eta}^i = \frac{\eta^i}{R^*T^*}, \quad \tilde{\varphi}^{\mathrm{s}} = \frac{\varphi^{\mathrm{s}}F^*}{R^*T^*}, \\
&\tilde{t}_0 = \frac{t_0D^*}{L^{*2}}, \quad \tilde{t}_{\mathrm{e}} = \frac{t_{\mathrm{e}}D^*}{L^{*2}}, \quad \tilde{\bar{c}}_0^{\mathrm{ext}} = \frac{\bar{c}_0^{\mathrm{ext}}}{c^*}, \quad \tilde{\bar{c}}_{\mathrm{e}}^{\mathrm{ext}} = \frac{\bar{c}_{\mathrm{e}}^{\mathrm{ext}}}{c^*}, \qquad (100) \\
&\tilde{H} = \frac{H}{L^*}, \\
&\tilde{c}_0^{\mathrm{H_2O}} = \frac{c_0^{\mathrm{H_2O}}}{c^*}, \quad \tilde{c}_0^i = \frac{c_0^i}{c^*}, \quad \tilde{p}_0 = \frac{p_0}{R^*T^*c^*}, \quad \tilde{\varphi}_0 = \frac{\varphi_0F^*}{R^*T^*}, \\
&\tilde{\mu} = \frac{\mu}{R^*T^*c^*}, \quad \tilde{\lambda} = \frac{\lambda}{R^*T^*c^*}, \quad \tilde{V}_{\mathrm{m}}^{\mathrm{H_2O}} = V_{\mathrm{m}}^{\mathrm{H_2O}}c^*, \quad \tilde{n}_0 = n_0, \\
&\tilde{z}^i = z^i, \quad \tilde{z}^{\mathrm{C^-}} = z^{\mathrm{C^-}}, \quad \tilde{c}^{\mathrm{C^-}} = \frac{c^{\mathrm{C^-}}}{c^*}, \quad \tilde{D}^{\mathrm{H_2O}} = \frac{D^{\mathrm{H_2O}}}{D^*}, \quad \tilde{D}^i = \frac{D^i}{D^*}, \\
&\tilde{R} = \frac{R}{R^*}, \quad \tilde{F} = \frac{F}{F^*}, \quad \tilde{T} = \frac{T}{T^*}.
\end{aligned}
$$

5.2.7. Parameters

The set of parameters used below is listed in Table 3. The constitutive parameters have been taken from Table 5.1 in Acartürk [4] and normalized. It is noted in this context that some of the parameters are defined differently in the latter work than in the present work, so that some conversion between the parameters is involved. This applies in particular to $D^{\mathrm{H_2O}}$, which is equal to $RTk^F/(\gamma^{FR}V_{\mathrm{m}}^{\mathrm{H_2O}})$ in the work of Acartürk [4] (the quantities k^F and γ^{FR} are defined in [4]).

Table 3. The parameters used for the hydrogel example.

Quantity	Value
$\tilde{t}_0$	0
$\tilde{t}_e$	5
$\tilde{\bar{c}}_0^{ext}$	0.9
$\tilde{\bar{c}}_e^{ext}$	0.1
$\tilde{H}$	1
$\tilde{c}_0^{H_2O}$	41.509
$\tilde{c}_0^{A^+}$	0.75415
$\tilde{c}_0^{B^-}$	0.60415
$\tilde{p}_0$	0.011077
$\tilde{\varphi}_0$	−0.11088
$\tilde{\mu}$	0.040360
$\tilde{\lambda}$	0.016144
$\tilde{V}_m^{H_2O}$	0.018069
$\tilde{n}_0$	0.25
$\tilde{z}^{A^+}$	1
$\tilde{z}^{B^-}$	−1
$\tilde{z}^{C^-}$	−1
$\tilde{c}^{C^-}$	0.15
$\tilde{D}^{H_2O}$	14.673
$\tilde{D}^{A^+}$	0.05
$\tilde{D}^{B^-}$	0.08
$\tilde{R}$	1
$\tilde{F}$	1
$\tilde{T}$	1

The initial values appearing in Table 3 were computed from the condition that the initial state is an equilibrium state, which leads to the following equations

$$c_0^{H_2O} = \frac{1-n_0}{V_m^{H_2O}} \tag{101}$$

$$c_0^{A^+} = -\frac{1}{2}\frac{z^{C^-}c^{C^-}}{z^{A^+}} + \frac{1}{2|z^{A^+}|}\sqrt{\left(z^{C^-}c^{C^-}\right)^2 - z^{A^+}z^{B^-}\left(2\bar{c}_0^{ext}c_0^{H_2O}V_m^{H_2O}\right)^2} \tag{102}$$

$$c_0^{B^-} = -\frac{1}{2}\frac{z^{C^-}c^{C^-}}{z^{B^-}} + \frac{1}{2|z^{B^-}|}\sqrt{\left(z^{C^-}c^{C^-}\right)^2 - z^{A^+}z^{B^-}\left(2\bar{c}_0^{ext}c_0^{H_2O}V_m^{H_2O}\right)^2} \tag{103}$$

$$p_0 = \frac{RT}{V_m^{H_2O}}\left(\frac{c_0^{A^+}+c_0^{B^-}}{c_0^{H_2O}} - 2V_m^{H_2O}\bar{c}_0^{ext}\right) \tag{104}$$

$$\varphi_0 = \frac{RT}{Fz^{A^+}}\ln\left(\frac{\bar{c}_0^{ext}c_0^{H_2O}V_m^{H_2O}}{c_0^{A^+}}\right). \tag{105}$$

The corresponding normalized values given in Table 3 are subject to rounding. However, in the simulations, values accurate to within numerical accuracy have been used. This also applies to $\tilde{\lambda}$, $\tilde{\mu}$ and $\tilde{D}^{H_2O}$.

5.2.8. Spatial Discretization and Temporal Discretization

Again, the α family with $\alpha = 1/2$ is used for temporal discretization, and the spatial discretization is performed in the two-dimensional axisymmetric setting. The particular quadrilateral finite elements employed for the analysis are compiled in Table 4. No elements are given for $\mathbf{I}^{H_2O}$ and $\mathbf{I}^i$ in this table because only the reduced formulation is considered in the numerical example below. It is noted that there are no interface terms coupling the unknowns associated with the discontinuous finite elements of type DGP_1 between neighboring cells. This means that the unknowns associated with these elements are local to the cell and can be eliminated with little cost by the direct linear solver. Another possibility would be to use discontinuous Lagrange elements of type DGQ_2 for c^{H_2O}, c^i and φ with the support points coinciding with the quadrature points. However, to fully benefit from this approach where the respective unknowns are local to the quadrature points, changes to the implementation would be necessary, which have not been implemented yet.

Table 4. Finite elements used for example 2.

Variable	Finite Element
$\mathbf{u}$	Q_2
$c^{H_2O}, c^i, p, \varphi$	DGP_1
$I_N^{H_2O}, I_N^i$	Q_2
η^{H_2O}, η^i	Q_2
φ^s	Q_2

5.2.9. Example Calculations and Results

The implementation of the constitutive equations and the numerical procedures was first validated against a result obtained by Acartürk [4], as can be seen in Appendix B. Subsequently, spatial and temporal convergence studies have been performed for the reduced formulation. In the latter case, the starting point is to take $N^t = 4$ equally spaced time increments for the entire simulation together with a coarse finite element mesh consisting of a single cell. With regard to the definition and evaluation of errors, exactly the same approach as in Section 5.1.10 is used. However, for this example, the convergence behavior in time is studied with $m^{t,\max} = 8$ and $m_h = 3$, while the spatial convergence study is conducted with $m^{h,\max} = 7$ and $m_t = 2$. In the latter case, this results in 577,033 unknowns for the finest mesh with $m^h = 7$.

The deformed shape of the hydrogel cylinder is shown in Figure 6 together with the cation concentration $\tilde{c}^{A^+}$ and the outline of the undeformed cylinder; whilst Figure 7a,b show the results of the temporal and spatial convergence study, respectively. The expected rates of convergence of $k^t = 2$ and $k^h = 2$ are clearly observed as for the first example.

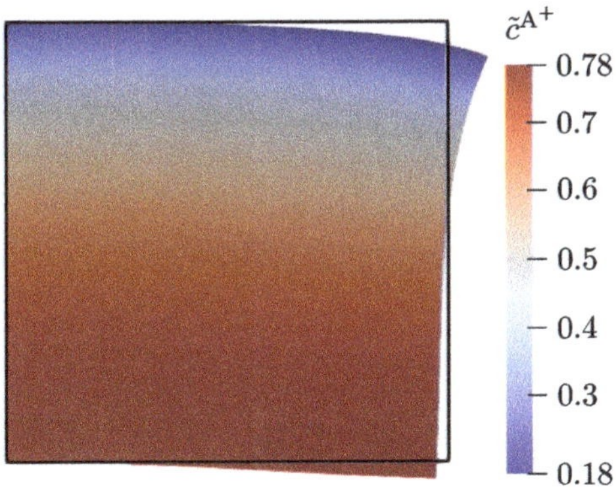

Figure 6. Deformed shape of the hydrogel cylinder at time $\tilde{t}^e$ together with cation concentration $\tilde{c}^{A^+}$ and outline of the undeformed shape (result obtained with $m_t = 2$ and $m_h = 7$).

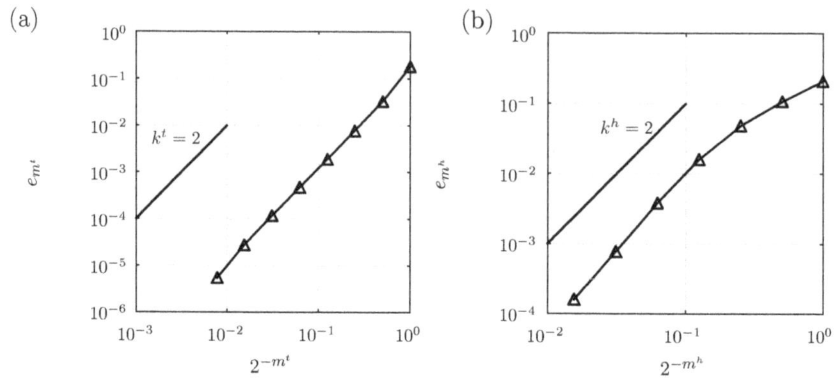

Figure 7. Convergence results for example 2: (**a**) temporal convergence, (**b**) spatial convergence.

6. Concluding Remarks

In the present contribution, a systematic approach to the thermodynamically consistent modeling of isothermal dissipative continuum problems using the concept of standard dissipative continua is proposed and applied to two example problems. The formulation does explicitly allow for different spatial regions, which are associated with different physics, as well as for the description of interfacial processes, which may be coupled to the physics in the volume. An important conceptual feature of the approach is the distinction between state variables, process variables and Lagrangian multipliers. While the state variables have the usual significance in that they describe the thermodynamic state of the system under consideration, the process variables are used to constrain the ways in which the thermodynamic state can change; and the latter constraints are incorporated with the help of the Lagrangian multipliers. Due to the variational structure of the formulation, a systematic elimination of variables is possible under certain circumstances, thus reducing the number of unknown variables, which is an important aspect for numerical solution procedures.

The variational approach is also beneficial in view of the temporal and spatial discretization of the space–time continuous problem. With regard to temporal discretization, it is, at least for a certain class of problems, possible to use generic discretization approaches with known convergence properties. Similarly, when using the finite element method for spatial discretization, much of the classical theory applies.

Albeit a large amount of formalization is clearly involved in the presented formulation, it is expected that the associated systematic approach substantially reduces the time penalty associated with implementing complex multiphysics models. At the same time, it likely reduces the potential for error both, during the formulation of multiphysics models as well as during the implementation into program code. In particular, it appears possible to solve a large class of problems using a single, well-tested implementation.

Some of the above aspects were demonstrated by considering two example problems. In this context, it was empirically shown that optimal rates of convergence in space and time can be achieved. For the purposes of this work, the example problems were kept simple. However, applications to more complex problems will be described in forthcoming contributions.

Funding: Financial support from the Deutsche Forschungsgemeinschaft (DFG) under Grants STA 1593/1-1 and STA 1593/2-1 is gratefully acknowledged.

Data Availability Statement: The source code for the library GalerkinTools and the corresponding documentation are available from the following repository: https://github.com/sebastian-stark/GalerkinTools (accessed on 26 February 2023); The source code for the library IncrementalFE and the corresponding documentation are available from the following repository: https:

//github.com/sebastian-stark/IncrementalFE (accessed on 26 February 2023); The source code used for the second example is available from the following repository: https://github.com/sebastian-stark/hydrogel_model_concentration_change (accessed on 26 February 2023); The source code used for the first example is in part available from the author upon request (the full source code cannot be made publicly available due to the use of a software library, which cannot be made available for legal reasons).

Acknowledgments: The author wishes to thank B.D. Reddy for an invitation for a research visit at the Centre for Research in Computational and Applied Mechanics at the University of Cape Town, during which part of the work underlying the present contribution was conducted.

Conflicts of Interest: The author declares no conflict of interest.

Appendix A. Validation of the Implementation for Example 1

In order to verify the correct implementation of the constitutive relations for example 1, some results were compared to those obtained by Hong [42], with Figure A1 showing a representative example. In particular, a laterally free plate of viscoelastic dielectric elastomer is considered, with the fringing fields neglected. An electric voltage is applied across the electrodes on the bottom and top faces of this plate. The resulting nominal electric field in the plate is $\tilde{E} = \tilde{\varphi}/\tilde{H}$, with $\tilde{H} = 1$ being the normalized thickness of the plate. The nominal electric field is increased at a rate of $\mathrm{d}\tilde{E}/\mathrm{d}\tilde{t} = 0.2$ until instability takes place. The material parameters used by Hong [42] coincide with the parameters given in Table 1 (note that the definition of the viscosity used by Hong [42] differs by a factor of 2 from the one used in the present work). For the comparisons, the total time interval was split into 1024 equally spaced time increments, and the α-family with $\alpha = 1/2$ was used for temporal discretization. Since the fields are homogeneous, the use of a single finite element is sufficient. Figure A1 shows the results for the total lateral stretch λ and the inelastic lateral stretch λ^{i}. It is seen that the results obtained with all three formulations are indistinguishable; and these results are consistent with the results of Hong [42], which confirms the correct implementation for at least the case of homogeneous uniaxial fields.

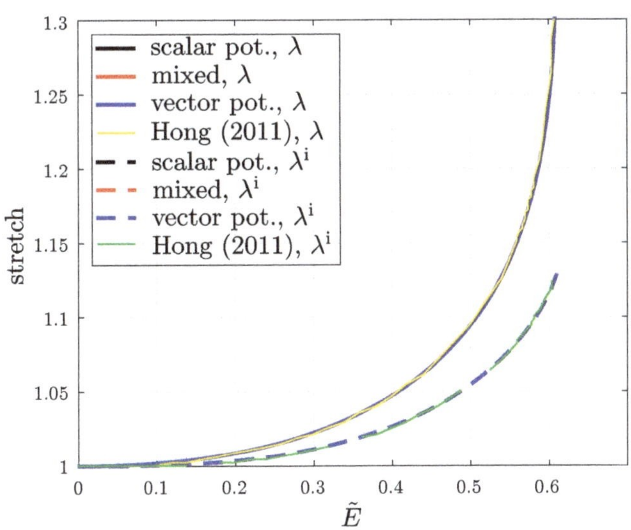

Figure A1. Comparison between the present formulation and the results obtained by Hong [42].

Appendix B. Validation of the Implementation for Example 2

In order to verify the correct implementation of the constitutive relations for example 2, an example problem described by Acartürk [4] is considered. The problem involves a block of hydrogel material with a width of 0.2 mm and a height of 1 mm in a plane strain setting. The normal mechanical displacement is constrained to zero on the lateral surfaces of the block as well as on its bottom surface, while the top surface is mechanically free. No matter is allowed to flow across the lateral surfaces and the bottom surfaces, while the top surface is in contact with a solution bath in the same way as shown in Figure 5. The ion concentration is linearly ramped from $\tilde{c}^{\text{ext}} = 0.9$ to $\tilde{c}^{\text{ext}} = 0.1$ between time $\tilde{t}_0 = 0$ and $\tilde{t}_1 = 0.5$. Subsequently, the external ion concentration is kept constant until the end of the simulation at time $\tilde{t}_e = 200$. In the present work, the calculation was performed with 80 finite elements in the axial direction. For the time stepping, an initial grid was created with 8 equally spaced time increments for the linear ramp and another 8 time increments for the subsequent step with constant external concentration. In the case of the latter, no equal time increment spacing was chosen. Rather, the time increment size was increased by a factor of 3 between subsequent time increments. For the actual computation, this initial temporal grid was uniformly refined six times, thus resulting in 1024 time increments in total. The resulting numerical solution is compared to the variant (SIb) discussed in Acartürk [4]. For this variant, the net electric current is constrained to zero; and for the particular one-dimensional problem with a monovalent salt considered herein, this is equivalent to the requirement of local electroneutrality used in this work. It is noted in this context that a number of different formulations were discussed by Acartürk [4], which should theoretically be equivalent. However, different results were obtained by Acartürk [4]; and this suggests that there are either errors in the implementation or other numerical issues for some of the formulations. The choice to consider the variant (SIb) for comparison is motivated by the fact that the results of this variant agree very well with the results of the present formulation. In particular, Figure A2 shows a comparison of the normal displacement $\tilde{u}_Z$ of the top surface of the hydrogel block over time. Excellent agreement is evident for this case. Figure A3 shows comparisons for the cation concentrations (with regard to the actual volume of the electrolyte) at different instants of time. Again, good agreement is observed.

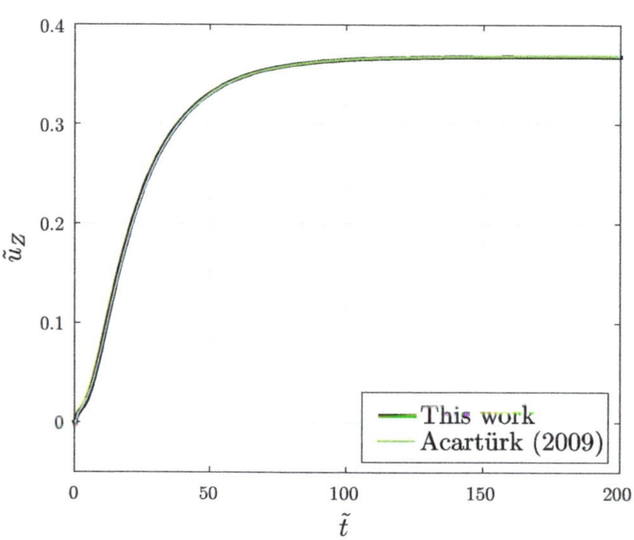

Figure A2. Comparison of the results for the normal displacement of the top surface of the hydrogel block [4].

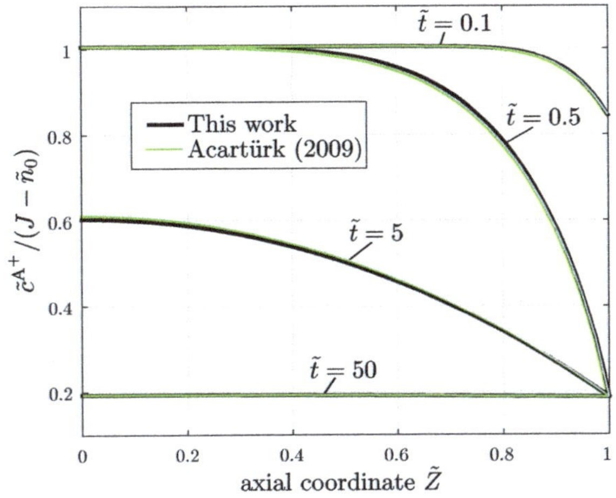

Figure A3. Comparison of the results for the cation concentration along the axial coordinate $\tilde{Z}$ at different times [4].

References

1. Landis, C. Fully coupled, multi-axial, symmetric constitutive laws for polycrystalline ferroelectric ceramics. *J. Mech. Phys. Solids* **2002**, *50*, 127–152. [CrossRef]
2. Miehe, C.; Rosato, D.; Kiefer, B. Variational principles in dissipative electro-magneto-mechanics: A framework for the macro-modeling of functional materials. *Int. J. Numer. Methods Eng.* **2011**, *86*, 1225–1276. [CrossRef]
3. Bucci, G.; Chiang, Y.M.; Carter, W.C. Formulation of the coupled electrochemical-mechanical boundary-value problem, with applications to transport of multiple charged species. *Acta Mater.* **2016**, *104*, 33–51. [CrossRef]
4. Acartürk, A.Y. Simulation of Charged Hydrated Porous Materials. Ph.D. thesis, University of Stuttgart, Stuttgart, Germany, 2009.
5. Simo, J.C.; Honein, T. Variational Formulation, Discrete Conservation Laws, and Path-Domain Independent Integrals for Elasto-Viscoplasticity. *J. Appl. Mech.* **1990**, *57*, 488–497. [CrossRef]
6. Ortiz, M.; Stainier, L. The variational formulation of viscoplastic constitutive updates. *Comput. Methods Appl. Mech. Eng.* **1999**, *171*, 419–444. [CrossRef]
7. Hackl, K.; Fischer, F.D. On the relation between the principle of maximum dissipation and inelastic evolution given by dissipation potentials. *Proc. R. Soc. Lond. A Math. Phys. Eng. Sci.* **2008**, *464*, 117–132. [CrossRef]
8. Yang, Q.; Stainier, L.; Ortiz, M. A variational formulation of the coupled thermo-mechanical boundary-value problem for general dissipative solids. *J. Mech. Phys. Solids* **2006**, *54*, 401–424. [CrossRef]
9. Carstensen, C.; Hackl, K.; Mielke, A. Non-convex potentials and microstructures in finite-strain plasticity. *Proc. R. Soc. Lond. A Math. Phys. Eng. Sci.* **2002**, *458*, 299–317. [CrossRef]
10. Ortiz, M.; Repetto, E.A. Nonconvex energy minimization and dislocation structures in ductile single crystals. *J. Mech. Phys. Solids* **1999**, *47*, 397–462. [CrossRef]
11. Halphen, B.; Nguyen, Q.S. Sur les matériaux standard généralisés. *J. De Mécanique* **1975**, *14*, 39–63.
12. Germain, P.; Nguyen, Q.S.; Suquet, P. Continuum Thermodynamics. *J. Appl. Mech.* **1983**, *50*, 1010–1020. [CrossRef]
13. Biot, M.A. Theory of Finite Deformations of Porous Solids. *Indiana Univ. Math. J.* **1972**, *21*, 597–620. [CrossRef]
14. Miehe, C. Strain-driven homogenization of inelastic microstructures and composites based on an incremental variational formulation. *Int. J. Numer. Methods Eng.* **2002**, *55*, 1285–1322. [CrossRef]
15. Miehe, C.; Schotte, J.; Lambrecht, M. Homogenization of inelastic solid materials at finite strains based on incremental minimization principles. Application to the texture analysis of polycrystals. *J. Mech. Phys. Solids* **2002**, *50*, 2123–2167. [CrossRef]
16. Miehe, C. A multi-field incremental variational framework for gradient-extended standard dissipative solids. *J. Mech. Phys. Solids* **2011**, *59*, 898–923. [CrossRef]
17. Miehe, C. Variational gradient plasticity at finite strains. Part I: Mixed potentials for the evolution and update problems of gradient-extended dissipative solids. *Comput. Methods Appl. Mech. Eng.* **2014**, *268*, 677–703. [CrossRef]
18. Miehe, C.; Welschinger, F.; Aldakheel, F. Variational gradient plasticity at finite strains. Part II: Local-global updates and mixed finite elements for additive plasticity in the logarithmic strain space. *Comput. Methods Appl. Mech. Eng.* **2014**, *268*, 704–734. [CrossRef]
19. Miehe, C.; Mauthe, S.; Hildebrand, F. Variational gradient plasticity at finite strains. Part III: Local-global updates and regularization techniques in multiplicative plasticity for single crystals. *Comput. Methods Appl. Mech. Eng.* **2014**, *268*, 735–762. [CrossRef]

20. McBride, A.T.; Reddy, B.D.; Steinmann, P. Dissipation-consistent modelling and classification of extended plasticity formulations. *J. Mech. Phys. Solids* **2018**, *119*, 118–139. [CrossRef]
21. Miehe, C.; Rosato, D. A rate-dependent incremental variational formulation of ferroelectricity. *Int. J. Eng. Sci.* **2011**, *49*, 466–496. [CrossRef]
22. Miehe, C.; Kiefer, B.; Rosato, D. An incremental variational formulation of dissipative magnetostriction at the macroscopic continuum level. *Int. J. Solids Struct.* **2011**, *48*, 1846–1866. [CrossRef]
23. Miehe, C.; Mauthe, S.; Teichtmeister, S. Minimization principles for the coupled problem of Darcy-Biot-type fluid transport in porous media linked to phase field modeling of fracture. *J. Mech. Phys. Solids* **2015**, *82*, 186–217. [CrossRef]
24. Miehe, C.; Hildebrand, F.E.; Böger, L. Mixed variational potentials and inherent symmetries of the Cahn-Hilliard theory of diffusive phase separation. *Proc. R. Soc. Lond. A Math. Phys. Eng. Sci.* **2014**, *470*, 20130641. [CrossRef]
25. Miehe, C.; Mauthe, S.; Ulmer, H. Formulation and numerical exploitation of mixed variational principles for coupled problems of Cahn-Hilliard-type and standard diffusion in elastic solids. *Int. J. Numer. Methods Eng.* **2014**, *99*, 737–762. [CrossRef]
26. Miehe, C.; Dal, H.; Schänzel, L.M.; Raina, A. A phase-field model for chemo-mechanical induced fracture in lithium-ion battery electrode particles. *Int. J. Numer. Methods Eng.* **2016**, *106*, 683–711. [CrossRef]
27. Alzetta, G.; Arndt, D.; Bangerth, W.; Boddu, V.; Brands, B.; Davydov, D.; Gassmoeller, R.; Heister, T.; Heltai, L.; Kormann, K.; et al. The deal.II Library, Version 9.0. *J. Numer. Math.* **2018**, *26*, 173–183. [CrossRef]
28. Bangerth, W.; Hartmann, R.; Kanschat, G. deal.II—A General Purpose Object Oriented Finite Element Library. *ACM Trans. Math. Softw.* **2007**, *33*, 24/1–24/27. [CrossRef]
29. Biot, M.A. Theory of Stress-Strain Relations in Anisotropic Viscoelasticity and Relaxation Phenomena. *J. Appl. Phys.* **1954**, *25*, 1385–1391. [CrossRef]
30. Biot, M.A. Variational Principles in Irreversible Thermodynamics with Application to Viscoelasticity. *Phys. Rev.* **1955**, *97*, 1463–1469. [CrossRef]
31. Abed-Meraim, F.; Nguyen, Q.S. A quasi-static stability analysis for Biot's equation and standard dissipative systems. *Eur. J. Mech.—A/Solids* **2007**, *26*, 383–393. [CrossRef]
32. Rockafellar, R.T. *Convex Analysis*; Princeton University Press: Princeton, NJ, USA, 1970.
33. Bathe, K.J. The inf−sup condition and its evaluation for mixed finite element methods. *Comput. Struct.* **2001**, *79*, 243–252. [CrossRef]
34. Auricchio, F.; da Veiga, L.B.; Brezzi, F.; Lovadina, C. Mixed Finite Element Methods. In *Encyclopedia of Computational Mechanics Second Edition*; John Wiley & Sons, Ltd.: Hoboken, NJ, USA, 2017; pp. 1–53. [CrossRef]
35. Stark, S. On a certain class of one step temporal integration methods for standard dissipative continua. *Comput. Mech.* **2021**, *67*, 265–287. [CrossRef]
36. Davis, T.A. Algorithm 832: UMFPACK V4.3—An Unsymmetric-pattern Multifrontal Method. *ACM Trans. Math. Softw.* **2004**, *30*, 196–199. [CrossRef]
37. Schenk, O.; Gärtner, K. Solving unsymmetric sparse systems of linear equations with PARDISO. *Future Gener. Comput. Syst.* **2004**, *20*, 475–487. [CrossRef]
38. Schenk, O.; Gärtner, K. On fast factorization pivoting methods for symmetric indefinite systems. *Electron. Trans. Numer. Anal.* **2006**, *23*, 158–179.
39. Karypis, G.; Kumar, V. A Fast and High Quality Multilevel Scheme for Partitioning Irregular Graphs. *SIAM J. Sci. Comput.* **1998**, *20*, 359–392. [CrossRef]
40. Amestoy, P.R.; Duff, I.S.; Koster, J.; L'Excellent, J.Y. A Fully Asynchronous Multifrontal Solver Using Distributed Dynamic Scheduling. *SIAM J. Matrix Anal. Appl.* **2001**, *23*, 15–41. [CrossRef]
41. Amestoy, P.R.; Guermouche, A.; L'Excellent, J.Y.; Pralet, S. Hybrid scheduling for the parallel solution of linear systems. *Parallel Comput.* **2006**, *32*, 136–156. [CrossRef]
42. Hong, W. Modeling viscoelastic dielectrics. *J. Mech. Phys. Solids* **2011**, *59*, 637–650. [CrossRef]
43. Stark, S.; Semenov, A.; Balke, H. On the boundary conditions for the vector potential formulation in electrostatics. *Int. J. Numer. Methods Eng.* **2015**, *102*, 1704–1732. [CrossRef]
44. deal.II Documentation. Available online: https://www.dealii.org/current/doxygen/deal.II/ (accessed on 28 January 2023).
45. Ruas, V. Mixed finite element methods with discontinuous pressures for the axisymmetric Stokes problem. *ZAMM—J. Appl. Math. Mech./Z. Für Angew. Math. Und Mech.* **2003**, *83*, 249–264. [CrossRef]

axioms

MDPI

Article

Elasticity Problem with a Cusp between Thin Inclusion and Boundary

Alexander Khludnev

Lavrentyev Institute of Hydrodynamics of SB RAS, Novosibirsk State University, Novosibirsk 630090, Russia; khlud@hydro.nsc.ru

Abstract: This paper concerns an equilibrium problem for an an elastic body with a thin rigid inclusion crossing an external boundary of the body at zero angle. The inclusion is assumed to be exfoliated from the surrounding elastic material that provides an interfacial crack. To avoid nonphysical interpenetration of the opposite crack faces, we impose inequality type constraints. Moreover, boundary conditions at the crack faces depend on a positive parameter describing a cohesion. A solution existence of the problem with different conditions on the external boundary is proved. Passages to the limit are analyzed as the damage parameter tends to infinity and to zero. Finally, an optimal control problem with a suitable cost functional is investigated. In this case, a part of the rigid inclusion is located outside of the elastic body, and a control function is a shape of the inclusion.

Keywords: elastic body; thin inclusion; cusp; non-penetration boundary condition; damage parameter; optimal control

MSC: 35J88; 74G22

1. Introduction

The engineering practice demonstrates a big variety of composite structures having thin inclusions. In particular, thin inclusions may cross an external boundary of the elastic body at zero angle. It is well known that, in general cases, Korn's inequalities are not valid in domains with non-smooth boundaries. This implies difficulties with a solution existence of such problems. This paper focuses on the equilibrium problem for a 2D elastic body with a thin rigid exfoliated inclusion crossing the external boundary of the body at zero angle. The exfoliation implies a presence of the crack between the inclusion and the elastic body. Moreover, the zero angle provides a non-smooth boundary in the mathematical formulation of the problem. Consequently, a proof of the solution existence requires additional arguments. We impose inequality type boundary conditions at the crack faces. In addition, these boundary conditions depend on a positive damage parameter characterizing a cohesion between the crack faces. Over the last decades, many papers have been published concerning problems for elastic bodies with exfoliated thin inclusions and inequality type boundary conditions. We refer the reader to [1–9]. Boundary value problems with inequality type boundary conditions for cohesive cracks can be found in [10–13]. The results for problems with a zero angle between the inclusion and the external boundaries are presented in [14], where a fictitious domain method was used to prove a solution existence. As for derivation of suitable models for thin inclusions in elastic structures, see [15–19] and the references therein. There are a number of applied papers related to thin inclusions in elastic bodies [20–26], as well as books with general approaches to the description of nonhomogeneous bodies [27,28].

The model considered in this paper belongs to the class of problems with a free boundary. The results obtained may be useful for other models with free boundaries, see for example [29], as well as for models of functionally graded materials [30,31].

From the practical point of view, the obtained results can be used for the modeling and analysis of different elastic and nonelastic structures having non-smooth boundaries.

This paper is structured as follows: In Section 2, we prove a solution existence of the problem. Variational and differential formulations of the problem are discussed. Passages to limits, as the damage parameter tends to infinity and to zero, are investigated in Sections 3 and 4. Mixed boundary conditions on the external boundary are considered in Section 5. A case of the inclusion partially extending beyond the elastic body is analyzed in Section 6. A solution existence of the optimal control problem with a suitable cost functional is proved.

2. Problem Formulation

Bounded domain in $\mathbb{R}^2$ with a smooth boundary Γ is denoted by Ω, and $\gamma \subset \Omega$ is a smooth curve such that $\bar{\gamma} \cap \Gamma = (0,0)$, $\Omega_\gamma = \Omega \setminus \bar{\gamma}$. The domain Ω_γ fits to an elastic body, and γ corresponds to a thin rigid inclusion. We assume that the angle between Γ and γ at the point $(0,0)$ is equal to zero for the undeformed state of the elastic body, see Figure 1. Denote $\Gamma_0 = \Gamma \setminus \{(0,0)\}$ and introduce Sobolev space

$$H^1_{\Gamma_0}(\Omega_\gamma) = \{v \in H^1(\Omega_\gamma) \mid v = 0 \text{ on } \Gamma_0\}.$$

Assume that $C = \{c_{ijkl}\}$ is a given elasticity tensor with the usual properties of symmetry and positive definiteness, $c_{ijkl} \in L^\infty_{loc}(\mathbb{R}^2)$, $i,j,k,l = 1,2$. Despite the cusp of the domain Ω_γ, Korn's inequality is fulfilled in the space $H^1_{\Gamma_0}(\Omega_\gamma)^2$. Indeed, consider a fictitious domain Ω_0 with a smooth boundary $\partial\Omega_0$ as depicted in Figure 2 assuming that angles between $\partial\Omega_0$ and Γ at the points x^1, x^2 are nonzero. Extended domain $\Omega_e = \Omega_\gamma \cup \Omega_0 \cup \gamma_1 \cup \gamma_2$ has the smooth cut γ. Let $v \in H^1_{\Gamma_0}(\Omega_\gamma)^2$. Since $v = 0$ on Γ_0, this function can be extended by zero to Ω_0. Denote by $\tilde{v}$ the extended function defined in Ω_e. It is clear that Korn's inequality holds for all such extended functions $\tilde{v}$. Hence, it is valid for all $v \in H^1_{\Gamma_0}(\Omega_\gamma)^2$, since $\tilde{v}$ is zero in Ω_0, i.e., there exists a constant $c_0 > 0$ such that

$$\int\limits_{\Omega_\gamma} \sigma(v)\varepsilon(v) \geq c_0 \|v\|^2_{H^1_{\Gamma_0}(\Omega_\gamma)^2} \quad \forall v \in H^1_{\Gamma_0}(\Omega_\gamma)^2. \tag{1}$$

Here $\sigma(v)$ is defined according to Hooke's law $\sigma(v) = C\varepsilon(v)$, $\varepsilon(v) = \{\varepsilon_{ij}(v)\}$, $\varepsilon_{ij}(v) = \frac{1}{2}(v_{i,j} + v_{j,i})$, $i,j = 1,2$. To simplify the formulae, we write $\sigma(v)\varepsilon(v)$ instead of $\sigma_{ij}(v)\varepsilon_{ij}(v)$.

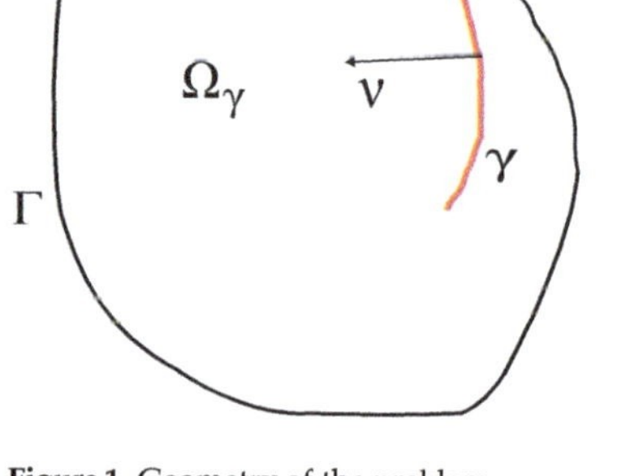

Figure 1. Geometry of the problem.

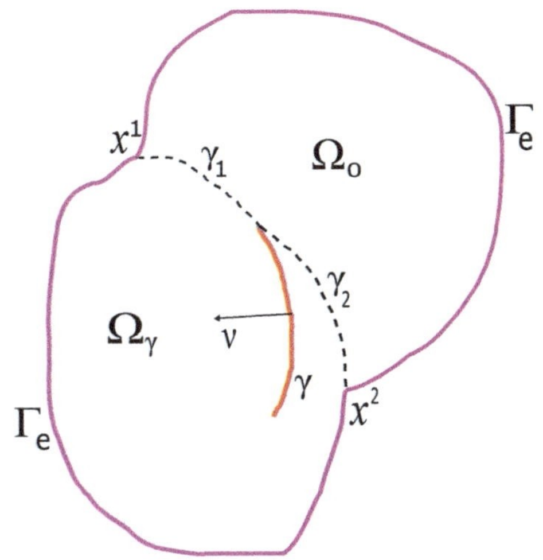

Figure 2. Fictitious domain Ω_0.

Denote by $R_0(\gamma)$ the space of infinitesimal rigid rotations,

$$R_0(\gamma) = \{\rho = (\rho_1, \rho_2) \mid \rho(x) = b(-x_2, x_1),\ b \in \mathbb{R}, x = (x_1, x_2) \in \gamma\}.$$

Let $f \in L^2(\Omega)^2$ be a given external force acting on the elastic body. Introduce a set of admissible displacements

$$S = \{v \in H^1_{\Gamma_0}(\Omega_\gamma)^2 \mid [v_\nu] \geq 0 \text{ on } \gamma;\ v|_{\gamma^-} \in R_0(\gamma)\},$$

where $v_\nu = v\nu$, $[h] = h^+ - h^-$; $h^\pm$ are traces of the function h on the crack faces $\gamma^\pm$, respectively. The signs $\pm$ fit to positive and negative crack faces with respect to the outward unit normal vector ν to γ.

An equilibrium problem for the body Ω_γ and the inclusion γ is formulated as follows: unknown functions are the displacement field $u^\alpha = (u_1^\alpha, u_2^\alpha)$, the stress tensor $\sigma = \{\sigma_{ij}\}$, $i, j = 1, 2$, defined in Ω_γ, as well as $\rho_0^\alpha \in R_0(\gamma)$, satisfying the following equations and boundary conditions

$$-\text{div}\, \sigma = f,\ \sigma = C\varepsilon(u^\alpha) \text{ in } \Omega_\gamma, \tag{2}$$

$$u^\alpha = 0 \text{ on } \Gamma_0;\ u^\alpha = \rho_0^\alpha \text{ on } \gamma^-, \tag{3}$$

$$[u_\nu^\alpha] \geq 0, -\sigma_\nu^+ + \frac{1}{\alpha}[u_\nu^\alpha] \geq 0,\ -\sigma_\tau^+ + \frac{1}{\alpha}[u_\tau^\alpha] = 0 \text{ on } \gamma, \tag{4}$$

$$[u_\nu^\alpha](-\sigma_\nu^+ + \frac{1}{\alpha}[u_\nu^\alpha]) = 0 \text{ on } \gamma, \tag{5}$$

$$\int_\gamma [\sigma\nu]\rho = 0\ \ \forall \rho \in R_0(\gamma). \tag{6}$$

Here $\alpha > 0$ is a damage parameter characterizing a cohesion between the crack faces; $\sigma_\nu = \sigma_{ij}\nu_j\nu_i$, $\sigma_\tau = \sigma_{ij}\nu_j\tau_i$, $\nu = (\nu_1, \nu_2)$, $\tau = (-\nu_2, \nu_1)$.

Relations (2) are the equilibrium equation and constitutive law (Hooke's law). The first inequality in (4) provides a mutual non-penetration between the crack faces $\gamma^\pm$. The identity (6) provides a zero moment acting on the inclusion γ. The contact set between the crack faces is unknown a priori, and the model (2)–(6) corresponds to a free boundary approach.

The problem (2)–(6) has a unique solution. Indeed, consider the energy functional $G_\alpha : H^1_{\Gamma_0}(\Omega_\gamma)^2 \to \mathbb{R}$,

$$G_\alpha(v) = \frac{1}{2}\int_{\Omega_\gamma} \sigma(v)\varepsilon(v) - \int_{\Omega_\gamma} fv + \frac{1}{2\alpha}\int_\gamma [v]^2.$$

Then the minimization problem

$$\inf_{v\in S} G_\alpha(v) \tag{7}$$

has a solution. To prove this statement, it suffices to use Korn's inequality (1) and note that the set S is weakly closed. Indeed, we have $[v_\nu] \in H^{1/2}(\gamma)$. Hence, the set S is closed and consequently weakly closed. The solution of the problem (7) satisfies the variational inequality

$$u^\alpha \in S, \tag{8}$$

$$\int_{\Omega_\gamma} \sigma(u^\alpha)\varepsilon(\bar{u} - u^\alpha) - \int_{\Omega_\gamma} f(\bar{u} - u^\alpha) + \tag{9}$$

$$+\frac{1}{\alpha}\int_\gamma [u^\alpha][\bar{u} - u^\alpha] \geq 0 \ \ \forall \bar{u} \in S.$$

The following statement takes place.

Theorem 1. *For smooth solutions, problem formulations* (2)–(6) *and* (8) *and* (9) *are equivalent.*

Proof. To simplify notations, we omit the symbol α. We first check that the equilibrium equation follows from (8) and (9), see (2). To this end, we have to substitute in (9) test functions of the form $\bar{u} = u \pm v$, $v \in C_0^\infty(\Omega_\gamma)^2$. Next, we choose test functions $\bar{u} = u \pm v$, $[v_\nu] = 0$ on γ, $v \in S$, and substitute in (9). This implies

$$\int_{\Omega_\gamma} \sigma(u)\varepsilon(v) - \int_{\Omega_\gamma} fv + \frac{1}{\alpha}\int_\gamma [u][v] = 0,$$

and consequently, taking into account the equilibrium equation, we obtain

$$-\int_\gamma [\sigma_\nu]v_\nu - \int_\gamma [\sigma_\tau v_\tau] + \frac{1}{\alpha}\int_\gamma [u_\tau][v_\tau] = 0. \tag{10}$$

Since v_τ^+ is arbitrary on γ, from (10) we derive the third relation of (4). The relation (10) can be written in the form

$$-\int_\gamma [\sigma_\nu]v_\nu - \int_\gamma [\sigma_\tau]v_\tau^- + \int_\gamma [\sigma_\tau]v_\tau^- + \int_\gamma (\sigma_\tau^- - \frac{1}{\alpha}[u_\tau])v_\tau^- = 0 \tag{11}$$

which gives

$$-\int_\gamma [\sigma\nu]v^- + \int_\gamma v_\tau^-(\sigma_\tau^+ - \frac{1}{\alpha}[u_\tau]) = 0 \tag{12}$$

providing, by the third relation of (4), the identity (6). □

Now we can choose test functions in (9) in the form $\bar{u} = u + v, v \in H^1_\Gamma(\Omega_\gamma)^2, v_\nu^+ \geq 0$ on γ, supp $v \subset \bar{Q}$, see Figure 3. It provides the following relation

$$\int_{\Omega_\gamma} \sigma(u)\varepsilon(v) - \int_{\Omega_\gamma} fv + \frac{1}{\alpha}\int_\gamma [u]v^+ \geq 0.$$

Consequently, integrating by parts, we have

$$\int_\gamma (\sigma_\nu^+ v_\nu^+ + \sigma_\tau^+ v_\tau^+) - \frac{1}{\alpha}\int_\gamma [u_\nu]v_\nu^+ - \frac{1}{\alpha}\int_\gamma [u_\tau]v_\tau^+ \leq 0. \tag{13}$$

In view of the choice of v and the last relation of (4), from (13) the second relation of (4) follows.

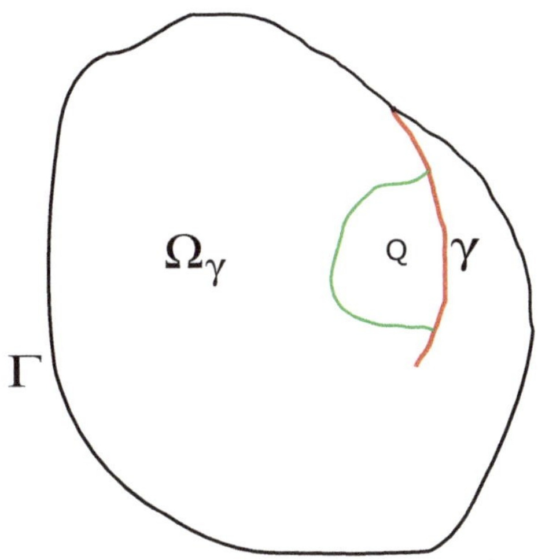

Figure 3. Neighborhood Q.

It remains to check the condition (5). To this end, suppose that at a given point $x^0 \in \gamma$ we have $[u_\nu(x^0)] > 0$. Take test functions in (9) of the following form: $\bar{u} = u \pm \beta\psi$, supp $\psi \subset \bar{Q}$, β is a small parameter and Q is a small neighborhood of the point x^0, ψ is a quite smooth function, see Figure 3. We obtain

$$\int_{\Omega_\gamma} \sigma(u)\varepsilon(\psi) - \int_{\Omega_\gamma} f\psi + \frac{1}{\alpha}\int_\gamma [u]\psi^+ = 0,$$

consequently, by the third relation of (4),

$$\int_\gamma \sigma_\nu^+ \psi_\nu^+ - \frac{1}{\alpha}\int_\gamma [u_\nu]\psi_\nu^+ = 0,$$

and thus $\sigma_\nu^+(x^0) - \frac{1}{\alpha}[u_\nu(x^0)] = 0$, i.e., $[u_\nu(x^0)](\sigma_\nu^+(x^0) - \frac{1}{\alpha}[u_\nu(x^0)]) = 0$. On the other hand, assuming that $-\sigma_\nu^+(x^0) + \frac{1}{\alpha}[u_\nu(x^0)] < 0$, we easily derive $[u_\nu(x^0)] = 0$, and (5) easily follows. Thus, from (8) and (9) we have derived all equations and boundary conditions (2)–(6).

Now we prove the converse statement. Let (2)–(6) be fulfilled. We take $\bar{u} \in S$ and multiply the first equation from (2) by $\bar{u} - u$. Integrating over Ω_γ, one obtains

$$\int\limits_{\Omega_\gamma} (\text{div}\, \sigma + f)(\bar{u} - u) = 0,$$

and consequently,

$$\int\limits_{\Omega_\gamma} \sigma(u)\varepsilon(\bar{u} - u) - \int\limits_{\Omega_\gamma} f(\bar{u} - u) \pm \frac{1}{\alpha} \int\limits_{\gamma} [u][\bar{u} - u] + \\ + \int\limits_{\gamma} [\sigma\nu(\bar{u} - u)] = 0. \tag{14}$$

To derive the variational inequality (9) from (14), it suffices to prove that

$$-\int\limits_{\gamma} [\sigma\nu(\bar{u} - u)] + \frac{1}{\alpha} \int\limits_{\gamma} [u][\bar{u} - u] \geq 0. \tag{15}$$

But the inequality (15) easily follows from boundary conditions (4)–(5). Thus, the equivalence of (8) and (9) and (2)–(6) is completely proved.

In addition to (2)–(6), we can provide one more differential formulation of the problem (8) and (9). It reads as follows (again omitting the symbol α): it is necessary to find a displacement field $u = (u_1, u_2)$, a stress tensor $\sigma = \{\sigma_{ij}\}, i, j = 1, 2$, defined in Ω_γ, and a thin inclusion displacement $\rho_0 \in R_0(\gamma)$ defined on γ such that

$$-\text{div}\, \sigma = f,\ \sigma = C\varepsilon(u) \ \text{ in } \Omega_\gamma, \tag{16}$$

$$u = 0 \ \text{ on } \Gamma_0, \tag{17}$$

$$[u_\nu] \geq 0,\ u^- = \rho_0 \ \text{ on } \gamma, \tag{18}$$

$$-\int\limits_{\gamma} [\sigma\nu \cdot u] + \frac{1}{\alpha} \int\limits_{\gamma} [u]^2 = 0, \tag{19}$$

$$-\int\limits_{\gamma} [\sigma\nu \cdot \bar{u}] + \frac{1}{\alpha} \int\limits_{\gamma} [u][\bar{u}] \geq 0 \ \ \forall \bar{u} \in S. \tag{20}$$

Let us check that formulations (16)–(20) and (8) and (9) are equivalent for smooth solutions. Assume that (8) and (9) take place. This provides the equilibrium equation, see (2). From (8) and (9) we easily derive

$$\int\limits_{\Omega_\gamma} \sigma(u)\varepsilon(u) - \int\limits_{\Omega_\gamma} fu + \frac{1}{\alpha} \int\limits_{\gamma} [u]^2 = 0. \tag{21}$$

Making the integration by parts in (21), we obtain (19). By (21), the variational inequality (9) can be rewritten as

$$\int\limits_{\Omega_\gamma} \sigma(u)\varepsilon(\bar{u}) - \int\limits_{\Omega_\gamma} f\bar{u} + \frac{1}{\alpha} \int\limits_{\gamma} [u][\bar{u}] \geq 0 \ \ \forall \bar{u} \in S,$$

thus, integrating by parts, the inequality (20) is obtained. Consequently, all relations (16)–(20) are derived from (8) and (9).

Conversely, let (16)–(20) be fulfilled. We take $\bar{u} \in S$ and multiply the first equation from (16) by $\bar{u} - u$. Integrating over Ω_γ, we obtain

$$\int_{\Omega_\gamma} (\text{div}\, \sigma + f)(\bar{u} - u) = 0.$$

Thus,

$$\int_\gamma [\sigma\nu(\bar{u} - u)] + \int_{\Omega_\gamma} \sigma(u)\varepsilon(\bar{u} - u) - \int_{\Omega_\gamma} f(\bar{u} - u) \pm \frac{1}{\alpha} \int_\gamma [u][\bar{u} - u] = 0. \tag{22}$$

We see that for obtaining the variational inequality (9) from (22), it is enough to prove the inequality

$$\int_\gamma [\sigma\nu(\bar{u} - u)] - \frac{1}{\alpha} \int_\gamma [u][\bar{u} - u] \leq 0. \tag{23}$$

But the inequality (23) easily follows from (19)–(20). Thus, the equivalence of (8) and (9) and (16)–(20) is proved for smooth solutions.

3. Passage to Limit in (8) and (9) as $\alpha \to \infty$

In this section, we justify a passage to limit in the model (8) and (9) as $\alpha \to \infty$. It turns out that the limit model fits to zero friction at the positive crack face γ^+.

From (9), it follows

$$\int_{\Omega_\gamma} \sigma(u^\alpha)\varepsilon(u^\alpha) - \int_{\Omega_\gamma} f u^\alpha + \frac{1}{\alpha} \int_\gamma [u^\alpha]^2 = 0. \tag{24}$$

By Korn's inequality valid in the space $H^1_{\Gamma_0}(\Omega_\gamma)^2$, the relation (24) implies a uniform in α estimate

$$\|u^\alpha\|_{H^1_{\Gamma_0}(\Omega_\gamma)^2} \leq c.$$

Choosing a subsequence, if necessary, we assume that as $\alpha \to \infty$

$$u^\alpha \to u \text{ weakly in } H^1_{\Gamma_0}(\Omega_\gamma)^2, \tag{25}$$

$$[u^\alpha] \to [u] \text{ weakly in } L^2(\gamma)^2, \tag{26}$$

$$u|_{\gamma^-} = \rho^\infty \in R_0(\gamma). \tag{27}$$

By (25)–(27), a passage to the limit as $\alpha \to \infty$ can be fulfilled in (8) and (9) which implies

$$u \in S, \int_{\Omega_\gamma} \sigma(u)\varepsilon(\bar{u} - u) - \int_{\Omega_\gamma} f(\bar{u} - u) \geq 0 \ \forall \bar{u} \in S. \tag{28}$$

Thus, we arrive at the following assertion.

Theorem 2. *Solutions of the problems* (8) *and* (9) *converge in the sense* (25)–(27) *to the solution of* (28) *as* $\alpha \to \infty$.

The problem (28) admits a differential formulation. It is necessary to find a displacement field $u = (u_1, u_2)$, a stress tensor $\sigma = \{\sigma_{ij}\},\ i,j = 1,2,$ defined in Ω_γ, and $\rho^\infty \in R_0(\gamma)$ such that

$$-\mathrm{div}\,\sigma = f,\ \sigma = C\varepsilon(u) \text{ in } \Omega_\gamma, \tag{29}$$

$$u = 0 \text{ on } \Gamma_0;\ u = \rho^\infty \text{ on } \gamma^-, \tag{30}$$

$$[u_\nu] \ge 0,\ \sigma_\nu^+ \le 0,\ \sigma_\tau^+ = 0,\ [u_\nu]\sigma_\nu^+ = 0 \text{ on } \gamma, \tag{31}$$

$$\int\limits_\gamma [\sigma\nu]\rho = 0 \ \ \forall \rho \in R_0(\gamma). \tag{32}$$

We can prove the following assertion.

Theorem 3. *For smooth solutions, problem formulations* (28) *and* (29)–(32) *are equivalent.*

We do not prove this theorem since the arguments used are simpler as compared to those of Theorem 1.

The model (29)–(32) is characterized by zero friction at the positive crack face γ^+.

4. Passage to Limit in (8) and (9) as $\alpha \to 0$

This section concerns a passage to limit as $\alpha \to 0$ in the model (8) and (9). We will prove that the limit model corresponds to the case without exfoliation of the rigid inclusion from the surrounding elastic body, i.e., to the case without a crack between γ and the elastic body.

Since the relation (24) takes place, we have the uniform in α estimate

$$\|u^\alpha\|_{H^1_{\Gamma_0}(\Omega_\gamma)^2} \le c. \tag{33}$$

Moreover, (24), (33) imply

$$\int\limits_\gamma [u^\alpha]^2 \le c\alpha. \tag{34}$$

Introduce a set of admissible displacements for the limit problem

$$S_0 = \{v \in H^1_{\Gamma_0}(\Omega_\gamma)^2 \mid \ v|_\gamma \in R_0(\gamma)\}.$$

Note that we have $[v] = 0$ on γ for $v \in S_0$. By (33), (34), we can assume that as $\alpha \to 0$,

$$u^\alpha \to u \text{ weakly in } H^1_{\Gamma_0}(\Omega_\gamma)^2, \tag{35}$$

$$[u^\alpha] \to [u] \text{ weakly in } L^2(\gamma)^2, \tag{36}$$

$$u|_\gamma = \rho^0 \in R_0(\gamma). \tag{37}$$

In particular, we have $[u] = 0$ on γ.

Take in (9) test functions of the form $\bar{u} = u^\alpha \pm v$, $v \in S_0$, and pass to the limit as $\alpha \to 0$ taking into account (35)–(37). It gives

$$u \in S_0,\ \int\limits_{\Omega_\gamma} \sigma(u)\varepsilon(v) - \int\limits_{\Omega_\gamma} fv = 0 \ \ \forall v \in S_0. \tag{38}$$

Hence, the following assertion has been proved.

Theorem 4. *Solutions of the problems* (8) *and* (9) *converge in the sense* (35)–(37) *to the solution of* (38) *as* $\alpha \to 0$.

Notice that the problem (38) corresponds to minimization of the energy functional over the set S_0,

$$\inf_{v \in S_0} \{\frac{1}{2} \int_{\Omega_\gamma} \sigma(v)\varepsilon(v) - \int_{\Omega_\gamma} fv\}. \tag{39}$$

The minimization problem (39) has a unique solution satisfying (38).

To conclude this section, we provide a differential formulation of the problem (38): find a displacement field $u = (u_1, u_2)$, a stress tensor $\sigma = \{\sigma_{ij}\},\ i,j = 1,2,$ defined in Ω_γ, and $\rho^0 \in R_0(\gamma)$ such that

$$-\text{div}\,\sigma = f,\ \sigma = C\varepsilon(u) \text{ in } \Omega_\gamma, \tag{40}$$

$$u = 0 \text{ on } \Gamma_0;\ u = \rho^0 \text{ on } \gamma, \tag{41}$$

$$\int_\gamma [\sigma\nu]\rho = 0 \ \ \forall \rho \in R_0(\gamma). \tag{42}$$

We see that the limit problem (40)–(42) fits to the rigid inclusion without exfoliation from the surrounding elastic body.

Problems (38) and (40)–(42) are equivalent for smooth solutions. The proof of this statement is simpler compared with that of Theorem 1.

5. Mixed Boundary Conditions on External Boundary Γ_0

Along with the problem (2)–(6), it is possible to consider mixed boundary conditions on Γ_0. Denote by n a unit normal vector to Γ. Like in the previous sections, the angle between Γ and γ at the point $(0,0)$ is zero. Suppose that γ_1 is a smooth part of Γ as depicted in Figure 4, meas $\Gamma \setminus \gamma_1 > 0$. Problem formulation is as follows: unknown functions are the displacement field $u^\alpha = (u_1^\alpha, u_2^\alpha)$, the stress tensor $\sigma = \{\sigma_{ij}\},\ i,j = 1,2,$ defined in Ω_γ, as well as $\rho^\alpha \in R_0(\gamma)$, satisfying the following equations and boundary conditions

$$-\text{div}\,\sigma = f,\ \sigma = C\varepsilon(u^\alpha) \text{ in } \Omega_\gamma, \tag{43}$$

$$u^\alpha = 0 \text{ on } \Gamma \setminus \gamma_1;\ \sigma n = 0 \text{ on } \gamma_1;\ u^\alpha = \rho^\alpha \text{ on } \gamma^-, \tag{44}$$

$$[u_\nu^\alpha] \geq 0, -\sigma_\nu^+ + \frac{1}{\alpha}[u_\nu^\alpha] \geq 0,\ -\sigma_\tau^+ + \frac{1}{\alpha}[u_\tau^\alpha] = 0 \text{ on } \gamma, \tag{45}$$

$$[u_\nu^\alpha](-\sigma_\nu^+ + \frac{1}{\alpha}[u_\nu^\alpha]) = 0 \text{ on } \gamma, \tag{46}$$

$$\int_\gamma [\sigma\nu]\rho = 0 \ \ \forall \rho \in R_0(\gamma). \tag{47}$$

We are planning to solve the problem (43)–(47) by minimizing a suitable functional. To this end, preliminary arguments are needed. Introduce the space

$$H^1_{\Gamma\setminus\gamma_1}(\Omega_\gamma) = \{v \in H^1(\Omega_\gamma) \mid v = 0 \text{ on } \Gamma \setminus \gamma_1\}.$$

By adding a fictitious domain Ω_0, consider an extended domain $\Omega^e = \Omega_\gamma \cup \Omega_0 \cup \gamma_2$ with a smooth cut $\gamma \cup \gamma_1 \cup \{(0,0)\}$ and Lipschitz external boundary Γ_e, see Figure 2. Taking $v \in H^1_{\Gamma\setminus\gamma_1}(\Omega_\gamma)^2$, we can extend this function by zero to Ω_0. The extended function is equal to zero on Γ_e and belongs to the space $H^1_{\Gamma_e}(\Omega^e)^2$, where

$$H^1_{\Gamma_e}(\Omega^e) = \{v \in H^1(\Omega^e) \mid v = 0 \text{ on } \Gamma_e\}.$$

Consequently, Korn's inequality holds for such extended functions. This implies that Korn's inequality is valid in the space $H^1_{\Gamma\setminus\gamma_1}(\Omega_\gamma)^2$.

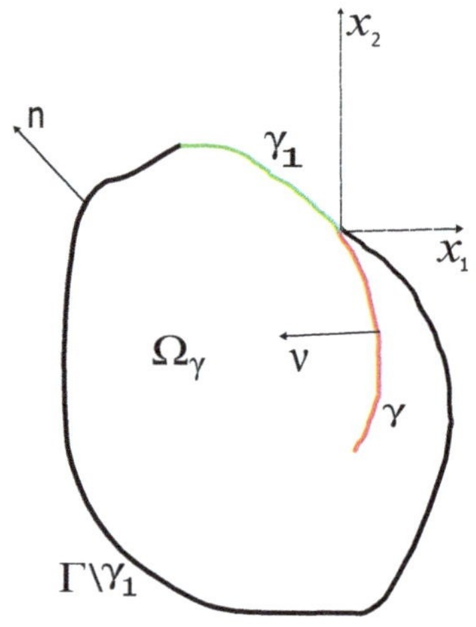

Figure 4. Partition of the external boundary.

To proceed, we introduce a set of admissible displacements

$$S_N = \{v \in H^1_{\Gamma\setminus\gamma_1}(\Omega_\gamma)^2 \mid [v_\nu] \geq 0 \text{ on } \gamma;\ v|_{\gamma^-} \in R_0(\gamma)\}.$$

The set S_N is closed and convex; hence, it is weakly closed. The above arguments imply that the problem

$$\inf_{v\in S_N} \{\frac{1}{2}\int\limits_{\Omega_\gamma} \sigma(v)\varepsilon(v) - \int\limits_{\Omega_\gamma} fv + \frac{1}{2\alpha}\int\limits_{\gamma} [v]^2\}$$

has (a unique) solution satisfying the following variational inequality

$$u^\alpha \in S_N, \tag{48}$$

$$\int\limits_{\Omega_\gamma} \sigma(u^\alpha)\varepsilon(v-u^\alpha) - \int\limits_{\Omega_\gamma} f(v-u^\alpha) + \tag{49}$$

$$+\frac{1}{\alpha}\int\limits_{\gamma} [u^\alpha][v-u^\alpha] \geq 0 \quad \forall v \in S_N.$$

The following statement holds.

Theorem 5. *For smooth solutions, problem formulations* (43)–(47) *and* (48)–(49) *are equivalent.*

The arguments are omitted since they are similar to those of Theorem 1.

6. Optimal Control of the Inclusion Shape

We devote this section to the case of the rigid inclusion crossing the boundary Γ and partially located outside of the elastic body. Denote by γ, γ_e internal and external parts of the rigid inclusion $\gamma_0 = \gamma \cup \gamma_e \cup \{(0,0)\}$, $\Gamma \cap \gamma_0 = (0,0)$, see Figure 5. The part γ of the inclusion γ_0 is assumed to be a Lipschitz curve and γ_e is a continuous one. The angle between γ_0 and Γ at the point $(0,0)$ is zero. Tip points of the inclusion γ_0 are $x^0 = (-1,-1)$ and $z^0 = (1,1)$. Moreover, $y^0 \in \gamma$, $y^0 = (-1/2,-1)$. We suppose that the inclusion shape located between the points x^0 and y^0 may change. The aim of this section is to analyze an optimal control problem assuming that a control function is a shape of the inclusion located between x^0, y^0, and a cost functional is a displacement of the inclusion at the tip point z^0. To be more precise, consider a bounded and weakly closed set $\Xi \subset H_0^2(-1/2, -1)$ assuming that the inclusion shape located between the points x^0 and y^0 is described as a graph of the function

$$x_2 = \xi(x_1) - 1, \quad x_1 \in (-1/2, -1), \ \xi \in \Xi.$$

In this case, the curve γ corresponding to ξ is denoted by γ_ξ, and Ω_{γ_ξ} is denoted by Ω_ξ. An equilibrium problem for the body Ω_ξ with a given function ξ and a fixed damage parameter α is formulated as follows: unknown functions are the displacement field $u^\xi = (u_1^\xi, u_2^\xi)$, the stress tensor $\sigma = \{\sigma_{ij}\}$, $i, j = 1, 2$, defined in Ω_ξ, as well as $\rho_0^\xi \in R_0(\gamma_\xi)$, satisfying the following equations and boundary conditions

$$-\text{div}\, \sigma = f, \ \sigma = C\varepsilon(u^\xi) \text{ in } \Omega_\xi, \tag{50}$$

$$u^\xi = 0 \text{ on } \Gamma_0; \ u^\xi = \rho_0^\xi \text{ on } \gamma_\xi^-, \tag{51}$$

$$[u_\nu^\xi] \geq 0, -\sigma_\nu^+ + \frac{1}{\alpha}[u_\nu^\xi] \geq 0, \ -\sigma_\tau^+ + \frac{1}{\alpha}[u_\tau^\xi] = 0 \text{ on } \gamma_\xi, \tag{52}$$

$$[u_\nu^\xi](-\sigma_\nu^+ + \frac{1}{\alpha}[u_\nu^\xi]) = 0 \ \text{ on } \gamma_\xi, \tag{53}$$

$$\int_{\gamma_\xi} [\sigma\nu]\rho = 0 \ \ \forall \rho \in R_0(\gamma_\xi). \tag{54}$$

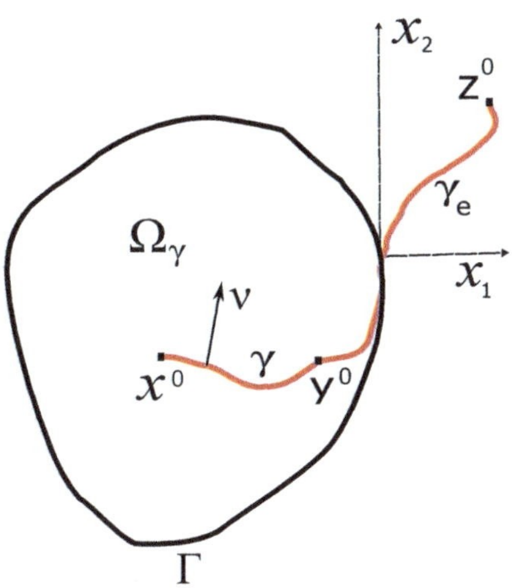

Figure 5. Inclusion $\gamma_0 = \gamma \cup \gamma_e \cup \{(0,0)\}$.

The problem (50)–(54) can be written in the variational form. To this end, introduce a set of admissible displacements

$$S_\xi = \{v \in H^1_{\Gamma_0}(\Omega_\xi)^2 \mid [v_\nu] \geq 0 \text{ on } \gamma_\xi; \ v|_{\gamma_\xi^-} \in R_0(\gamma_\xi)\}.$$

Then the problem (50)–(54) is equivalent to the following variational inequality

$$u^\xi \in S_\xi, \tag{55}$$

$$\int_{\Omega_\xi} \sigma(u^\xi)\varepsilon(v-u^\xi) - \int_{\Omega_\xi} f(v-u^\xi) + \\ + \frac{1}{\alpha}\int_{\gamma_\xi} [u^\xi][v-u^\xi] \geq 0 \;\; \forall v \in S_\xi. \tag{56}$$

Moreover, we know that the problem (55) and (56) corresponds to minimization of the energy functional over the set S_ξ,

$$\inf_{v\in S_\xi}\{\frac{1}{2}\int_{\Omega_\xi} \sigma(v)\varepsilon(v) - \int_{\Omega\xi} fv + \frac{1}{2\alpha}\int_{\gamma_\xi}[v]^2\}. \tag{57}$$

According to Section 2, the set S_ξ is weakly closed, and the energy functional is coercive on S_ξ for any fixed $\xi \in \Xi$. Hence, the problem (57) indeed has a solution u^ξ satisfying (55) and (56).

Note that a displacement of the γ_e- points is defined according to the function ρ_0^ξ from (51). If

$$\rho_0^\xi(x) = (c^1, c^2) + b(-x_2, x_1),\; x = (x_1, x_2) \in \gamma_\xi,$$

then

$$\rho_0^\xi(x) = (c^1, c^2) + b(-x_2, x_1),\; x = (x_1, x_2) \in \gamma_e.$$

In particular, we can find a displacement of the inclusion γ_0 at the tip point z^0, i.e., $\rho_0^\xi(1,1) = (\rho_{01}^\xi(1,1), \rho_{02}^\xi(1,1))$. Thus, for any $\xi \in \Xi$ a value of a cost functional

$$J(\xi) = |\rho_{02}^\xi(1,1)|$$

can be defined. An optimal control problem to be analyzed below is formulated as follows

$$\inf_{\xi\in\Xi} J(\xi). \tag{58}$$

We see that the inclusion shape is defined by the function ξ. Solving optimal control problem (58), we find the best inclusion shape that minimizes the cost functional. The following statement takes place.

Theorem 6. *There exists a solution of the optimal control problem* (58).

Proof. Consider a minimizing sequence $\xi^m \in \Xi$. By boundedness of Ξ and the imbedding theorem, we can assume that as $m \to \infty$,

$$\xi^m \to \xi \;\; \text{weakly in } H_0^2(-1/2,-1),\; \xi \in \Xi, \\ \xi^m \to \xi \text{ strongly in } C^1[-1/2,-1]. \tag{59}$$

Introduce the notation

$$S^m = \{v \in H^1_{\Gamma_0}(\Omega_m)^2 \mid [v_\nu] \geq 0 \text{ on } \gamma_{\xi_m}; \\ v|_{\gamma^-_{\xi^m}} \in R_0(\gamma_{\xi^m})\},$$

where $\Omega_m = \Omega \setminus \bar{\gamma}_{\xi^m}$. For any m, a solution of the problem

$$u^m \in S^m, \tag{60}$$

$$\int\limits_{\Omega_m} \sigma(u^m)\varepsilon(v - u^m) - \int\limits_{\Omega_m} f(v - u^m) + \tag{61}$$

$$+\frac{1}{\alpha} \int\limits_{\gamma_{\xi^m}} [u^m][v - u^m] \geq 0 \;\; \forall v \in S^m$$

can be found. We can provide a transformation of the independent variables

$$\begin{cases} x_1 &= y_1 \\ x_2 &= y_2 - \varphi(y)(\xi^m(y_1) - \xi(y_1)), \end{cases} \tag{62}$$

where $x = (x_1, x_2) \in \Omega_\xi$, $y = (y_1, y_2) \in \Omega_m$. A smooth function φ with compact support in Ω_ξ is chosen in such a way that $\varphi = 1$ in a neighborhood of the union

$$\bigcup \{(y_1, y_2) \mid y_2 = \xi^m(y_1) - 1, \; y_1 \in [-1/2, -1]\},$$

where all functions ξ, ξ^m are extended by zero outside of $[-1/2, -1]$. Denote

$$u_m(x) = u^m(y), x \in \Omega_\xi, \; y \in \Omega_m.$$

Next, we can use the arguments of paper [32] where a perturbation of the inclusion shapes is analyzed, and obtain a priori estimates from (60) and (61) being uniform in m,

$$\|u_m\|_{H^1_{\Gamma_0}(\Omega_\xi)^2} \leq c. \tag{63}$$

By (63), we assume that as $m \to \infty$,

$$u_m \to u \;\; \text{weakly in} \;\; H^1_{\Gamma_0}(\Omega_\xi)^2,$$

and moreover, it is proved

$$u_m \to u \text{ strongly in } H^1_{\Gamma_0}(\Omega_\xi)^2. \tag{64}$$

Making a transformation of the independent variables (62) in (60) and (61) and passing to the limit as $m \to \infty$, by (64), we obtain

$$u \in S_\xi, \tag{65}$$

$$\int\limits_{\Omega_\xi} \sigma(u)\varepsilon(v - u) - \int\limits_{\Omega_\xi} f(v - u) + \tag{66}$$

$$+\frac{1}{\alpha} \int\limits_{\gamma_\xi} [u][v - u] \geq 0 \;\; \forall v \in S_\xi$$

which means $u = u^\xi$. It is turned out (see [32]) that if

$$\rho^m = u^m \;\; \text{on} \;\; \gamma^-_{\xi^m},$$

then as $m \to \infty$,

$$\rho_m(x) \to \rho_0^\xi(x) \tag{67}$$

for all $x \in \gamma$, and consequently, for all $x \in \gamma_e$, where $\rho_0^\xi = (\rho_{01}^\xi, \rho_{02}^\xi) = u^\xi|_{\gamma_\xi^-}$. Then, by (67),

$$\inf_{\tilde{\xi}\in\Xi} J(\tilde{\xi}) = \lim_{m\to\infty} \inf J(\xi^m) = \lim_{m\to\infty} \inf |\rho_{m2}(1,1)| = |\rho_{02}^\xi(1,1)| =$$
$$= J(\xi) \geq \inf_{\tilde{\xi}\in\Xi} J(\tilde{\xi}).$$

Thus, the limit function ξ from (59) is a solution of the optimal control problem (58). Theorem 6 is proved. □

7. Conclusions

This paper provides a rigorous mathematical analysis of the problem for an elastic body with a thin rigid inclusion crossing the external boundary of the body at zero angle. It is supposed that the inclusion is exfoliated from the surrounding body which implies a presence of the interfacial crack. Inequality type constraints are imposed at the crack faces proving a mutual non-penetration between them. In addition to this factor, boundary conditions depend on a positive damage parameter describing the adhesion between the opposite crack faces. These boundary conditions imply that the problem considered refers to the problem with an unknown set of a contact. The solution existence of the problem is proved, and asymptotic analysis is fulfilled with respect to the damage parameter assuming that this parameter tends to infinity and to zero. Therefore, in the frame of a high–level mathematical model, we prove a correctness of the boundary value problem and analyze the limit models. Moreover, the existence of a solution to the optimal control problem is proved which allows us to find the optimal shape of the rigid inclusion. The approaches used in this paper can be useful for the analysis of various complex elastic and inelastic structures formulated in terms of free boundary problems, and in particular, for those having zero angles of the boundary.

Funding: This work is supported by the Mathematical Center in Akademgorodok under agreement No. 075-15-2022-282 with the Ministry of Science and Higher Education of the Russian Federation.

Data Availability Statement: No new data were created or analyzed in this study. Data sharing is not applicable to this article.

Conflicts of Interest: The authors declare no conflict of interest.

References

1. Lazarev, N. Shape sensitivity analysis of the energy integrals for the Timoshenko-type plate containing a crack on the boundary of a rigid inclusion. *Z. Angew. Math. Phys.* **2015**, *66*, 2025–2040. [CrossRef]
2. Lazarev, N.; Itou, H. Optimal location of a rigid inclusion in equilibrium problems for inhomogeneous Kirchhoff-Love plates with a crack. *Math. Mech. Solids* **2019**, *24*, 3743–3752. [CrossRef]
3. Khludnev, A.M. On the crossing bridge between two Kirchhoff-Love plates. *Axioms* **2023**, *12*, 120. [CrossRef]
4. Rudoy, E.; Shcherbakov, V. First-order shape derivative of the energy functional for elastic plates with rigid inclusions and interfacial cracks. *Appl. Math. Optim.* **2021**, *84*, 2775–2802. [CrossRef]
5. Rudoy, E.M. On numerical solving a rigid inclusions problem in 2D elasticity. *Z. Angew. Math. Phys.* **2017**, *68*, 19. [CrossRef]
6. Khludnev, A.M.; Fankina, I.V. Equilibrium problem for elastic plate with thin rigid inclusion crossing an external boundary. *Z. Angew. Math. Phys.* **2021**, *72*, 121. [CrossRef]
7. Shcherbakov, V.V. Shape optimization of rigid inclusions in elastic plates with cracks. *Z. Angew. Math. Phys.* **2016**, *67*, 71. [CrossRef]
8. Shcherbakov, V.V. Energy release rates for interfacial cracks in elastic bodies with thin semirigid inclusions. *Z. Angew. Math. Phys.* **2017**, *68*, 26. [CrossRef]
9. Furtsev, A.I. On contact between a thin obstacle and a plate containing a thin inclusion. *J. Math. Sci.* **2019**, *237*, 530–545. [CrossRef]
10. Khludnev, A.M. On modeling thin inclusions in elastic bodies with a damage parameter. *Math. Mech. Solids* **2019**, *24*, 2742–2753. [CrossRef]
11. Khludnev, A.M. On thin Timoshenko inclusions in elastic bodies with defects. *Arch. Appl. Mech.* **2019**, *89*, 1691–1704. [CrossRef]
12. Kovtunenko, V.A.; Kunisch, K. Shape derivative for penalty-constrained nonsmooth-nonconvex optimization: Cohesive crack problem. *J. Optim. Theory Appl.* **2022**, *194*, 597–635. [CrossRef]

13. Almi, S. Energy release rate and quasi-static evolution via vanishing viscosity in a fracture model depending on the crack opening. *ESAIM Control Optim. Calc. Var.* **2017**, *23*, 791–826. [CrossRef]
14. Khludnev, A.M.; Popova, T.S. Timoshenko inclusions in elastic bodies crossing an external boundary at zero angle. *Acta Mech. Solida Sin.* **2017**, *30*, 327–333. [CrossRef]
15. Rudoy, E. Asymptotic justification of models of plates containing inside hard thin inclusions. *Technologies* **2020**, *8*, 59. [CrossRef]
16. Furtsev, A.; Rudoy, E. Variational approach to modeling soft and stiff interfaces in the Kirchhoff-Love theory of plates. *Int. J. Solids Struct.* **2020**, *202*, 562–574. [CrossRef]
17. Serpilli, M. Asymptotic interface models in magneto-electro-thermoelastic composites. *Meccanica* **2017**, *52*, 1407–1424. [CrossRef]
18. Serpilli, M.; Rizzoni, R.; Lebon, F.; Dumont, S. An asymptotic derivation of a general imperfect interface law for linear multiphysics composites. *Int. J. Solids Struct.* **2019**, *180–181*, 97–107. [CrossRef]
19. Gaudiello, A.; Sili, A. Limit models for thin heterogeneous structures with high contrast. *J. Differ. Equ.* **2021**, *302*, 37–63. [CrossRef]
20. Mallick, P. *Fiber-Reinforced Composites. Materials, Manufacturing, and Design*; Marcel Dekker: New York, NY, USA, 1993.
21. Pasternak, I.M. Plane problem of elasticity theory for anisotropic bodies with thin elastic inclusions. *J. Math. Sci.* **2012**, *186*, 31–47. [CrossRef]
22. Caillerie, D. The effect of a thin inclusion of high rigidity in an elastic body. *Math. Meth. Appl. Sci.* **1980**, *2*, 251–270. [CrossRef]
23. Goudarzi, M.; Dal Corso, F.; Bigoni, D.; Simone, A. Dispersion of rigid line inclusions as stiffeners and shear band instability triggers. *Int. J. Solids Struct.* **2021**, *210–211*, 255–272. [CrossRef]
24. El Jarroudi, M. Homogenization of an elastic material reinforced with thin rigid von Karman ribbons. *Math. Mech. Solids* **2018**, *24*, 1–27. [CrossRef]
25. Hu, K.X.; Chandra, A.; Huang, Y. On crack, rigid-line fiber, and interface interactions. *Mech. Mater.* **1994**, *19*, 15–28. [CrossRef]
26. Pingle, P.; Sherwood, J.; Gorbatikh, L. Properties of rigid-line inclusions as building blocks of naturally occurring composites. *Compos. Sci. Technol.* **2008**, *68*, 2267–2272. [CrossRef]
27. Kozlov, V.A.; Ma'zya, V.G.; Movchan, A.B. *Asymptotic Analysis of Fields in a Multi-Structure*; Oxford Mathematical Monographs; Oxford University Press: New York, NY, USA, 1999.
28. Panasenko, G. *Multi-Scale Modelling for Structures and Composites*; Springer: New York, NY, USA, 2005.
29. Boureghda, A.; Djellab, N. Du Fort-Frankel Finite difference scheme for solving of oxygen diffusion problem inside one cell. *J. Comput. Theor. Transport.* **2023**. [CrossRef]
30. Amar, L.H.H.; Bourada, F.; Bousahla, A.A.; Tounsi, A.; Benrahou, K.H.; Albalawi, H.; Tounsi, A. Buckling analysis of FG plates via 2D and quasi-3D refined shear deformation theories. *Struct. Engin. Mech.* **2023**, *85*, 765–780.
31. Tounsi, A.; Bousahla, A.A.; Tahir, S.I.; Mostefa, A.H.; Bourada, F.; Al-Osta, M.A.; Tounsi, A. Influences of different boundary conditions and hygro-thermal environment on the free vibration responses of FGM sandwich plates resting on viscoelastic foundation. *Int. J. Struct. Stab. Dyn.* **2023** , 2450117. [CrossRef]
32. Khludnev, A.M. Shape control of thin rigid inclusions and cracks in elastic bodies. *Arch. Appl. Mech.* **2013**, *83*, 1493–1509. [CrossRef]

axioms

MDPI

Article

A Quasi-Explicit Method Applied to Missing Boundary Data Reconstruction for the Stokes System

Abdulaziz H. Alharbi [1,*], Fadhel Jday [1,2], Abdulrahman B. Albidah [3] and Ali M. Alhartomi [4]

1 Department of Mathematics, Jamoum University College, Umm Al-Qura University, Makkah 25375, Saudi Arabia; fmjday@uqu.edu.sa
2 ENIT-LAMSIN, University of Tunis El Manar, Tunis 1002, Tunisia
3 Department of Mathematics, College of Science Al-Zulfi, Majmaah University, Al-Majmaah 11952, Saudi Arabia; a.albedah@mu.edu.sa
4 Department of Mathematics, Al-Leith University College, Umm Al-Qura University, Makkah 24382, Saudi Arabia; amhartomi@uqu.edu.sa
* Correspondence: ahhrbe@uqu.edu.sa

Abstract: In this paper, we study the data completion problem for the Cauchy–Stokes equation in a cylindrical domain, Ω. Neumann and Dirichlet boundary conditions are prescribed on part of the overdetermined boundary, Γ_0, and the goal is to complete the data on the other part of the boundary, Γ_a. Here, Γ_0 and Γ_a represent the side faces of the cylinder Ω. This problem is known to be ill-posed and is formulated as an optimal control problem with a regularized cost function. To directly approximate the missing data on Γ_a, we employ the method of factorization of elliptic boundary value problems. This technique allows the factorization of a boundary value problem into a product of parabolic problems. It is successfully applied to the optimality system in this work, yielding new and significant results.

Keywords: elliptic boundary value problems; factorization method; Dirichlet–Neumann operator; Stokes problem

MSC: 34A12; 35J40; 35J50

1. Introduction

Completing the Navier–Stokes equations' missing boundary data is a crucial task in many engineering and scientific fields. When predicting the weather and modeling the climate for accurate weather and climate forecasts, accurate simulations of oceanic and atmospheric circulation are necessary. However, measurements of boundary conditions, including the temperature gradients, pressure, and wind velocity, are frequently lacking. Refining the numerical models employed in projections requires us to fill this data gap (see [1,2]). Measurement method limitations might result in incomplete boundary data in engineering domains such as hydrodynamics and aerodynamics. For example, not all boundary conditions are understood in detail for wind tunnel studies. When these missing data are filled in, accurate simulations are guaranteed, which is essential in developing effective systems like turbines, cars, and airplanes (see [3]). In the field of biomedical engineering, when simulating physiological flows like blood circulation in arteries or respiratory system airflow, one frequently encounters unidentified boundary conditions like pressure or wall shear stress. By filling in these missing data, the simulations are improved and medical devices like artificial valves and stents can be designed more effectively [4]. In environmental engineering, the modeling of water flows in natural settings, such as rivers, lakes, or coastal regions, often involves inaccessible areas where boundary data are missing. Completing these data is essential in simulating pollutant dispersion, sediment transport, and flood dynamics, thereby informing environmental management and disaster preparedness; see [5].

In applications such as drag reduction in aerodynamics or mixing enhancement in chemical reactors, missing boundary data present significant challenges for active flow control. Resolving this issue is essential in designing effective control strategies that optimize system performance; see [6].

The problem of missing boundary data is often addressed using inverse problems, where unknown boundary conditions are inferred from available measurements. Techniques such as data assimilation, regularization methods, and physics-informed neural networks are commonly employed to reconstruct the missing information, ensuring accurate and reliable simulations.

For example, in the context of the Navier–Stokes equations, stability estimates have been utilized in inverse problems to recover boundary coefficients from measurements. These approaches are critical in ensuring the accuracy and reliability of simulations across a range of applications.

In summary, completing missing boundary data in the Navier–Stokes equations is fundamental for accurate modeling and simulation in various fields, including weather forecasting, industrial design, biomedical engineering, environmental management, and fluid system optimization.

This work focuses on the Cauchy–Stokes problem within a cylindrical domain Ω, where data are provided on a portion of Ω's boundary. Notably, there is limited literature on the Cauchy–Stokes problem. For instance, ref. [7] addresses this issue by modeling the data recovery process as a least-squares tracking problem. Moreover, alternating iterative algorithms have been applied in [8,9] for elliptic equations and in [10–13] for stationary Stokes systems. The Poincaré–Steklov operator is employed in [14] as another method to tackle this problem.

In this paper, we present the factorization method, which reformulates the elliptic boundary value problem as a parabolic one. This technique provides a direct means of computing the missing boundary data for any specified Cauchy data.

This technique consists of embedding the initial problem in a family of similar problems depending on a parameter, and these are solved recursively. It can be viewed as an infinite-dimensional generalization of the block Gauss LU factorization. It has been used by Bellman [15] and Lions [16] (in the infinite-dimensional case) to derive the optimal feedback law in linear-quadratic optimal control problems. The method applied to the Poisson equation has been presented in [17,18], and it has recently been used by Bouarroudj et al. in [19,20] to analyze boundary-value problems for fourth-order partial differential equations Moreover, it has already been used to solve the electrocardiographic imaging (ECGI) problem in the work by Addouche et al. [21]. The Cauchy–Stokes systems have been presented in [22], which are the same as in [23,24]. Moreover, we have Dirichlet and Neumann data on the whole boundary of Ω (see Figure 1), and we search for the speed and the pressure in Ω. This problem is well-posed and has a unique weak solution. In our work, we solve an inverse problem: a data completion problem for the Stokes equation in Ω. The velocity $\mathcal{U}$ (a Dirichlet datum) and a force $\mathcal{F}$ are given on part of the boundary of Ω, accessible via direct measurement, while no condition is given on Γ_a (inaccessible via direct measurements). The data completion problem consists of recovering a boundary condition on Γ_a to directly obtain an approximation of the missing data. This problem is known to be severely ill-posed (see Hadamard [25]); it is set as an optimal control problem with a cost function.

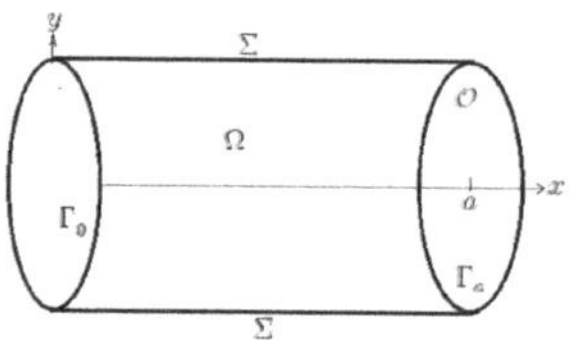

Figure 1. Schematic representation of the cylindrical domain Ω.

This paper is organized as follows. In Section 2, we introduce the cylindrical geometry of the domain Ω and establish key notations, Sobolev spaces, and the forward Stokes problem. The inverse problem is then rigorously formulated as a Cauchy–Stokes data completion task. Section 3 transforms this ill-posed inverse problem into a well-posed optimal control framework, defining the energy-like error functional and proving its convexity. Section 4 presents the core theoretical advancements, including the factorization method's application to derive decoupled Riccati equations for the Dirichlet-to-Neumann (D) and Neumann-to-Dirichlet (Q) operators, alongside critical theorems governing the optimality system. Section 5 provides the detailed proof of Theorem 1, elucidating the structure and evolution of the operator D. In Section 6, we solve the optimal control problem non-iteratively using the factorization method, proving Theorems 2 and 3 to characterize the missing boundary data and establish compatibility conditions. Finally, Section 7 concludes with insights into the method's efficiency, numerical prospects, and extensions to non-cylindrical domains. This revised structure emphasizes the interplay between theoretical analysis and computational strategy, offering a cohesive pathway from problem formulation to solution.

2. Preliminaries

2.1. Notations

Let Ω be the open-bounded cylinder $\Omega =]0, a[\times \mathcal{O}$ in $\mathbb{R}^n$, where $a > 0$, and $\mathcal{O}$ is a bounded open set in $\mathbb{R}^{n-1}$, representing the cross-section of the cylinder. Let $\Sigma =]0, a[\times \partial\mathcal{O}$ denote the lateral boundary and $\Gamma_0 = \{0\} \times \mathcal{O}$ and $\Gamma_a = \{a\} \times \mathcal{O}$ be the faces of the cylinder. A general point $(x_1, x_2, \ldots, x_n)$ is also denoted by $(x, \mathbf{y})$, where $x = x_1$ is the coordinate along the axis of the cylinder, and $\mathbf{y} = (x_2, \ldots, x_n)$ represents the coordinates in the cross-section, perpendicular to the axis. The cylindrical geometry simplifies the presentation of the factorization method, but the method can be easily generalized to regular non-cylindrical domains.

Firstly, to emphasize the role of the component along the axis of the cylinder, which will play a crucial role in the factorization method, we introduce the following notations.

- For a given vector field Θ, we denote by Θ_x the component of Θ along the axis of the cylinder and by $\Theta_{\mathbf{y}}$ its components with respect to the coordinates in the cross-section.
- ∇ represents the gradient vector, where $\nabla_x = \dfrac{\partial}{\partial x_1}$, and $\nabla_{\mathbf{y}}$ denotes the components with respect to the coordinates in the cross-section.
- For a given vector field Θ, we define the divergence as

$$div(\Theta) = \sum_{i=1}^{n} \frac{\partial \Theta}{\partial x_i},$$

with

$$div_x(\Theta) = \frac{\partial \Theta}{\partial x_1}, \quad div_{\mathbf{y}}(\Theta) = \sum_{i=2}^{n} \frac{\partial \Theta}{\partial x_i}.$$

Secondly, we introduce the following notations.

- ν represents the fluid kinematic viscosity.
- The strain tensor is given by

$$T(\mathbf{u}) = \frac{1}{2}(\nabla \mathbf{u} + (\nabla \mathbf{u})^t),$$

where

$$(T(\mathbf{u}))_{ij} = \frac{1}{2}\left(\frac{\partial \mathbf{u}_{x_i}}{\partial x_j} + \frac{\partial \mathbf{u}_{x_j}}{\partial x_i}\right), \quad 1 \le i,j \le n.$$

- The stress tensor is defined as

$$\sigma(\mathbf{u}) = 2\nu T(\mathbf{u}) - pI.$$

- I denotes the identity matrix.
- N is the outward unit normal vector; in our case, $N = (-1,0,\ldots,0)$ on Γ_0 and $N = (1,0,\ldots,0)$ on Γ_a.
- We denote by $\nabla \mathbf{u} : \nabla v$ the trace of their product, which is defined as

$$\nabla \mathbf{u} : \nabla v = \mathrm{tr}(\nabla \mathbf{u} \nabla v) = \sum_{i=1}^{n} \nabla u_{x_i} \nabla v_{x_i} = \sum_{i,j=1}^{n} \frac{\partial u_{x_i}}{\partial x_j}\frac{\partial v_{x_j}}{\partial x_i},$$

where

$$\nabla \mathbf{u} = \begin{pmatrix} \nabla u_{x_1} \\ \vdots \\ \nabla u_{x_n} \end{pmatrix} = \begin{pmatrix} \frac{\partial u_{x_1}}{\partial x_1} & \cdots & \frac{\partial u_{x_1}}{\partial x_n} \\ \vdots & \ddots & \vdots \\ \frac{\partial u_{x_n}}{\partial x_1} & \cdots & \frac{\partial u_{x_n}}{\partial x_n} \end{pmatrix}.$$

The Laplacian of $\mathbf{u}$ is given by

$$\Delta \mathbf{u} = \begin{pmatrix} \Delta u_{x_1} \\ \vdots \\ \Delta u_{x_n} \end{pmatrix}.$$

Finally, we define the following Sobolev space.

- The Sobolev space $H_{00}^{1/2}(\mathcal{O})$ is defined, as stated in Theorem 11.7 (p. 72) of [16], as the $\frac{1}{2}$-interpolation between $H_0^1(\mathcal{O})$ and $L^2(\mathcal{O})$. Its dual space is denoted by $\left(H_{00}^{1/2}(\mathcal{O})\right)'$.

2.2. Forward Problem

The direct problem is defined as follows: for a given $\mathcal{U} \in H_{00}^{1/2}(\Gamma_0)$ and $\mathcal{G} \in \left(H_{00}^{1/2}(\Gamma_a)\right)'$, find the velocity $\mathbf{u} \in H^1(\Omega)$ and the pressure $p \in L^2(\Omega)$ satisfying

$$(\mathcal{P})\begin{cases} -\nu\Delta \mathbf{u} + \nabla p = 0 & \text{in } \Omega, \\ div(\mathbf{u}) = 0 & \text{in } \Omega, \\ \mathbf{u} = 0 & \text{on } \Sigma, \\ \mathbf{u} = \mathcal{U} & \text{on } \Gamma_0, \\ \sigma(\mathbf{u}) \cdot N = \mathcal{G} & \text{on } \Gamma_a. \end{cases} \tag{1}$$

Physical Interpretation

In Problem $(\mathcal{P})$ (Equation (1)), the unknowns $\mathbf{u}$ and p represent the following.

- **Velocity field ($\mathbf{u}$)**: $\mathbf{u} \in H^1(\Omega)$ describes the fluid motion in Ω, satisfying the following:
  - No-slip condition, $\mathbf{u} = 0$ on Σ;

- Prescribed velocity, $\mathbf{u} = \mathcal{U}$ on Γ_0;
- Traction condition, $\sigma(\mathbf{u}) \cdot N = \mathcal{G}$ on Γ_a.

- **Pressure field (p)**: $p \in L^2(\Omega)$ enforces incompressibility ($\text{div}(\mathbf{u}) = 0$) and balances viscous forces through ∇p.

We need the following lemma that provides a general integration by parts formula.

Lemma 1 ([14,26]). *If $u \in H^1(\Omega)$, such that $div(u) = 0$ in Ω, then $\Delta u = 2\nabla \cdot T(u)$ and*

$$-\int_\Omega \nu \Delta u \cdot v \, dx = \int_\Omega 2\nu T(u) : T(v) \, dx - \int_{\partial\Omega} 2\nu T(u) \, N \cdot v \, dx, \text{ for all } v \in H^1(\Omega).$$

Let the space $Y = \{\mathbf{u} \in H^1(\Omega) : div(\mathbf{u}) = 0 \text{ and } \Omega, \ \mathbf{u} = 0 \text{ on } \Sigma \cup \Gamma_0\}$. Then, a mixed formulation of the Stokes equations is obtained by multiplying the first equation of $(\mathcal{P})$ by a test function $v \in Y$, by integration over Ω, and by applying Lemma 1 as well as the divergence theorem. Then,

$$\int_\Omega 2\nu T(\mathbf{u}) : T(v) \, dx - \int_\Omega p \, div(v) \, dx = \int_{\partial\Omega} (2\nu T(\mathbf{u}) \, N) \cdot v \, dx - \int_{\partial\Omega} (p \, N) v \, dx.$$

Using the boundary conditions where $\mathbf{u} \in Y$ satisfies the constraint $\mathbf{u}_{|\Gamma_0} = \mathcal{U}$, we obtain

$$\begin{aligned} \int_\Omega 2\nu T(\mathbf{u}) : T(v) \, dx &= \int_{\partial\Omega} (2\nu T(\mathbf{u}) - p) \, N \cdot v \, dx \\ &= \int_{\Gamma_a} (2\nu T(\mathbf{u}) - p) \, N \cdot v \, dx \\ &= \int_{\Gamma_a} \mathcal{G} v \, dx. \end{aligned}$$

We write, for all $(\mathbf{u}, v) \in Y \times Y$,

$$a(\mathbf{u}, v) = \int_\Omega 2\nu T(\mathbf{u}) : T(v) \, dx \text{ and } l(v) = \int_{\Gamma_a} \mathcal{G} v \, dx.$$

So, $\mathbf{u}$ is a weak solution of $(\mathcal{P})$ if and only if $a(\mathbf{u}, v) - l(v) = 0$, for all $v \in Y$.

The well-posedness of the above variational formulation is given by the Lax–Milgram theorem (see [16] for more details).

2.3. The Inverse Problem

Assuming a given velocity $\mathcal{U} \in H^{1/2}_{00}(\Gamma_0)$ and a force $\mathcal{F} \in \left(H^{1/2}_{00}(\Gamma_0)\right)'$ on Γ_0, the data completion problem for the Stokes operator can be formulated as a Cauchy problem.

Find the velocity $\mathbf{u} \in \mathcal{H}$ and the pressure $p \in \mathcal{P}$ satisfying

$$(\mathcal{PI}) \begin{cases} -\nu\Delta\mathbf{u} + \nabla p = 0 & \text{in } \Omega, \\ div(\mathbf{u}) = 0 & \text{in } \Omega, \\ \mathbf{u} = 0 & \text{on } \Sigma, \\ \mathbf{u} = \mathcal{U} & \text{on } \Gamma_0, \\ \sigma(\mathbf{u}) \cdot N = \mathcal{F} & \text{on } \Gamma_0. \end{cases} \tag{2}$$

We have on Γ_0

$$\sigma(\mathbf{u}) \cdot N = \mathcal{F} \quad \text{on } \Gamma_0 \Rightarrow \begin{cases} p(0) - 2\nu \frac{\partial u_{x_1}}{\partial x_1}(0) = \mathcal{F}_{x_1}, \\ -\nu(\frac{\partial u_{x_j}}{\partial x_1}(0) + \frac{\partial u_{x_1}}{\partial x_j}(0)) = \mathcal{F}_{x_j}, \ j = 2, \ldots, n. \end{cases}$$

This can be expressed as follows:

$$\begin{aligned} & p(0) - 2\nu\frac{\partial u_x}{\partial x}(0) = \mathcal{F}_x, \\ & -\nu(\frac{\partial \mathbf{u_y}}{\partial x}(0) + (\nabla_\mathbf{y})u_x(0)) = \mathcal{F}_\mathbf{y}, \end{aligned} \tag{3}$$

where $\nabla_\mathbf{y} = (\partial_{x_2}, \ldots, \partial_{x_n})^t$ is the gradient operator defined on the section of the cylinder; $u_x = u_{x_1}$ and $\mathbf{u_y} = (u_{x_2}, \ldots, u_{x_n})^t$ are the components of the vector u.

This problem is known to be ill-posed in the sense that the dependence of $(\mathbf{u}, p)$ on the data $(\mathcal{U}, \mathcal{F})$ is not continuous and the solution does not exist for any pair of data; see [25].

The Cauchy data $(\mathcal{U}, \mathcal{F})$ are called compatible if the problem (2) has a solution.

In order to reconstruct the unknown boundary data $\mathbf{u}_{|\Gamma_a}$ and $\sigma(\mathbf{u}) \cdot N_{|\Gamma_a}$ on Γ_a, we will use the factorization method (see [27–29] for the Laplace equation). The inverse problem is formulated as an optimization one.

2.4. Data Completion Problem

The considered data completion problem $(\mathcal{P}_0)$ can be stated as follows: for given compatible data $(\mathcal{U}, \mathcal{F}) \in H_{00}^{1/2}(\Gamma_0) \times (H_{00}^{1/2}(\Gamma_0))'$, for which the existence and uniqueness of the solution are guaranteed, find the unknown boundary data $(V, G) \in H_{00}^{1/2}(\Gamma_a) \times (H_{00}^{1/2}(\Gamma_a))'$ such that

$$(\mathcal{P}_0)\begin{cases} -\nu\Delta\mathbf{u} + \nabla p = 0 & \text{in } \Omega, \\ div(\mathbf{u}) = 0 & \text{in } \Omega, \\ \mathbf{u} = 0 & \text{on } \Sigma, \\ \mathbf{u} = \mathcal{U} & \text{on } \Gamma_0, \\ \sigma(\mathbf{u}) \cdot N = \mathcal{F} & \text{on } \Gamma_0, \\ \mathbf{u} = V & \text{on } \Gamma_a, \\ \sigma(\mathbf{u}) \cdot N = G & \text{on } \Gamma_a. \end{cases} \tag{4}$$

To solve this problem, the unknown data (V, G) will be characterized as the minimum of an energy-like functional; see [8,30,31].

2.5. Optimal Control Problem

The data completion problem $(\mathcal{P}_0)$ is transformed into an optimal control problem following the approach used in [8]. It has two states and translates into the two following Stokes problems. Find $\mathbf{u}^N$ and $\mathbf{u}^D$ solutions of

$$(\mathcal{P}_1)\begin{cases} -\nu\Delta\mathbf{u}^N + \nabla p^N = 0 & \text{in } \Omega, \\ div(\mathbf{u}^N) = 0 & \text{in } \Omega, \\ \mathbf{u}^N = 0 & \text{on } \Sigma, \\ \sigma(\mathbf{u}^N) \cdot N = \mathcal{F} & \text{on } \Gamma_0, \\ \mathbf{u}^N = v & \text{on } \Gamma_a. \end{cases}$$

$$(\mathcal{P}_2)\begin{cases} -\nu\Delta\mathbf{u}^D + \nabla p^D = 0 & \text{in } \Omega, \\ div(\mathbf{u}^D) = 0 & \text{in } \Omega, \\ \mathbf{u}^D = 0 & \text{on } \Sigma, \\ \mathbf{u}^D = \mathcal{U} & \text{on } \Gamma_0, \\ \sigma(\mathbf{u}^D) \cdot N = g & \text{on } \Gamma_a. \end{cases}$$

The unknown data (V, G) appearing in the problem $(\mathcal{P}_0)$ can be characterized as the solution of the following minimization problem:

$$(V, G) = arg \min\{E(v, g); (v, g) \in \mathcal{U}_{ad}\}$$

where E is the following energy-like error functional defined on $U_{ad} = \left(H_{00}^{1/2}(\mathcal{O})\right) \times \left(H_{00}^{1/2}(\mathcal{O})\right)'$ by

$$E(v,g) = \frac{1}{2}\int_{\Omega} \sigma(\mathbf{u}^N(v) - \mathbf{u}^D(g)) : \nabla(\mathbf{u}^N(v) - \mathbf{u}^D(g))dx. \tag{5}$$

Lemma 2. *The functional E defined by Equation (5) is an energy functional that is positive, and, if $\mathcal{U}$ and $\mathcal{F}$ are compatible, then there exists a unique solution that is the minimum of the functional E.*

$$E(v,g) = \frac{1}{2}\int_{\Omega} \sigma(\mathbf{u}^N(v) - \mathbf{u}^D(g)) : \nabla(\mathbf{u}^N(v) - \mathbf{u}^D(g))dx.$$

We write $\tilde{u} = (\mathbf{u}^N(v) - \mathbf{u}^D(g))dx$ and $\tilde{p} = p^N - p^D$.

Then,

$$\begin{aligned} E(v,g) &= \frac{1}{2}\int_{\Omega} \sigma(\tilde{u}) : \nabla(\tilde{u})dx \\ &= \frac{1}{2}\int_{\Omega} (\nabla\tilde{u} + (\nabla\tilde{u})^t - \tilde{p}I) : \nabla\tilde{u}dx \\ &= \frac{1}{2}\int_{\Omega} (\nabla\tilde{u} : \nabla\tilde{u} + (\nabla\tilde{u})^t : \nabla\tilde{u} - \underbrace{\tilde{p}\ div\ \tilde{u}}_{0} dx \\ &= \frac{1}{2}\int_{\Omega} \sum_{i,j=1}^{n} (\frac{\partial\tilde{u}_{x_i}}{\partial x_j}\frac{\partial\tilde{u}_{x_j}}{\partial x_i} + (\frac{\partial\tilde{u}_{x_i}}{\partial x_j})^2)dx. \end{aligned}$$

We have

$$\begin{aligned} \sum_{i,j=1}^{n} (\frac{\partial\tilde{u}_{x_i}}{\partial x_j} + \frac{\partial\tilde{u}_{x_j}}{\partial x_i})^2 &= \sum_{i,j=1}^{n} (\frac{\partial\tilde{u}_{x_i}}{\partial x_j})^2 + (\frac{\partial\tilde{u}_{x_j}}{\partial x_i})^2 + 2\frac{\partial\tilde{u}_{x_i}}{\partial x_j}\frac{\partial\tilde{u}_{x_j}}{\partial x_i} \\ &= 2\Big(\sum_{i,j=1}^{n} (\frac{\partial\tilde{u}_{x_i}}{\partial x_j})^2 + \frac{\partial\tilde{u}_{x_i}}{\partial x_j}\frac{\partial\tilde{u}_{x_j}}{\partial x_i}\Big), \end{aligned}$$

and then

$$E(v,g) = \frac{1}{4}\int_{\Omega} \sum_{i,j=1}^{n} (\frac{\partial\tilde{u}_{x_i}}{\partial x_j} + \frac{\partial\tilde{u}_{x_j}}{\partial x_i})^2 dx.$$

So, $E(v,g)$ is positive energy. For the existence of a minimum of E when (U,F) is a compatible pair, see [14].

3. Brief Sketch of the Factorization Method

In this section, we apply the factorization method to the states $\mathbf{u}^N$, $\mathbf{u}^D$. We embed the control problem in a family of similar problems defined on the Ω_s subdomain of Ω. For this, we define $\Gamma_s = \{x = s\} \times \mathcal{O}$ as a mobile border that will move from $x = 0$ to $x = a$. At each position $x = s$, one can thus define a subdomain Ω_s of surface side Σ_s delimited by surfaces Γ_0 and Γ_s (see Figure 2).

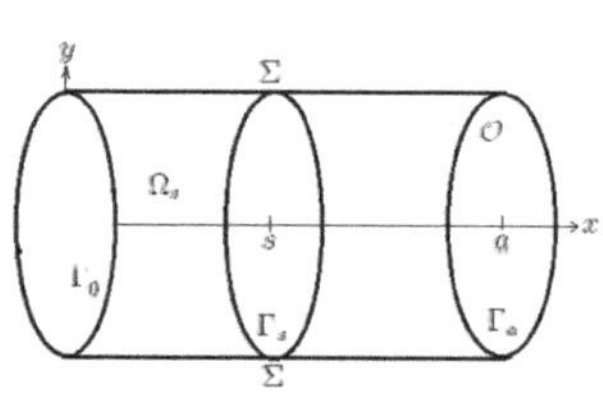

Figure 2. Schematic representation of the moving domain Ω_s.

For given boundary data $(\psi, \varphi) \in H^{1/2}_{00}(\Gamma_s) \times \left(H^{1/2}_{00}(\Gamma_s)\right)'$, we define $\mathbf{u}^{N_s}$ and $\mathbf{u}^{D_s}$ as the solutions to the following two problems in Ω_s:

$$(\mathcal{P}_1^s)\begin{cases} -\nu\Delta\mathbf{u}^{N_s} + \nabla p^{N_s} = 0 & \text{in } \Omega_s, \\ div(\mathbf{u}^{N_s}) = 0 & \text{in } \Omega_s, \\ \mathbf{u}^{N_s} = 0 & \text{on } \Sigma_s, \\ \mathbf{u}^{N_s} = \psi & \text{on } \Gamma_s, \\ \sigma(\mathbf{u}^{N_s}) \cdot N = \mathcal{F} & \text{on } \Gamma_0. \end{cases}$$

$$(\mathcal{P}_2^s)\begin{cases} -\nu\Delta\mathbf{u}^{D_s} + \nabla p^{D_s} = 0 & \text{in } \Omega_s, \\ div(\mathbf{u}^{D_s}) = 0 & \text{in } \Omega_s, \\ \mathbf{u}^{D_s} = 0 & \text{on } \Sigma_s, \\ \mathbf{u}^{D_s} = \mathcal{U} & \text{on } \Gamma_0, \\ \sigma(\mathbf{u}^{D_s}) \cdot N = \varphi & \text{on } \Gamma_s, \end{cases}$$

- **Dirichlet to Neumann mapping**
  By splitting the problem $(\mathcal{P}_1^s)$ into two well-posed subproblems, we can write $\mathbf{u}^{N_s}$ as the sum of two functions γ_N^s and β_N^s depending linearly on ψ and $\mathcal{F}$. The functions γ_N^s and β_N^s are solutions of the following two problems:

$$\begin{cases} -\nu\Delta\gamma_N^s + \nabla q^{N_s} = 0 & \text{in} & \Omega_s, \\ div(\gamma_N^s) = 0 & \text{in} & \Omega_s, \\ \gamma_N^s = 0 & \text{on} & \Sigma_s, \\ \sigma(\gamma_N^s) \cdot N = 0 & \text{on} & \Gamma_0, \\ \gamma_N^s = \psi & \text{on} & \Gamma_s. \end{cases} \quad \text{and} \quad \begin{cases} -\nu\Delta\beta_N^s + \nabla l^{N_s} = 0 & \text{in} & \Omega_s, \\ div(\beta_N^s) = 0 & \text{in} & \Omega_s, \\ \beta_N^s = 0 & \text{on} & \Sigma_s, \\ \sigma(\beta_N^s) \cdot N = \mathcal{F} & \text{on} & \Gamma_0, \\ \beta_N^s = 0 & \text{on} & \Gamma_s, \end{cases} \tag{6}$$

  where $\mathbf{u}^{N_s} = \gamma_N^s + \beta_N^s$, $p^{N_s} = q^{N_s} + l^{N_s}$.
  Without loss of generality, we assume in what follows that $\nu = 1$ (the pressure p and velocity u can be rescaled proportionally to ν). For every $s \in \,]0, a]$, we define the Dirichlet to Neumann mapping $D(s) : H^{1/2}_{00}(\Gamma_s) \longrightarrow \left(H^{1/2}_{00}(\Gamma_s)\right)'$ by

$$D(x = s)\psi = \frac{\partial\gamma_N^s}{\partial x} \mid \Gamma_s. \tag{7}$$

  We also define the residual part ω_N by $\omega_N(s) = \frac{\partial\beta_N^s}{\partial x}$. We have

$$\frac{\partial\mathbf{u}^{N_s}}{\partial x} \,|_{\Gamma_s} = D(s)\psi + \omega_N(s). \tag{8}$$

  Henceforth, we denote $\mathbf{u}^N$ (instead of $\mathbf{u}^{N_s}$) and rewrite Equation (3) in the form

$$\frac{\partial\mathbf{u}^N}{\partial x} = D\mathbf{u}^N + \omega_N \Rightarrow \begin{pmatrix} \frac{\partial u_x^N}{\partial x} \\ \\ \frac{\partial \mathbf{u}_\mathbf{y}^N}{\partial x} \end{pmatrix} = D\begin{pmatrix} u_x^N \\ \\ \mathbf{u}_\mathbf{y}^N \end{pmatrix} + \begin{pmatrix} \omega_{N,x} \\ \\ \omega_{N,\mathbf{y}} \end{pmatrix}, \tag{9}$$

  where $(u_x^N, \mathbf{u}_\mathbf{y}^N)^t$ and $(\omega_{N,x}, \omega_{N,\mathbf{y}})^t$ are the components of the vectors $\mathbf{u}^N$ and ω_N.
  We can represent D as follows:

$$D := \begin{pmatrix} D_{xx} & D_{x\mathbf{y}} \\ D_{\mathbf{y}x} & D_{\mathbf{y}\mathbf{y}} \end{pmatrix}, \tag{10}$$

where $D_{\mathbf{xy}} = (D_{12}, D_{13}, \ldots, D_{1n})$, $D_{\mathbf{y}x} = (D_{21}, D_{31}, \ldots, D_{n1})^t$, and $D_{\mathbf{yy}}$ is the part $(D_{ij}, 2 \leq i, j \leq n)$. From (9), we obtain

$$\frac{\partial u_x^N}{\partial x} = D_{xx}u_x^N + D_{x\mathbf{y}}\mathbf{u}_{\mathbf{y}}^N + \omega_{N,x}, \tag{11}$$

and

$$\frac{\partial \mathbf{u}_{\mathbf{y}}^N}{\partial x} = D_{\mathbf{y}x}u_x^N + D_{\mathbf{yy}}\mathbf{u}_{\mathbf{y}}^N + \omega_{N,\mathbf{y}}. \tag{12}$$

- **Neumann to Dirichlet mapping**
By splitting the problem $(\mathcal{P}_2^s)$ into two well-posed subproblems, we can write $\mathbf{u}^{D_s}$ as the sum of two functions γ_D^s and β_D^s depending linearly on φ. The functions γ_D^s and β_D^s are solutions of the following two problems:

$$\begin{cases} -\nu\Delta\gamma_D^s + \nabla q_D^s = 0 & \text{in} \quad \Omega_s, \\ div(\gamma_D^s) = 0 & \text{in} \quad \Omega_s, \\ \gamma_D^s = 0 & \text{on} \quad \Sigma_s, \\ \gamma_D^s = 0 & \text{on} \quad \Gamma_0, \\ \sigma(\gamma_D^s)\cdot N = \varphi & \text{on} \quad \Gamma_s, \end{cases} \quad \text{and} \quad \begin{cases} -\nu\Delta\beta_D^s + \nabla l_D^s = 0 & \text{in} \quad \Omega_s, \\ div(\beta_D^s) = 0 & \text{in} \quad \Omega_s, \\ \beta_D^s = 0 & \text{on} \quad \Sigma_s, \\ \beta_D^s = \mathcal{U} & \text{on} \quad \Gamma_0, \\ \sigma(\beta_D^s)\cdot N = 0 & \text{on} \quad \Gamma_s. \end{cases} \tag{13}$$

We use the same methodology as in the previous section. We define the Neumann to Dirichlet mapping $Q(s) : \left(H_{00}^{1/2}(\Gamma_s)\right)' \longrightarrow H_{00}^{1/2}(\Gamma_s)$ by

$$Q(x=s)\varphi = \gamma_{D|\Gamma_s}^s$$

where $Q(0) = 0$. We also define the residual part $\omega_D(s) = \beta_{D|\Gamma_s} \in H_{00}^{1/2}(\Gamma_a)$, where $\omega_D(0) = \mathcal{U}$. We have

$$\mathbf{u}^{D_s}{}_{|\Gamma_s} = Q(s)\varphi + \omega_D(s).$$

4. Main Results

The factorization method plays a central role in this work by decomposing the original boundary value problem, defined on a cylindrical domain, into a family of coupled subproblems along the cylinder axis. By introducing a mobile boundary Γ_s, this approach transforms the state equation into a system of decoupled Riccati-type differential equations for the Dirichlet-to-Neumann (D) and Neumann-to-Dirichlet (Q) operators, as well as the associated residual functions. This factorization enables the explicit expression of the cost function in terms of the controls v and g, thereby avoiding the direct resolution of complex global problems. It provides a recursive and geometrically adaptive strategy, particularly effective for optimal control and inverse problems, such as in electrocardiography, where reconstructing data on inaccessible boundaries requires a robust and numerically stable approach.

Theorem 1. *The Dirichlet-to-Neumann operator D, the Neumann-to-Dirichlet operator Q, and the residual functions ω_D and ω_Q satisfy decoupled Riccati-type differential equations along the cylinder axis.*

Theorem 2. *For a pair $(v, g) \in H_{00}^{1/2}(\Gamma_a) \times (H_{00}^{1/2}(\Gamma_a))'$,*

$$\frac{\partial E}{\partial v}(h) = \int_{\Gamma_a} \sigma(\gamma_N^h)\cdot N(\boldsymbol{u}^N - \boldsymbol{u}^D)d\Gamma_a, \textit{ for all } h \in H_{00}^{1/2}(\Gamma_a),$$

$$\frac{\partial E}{\partial g}(k) = \int\limits_{\Gamma_a} \sigma(u^D - u^N) \cdot N\gamma_D^k d\Gamma_a, \textit{ for all } k \in (H_{00}^{1/2}(\Gamma_a))',$$

where γ_N^h *and* γ_D^k *are the solutions of*

$$\begin{cases} -\Delta\gamma_N^h + \nabla q_N^h = 0 & in \quad \Omega, \\ div(\gamma_N^h) = 0 & in \quad \Omega, \\ \gamma_N^h = 0 & on \quad \Sigma, \\ \sigma(\gamma_N^h)\cdot N = 0 & on \quad \Gamma_0, \\ \gamma_N^h = h & on \quad \Gamma_a, \end{cases}, \quad \begin{cases} -\Delta\gamma_D^k + \nabla q_D^k = 0 & in \quad \Omega, \\ div(\gamma_D^k) = 0 & in \quad \Omega, \\ \gamma_D^k = 0 & on \quad \Sigma, \\ \sigma(\gamma_D^k)\cdot N = k & on \quad \Gamma_a, \\ \gamma_D^k = 0 & on \quad \Gamma_0. \end{cases}$$

Theorem 3. *For a compatible datum $(\mathcal{U}, \mathcal{F})$, the optimum of E is attained for v and g, the unknown Cauchy data on the inaccessible boundary part where direct measurement is unavailable. These variables satisfy the system*

$$\begin{cases} (I - Q(a)D'')v = Q(a)\omega_N' + \omega_D \\ (I - D''Q(a))g = D''\omega_D + \omega_N' \end{cases}$$

where

$$D'' = \begin{pmatrix} 0 & 2(-\nabla_y)^t \\ D_{yx} & D_{yy} + \nabla_y \end{pmatrix} \textit{ and } \omega_N' = \begin{pmatrix} -p^N \\ \\ \omega_{N,y} \end{pmatrix}$$

5. Proof of Theorem 1

5.1. The Dirichlet-to-Neumann Operator and the Residual Function ω_N

We consider, for $x < s$, that the restriction of $\mathbf{u}^{N_s}(\psi)$ to Ω_x is a solution to the problem $(\mathcal{P}_1^s)$. By the same argument as previously made, we have the relation

$$\frac{\partial \mathbf{u}^{N_s}}{\partial x}(x, \psi) = D(x)\mathbf{u}^{N_s}(x, \psi) + \omega_N(x).$$

From Equation (9), we obtain

$$\frac{\partial u_x^N}{\partial x} = D_{xx}u_x^N + D_{xy}\mathbf{u}_\mathbf{y}^N + \omega_{N,x} \tag{14}$$

and

$$\frac{\partial \mathbf{u}_\mathbf{y}^N}{\partial x} = D_{\mathbf{y}x}u_x^N + D_{\mathbf{yy}}\mathbf{u}_\mathbf{y}^N + \omega_{N,\mathbf{y}}. \tag{15}$$

From the second equation of the problem $(\mathcal{P}_1^s)$, we have

$$\frac{\partial u_x^N}{\partial x} = -div_\mathbf{y}\mathbf{u}_\mathbf{y}^N \tag{16}$$

From Equations (14) and (16), we deduce that $D_{xx} = 0$, $D_{xy} = (-\frac{\partial}{\partial x_2}, \ldots, -\frac{\partial}{\partial x_n})$ and $\omega_{N,x} = 0$. Then, the first line of D is $(0,\ (-\nabla_\mathbf{y})^t)$.

Using the equation satisfied by $\mathbf{u}^N$ in the problem $(\mathcal{P})$, we have

$$-\Delta\mathbf{u}^N + \nabla p^N = 0 \Rightarrow -\Delta\begin{pmatrix} u_x^N \\ \mathbf{u}_\mathbf{y}^N \end{pmatrix} + \begin{pmatrix} \frac{dp^N}{dx} \\ \nabla_\mathbf{y} p^N \end{pmatrix} = \begin{pmatrix} 0 \\ 0 \end{pmatrix}$$

and then

$$\begin{cases} -\Delta u_x^N + \frac{dp^N}{dx} = 0, \\ -\Delta \mathbf{u_y}^N + \nabla_{\mathbf{y}} p^N = 0. \end{cases}.$$

The operator $-\Delta = -\frac{d^2}{dx^2} - \Delta_{\mathbf{y}}$ is decomposed into

$$\frac{d^2 u_x^N}{dx^2} = -\Delta_{\mathbf{y}} u_x^N + \frac{dp^N}{dx} \tag{17}$$

$$\frac{d^2 \mathbf{u_y}^N}{dx^2} = -\Delta_{\mathbf{y}} \mathbf{u_y}^N + \nabla_{\mathbf{y}} p^N. \tag{18}$$

The derivative of (15) with respect to x gives

$$\frac{\partial^2 \mathbf{u_y}^N}{\partial x^2} = \frac{\partial D_{\mathbf{y}x}}{\partial x} u_x^N + D_{\mathbf{y}x} \frac{\partial u_x^N}{\partial x} + \frac{\partial D_{\mathbf{yy}}}{\partial x} \mathbf{u_y}^N + D_{\mathbf{yy}} \frac{\partial \mathbf{u_y}^N}{\partial x} + \frac{\partial \omega_{N,\mathbf{y}}}{\partial x}.$$

Using (14), (15), and (18), we obtain

$$(-\Delta_{\mathbf{y}} - \frac{\partial D_{\mathbf{yy}}}{\partial x} - D_{\mathbf{yy}}^2 + D_{\mathbf{y}x} div_{\mathbf{y}}) \mathbf{u_y}^N - (D_{\mathbf{yy}} D_{\mathbf{y}x} + \frac{\partial D_{\mathbf{y}x}}{\partial x}) u_x^N + \nabla_{\mathbf{y}} p^N - D_{\mathbf{yy}} \omega_{N,\mathbf{y}} - \frac{\partial \omega_{N,\mathbf{y}}}{\partial x} = 0. \tag{19}$$

where $p^N = q^N + l^N$.

Let us introduce the operators K_N and H_N:

$$p^N = K_N(x) u_x^N + H_N(x) \mathbf{u_y}^N + l^N \tag{20}$$

K_N and H_N are defined on the section Γ_s, dependent only on x. We have

$$\nabla_{\mathbf{y}} p^N = H_N \nabla_{\mathbf{y}} \mathbf{u_y}^N + K_N \nabla_{\mathbf{y}} u_x^N + \nabla_y l^N \tag{21}$$

and

$$\frac{\partial p^N}{\partial x} = \frac{\partial H_N}{\partial x} \mathbf{u_y}^N + H_N \frac{\partial \mathbf{u_y}^N}{\partial x} + \frac{\partial K_N}{\partial x} u_x^N + K_N \frac{\partial u_x^N}{\partial x} + \frac{\partial l^N}{\partial x}$$

Using (14) and (15), we obtain

$$\frac{\partial p^N}{\partial x} = (\frac{\partial H_N}{\partial x} + H_N D_{\mathbf{yy}} - K_N div_{\mathbf{y}}) \mathbf{u_y}^N + (\frac{\partial K_N}{\partial x} + H_N D_{\mathbf{y}x}) u_x^N + H_N \omega_{N,\mathbf{y}} + \frac{\partial l^N}{\partial x} \tag{22}$$

Substituting (21) into Equation (19), we find

$$\begin{aligned} &(-\Delta_{\mathbf{y}} + \nabla_{\mathbf{y}} H_N - \frac{\partial D_{\mathbf{yy}}}{\partial x} - D_{\mathbf{yy}}^2 + div_{\mathbf{y}} D_{\mathbf{y}x}) \mathbf{u_y}^N + (\nabla_{\mathbf{y}} K_N - D_{\mathbf{yy}} D_{\mathbf{y}x} - \frac{\partial D_{\mathbf{y}x}}{\partial x}) u_x^N + \\ &\nabla_{\mathbf{y}} l^N - D_{\mathbf{yy}} \omega_{N,\mathbf{y}} - \frac{\partial \omega_{N,\mathbf{y}}}{\partial x} = 0. \end{aligned} \tag{23}$$

We also take the derivative of (16) with respect to x, and we obtain

$$-\frac{\partial^2 u_x^N}{\partial x^2} = -\frac{\partial}{\partial x}(-div_{\mathbf{y}} \mathbf{u_y}^N) = div_{\mathbf{y}}(D_{\mathbf{y}x} u_x^N + D_{\mathbf{yy}} \mathbf{u_y}^N + \omega_{N,\mathbf{y}}). \tag{24}$$

By substituting $\frac{\partial^2 u_x^N}{\partial x^2}$ and $\frac{dp^N}{dx}$ using (24) and (22) in Equation (17), we obtain

$$\begin{aligned} &(\frac{\partial H_N}{\partial x} + H_N D_{\mathbf{yy}} - K_N div_{\mathbf{y}} + div_{\mathbf{y}} D_{\mathbf{yy}}) \mathbf{u_y}^N + (H_N D_{\mathbf{y}x} + \frac{\partial K_N}{\partial x} + div_{\mathbf{y}} D_{\mathbf{y}x} - \Delta_{\mathbf{y}}) u_x^N \\ &= -H_N \omega_{1,y} - div_{\mathbf{y}} \omega_{N,\mathbf{y}} - \frac{\partial l^N}{\partial x}. \end{aligned} \tag{25}$$

According to the definition of the operator D, we have

$$\frac{\partial \gamma_N}{\partial x}(s) = D(s)\gamma_N(s) \quad (26)$$

and then

$$\frac{\partial \gamma_{N,\mathbf{y}}}{\partial x}(s) = D_{\mathbf{y}x}(s)\gamma_{N,x}(s) + D_{\mathbf{yy}}(s)\gamma_{N,\mathbf{y}}(s) \quad (27)$$

where $\gamma_N = (\gamma_{N,x}, \gamma_{N,\mathbf{y}})$.

From Equation (3) and using the condition

$$\sigma(\gamma_N(s)) \cdot N = 0 \text{ on } \Gamma_0 \quad (28)$$

we have

$$\frac{\partial \gamma_{N,\mathbf{y}}}{\partial x}(0) = -\nabla_{\mathbf{y}}\gamma_{N,x}(0). \quad (29)$$

From Equation (27), we obtain

$$-\nabla_{\mathbf{y}}\gamma_{N,x}(0) = D_{\mathbf{y}x}(0)\gamma_{N,x}(0) + D_{\mathbf{yy}}(0)\gamma_{N,\mathbf{y}}(0) \quad (30)$$

and, by identification, we find

$$D_{\mathbf{yy}}(0) = 0 \text{ and } D_{\mathbf{y}x}(0) = -\nabla_{\mathbf{y}}. \quad (31)$$

Then, the matrix operator $D(0)$ is represented by

$$D(0) = \begin{pmatrix} 0 & (-\nabla_{\mathbf{y}})^t \\ -\nabla_{\mathbf{y}} & 0 \end{pmatrix}.$$

From Equation (3), we have

$$\begin{aligned} p^N(0) - 2\frac{\partial u_x^N}{\partial x}(0) &= \mathcal{F}_x \Rightarrow p^N(0) + 2div_{\mathbf{y}}\mathbf{u}_{\mathbf{y}}^N(0) = \mathcal{F}_x \\ &\Rightarrow p^N(0) = \mathcal{F}_x - 2div_{\mathbf{y}}\mathbf{u}_{\mathbf{y}}^N(0) \end{aligned} \quad (32)$$

Writing relation (20) at $x = 0$,

$$p^N(0) = H_N(0)\mathbf{u}_{\mathbf{y}}^N(0) + K_N(0)u_x^N(0) + l^N(0). \quad (33)$$

So, by identification, we obtain

$$H_N(0) = -2div_{\mathbf{y}}, \quad K_N(0) = 0 \text{ and } l^N(0) = \mathcal{F}_x. \quad (34)$$

Writing the relation (15) at $x = 0$,

$$\frac{\partial \mathbf{u}_{\mathbf{y}}^N}{\partial x}(0) = D_{\mathbf{y}x}(0)u_x^N(0) + D_{\mathbf{yy}}(0)\mathbf{u}_{\mathbf{y}}^N(0) + \omega_{N,\mathbf{y}}(0) \quad (35)$$

and, from Equation (3), we have

$$\frac{\partial \mathbf{u}_{\mathbf{y}}^N}{\partial x}(0) = -\nabla_{\mathbf{y}}u_x^N(0) - \mathcal{F}_{\mathbf{y}}(0) \quad (36)$$

and thus

$$\omega_{N,\mathbf{y}}(0) = -\mathcal{F}_{\mathbf{y}}(0). \quad (37)$$

By (23) and (25), and taking into account that u_x^N, $\mathbf{u}_\mathbf{y}^N$ are arbitrary, we obtain the following decoupled system:

$$\begin{cases} \frac{\partial D_{\mathbf{yy}}}{\partial x} + \Delta_\mathbf{y} - \nabla_y H_N + D_{\mathbf{yy}}^2 - D_{\mathbf{y}x} div_\mathbf{y} &= 0; \quad D_{\mathbf{yy}}(0) = 0, \\ -\frac{\partial D_{\mathbf{y}x}}{\partial x} + \nabla_\mathbf{y} K_N - D_{\mathbf{yy}} D_{\mathbf{y}x} &= 0; \quad D_{\mathbf{y}x}(0) = -\nabla_\mathbf{y}, \\ \frac{\partial H_N}{\partial x} + H_N D_{\mathbf{yy}} - K_N div_\mathbf{y} + D_{\mathbf{yy}} div_\mathbf{y} &= 0; \quad H_N(0) = -2div_\mathbf{y}, \\ \frac{\partial K_N}{\partial x} + H_N D_{\mathbf{y}x} + D_{\mathbf{y}x} div_\mathbf{y} - \Delta_\mathbf{y} &= 0; \quad K_N(0) = 0. \end{cases} \tag{38}$$

$$\begin{cases} -\frac{\partial \omega_{N,\mathbf{y}}}{\partial x} - D_{\mathbf{yy}} \omega_{N,\mathbf{y}} + \nabla_y l^N &= 0; \quad \omega_{N,\mathbf{y}}(0) = -\mathcal{F}_\mathbf{y}(0), \\ \frac{\partial l^N}{\partial x} + H_N \omega_{N,\mathbf{y}} + div_\mathbf{y} \omega_{N,\mathbf{y}} &= 0; \quad l^N(0) = \mathcal{F}_x. \end{cases} \tag{39}$$

After solving these equations, we find $\mathbf{u}^N$ via the backward integration of the implicit differential equation:

$$\frac{\partial \mathbf{u}^N}{\partial x} = D\mathbf{u}^N + \omega_N, \qquad \frac{\partial \mathbf{u}^N}{\partial x}(a) = D(a)v + \omega_N(a)$$

where

$$D = \begin{pmatrix} 0 & (-\nabla_\mathbf{y})^t \\ D_{\mathbf{y}x} & D_{\mathbf{yy}} \end{pmatrix}, \qquad \omega_N = \begin{pmatrix} 0 \\ \omega_{N,\mathbf{y}} \end{pmatrix} \tag{40}$$

and we obtain

$$p^N = u_x^N + H_N \mathbf{u}_\mathbf{y}^N + l^N.$$

The system (38) can be written in the following form:

$$\frac{d\mathcal{D}}{dx} + \mathcal{D}\begin{pmatrix} I & 0 \\ 0 & 0 \end{pmatrix}\mathcal{D} + \mathcal{D}\begin{pmatrix} 0 & 0 \\ -\operatorname{div}_\mathbf{y} & 0 \end{pmatrix} + \begin{pmatrix} 0 & -\nabla_\mathbf{y} \\ 0 & 0 \end{pmatrix}\mathcal{D} = \begin{pmatrix} -\Delta_\mathbf{y} & 0 \\ 0 & \Delta_\mathbf{y} \end{pmatrix} \tag{41}$$

$$\mathcal{D}(0) = \begin{pmatrix} 0 & -\nabla_\mathbf{y} \\ -\operatorname{div}_\mathbf{y} & 0 \end{pmatrix}, \tag{42}$$

where

$$\mathcal{D} = \begin{pmatrix} D_{\mathbf{yy}} & D_{\mathbf{y}x} \\ H_N & K_N \end{pmatrix},$$

is the operator matrix relating the Dirichlet condition to the normal derivative of the tangential component of the velocity and the pressure.

5.2. The Neumann-to-Dirichlet Operator and the Residual Function ω_D

We consider, for $x < s$, that the restriction of $\mathbf{u}^{D_s}(\varphi)$ to Ω_x is a solution to the problem $(\mathcal{P}_2^s)$. By the same computations as those previously used, we have the relation

$$\mathbf{u}^{D_s}(x,\varphi) = Q(x)\varphi + \omega_D(x). \tag{43}$$

We denote by $\mathbf{u}^{D_s}$, Q and ω_D the applications $\mathbf{u}^{D_s}(x)$, $Q(x)$ and $\omega_D(x)$, respectively.

$$\mathbf{u}^{D_s} = Q\varphi + \omega_D \tag{44}$$

In the same way as in the previous section, we will note $\mathbf{u}^D$ instead of $\mathbf{u}^{D_s}$.

$$\mathbf{u}^D = Q\varphi + \omega_D \Rightarrow \begin{pmatrix} \mathbf{u}_x^D \\ \mathbf{u}_{\mathbf{y}}^D \end{pmatrix} = \begin{pmatrix} Q_{xx} & Q_{x\mathbf{y}} \\ Q_{\mathbf{y}x} & Q_{\mathbf{y}\mathbf{y}} \end{pmatrix} \begin{pmatrix} \varphi_x \\ \varphi_{\mathbf{y}} \end{pmatrix} + \begin{pmatrix} \omega_{D,x} \\ \omega_{D,\mathbf{y}} \end{pmatrix}$$

$$\Rightarrow \begin{cases} \mathbf{u}_x^D = Q_{xx}\varphi_x + Q_{x\mathbf{y}}\varphi_{\mathbf{y}} + \omega_{D,x} \\ \mathbf{u}_{\mathbf{y}}^D = Q_{\mathbf{y}x}\varphi_x + Q_{\mathbf{y}\mathbf{y}}\varphi_{\mathbf{y}} + \omega_{D,\mathbf{y}} \end{cases} \tag{45}$$

Then,

$$\frac{d\mathbf{u}_x^D}{dx} = \frac{dQ_{xx}}{dx}\varphi_x + Q_{xx}\frac{d\varphi_x}{dx} + \frac{dQ_{x\mathbf{y}}}{dx}\varphi_{\mathbf{y}} + Q_{x\mathbf{y}}\frac{d\varphi_{\mathbf{y}}}{dx} + \frac{d\omega_{D,x}}{dx} \tag{46}$$

and

$$\frac{d\mathbf{u}_{\mathbf{y}}^D}{dx} = \frac{dQ_{\mathbf{y}x}}{dx}\varphi_x + Q_{\mathbf{y}x}\frac{d\varphi_x}{dx} + \frac{dQ_{\mathbf{y}\mathbf{y}}}{dx}\varphi_{\mathbf{y}} + Q_{\mathbf{y}\mathbf{y}}\frac{d\varphi_{\mathbf{y}}}{dx} + \frac{d\omega_{D,\mathbf{y}}}{dx}. \tag{47}$$

We will express $\frac{d\varphi_x}{dx}$ and $\frac{d\varphi_{\mathbf{y}}}{dx}$ according to φ_x and $\varphi_{\mathbf{y}}$ and replace them in Equations (46) and (47).

We have

$$\sigma(\mathbf{u}^D) \cdot N = 2T(\mathbf{u}^D) \cdot N - p^D \cdot I \cdot N = \varphi \quad \text{on } \Gamma_s$$

where $N = (1, 0, \ldots, 0)$ on Γ_s, so

$$\begin{cases} 2\frac{\partial \mathbf{u}_x^D}{\partial x} - p^D = \varphi_x \\ \\ \frac{\partial \mathbf{u}_{\mathbf{y}}^D}{\partial x} + \nabla_{\mathbf{y}}\mathbf{u}_x^D = \varphi_{\mathbf{y}} \end{cases} \tag{48}$$

and then

$$\begin{cases} \frac{d\varphi_x}{dx} = 2\frac{d^2\mathbf{u}_x^D}{dx^2} - \frac{dp^D}{dx} \\ \\ \frac{d\varphi_{\mathbf{y}}}{dx} = \frac{d^2\mathbf{u}_{\mathbf{y}}^D}{dx^2} + \nabla_{\mathbf{y}}\frac{d\mathbf{u}_x^D}{dx}. \end{cases} \tag{49}$$

From Equations (17) and (18), we obtain

$$\begin{cases} \frac{d\varphi_x}{dx} = -2\Delta_{\mathbf{y}}\mathbf{u}_x^D + \frac{dp^D}{dx}, \\ \\ \frac{d\varphi_{\mathbf{y}}}{dx} = -\Delta_{\mathbf{y}}\mathbf{u}_{\mathbf{y}}^D + \nabla_{\mathbf{y}}p^D + \nabla_{\mathbf{y}}\frac{d\mathbf{u}_x^D}{dx}. \end{cases} \tag{50}$$

From Equations (45) and (48), substituting $\mathbf{u}_x^D$, $\mathbf{u}_{\mathbf{y}}^D$ and $\frac{d\mathbf{u}_x^D}{dx}$ in (50), we obtain

$$\begin{cases} \frac{d\varphi_x}{dx} = -2\Delta_{\mathbf{y}}(Q_{xx}\varphi_x + Q_{x\mathbf{y}}\varphi_y + \omega_{D,x}) + \frac{dp^D}{dx}, \\ \\ \frac{d\varphi_{\mathbf{y}}}{dx} = -\Delta_{\mathbf{y}}(Q_{\mathbf{y}x}\varphi_x + Q_{\mathbf{y}\mathbf{y}}\varphi_y + \omega_{D,\mathbf{y}}) + \nabla_{\mathbf{y}}p^D + \nabla_{\mathbf{y}}(\frac{p^D}{2} + \frac{\varphi_x}{2}). \end{cases} \tag{51}$$

$$p^D = H_D(x)\varphi_{\mathbf{y}} + K_D(x)\varphi_x + l_D. \tag{52}$$

From Equation (48), we have

$$p^D(x) = 2\frac{\partial \mathbf{u}_x^D(x)}{\partial x} - \varphi_x(x)$$

and, from the second equation of problem $(\mathcal{P}_2)$, we also have

$$\frac{\partial \mathbf{u}_x^D}{\partial x} = -div_{\mathbf{y}}\mathbf{u}_{\mathbf{y}}^D$$

with

$$\mathbf{u}_{\mathbf{y}}^{D} = Q_{\mathbf{y}x}\varphi_x + Q_{\mathbf{yy}}\varphi_{\mathbf{y}} + \omega_{D,\mathbf{y}}$$

Then,

$$\begin{aligned} p^D(x) &= -2div_{\mathbf{y}}\mathbf{u}_{\mathbf{y}}^{D}(x) - \varphi_x(x) \\ &= -2div_{\mathbf{y}}\Big(Q_{\mathbf{y}x}(x)\varphi_x(x) + Q_{\mathbf{yy}}(x)\varphi_{\mathbf{y}}(x) + \omega_{D,y}(x)\Big) - \varphi_x(x), \ \ \forall x \in [0,a]. \end{aligned}$$

By identification with (52), we obtain $\forall x \in [0,a]$:

$$\begin{cases} H_D(x) = -2div_{\mathbf{y}}Q_{\mathbf{yy}}(x), \\ K_D(x) = -(I + 2div_{\mathbf{y}}Q_{\mathbf{y}x}(x)), \\ l_D(x) = -2div_{\mathbf{y}}\omega_{D,\mathbf{y}}(x). \end{cases} \tag{53}$$

Substituting (52) in (51), we obtain

$$\frac{d\varphi_x}{dx} = -2\Delta_{\mathbf{y}}(Q_{xx}\varphi_x + Q_{x\mathbf{y}}\varphi_y + \omega_{D,x}) + \frac{\partial H_D}{\partial x}\varphi_{\mathbf{y}} + H_D\frac{\partial \varphi_{\mathbf{y}}}{\partial x} + \frac{\partial K_D}{\partial x}\varphi_x + K_D\frac{\partial \varphi_x}{\partial x} + \frac{\partial l_D}{\partial x}$$

$$\frac{d\varphi_{\mathbf{y}}}{dx} = -\Delta_{\mathbf{y}}(Q_{\mathbf{y}x}\varphi_x + Q_{\mathbf{yy}}\varphi_y + \omega_{D,\mathbf{y}}) + \frac{3}{2}(\nabla_{\mathbf{y}}H_D\ \varphi_{\mathbf{y}} + \nabla_y K_D\ \varphi_x + \nabla_{\mathbf{y}}l_D) + \frac{1}{2}\nabla_{\mathbf{y}}\varphi_x$$

and then

$$\begin{cases} (I-K_D)\frac{d\varphi_x}{dx} = \Big(-2\Delta_{\mathbf{y}}Q_{xx} - H_D\Delta_{\mathbf{y}}Q_{\mathbf{y}x} + \frac{3}{2}H_D\nabla_{\mathbf{y}}K_D + \frac{1}{2}H_D\nabla_{\mathbf{y}} + \frac{\partial K_D}{\partial x}\Big)\varphi_x + \\ \Big(-2\Delta_{\mathbf{y}}Q_{x\mathbf{y}} + \frac{\partial H_D}{\partial x} - H_D\Delta_{\mathbf{y}}Q_{\mathbf{yy}} + \frac{3}{2}H_D\nabla_{\mathbf{y}}H_D\Big)\varphi_y - 2\Delta_{\mathbf{y}}\omega_{D,x} + H_D(-\Delta_{\mathbf{y}}\omega_{D,y} + \frac{3}{2}\nabla_{\mathbf{y}}l_D) + \frac{\partial l_D}{\partial x} \\ \\ \frac{d\varphi_y}{dx} = \Big(-\Delta_{\mathbf{y}}Q_{\mathbf{y}x} + \frac{3}{2}\nabla_{\mathbf{y}}K_D + \frac{1}{2}\nabla_{\mathbf{y}}\Big)\varphi_x + \Big(-\Delta_{\mathbf{y}}Q_{\mathbf{yy}} + \frac{3}{2}\nabla_{\mathbf{y}}H_D\Big)\varphi_y - \Delta_{\mathbf{y}}\omega_{D,y} + \frac{3}{2}\nabla_{\mathbf{y}}l_D \end{cases} \tag{54}$$

We multiply Equation (46) by $(I-K_D)$. From Equations (48) and (54), we obtain

$$\begin{aligned} &\Big[(I-K_D)\frac{dQ_{xx}}{dx} - 2Q_{xx}\Delta_{\mathbf{y}}Q_{xx} - Q_{xx}H_D\Delta_{\mathbf{y}}Q_{\mathbf{y}x} + \frac{3}{2}Q_{xx}H_D\nabla_{\mathbf{y}}K_D + \frac{1}{2}Q_{xx}H_D\nabla_{\mathbf{y}} + \\ &Q_{xx}\frac{dK_D}{dx} - (I-K_D)Q_{x\mathbf{y}}\Delta_{\mathbf{y}}Q_{\mathbf{y}x} + \frac{3}{2}(I-K_D)Q_{x\mathbf{y}}\nabla_{\mathbf{y}}K_D + \frac{1}{2}(I-K_D)Q_{x\mathbf{y}}\nabla_{\mathbf{y}} - \frac{(I-K_D)(I+K_D)}{2}\Big]\varphi_x + \\ \\ &\Big[(I-K_D)\frac{dQ_{x\mathbf{y}}}{dx} - 2Q_{xx}\Delta_{\mathbf{y}}Q_{x\mathbf{y}} + Q_{xx}\frac{\partial H_D}{\partial x} - Q_{xx}\Delta_{\mathbf{y}}H_D\ Q_{\mathbf{yy}} + \frac{3}{2}Q_{xx}H_D\nabla_{\mathbf{y}}H_D - \frac{1}{2}(I-K_D)H_D \\ &-(I-K_D)Q_{x\mathbf{y}}\Delta_{\mathbf{y}}Q_{\mathbf{yy}} + \frac{3}{2}(I-K_D)Q_{x\mathbf{y}}\nabla_{\mathbf{y}}H_D\Big]\varphi_{\mathbf{y}} + (I-K_D)\frac{d\omega_{D,x}}{dx} + Q_{xx}\frac{\partial l_D}{\partial x} - 2Q_{xx}\Delta_{\mathbf{y}}\omega_{D,x} - \\ \\ &Q_{xx}H_D\Delta_{\mathbf{y}}\omega_{D,y} + \frac{3}{2}Q_{xx}H_D\nabla_{\mathbf{y}}l_D - \frac{(I-K_D)l_D}{2} - (I-K_D)Q_{x\mathbf{y}}\Delta_{\mathbf{y}}\omega_{D,y} + \frac{3}{2}(I-K_D)Q_{x\mathbf{y}}\nabla_{\mathbf{y}}l_D = 0 \end{aligned} \tag{55}$$

Proceeding in the same way for Equation (47), we have

$$\begin{aligned} &\Big[(I-K_D)\frac{dQ_{\mathbf{y}x}}{dx} + Q_{\mathbf{y}x}\frac{dK_D}{dx} + (I-K_D)\nabla_y Q_{xx} - 2Q_{\mathbf{y}x}\Delta_{\mathbf{y}}Q_{xx} - Q_{\mathbf{y}x}\Delta_{\mathbf{y}}H_D Q_{\mathbf{y}x} + \\ &\frac{3}{2}Q_{\mathbf{y}x}K_D\nabla_{\mathbf{y}}H_D + \frac{1}{2}Q_{\mathbf{y}x}\nabla_{\mathbf{y}}H_D - (I-K_D)Q_{\mathbf{yy}}\Delta_{\mathbf{y}}Q_{\mathbf{y}x} + \frac{3}{2}(I-K_D)Q_{\mathbf{yy}}\nabla_{\mathbf{y}}K_D + \\ &\frac{1}{2}(I-K_D)Q_{\mathbf{yy}}\nabla_{\mathbf{y}}\Big]\varphi_x + \Big[(I-K_D)\frac{dQ_{\mathbf{yy}}}{dx} - 2Q_{\mathbf{y}x}\Delta_{\mathbf{y}}Q_{x\mathbf{y}} + Q_{\mathbf{y}x}\frac{dH_D}{dx} - Q_{\mathbf{y}x}\Delta_{\mathbf{y}}H_D Q_{\mathbf{yy}} + \\ &\frac{3}{2}Q_{\mathbf{y}x}H_D\nabla_{\mathbf{y}}H_D - (I-K_D)Q_{\mathbf{yy}}\Delta_{\mathbf{y}}Q_{\mathbf{yy}} + \frac{3}{2}(I-K_D)\nabla_{\mathbf{y}}H_D + (I-K_D)\nabla_{\mathbf{y}}Q_{x\mathbf{y}} - (I-K_D)\Big]\varphi_{\mathbf{y}} + \\ &(I-K_D)\frac{d\omega_{D,\mathbf{y}}}{dx} + Q_{\mathbf{y}x}\frac{\partial l_D}{\partial x} - 2Q_{\mathbf{y}x}\Delta_{\mathbf{y}}\omega_{D,x} - Q_{\mathbf{y}x}H_D\Delta_{\mathbf{y}}\omega_{D,\mathbf{y}} + \frac{3}{2}Q_{\mathbf{y}x}H_D\nabla_{\mathbf{y}}l_D - (I-K_D)Q_{\mathbf{yy}}\Delta_{\mathbf{y}}\omega_{D,y} + \\ &\frac{3}{2}(I-K_D)Q_{\mathbf{yy}}\nabla_{\mathbf{y}}l_D + (I-K_D)\nabla_{\mathbf{y}}\omega_{D,x} = 0 \end{aligned} \tag{56}$$

Taking into account that φ_x and $\varphi_{\mathbf{y}}$ are arbitrary in (55), (56), and by (53), we obtain the decoupled system

$$
\begin{cases}
\frac{dQ_{yx}}{dx} + \frac{1}{2}(I-K_D)\nabla_y Q_{xx} - Q_{yx}\Delta_y Q_{xx} - \frac{1}{2}Q_{yx}\Delta_y H_D Q_{yx} + \frac{3}{4}Q_{yx}K_D\nabla_y H_D \\
+\frac{1}{4}Q_{yx}\nabla_y H_D - \frac{1}{2}(I-K_D)Q_{yy}\Delta_y Q_{yx} + \frac{3}{4}(I-K_D)Q_{yy}\nabla_y K_D + \frac{1}{4}(I-K_D)Q_{yy}\nabla_y = 0 \\
\\
\frac{dQ_{yy}}{dx} - Q_{yx}\Delta_y Q_{xy} - \frac{1}{2}Q_{yx}\Delta_y H_D Q_{yy} + \frac{3}{4}Q_{yx}H_D\nabla_y H_D - \frac{1}{2}(I-K_D)Q_{yy}\Delta_y Q_{yy} + \\
\frac{3}{4}(I-K_D)\nabla_y H_D + \frac{1}{2}(I-K_D)\nabla_y Q_{xy} - (I-K_D) = 0 \\
\\
(I-K_D)\frac{dQ_{xx}}{dx} - 2Q_{xx}div_y\frac{dQ_{yx}}{dx} - 2Q_{xx}\Delta_y Q_{xx} - Q_{xx}H_D\Delta_y Q_{yx} + \frac{3}{2}Q_{xx}H_D\nabla_y K_D + \frac{1}{2}Q_{xx}H_D\nabla_y \\
-(I-K_D)Q_{xy}\Delta_y Q_{yx} + \frac{3}{2}(I-K_D)Q_{xy}\nabla_y K_D + \frac{1}{2}(I-K_D)Q_{xy}\nabla_y - \frac{(I-K_D)(I+K_D)}{2} = 0 \\
\\
(I-K_D)\frac{dQ_{xy}}{dx} - 2Q_{xx}div_y\frac{dQ_{yy}}{dx} - 2Q_{xx}\Delta_y Q_{xy} - Q_{xx}\Delta_y H_D\, Q_{yy} + \frac{3}{2}Q_{xx}H_D\nabla_y H_D \\
-\frac{1}{2}(I-K_D)H_D - (I-K_D)Q_{xy}\Delta_y Q_{yy} + \frac{3}{2}(I-K_D)Q_{xy}\nabla_y H_D = 0
\end{cases}
\tag{57}
$$

$$
\begin{cases}
2\frac{d\omega_{D,y}}{dx} - 2Q_{yy}\Delta_y\omega_{D,y} + 3Q_{yy}\nabla_y l_D - 2Q_{yx}\Delta_y\omega_{D,x} + (I-K_D)\nabla_y\omega_{D,x} = 0 \\
\\
(I-K_D)\frac{d\omega_{D,x}}{dx} - 2Q_{xx}div_y\frac{d\omega_{D,y}}{dx} - 2Q_{xx}\Delta_y\omega_{D,x} - Q_{xx}H_D\Delta_y\omega_{D,y} + \frac{3}{2}Q_{xx}H_D\nabla_y l_D \\
-\frac{(I-K_D)l_D}{2} - (I-K_D)Q_{xy}\Delta_y\omega_{D,y} + \frac{3}{2}(I-K_D)Q_{xy}\nabla_y l_D = 0
\end{cases}
\tag{58}
$$

with the following conditions:

$$Q(0) = 0, \ \ \omega_D(0) = \mathcal{U}, \tag{59}$$

After solving these equations, we find $\mathbf{u}^D$ via the backward integration of the implicit differential equation:

$$\mathbf{u}^D = Q\varphi + \omega_D, \qquad \mathbf{u}^D(a) = Q(a)g + \omega_D(a)$$

where

$$Q = \begin{pmatrix} Q_{xx} & Q_{xy} \\ Q_{yx} & Q_{yy} \end{pmatrix}, \qquad \omega_D = \begin{pmatrix} \omega_{D,x} \\ \omega_{D,y} \end{pmatrix}$$

and

$$p^D = H_D\varphi_y + K_D\varphi_x + l_D.$$

6. Solving the Optimal Control Problem Using the Factorization Method

In contrast to classical iterative methods that are widely used in the literature to solve optimal control or inverse problems, this work proposes a radically different non-iterative factorization approach. While existing techniques (e.g., conjugate gradient algorithms, Newton-type methods, or domain decomposition schemes) rely on successive updates and often costly convergence criteria, our method leverages the structural decomposition of the problem through decoupled Riccati equations. This originality entirely avoids iterative optimization loops by directly expressing the optimal solution via the operators D, Q and residual functions ω_D, ω_N. Furthermore, the geometrically adaptive formulation based on the mobile boundary Γ_s provides intrinsic numerical stability, particularly advantageous for non-cylindrical domains or ill-posed problems, where iterative methods struggle to ensure robustness and precision. This innovation introduces new possibilities in electrocardiography and distributed control, offering significant advantages through reduced computational costs.

Let us show now that the energy functional $E(v,g)$ can be expressed directly in terms of the control variables v and g using the operators D and Q. Thus, it is not pointless to introduce an adjoint state to derive the optimality condition.

Proof of Theorem 2. We have

$$E(v,g) = \frac{1}{2}\int_{\Omega} \sigma(\mathbf{u}^N(v) - \mathbf{u}^D(g)) : \nabla(\mathbf{u}^N(v) - \mathbf{u}^D(g))dx.$$

Using the Green formula and Lemma 1, the partial derivative of E with respect to v is given by (see [14,26])

$$\frac{\partial E}{\partial v}(h) = \int_{\Omega} 2T(\mathbf{u}^N - \mathbf{u}^D) : \nabla\gamma_N^h dx = \int_{\partial\Omega} \sigma(\gamma_N^h)\cdot N(\mathbf{u}^N - \mathbf{u}^D)dx.$$

Since $\sigma(\gamma_N^h)\cdot N = 0$ on Γ_0 and $\mathbf{u}^N = \mathbf{u}^D = 0$ on Σ, we obtain

$$\frac{\partial E}{\partial v}(h) = \int_{\Gamma_a} \sigma(\gamma_N^h)\cdot N(\mathbf{u}^N - \mathbf{u}^D)d\Gamma_a, \text{ for all } h \in H_{00}^{1/2}(\Gamma_a). \tag{60}$$

In a similar way, we derive the partial derivative of E with respect to g :

$$\frac{\partial E}{\partial g}(k) = \int_{\partial\Omega} \sigma(\mathbf{u}^D - \mathbf{u}^N)\cdot N\gamma_D^k dx.$$

Since $\gamma_D^k = 0$ on Γ_0 and Σ, we obtain

$$\frac{\partial E}{\partial g}(k) = \int_{\Gamma_a} \sigma(\mathbf{u}^D - \mathbf{u}^N)\cdot N\gamma_D^k d\Gamma_a, \forall k \in (H_{00}^{1/2}(\Gamma_a))'.$$

□

Proof of Theorem 3. From Equations (3) and (44), we have

$$\mathbf{u}^D(a) = Q(a)\sigma(\mathbf{u}^D)(a).N + \omega_D(a), \tag{61}$$

$$\frac{\partial \mathbf{u}^N}{\partial x}(a) = D(a)\mathbf{u}^N(a) + \omega_N(a).$$

where

$$\sigma(\mathbf{u}^D)\cdot N = \begin{pmatrix} 2\frac{\partial u_{D,x}}{\partial x} - p^D \\ \frac{\partial u_{D,\mathbf{y}}}{\partial x} + \nabla_{\mathbf{y}} u_{D,x} \end{pmatrix}$$

$$\frac{\partial \mathbf{u}^N}{\partial x}(a) = D(a)\mathbf{u}^N(a) + \omega_N(a) \Rightarrow \begin{pmatrix} \frac{\partial u_x^N}{\partial x} \\ \frac{\partial \mathbf{u}_{\mathbf{y}}^N}{\partial x} \end{pmatrix} = \begin{pmatrix} 0 & (-\nabla_{\mathbf{y}})^t \\ D_{\mathbf{y}x} & D_{\mathbf{y}\mathbf{y}} \end{pmatrix}\begin{pmatrix} u_x^N \\ \mathbf{u}_{\mathbf{y}}^N \end{pmatrix} + \begin{pmatrix} 0 \\ \omega_{N,\mathbf{y}} \end{pmatrix}$$

$$\Rightarrow \underbrace{\begin{pmatrix} 2\frac{\partial u_x^N}{\partial x} - p^N \\ \frac{\partial \mathbf{u}_{\mathbf{y}}^N}{\partial x} \end{pmatrix} + \begin{pmatrix} 0 \\ \nabla_{\mathbf{y}} u_x^N \end{pmatrix}}_{\sigma(\mathbf{u}^N)\cdot N} = \underbrace{\begin{pmatrix} 0 & 2(-\nabla_{\mathbf{y}})^t \\ D_{\mathbf{y}x} & D_{\mathbf{y}\mathbf{y}} \end{pmatrix}}_{D'}\begin{pmatrix} u_x^N \\ \mathbf{u}_{\mathbf{y}}^N \end{pmatrix} + \underbrace{\begin{pmatrix} -p^N \\ \omega_{N,\mathbf{y}} \end{pmatrix}}_{\omega_N'} + \begin{pmatrix} 0 \\ \nabla_{\mathbf{y}} u_x^N \end{pmatrix}$$

$$\Rightarrow \sigma(\mathbf{u}^N) \cdot N = D'\mathbf{u}^N + \omega_N' + \underbrace{\begin{pmatrix} 0 & 0 \\ \nabla_{\mathbf{y}} & 0 \end{pmatrix} \begin{pmatrix} u_x^N \\ \mathbf{u}_{\mathbf{y}}^N \end{pmatrix}}_{R\mathbf{u}^N}$$

$$\Rightarrow \sigma(\mathbf{u}^N)(a) \cdot N = \underbrace{(D' + R)}_{D''} \mathbf{u}^N(a) + \omega_N'(a). \tag{62}$$

Using (61) and (62), we obtain

$$\begin{aligned} \frac{\partial E}{\partial v}(h) &= \int_{\Gamma_a} (D''h)(v - Q\,g - \omega_D) d\Gamma_a, \\ \frac{\partial E}{\partial g}(k) &= \int_{\Gamma_a} (g - D''v - \omega_D')(Qk) d\Gamma_a. \end{aligned} \tag{63}$$

The relation (63) at the optimum of E is equivalent to

$$\tfrac{\partial E}{\partial v}(h) = 0, \text{ for all } h \in H_{00}^{1/2}(\Gamma_a), \quad \tfrac{\partial E}{\partial g}(k) = 0, \text{ for all } k \in (H_{00}^{1/2}(\Gamma_a))'$$

Then,

$$\left\langle D''h, v - Q\,g - \omega_2 \right\rangle_{\Gamma_a} = 0, \quad \left\langle g - D''v - \omega_N', Q\,k \right\rangle_{\Gamma_a} = 0$$

which is equivalent to

$$\begin{aligned} &\left\langle (D'')^t(v - Q\,g - \omega_D), h \right\rangle_{\Gamma_a} = 0, \text{ for all } h \in H_{00}^{1/2}(\Gamma_a) \\ &\left\langle Q^t\,(g - D''v - \omega_N'), k \right\rangle_{\Gamma_a} = 0, \text{ for all } k \in (H_{00}^{1/2}(\Gamma_a))' \end{aligned}$$

and we obtain

$$(D'')^t(v - Q\,g - \omega_D) = 0 \quad \textit{and} \quad Q^t\,(g - D''v - \omega_N') = 0,$$

where $(D'')^t$ and Q^t represent, respectively, the transposes of D'' and Q.

By construction, the two operators Q and D'' are injective, so

$$\left\{ \begin{array}{l} v - Q\,g - \omega_N = 0, \\ g - D''v - \omega_D' = 0. \end{array} \right.$$

$$\Rightarrow \left\{ \begin{array}{l} v - Q(D''v + \omega_N') - \omega_D = 0, \\ g - D''(Q\,g + \omega_D) - \omega_N' = 0. \end{array} \right.$$

$$\Rightarrow \left\{ \begin{array}{l} (I - QD'')v = Q\omega_N' + \omega_D, \\ (I - D''Q)g = D''\omega_D + \omega_N'. \end{array} \right.$$

Then, the optimum of E is reached for v and g, satisfying the above-mentioned system. □

Remark 1. *The compatibility of the data $(\mathcal{U}, \mathcal{F})$ with respect to the Cauchy problem is given by one of the three following assertions that are equivalent:*

1. $Q\omega_N' + \omega_D \in \mathcal{I}m(I - QD'')$,
2. $D''\omega_D + \omega_N' \in \mathcal{I}m(I - D''Q)$.

Algorithm Process

Step 1: Problem Setup

- Define cylindrical domain $\Omega = [0, a] \times \mathcal{O}$ with boundaries $\Gamma_0 = \{0\} \times \mathcal{O}$, $\Gamma_a = \{a\} \times \mathcal{O}$.
- Prescribe known data: Dirichlet velocity $\mathcal{U} \in H^{1/2}_{00}(\Gamma_0)$ and Neumann traction $\mathcal{F} \in (H^{1/2}_{00}(\Gamma_0))'$.
- Goal: Reconstruct missing velocity V and traction G on Γ_a.

Step 2: Optimal Control Formulation

- Define energy functional

$$E(v,g) = \frac{1}{2}\int_\Omega \sigma(u^N - u^D) : \nabla(u^N - u^D)\, dx,$$

where u^N (Neumann state) and u^D (Dirichlet state) solve

$$(\mathcal{P}_1) : \text{Stokes system with } \sigma(u^N) \cdot N = \mathcal{F} \text{ on } \Gamma_0$$
$$(\mathcal{P}_2) : \text{Stokes system with } u^D = \mathcal{U} \text{ on } \Gamma_0.$$

- Admissible controls: $(v, g) \in H^{1/2}_{00}(\Gamma_a) \times (H^{1/2}_{00}(\Gamma_a))'$.

Step 3: Factorization via Riccati Equations

- Introduce moving boundary $\Gamma_s = \{x = s\} \times \mathcal{O}$.
- Define operators for subdomains Ω_s:
  - Dirichlet-to-Neumann ($D(s)$) and Neumann-to-Dirichlet ($Q(s)$).
  - Residual functions $\omega_N(s), \omega_D(s)$.
- Solve decoupled Riccati Equations (41) and (57).
- Integrate residual Equations (40) and (58) with boundary conditions from $\mathcal{U}$ and $\mathcal{F}$.

Step 4: Solve Optimality System

- Compute terminal operators at $s = a$: $D(a)$, $Q(a)$ and the functions $\omega_N(a)$, $\omega_D(a)$ and p^N.
- Solve coupled system (39)

$$(I - Q(a)D'')v = Q(a)\omega_N' + \omega_D,$$
$$(I - D''Q(a))g = D''\omega_D + \omega_N'.$$

$$D'' = \begin{pmatrix} 0 & 2(-\nabla_{\mathbf{y}})^t \\ D_{\mathbf{y}x} & D_{\mathbf{yy}} + \nabla_{\mathbf{y}} \end{pmatrix} \text{ and } \omega_N' = \begin{pmatrix} -p^N \\ \\ \omega_{N,\mathbf{y}} \end{pmatrix}.$$

- Obtain optimal controls: $v = V$, $g = G$ on Γ_a.

Step 5: Reconstruct Missing Data

- Output reconstructed boundary data:

$$u|_{\Gamma_a} = V$$
$$\sigma(u) \cdot N|_{\Gamma_a} = G.$$

7. Conclusions

The method presented in this paper is an efficient technique to solve the data completion problem for the Cauchy–Stokes equation. Our approach is based on the factorization of elliptic boundary value problems, which allows the direct expression of the approximations of the missing data of the data completion problem, written as an optimal control problem. In this formulation, the Dirichlet-to-Neumann operator D and the Neumann-to-Dirichlet operator Q are independent of the data. So, if this problem must be solved for multiple data sets, for each new couple $(\mathcal{U}, \mathcal{F})$, we only have to solve the equations for the residual parts of D and Q, respectively. In addition, the proposed method leads to interesting analytical calculations to obtain high-quality information and offers several new perspectives and problems in the area of data completion problems.

In our future work, we will numerically test this method and we will try to extend it to more general geometries beyond cylinders.

Author Contributions: Conceptualization, F.J. and A.H.A.; methodology, F.J. and A.H.A.; validation, F.J., A.H.A. and A.M.A.; formal analysis, F.J., A.H.A. and A.B.A.; investigation, F.J. and A.H.A.; writing—original draft preparation, F.J. and A.H.A.; writing—review and editing, F.J., A.H.A., A.M.A. and A.B.A.; supervision, F.J. and A.H.A.; funding acquisition, A.H.A. All authors have read and agreed to the published version of the manuscript.

Funding: This research work was funded by Umm Al-Qura Universty, Saudi Arabia, under grant number 25UQU4340344GSSR01.

Data Availability Statement: All data supporting the findings of this study are available within the paper.

Acknowledgments: The authors extend their appreciation to Umm Al-Qura Universty, Saudi Arabia, for funding this research work through grant number 25UQU4340344GSSR01.

Conflicts of Interest: The authors declare that they have no conflicts of interest.

References

1. Xu, L.; Cheng, W.; Deng, Z.; Liu, J.; Wang, B.; Lu, B.; Wang, S.; Dong, L. Assimilation of the FY-4A AGRI Clear-Sky Radiance Data in a Regional Numerical Model and Its Impact on the Forecast of the "21·7" Henan Extremely Persistent Heavy Rainfall. *Adv. Atmos. Sci.* **2023**, *40*, 920–936. [CrossRef]
2. Eyre, J.R.; Bell, W.; Cotton, J.; English, S.J.; Forsythe, M.; Healy, S.B.; Pavelin, E.G.Assimilation of satellite data in numerical weather prediction. Part II: Recent years. *Q. J. R. Meteorol. Soc.* **2022**, *148*, 521–556. [CrossRef]
3. Shevelev, Y.D.; Egorov, N.A. Boundary Elements Method for Solving Aerodynamics Design Problems. *Math. Models Comput. Simul.* **2019**, *11*, 810–817. [CrossRef]
4. Ambrosi, D.; Quarteroni, A.; Rozza, G. *Modeling of Physiological Flows*; Springer: Berlin/Heidelberg, Germany, 2012.
5. Araghinejad, S. *Data-Driven Modeling: Using MATLAB in Water Resources and Environmental Engineering*; Water Science and Technology Library; Springer: Berlin/Heidelberg, Germany, 2013; Volume 67.
6. Blanchard, A.B.; Cornejo Maceda, G.Y.; Fan, D.; Li, Y.; Zhou, Y.; Noack, B.R.; Sapsis, T.P. Bayesian optimization for active flow control. *Acta Mech. Sin.* **2021**, *37*, 1786–1798. [CrossRef]
7. Johansson, T.; Lesnic, D. A variational conjugate gradient method for determining the fluid velocity of a slow viscous flows. *Appl. Anal.* **2006**, *85*, 1327–1341. [CrossRef]
8. Andrieux, S.; Baranger, T.N.; Abda, A.B. Solving Cauchy problems by minimizing an energy-like functional. *Inverse Probl.* **2006**, *22*, 115–133. [CrossRef]
9. Johansson, T.; Lesnic, D. Reconstruction of a stationary flow from incomplete boundary data using iterative methods. *Eur. J. Appl. Math.* **2006**, *17*, 651–663. [CrossRef]
10. Bastay, G.; Johansson, T.; Kozlov, V.A.; Lesnic, D. An alternating method for the stationary Stokes system. *ZAMM* **2006**, *86*, 268–280. [CrossRef]
11. Kozlov, V.A.; Mazya, V.G.; Fomin, A.V. An iterative method for solving the Cauchy problem for elliptic equations. *Comp. Math. Math. Phys.* **1991**, *31*, 45–52.

12. Zeb, A.; Elliott, L.; Ingham, D.B.; Lesnic, D. Boundary element two-dimensional solution of an inverse Stokes problem. *Eng. Anal. Bound. Elem.* **2000**, *24*, 75–88. [CrossRef]
13. Zeb, A.; Elliott, L.; Ingham, D.B.; Lessnic, D. An inverse Stokes problem using interior pressure data. *Eng. Anal. Bound. Elem.* **2002**, *26*, 739–745. [CrossRef]
14. Abda, A.B.; Saad, I.B.; Hassine, M. Data completion for Stokes System. *Comptes Rendus Mec.* **2009**, *337*, 703–708. [CrossRef]
15. Bellman, R. *Dynamic Programming*; Princeton University Press: Princeton, NJ, USA, 1957.
16. Lions, J.L. *Optimal Control of Systems Governed by Partial Differential Equations*; Springer: New York, NY, USA, 1971.
17. Henry, J.; Ramos, A. Factorization of second order elliptic boundary value problems by dynamic programming. *Nonlinear Anal.* **2004**, *59*, 629–647. [CrossRef]
18. Henry, J.; Ramos, A. Study of the initial value problems appearing in a method of factorization of second-order elliptic boundary value problems. *Nonlinear Anal.* **2008**, *68*, 2984–3008. [CrossRef]
19. Bouarroudj, N.; Henry, J.; Louro, B.; Orey, M. On a Direct Study of an Operator Riccati Equation Appearing in Boundary Value Problems Factorization. *Appl. Math. Sci.* **2008**, *46*, 2247–2257.
20. Bouarroudj, N.; Belaib, L.; Messirdi, B. New interpretation of elliptic Boundary value problems via invariant embedding approach and Yosida regularization. *Proyecciones J. Math.* **2018**, *37*, 749–764. [CrossRef]
21. Addouche, M.; Bouarroudj, N.; Jday, F.; Henry, J.; Zemzemi, N. Analysis of the ECGI inverse problem solution with respect to the measurement boundary size and the distribution of noise. *Math. Model. Nat. Phenom.* **2018**, *13*, 203. [CrossRef]
22. Jday, F. La Méthode de Factorisation des Problèmes Aux Limite. Application à la Reconstruction de Donnés Frontières. Ph.D. Thesis, ENIT, Tunis, Tunisia, 2012.
23. Henry, J.; Ramos, A.M. *Factorization of Boundary Value Problems Using the Invariant Embedding Method*; Elsevier: Amsterdam, The Netherlands, 2016; ISBN 978-1-78548-143-7.
24. Henry, J.; Ramos, A.M. *La Méthode de Factorisation des Problèmes Aux Limites par Plongement Invariant*; ISTE Editions Ltd.: London, UK, 2016; ISBN 978-1-78405-141-9.
25. Hadamard, J. *Lectures on Cauchy's Problem in Linear Partial Equations*; Dover: New York, NY, USA, 1953.
26. Abda, A.B.; Saad, I.B.; Hassine, M. Recovering boundary data: The Cauchy Stokes system. *Appl. Math. Model.* **2013**, *37*, 1–12. [CrossRef]
27. Henry, J.; Louro, B.; Soares, M.C. A factorization method for elliptic problems in a circular domain. *Comptes Rendus Acad. Sci. I Math.* **2004**, *339*, 175–180. [CrossRef]
28. Bouarroudj, N.; Belaib, L.; Messirdi, B. A Spectral Method for Fourth-Order Boundary Value Problmes. *Mathematica* **2018**, *60*, 111–118. [CrossRef]
29. Abda, A.B.; Henry, J.; Jday, F. Boundary data completion: The method of boundary value problem factorization. *Inverse Probl.* **2011**, *27*, 055014. [CrossRef]
30. Andrieux, S.; Baranger, T.N.; Abda, A.B. Data completion via an energy error functional. *Comptes Rendus Mec.* **2005**, *333*, 171–177. [CrossRef]
31. Kohn, R.; Vogelius, M. Determining conductivity by boundary measurements: II. Interior results. *Comm. Pure Appl. Math.* **1985**, *38*, 643–667. [CrossRef]

axioms

MDPI

Article

Variational Principle of the Unstable Nonlinear Schrödinger Equation with Fractal Derivatives

Kang-Jia Wang and Ming Li *

School of Physics and Electronic Information Engineering, Henan Polytechnic University, Jiaozuo 454003, China; kangjiaw@hpu.edu.cn
* Correspondence: mli@hpu.edu.cn

Abstract: The well-known nonlinear Schrödinger equation (NLSE) plays a crucial role in describing the temporal evolution of disturbances in marginally stable or unstable media. However, when the media is a fractal form, it becomes ineffective. Thus, the fractal modification to the NLSE is presented based on the fractal derivative in this work for the first time. The semi-inverse method is employed to establish the fractal variational principle. The entire process of deriving the fractal variational principle is presented in detail. To our knowledge, the fractal variational principle mentioned in this article is the first exploration and report to date. The fractal variational principle established in this paper is expected to deepen our understanding of the essence of physical phenomena in the fractal space and offer new ideas for the application and exploration of the variational approaches.

Keywords: fractal derivative; semi-inverse method; lagrange function; stationary condition; variational principle

MSC: 37J51; 37K58

1. Introduction

The importance of nonlinear partial differential equations (NPDEs) lies in their status as a fundamental discipline in modern mathematics, serving as a bridge between mathematics and other scientific fields involving in optics [1,2], thermodynamics [3–5], biomedical science [6,7], plasma physics [8,9] and others [10–14], and capable of describing various important and complex natural phenomena in the objective world. To better reflect the real life and some phenomena that occur in nature, solving NPDEs is particularly important. Therefore, many researchers always focus on researching how to obtain precise solutions. Many mathematicians and physicists have conducted in-depth research in this field, creating many special methods for solving the NPDEs, and these solutions have formed their own theories, for example the Kudryashov's approach [15,16], tanh-function technique [17,18], generalized auxiliary equation [19,20], Darboux transformation approach [21,22], Hirota bilinear method [23,24], and so on. In addition, the research on the variational principles of the NPDEs is also a hot topic, as the variational principles can help us gain a more intuitive and in-depth understanding of the solutions' physical properties. However, generally speaking, it is relatively difficult to find the variational principles of the NPDEs, and not all NPDEs can establish their variational principles. In this study, we first consider the unstable NLSE as follows [25]:

$$i\frac{\partial\psi}{\partial t}+\frac{\partial^2\psi}{\partial x^2}+2\alpha|\psi|^2\psi-2\beta\psi=0 \quad (1)$$

https://doi.org/10.3390/axioms14050376

which can be used to describe the temporal evolution of disturbances in marginally stable or unstable media, $i = \sqrt{-1}$, α, and β are non-zero arbitrary constants. In [25], the extended simple equation technique is adopted to find the different wave structures of Equation (1). In [26], the lie symmetries are explored. In [27], three different methods, the sine-cosine technique, exp(-ϕ(ξ))-expansion approach and the Riccati–Bernoulli sub-ODE approach are used to study the different wave structures. In [28], the modified Kudraysov method is employed to seek the abundant wave solutions. In [29], the new Jacobi elliptic function rational expansion method is adopted to construct the exact wave solutions. In [30], the improved modified Sardar sub-equation method is used to explore the diverse wave solutions. In [31], the $\exp_a$ and hyperbolic function methods are utilized to investigate the explicit exact solutions. In [32], the modified extended direct algebraic method is manipulated to plumb the abundant soliton solutions. In [33], the modified extended mapping method is utilized to seek for different optical soliton solutions. In [34], a modified mathematical method is proposed to look for the exact wave solutions. In [35], the modified exponential rational function method is consindered to study the exact traveling wave solutions. In [36], a new trial equation method is presented to develop the different kinds of soliton solutions. In [37], the extended rational sine-cosine/sinh-cosh approach is employed to explore the solitary and periodic wave solutions. In [38], the three-wave method, double exponential method, and the positive-quadratic function approach are used to find the abundant wave solutions. In [39], the improved auxiliary equation tool is adopted to develop the diverse wave structures. However, Equation (1) becomes powerless when the medium is the fractal form. Thus, we need to carry out the fractal modification for Equation (1) through the fractal derivative as follows:

$$i\frac{\partial \psi}{\partial t^{\gamma}} + \frac{\partial^2 \psi}{\partial x^{2\gamma}} + 2\alpha|\psi|^2\psi - 2\beta\psi = 0 \tag{2}$$

where $\gamma(0 < \gamma \leq 1)$ represents the two-scale fractal dimension, $\frac{\partial}{dx^{\gamma}}$, and $\frac{\partial}{dt^{\gamma}}$ are the fractal derivatives as follows [40,41]:

$$\frac{\partial}{\partial x^{\gamma}}\psi(x_0^{\gamma}, t^{\gamma}) = \Gamma(1+\gamma) \lim_{\substack{x - x_0 = \Delta x \\ \Delta x \neq 0}} \frac{\psi(x^{\gamma}, t^{\gamma}) - \psi(x_0^{\gamma}, t^{\gamma})}{(x - x_0)^{\gamma}} \tag{3}$$

$$\frac{\partial}{\partial t^{\gamma}}\psi(x^{\gamma}, t_0^{\gamma}) = \Gamma(1+\gamma) \lim_{\substack{t - t_0 = \Delta t \\ \Delta t \neq 0}} \frac{\psi(x^{\gamma}, t^{\gamma}) - \psi(x^{\gamma}, t_0^{\gamma})}{(t - t_0)^{\gamma}} \tag{4}$$

which admits the following chain rules [42]:

$$\frac{\partial^2}{\partial x^{2\gamma}} = \frac{\partial}{\partial x^{\gamma}}\frac{\partial}{\partial x^{\gamma}} \tag{5}$$

It should be noted that Equation (2) reduces into the classic unstable NLSE in Equation (1) for $\gamma = 1$. As we all know, the variational principle plays a crucial role in describing the nonlinear phenomena from a physical perspective. In addition, it is also the fundamental theoretical basis of the variational approaches. Thus, hereby in this study, we focus on constructing the fractal variational principle for Equation (2) by applying the semi-inverse method.

2. The Fractal Variational Principle

The function ψ can be written as follows:

$$\psi = \theta + i\varphi. \tag{6}$$

Tanking it into Equation (2) yields the following:

$$i\left(\frac{\partial\theta}{\partial t^{\gamma}} + i\frac{\partial\varphi}{\partial t^{\gamma}}\right) + \left(\frac{\partial^2\theta}{\partial x^{2\gamma}} + i\frac{\partial^2\varphi}{\partial x^{2\gamma}}\right) + 2\alpha\left(\theta^2 + \varphi^2\right)(\theta + i\varphi) - 2\beta(\theta + i\varphi) = 0, \tag{7}$$

which can be divided into the imaginary imaginary and real components, respectively, as follows:

$$\frac{\partial\theta}{\partial t^{\gamma}} + \frac{\partial\varphi}{\partial x^{2\gamma}} + 2\alpha\left(\theta^2 + \varphi^2\right)\varphi - 2\beta\varphi = 0, \tag{8}$$

and

$$-\frac{\partial\varphi}{\partial t^{\gamma}} + \frac{\partial\theta}{\partial x^{2\gamma}} + 2\alpha\left(\theta^2 + \varphi^2\right)\theta - 2\beta\theta = 0, \tag{9}$$

Then, we will employ the semi-inverse method to find the variational principle of Equations (8) and (9) as follows [43–50]:

$$J(\theta,\varphi) = \iint L\left(\theta, \theta_t^{(\gamma)}, \theta_x^{(\gamma)}, \varphi, \varphi_t^{(\gamma)}, \varphi_x^{(\gamma)}, \ldots\right) dt^{\gamma} dx^{\gamma}, \tag{10}$$

where $\theta_t^{(\gamma)} = \frac{\partial\theta}{\partial t^{\gamma}}$, $\theta_x^{(\gamma)} = \frac{\partial\theta}{\partial x^{\gamma}}$, $\varphi_t^{(\gamma)} = \frac{\partial\varphi}{\partial t^{\gamma}}$, $\varphi_x^{(\gamma)} = \frac{\partial\varphi}{\partial x^{\gamma}}$, and L is called the trial-Lagrange function (TLF) and the Euler—Lagrange equations of Equation (10) are the following:

$$\frac{\delta L}{\delta\varphi} = \frac{\partial L}{\partial\varphi} - \frac{\partial}{\partial x}\left(\frac{\partial L}{\partial\varphi_x^{(\gamma)}}\right) - \frac{\partial}{\partial t}\left(\frac{\partial L}{\partial\varphi_t^{(\gamma)}}\right). \tag{11}$$

and

$$\frac{\delta L}{\delta\theta} = \frac{\partial L}{\partial\theta} - \frac{\partial}{\partial x}\left(\frac{\partial L}{\partial\theta_x^{(\gamma)}}\right) - \frac{\partial}{\partial t}\left(\frac{\partial L}{\partial\theta_t^{(\gamma)}}\right), \tag{12}$$

In order to find the variational principles of Equations (8) and (9), the TLF can be assumed as follows:

$$L = \theta\frac{\partial\varphi}{\partial t^{\gamma}} + \frac{1}{2}\left(\frac{\partial\varphi}{\partial x^{\gamma}}\right)^2 + F\left(\theta, \varphi, \theta_t^{(\gamma)}, \theta_x^{(\gamma)}, \varphi_t^{(\gamma)}, \varphi_x^{(\gamma)}\right). \tag{13}$$

where $F\left(\theta, \varphi, \theta_t^{(\gamma)}, \theta_x^{(\gamma)}, \varphi_t^{(\gamma)}, \varphi_x^{(\gamma)}\right)$ is a undetermined function of $\theta, \varphi, \theta_t^{(\gamma)}, \theta_x^{(\gamma)}, \varphi_t^{(\gamma)}$, and $\varphi_x^{(\gamma)}$. By Equation (11), we have the following:

$$-\frac{\partial\theta}{\partial t^{\gamma}} - \frac{\partial^2\varphi}{\partial x^{2\gamma}} + \frac{\delta F}{\delta\varphi} = 0, \tag{14}$$

where $\frac{\delta F}{\delta\varphi}$ is the variational derivative in this study as follows:

$$\frac{\delta F}{\delta\varphi} = \frac{\partial F}{\partial\varphi} - \frac{\partial}{\partial t}\left(\frac{\partial F}{\partial\varphi_t^{(\gamma)}}\right) - \frac{\partial}{\partial x}\left(\frac{\partial F}{\partial\varphi_x^{(\gamma)}}\right). \tag{15}$$

A comparison between Equations (14) and (8) yields the following:

$$\frac{\delta F}{\delta\varphi} = \frac{\partial F}{\partial\varphi} - \frac{\partial}{\partial t}\left(\frac{\partial F}{\partial\varphi_t^{(\gamma)}}\right) - \frac{\partial}{\partial x}\left(\frac{\partial F}{\partial\varphi_x^{(\gamma)}}\right) = -2\alpha\left(\theta^2 + \varphi^2\right)\varphi + 2\beta\varphi, \tag{16}$$

To identify F, we can set:

$$\frac{\partial F}{\partial \varphi} = -2\alpha\left(\theta^2 + \varphi^2\right)\varphi + 2\beta\varphi, \tag{17}$$

$$\frac{\partial F}{\partial \varphi_t^{(\gamma)}} = 0, \tag{18}$$

$$\frac{\partial F}{\partial \varphi_x^{(\gamma)}} = 0, \tag{19}$$

From Equations (17)–(19), we can easily determine F as follows:

$$F = -\alpha\theta^2\varphi^2 - \frac{1}{2}\alpha\varphi^4 + \beta\varphi^2, \tag{20}$$

Now we can update the TLF as follows:

$$L = \theta\frac{\partial\varphi}{\partial t^\gamma} + \frac{1}{2}\left(\frac{\partial\varphi}{\partial x^\gamma}\right)^2 - \alpha\theta^2\varphi^2 - \frac{1}{2}\alpha\varphi^4 + \beta\varphi^2 + f\left(\theta, \varphi, \theta_t^{(\gamma)}, \theta_x^{(\gamma)}, \varphi_t^{(\gamma)}, \varphi_x^{(\gamma)}\right), \tag{21}$$

where $f\left(\theta, \varphi, \theta_t^{(\gamma)}, \theta_x^{(\gamma)}, \varphi_t^{(\gamma)}, \varphi_x^{(\gamma)}\right)$ is an undetermined function of $\theta, \varphi, \theta_t^{(\gamma)}, \theta_x^{(\gamma)}, \varphi_t^{(\gamma)}$, and $\varphi_x^{(\gamma)}$. By Equation (12), we have the following:

$$\frac{\partial\varphi}{\partial t^\gamma} - 2\alpha\theta\varphi^2 + \frac{\delta f}{\delta\theta} = 0, \tag{22}$$

where $\frac{\delta f}{\delta\varphi}$ is the variational derivative in this study as follows:

$$\frac{\delta f}{\delta\theta} = \frac{\partial f}{\partial\theta} - \frac{\partial}{\partial t}\left(\frac{\partial f}{\partial\theta_t^{(\gamma)}}\right) - \frac{\partial}{\partial x}\left(\frac{\partial f}{\partial\theta_x^{(\gamma)}}\right). \tag{23}$$

From Equations (9), (22), and (23), there are the following:

$$\frac{\delta f}{\delta\theta} = \frac{\partial f}{\partial\theta} - \frac{\partial}{\partial t}\left(\frac{\partial f}{\partial\theta_t^{(\gamma)}}\right) - \frac{\partial}{\partial x}\left(\frac{\partial f}{\partial\theta_x^{(\gamma)}}\right) = -\frac{\partial^2\theta}{\partial x^{2\gamma}} - 2\alpha\theta^3 + 2\beta\theta, \tag{24}$$

For identifying f, we can set:

$$\frac{\partial f}{\partial\theta} = -2\alpha\theta^3 + 2\beta\theta, \tag{25}$$

$$\frac{\partial f}{\partial\theta_t^{(\gamma)}} = 0, \tag{26}$$

$$-\frac{\partial}{\partial x}\left(\frac{\partial f}{\partial\theta_x^{(\gamma)}}\right) = -\frac{\partial^2\theta}{\partial x^{2\gamma}}, \tag{27}$$

Based on Equations (25)–(27), we can easily determine f as follows:

$$f = \frac{1}{2}\left(\frac{\partial\theta}{\partial x^\gamma}\right)^2 - \frac{1}{2}\alpha\theta^4 + \beta\theta^2 \tag{28}$$

Then, the TLF L can be found as follows:

$$L = \theta\frac{\partial\varphi}{\partial t^\gamma} + \frac{1}{2}\left(\frac{\partial\varphi}{\partial x^\gamma}\right)^2 + \frac{1}{2}\left(\frac{\partial\theta}{\partial x^\gamma}\right)^2 - \alpha\theta^2\varphi^2 - \frac{1}{2}\alpha\left(\varphi^4 + \theta^4\right) + \beta\left(\varphi^2 + \theta^2\right). \tag{29}$$

Thus, the variational principle is established as follows:

$$J(\theta,\varphi)=\iint\left\{\theta\frac{\partial\varphi}{\partial t^{\gamma}}+\frac{1}{2}\left(\frac{\partial\varphi}{\partial x^{\gamma}}\right)^{2}+\frac{1}{2}\left(\frac{\partial\theta}{\partial x^{\gamma}}\right)^{2}-\alpha\theta^{2}\varphi^{2}-\frac{1}{2}\alpha\left(\varphi^{4}+\theta^{4}\right)+\beta\left(\varphi^{2}+\theta^{2}\right)\right\}dt^{\gamma}dx^{\gamma}. \tag{30}$$

Proof. Computing the stationary conditions of Equation (30) with respect to φ and θ, we can obtain the Euler–Lagrange equations as follows:

$$\frac{\delta L}{\delta\varphi}:\ \frac{\partial\theta}{\partial t^{\gamma}}+\frac{\partial^{2}\varphi}{\partial x^{2\gamma}}+2\alpha\varphi\left(\theta^{2}+\varphi^{2}\right)-2\beta\varphi=0, \tag{31}$$

and

$$\frac{\delta L}{\delta\theta}:\ -\frac{\partial\varphi}{\partial t^{\gamma}}+\frac{\partial^{2}\theta}{\partial x^{2\gamma}}+2\alpha\theta\left(\varphi^{2}+\theta^{2}\right)-2\beta\theta=0. \tag{32}$$

Obviously, we can see Equations (31) and (32) equal to Equations (8) and (9), respectively, which fully confirms the correctness of the obtained variational principle in Equation (30).

Then, by Equation (6), we have the following:

$$\theta=\frac{\psi+\psi^{*}}{2}, \tag{33}$$

and

$$\varphi=-\frac{i(\psi-\psi^{*})}{2}. \tag{34}$$

Taking them into Equation (30) yields the fractal variational principle to Equation (2) as follows:

$$J(\psi,\psi^{*})=\iint\left\{-i(\psi+\psi^{*})\frac{\partial}{\partial t^{\gamma}}(\psi-\psi^{*})+2\frac{\partial\psi}{\partial x^{\gamma}}\frac{\partial\psi^{*}}{\partial x^{\gamma}}-2\alpha\psi^{2}(\psi^{*})^{2}+4\beta\psi\psi^{*}\right\}dt^{\gamma}dx^{\gamma}. \tag{35}$$

□

3. Proof of the Fractal Variational Principle

Proof. Calculating the functional stationary conditions of Equation (35) in regard to ψ^{*} and ψ, respectively, yields the following:

$$-i\left[\frac{\partial}{\partial t^{\gamma}}(\psi-\psi^{*})+\frac{\partial}{\partial t^{\gamma}}(\psi+\psi^{*})\right]-2\frac{\partial^{2}\psi}{\partial x^{2\gamma}}-4\alpha\psi^{2}\psi^{*}+4\beta\psi=0. \tag{36}$$

and

$$\frac{\delta L}{\delta\psi}:\ -i\left[\frac{\partial}{\partial t^{\gamma}}(\psi-\psi^{*})-\frac{\partial}{\partial t^{\gamma}}(\psi+\psi^{*})\right]-2\frac{\partial^{2}\psi^{*}}{\partial x^{2\gamma}}-4\alpha\psi(\psi^{*})^{2}+4\beta\psi^{*}=0, \tag{37}$$

After simple calculations, we have the following:

$$\frac{\delta L}{\delta\psi^{*}}:\ i\frac{\partial\psi}{\partial t^{\gamma}}+\frac{\partial^{2}\psi}{\partial x^{2\gamma}}+2\alpha|\psi|^{2}\psi-2\beta\psi=0, \tag{38}$$

and

$$\frac{\delta L}{\delta\psi}:\ i\frac{\partial\psi^{*}}{\partial t^{\gamma}}-\frac{\partial^{2}\psi^{*}}{\partial x^{2\gamma}}-2\alpha|\psi^{*}|^{2}\psi^{*}+2\beta\psi^{*}=0, \tag{39}$$

It is obvious that Equation (38) is the same with the fractal unstable NSLE given in Equation (2), thus confirming the correctness of the constructed fractal variational principle in Equation (35). □

4. Conclusions

The fractal unstable NLSE for the fractal media was proposed in this work for the first time. Taking advantage of the semi-inverse method, its fractal variational principle was developed and the entire construction process was displayed in detail. The correctness of the established fractal variational principle was also confirmed through the Euler–Lagrange equations, which were obtained by taking the stationary conditions. To the best of the author's knowledge, the fractal variational principle is first probed in this work and has never been reported in other literature yet. In addition, the extracted fractal variational principle can describe the nonlinear phenomena from a physical perspective in a fractal space, enabling a better understanding of the essence of physical phenomena and offer some new inspiration for the exploration of the analytical solutions and numerical scheme of the fractal NPDEs arising in physics.

Author Contributions: Conceptualization, K.-J.W.; methodology, K.-J.W.; software, K.-J.W.; writing—original draft preparation, K.-J.W., M.L.; writing—review and editing, K.-J.W., M.L.; data curation, M.L.; supervision, M.L. All authors have read and agreed to the published version of the manuscript.

Funding: This research received no external funding.

Data Availability Statement: The data that support the findings of this study are available from the corresponding author upon reasonable request.

Conflicts of Interest: The authors declare no conflict of interest.

References

1. Jhangeer, A.; Rezazadeh, H.; Seadawy, A.A. Study of travelling, periodic, quasiperiodic and chaotic structures of perturbed Fokas–Lenells model. *Pramana* **2021**, *95*, 41.
2. Wang, K.L. New perspective to the coupled fractional nonlinear Schrödinger equations in dual-core optical fibers. *Fractals* **2025**, *33*, 2550034.
3. Seadawy, A.R.; Rizvi, S.T.; Ali, I.; Younis, M.; Ali, K.; Makhlouf, M.M.; Althobaiti, A. Conservation laws, optical molecules, modulation instability and Painlevé analysis for the Chen–Lee–Liu model. *Opt. Quantum Electron.* **2021**, *53*, 172.
4. Sohail, M.; Nazir, U. Numerical computation of thermal and mass transportation in Williamson material utilizing modified fluxes via optimal homotopy analysis procedure. *Waves Random Complex Media* **2023**, 1–22. [CrossRef]
5. Waseem, F.; Sohail, M.; Ilyas, N.; Awwad, E.M.; Sharaf, M.; Khan, M.J.; Tulu, A. Entropy analysis of MHD hybrid nanoparticles with OHAM considering viscous dissipation and thermal radiation. *Sci. Rep.* **2024**, *14*, 1096.
6. Kumar, S.; Kumar, A.; Kharbanda, H. Abundant exact closed-form solutions and solitonic structures for the double-chain deoxyribonucleic acid (DNA) model. *Braz. J. Phys.* **2021**, *51*, 1043–1068.
7. Leonov, A.; Nagornov, O.; Tyuflin, S. Modeling of Mechanisms of Wave Formation for COVID-19 Epidemic. *Mathematics* **2022**, *11*, 167. [CrossRef]
8. Duran, S. Solitary wave solutions of the coupled konno-oono equation by using the functional variable method and the two variables (G'/G, $1/G$)-expansion method. *Adıyaman Univ. J. Sci.* **2020**, *10*, 585–594.
9. Seadawy, A.R. Stability analysis for Zakharov–Kuznetsov equation of weakly nonlinear ion-acoustic waves in a plasma. *Comput. Math. Appl.* **2014**, *67*, 172–180.
10. Wang, K.L. New computational approaches to the fractional coupled nonlinear Helmholtz equation. *Eng. Comput.* **2024**, *41*, 1285–1300.
11. Hosseini, K.; Hincal, E.; Sadri, K.; Rabiei, F.; Ilic, M.; Akgül, A.; Osman, M.S. The positive multi-complexiton solution to a generalized Kadomtsev-Petviashvili equation. *Partial. Differ. Equ. Appl. Math.* **2024**, *9*, 100647.
12. Hu, S.H.; Tian, B.; Du, X.X.; Liu, L.; Zhang, C.R. Lie symmetries, conservation laws and solitons for the AB system with time-dependent coefficients in nonlinear optics or fluid mechanics. *Pramana* **2019**, *93*, 38.

13. Akram, U.; Seadawy, A.R.; Rizvi, S.T.R.; Younis, M.; Althobaiti, S.; Sayed, S. Traveling wave solutions for the fractional Wazwaz–Benjamin–Bona–Mahony model in arising shallow water waves. *Results Phys.* **2021**, *20*, 103725.
14. Wang, K.J. An effective computational approach to the local fractional low-pass electrical transmission lines model. *Alex. Eng. J.* **2025**, *110*, 629–635.
15. Ayati, Z.; Hosseini, K.; Mirzazadeh, M. Application of Kudryashov and functional variable methods to the strain wave equation in microstructured solids. *Nonlinear Eng.* **2017**, *6*, 25–29.
16. Wang, K.J.; Zhu, H.W.; Shi, F.; Liu, X.L.; Wang, G.D.; Li, G. Lump wave, breather wave and other abundant wave solutions to the (2+1)-dimensional Sawada–Kotera–Kadomtsev Petviashvili equation of fluid mechanics. *Pramana* **2025**, *99*, 40.
17. Zaman, U.H.M.; Arefin, M.A.; Akbar, M.A.; Uddin, M.H. Utilizing the extended tanh-function technique to scrutinize fractional order nonlinear partial differential equations. *Partial. Differ. Equ. Appl. Math.* **2023**, *8*, 100563.
18. Darwish, A.; Ahmed, H.M.; Arnous, A.H.; Shehab, M.F. Optical solitons of Biswas–Arshed equation in birefringent fibers using improved modified extended tanh-function method. *Optik* **2021**, *227*, 165385.
19. Zayed, E.M.; Alngar, M.E.; El-Horbaty, M.M.; Biswas, A.; Kara, A.H.; Yıldırım, Y.; Belic, M.R. Cubic-quartic polarized optical solitons and conservation laws for perturbed Fokas-Lenells model. *J. Nonlinear Opt. Phys. Mater.* **2021**, *30*, 2150005.
20. Akram, G.; Sadaf, M.; Khan, M.A.U. Soliton dynamics of the generalized shallow water like equation in nonlinear phenomenon. *Front. Phys.* **2022**, *10*, 822042.
21. Ma, W.X. A novel kind of reduced integrable matrix mKdV equations and their binary Darboux transformations. *Mod. Phys. Lett. B* **2022**, *36*, 2250094.
22. Yang, D.Y.; Tian, B.; Wang, M.; Zhao, X.; Shan, W.R.; Jiang, Y. Lax pair, Darboux transformation, breathers and rogue waves of an N-coupled nonautonomous nonlinear Schrödinger system for an optical fiber or a plasma. *Nonlinear Dyn.* **2022**, *107*, 2657–2666.
23. Wang, K.J.; Liu, X.L.; Wang, W.D.; Li, S.; Zhu, H.W. Novel singular and non-singular complexiton, interaction wave and the complex multi-soliton solutions to the generalized nonlinear evolution equation. *Mod. Phys. Lett. B* **2025**, *39*, 2550135. [CrossRef]
24. Ahmad, S.; Saifullah, S.; Khan, A.; Inc, M. New local and nonlocal soliton solutions of a nonlocal reverse space-time mKdV equation using improved Hirota bilinear method. *Phys. Lett. A* **2022**, *450*, 128393.
25. Lu, D.; Seadawy, A.; Arshad, M. Applications of extended simple equation method on unstable nonlinear Schrödinger equations. *Optik* **2017**, *140*, 136–144.
26. Rafiq, M.H.; Raza, N.; Jhangeer, A. Nonlinear dynamics of the generalized unstable nonlinear Schrödinger equation: A graphical perspective. *Opt. Quantum Electron.* **2023**, *55*, 628.
27. Abdelrahman, M.A.E.; Ammar, S.I.; Abualnaja, K.M. New solutions for the unstable nonlinear Schrödinger equation arising in natural science. *Aims Math.* **2020**, *5*, 1893–1912.
28. Hosseini, K.; Kumar, D.; Kaplan, M.; Bejarbaneh, E.Y. New exact traveling wave solutions of the unstable nonlinear Schrödinger equations. *Commun. Theor. Phys.* **2017**, *68*, 761.
29. Tala-Tebue, E.; Djoufack, Z.I.; Fendzi-Donfack, E.; Kenfack-Jiotsa, A.; Kofané, T.C. Exact solutions of the unstable nonlinear Schrödinger equation with the new Jacobi elliptic function rational expansion method and the exponential rational function method. *Optik* **2016**, *127*, 11124–11130.
30. Khan, M.I.; Farooq, A.; Nisar, K.S.; Shah, N.A. Unveiling new exact solutions of the unstable nonlinear Schrödinger equation using the improved modified Sardar sub-equation method. *Results Phys.* **2024**, *59*, 107593.
31. Hosseini, K.; Zabihi, A.; Samadani, F.; Ansari, R. New explicit exact solutions of the unstable nonlinear Schrödinger's equation using the exp a and hyperbolic function methods. *Opt. Quantum Electron.* **2018**, *50*, 82.
32. Lu, D.; Seadawy, A.R.; Arshad, M. Bright–dark solitary wave and elliptic function solutions of unstable nonlinear Schrödinger equation and their applications. *Opt. Quantum Electron.* **2018**, *50*, 23.
33. Arshad, M.; Seadawy, A.R.; Lu, D.; Jun, W. Optical soliton solutions of unstable nonlinear Schröodinger dynamical equation and stability analysis with applications. *Optik* **2018**, *157*, 597–605. [CrossRef]
34. Iqbal, M.; Seadawy, A.R. Instability of modulation wave train and disturbance of time period in slightly stable media for unstable nonlinear Schrödinger dynamical equation. *Mod. Phys. Lett. B* **2020**, *34*, 2150010. [CrossRef]
35. Li, Y.; Lu, D.; Arshad, M. New exact traveling wave solutions of the unstable nonlinear Schrödinger equations and their applications. *Optik* **2021**, *226*, 165386.
36. Pandir, Y.; Ekin, A. Dynamics of combined soliton solutions of unstable nonlinear Schrodinger equation with new version of the trial equation method. *Chin. J. Phys.* **2020**, *67*, 534–543.
37. Montazeri, S.; Nazari, F.; Rezazadeh, H. Solitary and periodic wave solutions of the unstable nonlinear Schrödinger's equation. *Optik* **2024**, *297*, 171573.
38. Arshad, M.; Umer, M.A.; Xu, C.; Almehizia, A.A.; Yasin, F. Exploring conversation laws and nonlinear dynamics of the unstable nonlinear Schrödinger equation: Stability and applications. *Ain Shams Eng. J.* **2025**, *16*, 103210. [CrossRef]
39. Sarwar, A.; Arshad, M.; Farman, M.; Akgül, A.; Ahmed, I.; Bayram, M.; De la Sen, M. Construction of novel bright-dark solitons and breather waves of unstable nonlinear Schrödinger equations with applications. *Symmetry* **2022**, *15*, 99. [CrossRef]

40. He, J.H. Fractal calculus and its geometrical explanation. *Results Phys.* **2018**, *10*, 272–276.
41. Li, W.L.; Chen, S.H.; Wang, K.J. A variational principle of the nonlinear Schrödinger equation with fractal derivatives. *Fractals* **2025**. [CrossRef]
42. He, J.H. A Tutorial Review on Fractal Spacetime and Fractional Calculus. *Int. J. Theor. Phys.* **2014**, *53*, 3698–3718. [CrossRef]
43. He, J.H. Semi-inverse method and generalized variational principles with multi-variables in elasticity. *Appl. Math. Mech.* **2000**, *21*, 797–808.
44. He, J.H. Semi-Inverse method of establishing generalized variational principles for fluid mechanics with emphasis on turbomachinery aerodynamics. *Int. J. Turbo Jet Engines* **1997**, *14*, 23–31. [CrossRef]
45. Liang, Y.H.; Wang, K.J. Diverse wave solutions to the new extended (2+1)-dimensional nonlinear evolution equation: Phase portrait, bifurcation and sensitivity analysis, chaotic pattern, variational principle and Hamiltonian. *Int. J. Geom. Methods Mod. Phys.* **2025**, *22*, 2550158. [CrossRef]
46. He, J.H. Variational principle and periodic solution of the Kundu-Mukherjee-Naskar equation. *Results Phys.* **2020**, *17*, 103031. [CrossRef]
47. Liu, J.H.; Yang, Y.N.; Wang, K.J.; Zhu, H.W. On the variational principles of the Burgers-Korteweg-de Vries equation in fluid mechanics. *Europhys. Lett.* **2025**, *149*, 52001. [CrossRef]
48. He, J.H.; Qie, N.; He, C.H.; Saeed, T. On a strong minimum condition of a fractal variational principle. *Appl. Math. Lett.* **2021**, *119*, 107199. [CrossRef]
49. Wang, K.J.; Zhu, H.W.; Li, S.; Shi, F.; Li, G.; Liu, X.L. Bifurcation Analysis, Chaotic Behaviors, Variational Principle, Hamiltonian and Diverse Optical Solitons of the Fractional Complex Ginzburg-Landau Model. *Int. J. Theor. Phys.* **2025**, *64*, 134. [CrossRef]
50. Cao, X.Q.; Zhang, C.Z.; Hou, S.C.; Guo, Y.N.; Peng, K.C. Variational theory for (2+1)-dimensional fractional dispersive long wave equations. *Therm. Sci.* **2021**, *25*, 1277–1285. [CrossRef]

MDPI AG
Grosspeteranlage 5
4052 Basel
Switzerland
Tel.: +41 61 683 77 34

Axioms Editorial Office
E-mail: axioms@mdpi.com
www.mdpi.com/journal/axioms

www.ingramcontent.com/pod-product-compliance
Lightning Source LLC
Chambersburg PA
CBHW061549210926
51850CB00009B/2046

* 9 7 8 3 7 2 5 8 7 0 4 2 4 *